Management

FOR

DUMMIES®

2ND EDITION

Management

FOR

DUMMIES®

2ND EDITION

**by Richard Pettinger, MBA,
Bob Nelson, PhD and
Peter Economy, MBA**

A John Wiley and Sons, Ltd, Publication

Management For Dummies®, 2nd Edition

Published by
John Wiley & Sons, Ltd
The Atrium
Southern Gate
Chichester
West Sussex
PO19 8SQ
England

E-mail (for orders and customer service enquires): cs-books@wiley.co.uk

Visit our Home Page on www.wiley.com

For general information on our other products and services, please contact our Customer Care Department within the U.S. at 800-762-2974, outside the U.S. at 317-572-3993, or fax 317-572-4002.

For technical support, please visit www.wiley.com/techsupport.

Wiley also publishes its books in a variety of electronic formats. Some content that appears in print may not be available in electronic books.

British Library Cataloguing in Publication Data: A catalogue record for this book is available from the British Library

ISBN 978-0-470-97769-9 (paperback), ISBN 978-0-470-97840-5 (ebk), ISBN 978-0-470-97841-2 (ebk), ISBN 978-1-119-99179-3 (ebk)

Printed and bound in Great Britain by TJ International, Padstow, Cornwall

10 9 8 7 6

About the Authors

Richard Pettinger, MBA has taught since 1989 at University College London, where he is principal teaching fellow (reader) in management education and director of the Information Management for Business courses – part of a UK national initiative to bring about the required quality of management and technology education demanded for the future. Richard teaches general, strategic and operational management, change and organisational behaviour to a wide variety of domestic and international students on undergraduate, postgraduate and executive programmes.

Since 2005, Richard has been visiting professor at the Jagiellonian University Business School in Krakow, Poland, developing a wide range of teaching, learning and research initiatives.

Richard is the author of over forty books on all aspects of business and management. He also produces professional, conference and study papers.

Bob Nelson, PhD is founder and president of Nelson Motivation, Inc., a management training and products firm headquartered in San Diego, California. As a practising manager, researcher, and best-selling author, Bob is an internationally recognised expert in the areas of employee motivation, recognition and rewards, productivity and performance improvement, and leadership.

Bob has published 20 books and sold more than 2.5 million books on management, which have been translated in some 20 languages. He earned his BA in communications from Macalester College, his MBA in organisational behavior from UC Berkeley, and his PhD in management from the Peter F. Drucker Graduate Management Center of the Claremont Graduate University.

Visit his website at www.nelson-motivation.com or contact Bob directly at BobRewards@aol.com.

Peter Economy, MBA is associate editor of *Leader to Leader*, the award-winning magazine of the Peter F. Drucker Foundation for Nonprofit Leadership, and author of numerous books. Peter combines his writing expertise with more than 15 years of management experience to provide his readers with solid, hands-on information and advice. He received his bachelor's degree (with majors in economics and human biology) from Stanford University and his MBA at the Edinburgh Business School. Visit Peter at his website: www.petereconomy.com.

Dedication

To any manager who has struggled to do the job and every employee who has had to live with the consequences.

Acknowledgements

From Richard: I acknowledge three managers who have had great influence on the ways in which things have turned out: John Taylor, who set very high standards all round, and who remains a close colleague and friend; Jack Cadogan at the Manpower Services Commission who let me do things my way; and Graham Winch who started me off at UCL. I have had wonderful support and enthusiasm all the way through from Ram Ahronov, Peter Antonioni, Roger Cartwright, Kelvin Cheatle, Frances Kelly, Paul Griseri, Jacek Klich, Robert Pringle and Andrew Scott – great colleagues all. Thanks for the great work of Rachael Chilvers, Steve Edwards and everyone at Wiley in making this project into something that we can all be proud of. Finally, I would like to dedicate this book to my wife Rebecca, without whom nothing is possible.

From Bob: Thanks to Jim Reller, a delegator par excellence in my first corporate position at Control Data Corporation, who often gave out assignments with a disclaimer such as, 'I could probably do this task faster than you, but I believe you'll learn a lot from the process'; Dr. Ken Blanchard, also known as *The One Minute Manager,* who I worked with for more than ten years, demonstrated how to get the best efforts from people by using the softer side of management and never directly telling them what to do; and Dr. Peter F. Drucker who I worked with in my PhD studies at Claremont Graduate University.

Thanks for the ongoing love and support of my father Edward, my wife Jennifer, and my children, Daniel and Michelle.

From Peter: Richard Vaaler, contracting officer for the Department of Defense, taught the benefits of upholding high ethical standards and making things happen. At Horizons Technology, Inc., CFO Debbie Fritsch demonstrated the importance of hiring and developing superior employees and challenging authority. Pat Boyce, president, taught me to look beyond the obvious to ferret out the truth and also showed me the value of becoming one with your customers. Jim Palmer, chairman, embodied the value of painting the big picture — a vision for all employees to strive for.

These people taught more than just the technical skills of assigning work, conducting a performance appraisal, or disciplining an employee. They also emphasised the people side of management: how to motivate employees by example, reward them when they exceed your expectations, and make each customer feel like he or she is your only customer – even if you have thousands of others.

Thanks to my mother Betty Economy Gritis, my wife Jan, and my children, Peter J, Skylar Park, and Jackson Warren, for their everlasting love and for putting up with my crazy life. May the circle be unbroken.

Publisher's Acknowledgements

We're proud of this book; please send us your comments through our Dummies online registration form located at www.dummies.com/register/.

Some of the people who helped bring this book to market include the following:

Commissioning, Editorial, and Media Development

Project Editor: Steve Edwards
(Previous Edition: Rachael Chilvers)

Commissioning Editor: Sam Spickernell

Assistant Editor: Ben Kemble

Copy Editor: Charlie Wilson

Proofreader: Kate O'Leary

Technical Editor: Peter Clark

Production Manager: Daniel Mersey

Cover Photos: © Dimitri Vervitsiotis

Cartoons: Ed McLachlan

Composition Services

Senior Project Coordinator: Kristie Rees

Layout and Graphics: Samantha K. Cherolis, Joyce Haughey

Proofreaders: John Greenough, Jessica Kramer

Indexer: Ty Koontz

Contents at a Glance

Introduction 1

Part I: So You Want to Be a Manager 7

Chapter 1: You're a Manager – Now What? 9

Chapter 2: Lead, Follow or Get Out of the Way 29

Part II: Managing People 41

Chapter 3: Making the Million-Pound Decision: Recruitment and Selection............43

Chapter 4: Inspiring Employees to Better Performance....................................61

Chapter 5: Coaching, Mentoring and Development 79

Part III: Making Things Happen................................ 95

Chapter 6: Setting Goals and Targets...97

Chapter 7: Being an Expert at Performance Appraisal and Management 113

Chapter 8: Being an Expert Manager within Your Environment 129

Part IV: Working with (Other) People 141

Chapter 9: Knowing and Understanding Your Stakeholders............................143

Chapter 10: Communicating Effectively..155

Chapter 11: Working Together in Teams and Groups....................................169

Chapter 12: Managing Flexible Workers...183

Part V: Tough Times for Tough Managers 193

Chapter 13: Understanding and Managing Risk...195

Chapter 14: Dealing with Ethics and Office Politics......................................207

Chapter 15: Managing Change at Work...229

Chapter 16: Setting Standards and Enforcing Them: Employee Discipline............239

Chapter 17: Handling Resignations, Dismissals and Redundancies......................255

Part VI: Tools and Techniques for Managing 271

Chapter 18: Budgeting and Accounting 273

Chapter 19: Harnessing the Power of Technology 295

Chapter 20: Formulating Strategies for Being a Global Manager........................307

Chapter 21: Keeping Track of Management Trends.......................................319

Part VII: The Part of Tens 333

Chapter 22: Ten Common Management Mistakes 335

Chapter 23: Ten Common Management Myths 341

Chapter 24: Ten Great Ways to Engage Your Employees
(and Keep Them Engaged!) 347

Chapter 25: Ten (Plus Two) Classic Business Books
You Need to Know About 353

Index 359

Table of Contents

Introduction *1*

About This Book 2
How to Use This Book 3
Conventions Used in This Book 3
Foolish Assumptions 4
How This Book Is Organised 4
    Part I: So You Want to Be a Manager 4
    Part II: Managing People 4
    Part III: Making Things Happen 4
    Part IV: Working with (Other) People 5
    Part V: Tough Times for Tough Managers 5
    Part VI: Tools and Techniques for Managing 5
    Part VII: The Part of Tens 5
Icons Used in This Book 6
Where Do I Go from Here? 6

Part 1: So You Want to Be a Manager *7*

Chapter 1: You're a Manager – Now What? 9

Identifying the Different Styles of Management 10
    Macho management 11
    Participative management 12
    The best way 12
Recognising that Quick Fixes Don't Work 13
Meeting the Management Challenge 15
    The old rules don't work any more 16
    It's a new world 17
    Trust isn't a four-letter word 18
Explaining the New Functions of Management 19
    Energise 21
    Empower 22
    Support 23
    Communicate 23
Taking the First Steps towards Becoming a Manager 24
    Look and listen 25
    Do and learn 26

Chapter 2: Lead, Follow or Get Out of the Way 29
  Understanding the Differences between
    Management and Leadership 30
  Looking at What Leaders Do 31
    Inspire action 31
    Communicate 32
    Support and facilitate 33
  Surveying Leading Leadership Traits 35
    Optimism 35
    Confidence 36
    Integrity 36
    Decisiveness 37
  Fostering Collaborative Leadership 38

Part II: Managing People 41

Chapter 3: Making the Million-Pound Decision:
Recruitment and Selection 43
  Asking for the Right Stuff 44
  Defining the Job and the Person 46
  Finding Good People 47
  Being the Greatest Interviewer in the World 49
    Asking the right questions 50
    Interviewing do's 51
    Interviewing don'ts 53
  Evaluating Your Candidates 55
    Checking references 55
    Reviewing your notes 56
    Conducting second (or third) interviews 57
  Engaging the Best (and Leaving the Rest) 58
    Being objective 58
    Trusting your instincts 59
    Adjusting after the offer 60

Chapter 4: Inspiring Employees to Better Performance 61
  The Greatest Management Principle in the World 62
    Recognition isn't as simple as it looks 62
    Biscuit motivation 63
  Discovering What Employees Want 65
    Creating a supportive environment 67
    Having a good game plan 69
  Deciding What to Reward 69
  Starting with the Positive 71
  Making a Big Deal about Something Little 73

Money and Motivation 74
    Compensating with wages and salaries 74
    Realising when incentives become entitlements 74
    Working out what motivates your staff 75
    Realising that you hold the key to your employees' motivation ... 76

Chapter 5: Coaching, Mentoring and Development 79
Playing a Coach's Role 80
Coaching: A Rough Guide 82
Coaching Metaphors for Success in Business 83
Tapping into the Coach's Expertise 84
Developing and Mentoring Employees 86
Explaining How Employee Development Helps 86
Creating Career Development Plans 88
Helping Employees to Develop 89
Finding a Mentor, Being a Mentor 91
Balancing Development and Downsizing 92

Part III: Making Things Happen 95

Chapter 6: Setting Goals and Targets 97
If You Don't Know Where You're Going, How Do
  You Know When You Get There? 98
Identifying SMART Goals 101
Setting Goals: Less Is More 103
Communicating Your Goals to Your Team 105
Juggling Priorities 107
Using Your Power for Good: Making Your Goals Happen 110

**Chapter 7: Being an Expert at Performance
Appraisal and Management 113**
Taking the First Steps 114
Developing a System for Providing Immediate
  Performance Feedback 116
    Setting your checkpoints: The milestones 116
    Reaching your checkpoints: The actions 116
    Acting in sequence: The relationships 117
    Establishing your timeframe: The schedules 118
    Reducing shrinkage 118
Reading the Results 120
Appraising Performance: Why It Matters 121
Spelling Out the Performance Appraisal Process 123
Preparing for the No-Surprises Appraisal 126

Chapter 8: Being an Expert Manager within Your Environment 129

Scrutinising Your Environment 129
  Conducting a PESTEL analysis 130
  Doing a SWOT analysis..131
  Knowing your market 134
  Identifying other issues and dealing with them............................135
  Considering your company's reputation 136
  Reaching a conclusion 136
Recognising and Accepting Your Responsibilities...................................137
  Facing up to your obligations and actions 137
  Being, and going, green 138

Part IV: Working with (Other) People 141

Chapter 9: Knowing and Understanding Your Stakeholders 143

Getting On with People..143
  Pleasing who you can, when you can...144
  Inspiring confidence 144
  Handling discomfort 145
Recognising Your Stakeholders 145
  Financial backers 146
  Customers and clients..146
  Staff..148
  Suppliers 149
  Communities..150
Taking Everyone Else into Account 151
  The media 151
  Government and regulators 152
  Pressure groups, lobbies and vested interests..............................154

Chapter 10: Communicating Effectively 155

Viewing Communication as the Cornerstone of Your Business............156
Being at the Cutting Edge of Information and
  Communication Technology 158
  Speed and flexibility 159
  Gadgets and gizmos...159
  Videoconferencing...160
Badmouthing Bad Communication 161
  Knowing what causes bad communication 161
  Looking at barriers to good communication...................................162
  Poisoning the well of communication 163
Hearing It For Listening 164
Harnessing the Power of the Written Word 166

Chapter 11: Working Together in Teams and Groups **169**

Phasing Out the Old Hierarchy 170
Downsizing organisations 170
Moving towards co-operation 172
Empowering Your Teams 173
Recognising the value of an empowered workforce 173
Managing your teams 174
Identifying the Advantages of Teams 175
Smaller and nimbler 175
Innovative and adaptable 176
Setting Up and Supporting Your Teams 176
Formal teams 177
Informal teams 178
Self-managed teams 179
The real world 180
New technology and teams 181

Chapter 12: Managing Flexible Workers **183**

Making Room for a New Kind of Employee 184
Preparing to be flexible 185
Anticipating changes to the organisation's culture 186
Managing from a Distance 187
Managing Different Shifts and Patterns of Work 188
Taking up Telecommuting 190

Part V: Tough Times for Tough Managers .... _193_

Chapter 13: Understanding and Managing Risk **195**

Defining Risk 196
Your company and risk 197
The business environment and risk 198
Knowing What Can Go Wrong, and Why 198
Losses 199
Accidents 201
Crime 201
Realising What Can Really Go Wrong 202
Knowing What You Can, and Must, Do 204
Remembering That Risk Management Is Profitable 206

Chapter 14: Dealing with Ethics and Office Politics **207**

Doing the Right Thing: Ethics and You 208
Defining ethics 208
Creating a code of ethics 209
Living ethics 212

Evaluating Your Political Environment..213
    Assessing your organisation's political environment..................214
    Identifying key players..215
    Redrawing your organisation chart.......................................217
Scrutinising Communication: What's Real and What's Not?..................218
    Believing actions, not words...219
    Reading between the lines..219
    Probing for information..220
Uncovering the Unwritten Rules of Organisational Politics..................221
    Be friendly with all...222
    Help others get what they want..223
    Don't party at company parties..223
    Manage your manager...224
    Move ahead with your mentors...225
    Be trustworthy..226
Protecting Yourself...226
    Document for protection..226
    Don't make promises you can't keep......................................227
    Be visible...227

Chapter 15: Managing Change at Work......................229

Keeping Pace...229
    Choosing between legitimate urgency and crisis management...230
    Recognising and dealing with crises......................................230
Embracing Change..231
    Identifying the four stages of change....................................232
    Figuring out whether you're fighting change.............................233
Aiding Your Employees through Change 235
Encouraging Employee Initiative..236
Making Changes within Yourself..238

Chapter 16: Setting Standards and Enforcing Them: Employee Discipline........................239

Understanding the Need for Employee Discipline............................240
Following Procedures..241
Focusing on Performance, Not Personalities..................................243
Identifying the Two Tracks of Discipline.....................................244
    Dealing with performance problems: The first track...................244
    Dealing with misconduct: The second track.............................246
Disciplining Employees: A Suite in Five Parts................................248
    Describing the unacceptable behaviour..................................248
    Expressing the impact to the work unit..................................249
    Specifying the required changes..249
    Outlining the consequences..250
    Providing emotional support...250
    Putting it all together..251
Making and Implementing an Improvement Plan..........................252

Chapter 17: Handling Resignations, Dismissals and Redundancies **255**
Accepting Resignations 255
Dealing with Dismissals 256
　　Making employees redundant 257
　　Processing the types of dismissal 259
　　Gathering good reasons for firing 261
Easing into Dismissal 262
　　Trying to avoid the inevitable 263
　　Working up to dismissal 264
Heeding the Warning Before You Fire an Employee 265
Firing an Employee Fairly in Three Steps 267
Determining the Best Time to Dismiss 269

Part VI: Tools and Techniques for Managing **271**

Chapter 18: Budgeting and Accounting **273**
Exploring the Wonderful World of Budgets 273
Making a Budget 275
Budgeting and the Real World 277
　　Producing real budgets 279
　　Staying on budget 280
Understanding the Basics of Accounting 282
　　Working out the accounting equation 282
　　Knowing double-entry bookkeeping 285
Identifying the Most Common Types of Financial Statements 286
　　The balance sheet 286
　　The profit and loss account 288
　　The cash-flow statement 290
Analysing Business Health 290
　　Using financial ratios 290
　　Using other measures 292

Chapter 19: Harnessing the Power of Technology **295**
Using Technology to Your Advantage 296
　　Know your business 296
　　Create a technology-competitive advantage 297
　　Develop a plan 297
　　Get some help 298
Evaluating the Benefits and Drawbacks of Technology 299
Improving Efficiency and Productivity 301
Getting the Most Out of Information Technology 303
Planning and Implementation 305

Chapter 20: Formulating Strategies for Being a Global Manager . . . 307
Defining Globalisation 308
Having Global Knowledge and Expertise 309
Why Go Global (and Why Not)? 311
Knowing Where to Set Things Up, and Why 312
Working Out whether You'll Really Turn a Profit 313
Debunking Some Management Myths 314
Outsourcing: The Cure for All Ills 314
Keeping your contracts under control 315
Keeping your reputation intact 316
Recognising that outsourcing's hard work 316

Chapter 21: Keeping Track of Management Trends 319
Being a Professional Manager 320
Building the Basics 321
Adopting the Best of Management Trends 323
Outsourcing 323
Creating a learning organisation 324
Making a flat organisation 325
Unlocking open-book management 326
Using consultants 328
Managing Stress 330
Committing to Being an Expert Manager 332

Part VII: The Part of Tens 333

Chapter 22: Ten Common Management Mistakes 335
Not Making the Transition from Worker to Manager 335
Not Setting Clear Goals and Expectations 336
Failing to Delegate 336
Failing to Communicate 337
Not Making Time for Employees 337
Not Recognising Employee Achievements 338
Failing to Develop 338
Resisting Change 339
Going for the Quick Fix over the Lasting Solution 339
Taking It All Too Seriously 340

Chapter 23: Ten Common Management Myths 341
You Can't Trust Your Employees to Be Responsible 341
You Have to Constantly Watch Your Employees 342
When You Delegate, You Lose Control of a Task and Its Outcome 342
You're the Only One Who Has the Answers 343

You Can Do the Work Faster by Yourself..343
Delegation Dilutes Your Authority 344
Your Employees Get Recognition for Doing a Good Job, Not You........344
Delegation Decreases Your Flexibility 345
Your Employees Are Too Busy 345
Your Workers Don't See the Big Picture...346

**Chapter 24: Ten Great Ways to Engage Your Employees
(and Keep Them Engaged!).** **347**

Being Supportive and Involved..348
Handling Mistakes Expertly...348
Granting Autonomy 348
Allowing Flexible Working Hours 349
Offering Training and Development...349
Giving Your Time..350
Providing Opportunities for Work and Job Enlargement.....................350
Giving Praise and Recognition Where It's Due 351
Solving Problems Quickly..351
Rewarding Employees Fairly..352

**Chapter 25: Ten (Plus Two) Classic Business Books
You Need to Know About** **353**

In Search of Excellence 353
Managing for Results..354
The Human Side of Enterprise 354
The Peter Principle...354
Competitive Strategy..355
The One Minute Manager 355
Management Stripped Bare 356
In Search of European Excellence 356
The Fifth Discipline: The Art and Practice
    of the Learning Organization..356
Understanding Organisations 357
Body and Soul: The Body Shop Story 357
Maverick 358

Index *359*

Introduction

Congratulations! As a result of your astute choice of material, you're about to read a completely fresh approach to the topic of management. If you've already read other books about management, you've surely noticed that most of them fall into one of four categories: (1) textbooks; (2) deadly boring tomes that make great paperweights; (3) 'I did it my way' – the war stories of successful and/or high-profile individuals (some of these are admittedly excellent, but others are little more than cynical attempts to cash in on transient fame/notoriety); or (4) recycled platitudes glazed with a thin sugar-coating of pop psychobabble, which sounds great on paper, but fails abysmally in the real world, and is as superficial as a coat of paint.

Management For Dummies is different. First, this book is fun, which reflects our strong belief and experience that management ought to be fun – that you ought to be working in a job and a company that you enjoy as well as, of course, producing excellent results.

Second, popular business books seem to be here today and gone tomorrow. Like it or not, many managers (and the companies they work for) seem to be ruled by the business fad of the month. Following fads isn't a sustainable approach to management. So you need the practical advice we offer in this book.

When we produced the previous edition of this book four years ago, everything in the garden was rosy, and we were all looking forward to hundreds of years of high and increasing levels of profitability and prosperity. How times change! Because since we produced that edition we've experienced

- ✔ An economic and financial crisis that is going to take many years to recover from
- ✔ A political crisis leading to a collective loss of confidence and period of great uncertainty, which is also going to last for some time

And these things didn't just happen! They happened because of decisions taken by the people in charge – the managers. Of course, managers took decisions on the basis of what they thought would happen; or rather, what they hoped (prayed?) would happen. Clearly this wasn't, and isn't, good enough. You've got to know what will happen to be as sure as you possibly can that things will turn out in particular ways. And you can only do so by putting in the hard graft – not just becoming a manager, but becoming an expert manager, a professional manager, someone who knows and understands what they're doing and why.

Never has managerial expertise been so important. People can't afford another financial crisis like the one the UK is still going through now. And that's where this book comes in. In *Management For Dummies* we get away from fads and fashions by concentrating on tried and tested solutions to the most common situations that real supervisors and managers face: solutions that stand up over time and that you can use in turbulent times. You find no mumbo-jumbo or superficiality here – just practical solutions to everyday problems.

Management For Dummies provides a comprehensive overview of the fundamentals of effective management, presented in a fun and interesting format. Everyone knows from personal experience that managing can be an intimidating job. New managers especially are often at a loss as to what they need to do. Don't worry. Relax. Help is at your fingertips.

About This Book

Management For Dummies is perfect for all levels of managers. New managers and managers-to-be can find everything they need to know to be successful. Experienced managers are challenged to shift their perspectives and to take a fresh look at their management philosophies and techniques. Despite the popular saying about teaching old dogs new tricks, you can always make changes that ease your job – and the jobs of your employees – and make them more enjoyable and a lot more effective.

But even the most experienced manager can feel overwhelmed from time to time – new tricks or not. For Bob, it was when he was giving an important business presentation to a group of international executives, one of whom pointed out that his flies were undone. Although Bob did score bonus points for getting his audience's attention with this novel fashion statement, he could've done so in a more conventional way.

For Peter, it was when he reprimanded an employee for arriving late at work only to later discover that she'd stopped off to buy him a cake in celebration of Boss's Day. Needless to say, the event wasn't quite as festive as it could've been!

For Richard, it was when he turned up to give a presentation to a group of managers and executives from the central banking sector. Just before he was due to go on, he was told that he'd been given the wrong brief and was asked to speak on a different subject altogether. He survived – but it was the longest two hours of his life!

Whether you're new to the job or are faced with a new task in an old job, all managers feel overwhelmed sometimes. The secret to dealing with such feelings is to discover what you can do better (or differently) to obtain the results you want. When you do make a mistake, pick yourself up, laugh it off and learn from it.

How to Use This Book

Despite the obvious resemblance of this book to one of the yellow bricks on Dorothy's road to Oz, the proper way to use this book isn't as a doorstop or a makeshift paperweight. You can use this book in one of two ways:

- ✔ If you want to find out about a specific topic, such as delegating tasks or recruiting employees, you can flick to that section and get your answers quickly. Faster than you can say, 'Where's that report I asked for last week?' you'll have your answer.

- ✔ If you want a crash course in management, read this book from cover to cover. Forget going back to college to get your MBA – you can save your money and take a trip to the South of France instead.

This book is unique because you can read each chapter without having to read what comes before. Or you can read each chapter without reading what comes after. Or you can read the book backwards. Or you can just carry it around with you to impress your peers.

Conventions Used in This Book

For Dummies books avoid jargon, dense reams of text and fiddly footnotes. To make your reading experience even easier, we use a couple of simple conventions. Italics introduce new terms, which are always followed by a definition; and we use `monofont` text for web addresses.

Foolish Assumptions

As we wrote this book, we made a few assumptions about you, our readers. For example, we assumed that you're already a manager – or a manager-to-be – and that you're truly motivated to discover some new approaches to managing organisations and to leading people. We also assumed that you're ready, willing and able to commit yourself to becoming a better manager.

How This Book Is Organised

Management For Dummies is organised into seven parts. Each part covers a major area of management practice. The chapters within each part cover specific topics in detail. Following is a summary of what you'll find in each part.

Part 1: So You Want to Be a Manager

Successful managers master many basic skills. This part begins with a discussion of what managers are and what they do, and then looks at the most basic management skills: organisation, people skills and leadership.

Part II: Managing People

The heart of management boils down to getting tasks done through others. This process starts with attracting, recruiting and keeping talented workers and extends to motivating and coaching them to go above and beyond expectations.

Part III: Making Things Happen

Making things happen is another important aspect of managing that starts with knowing where you're going and how to tell when you've arrived. In this part, we consider goal setting, measuring and monitoring employee performance and conducting performance appraisals.

Part IV: Working with (Other) People

Successful managers have discovered that building bridges to other workers and managers – both inside and outside the organisation – is important. This part covers communicating, making presentations, building high-performance teams and building effective relationships with your stakeholders.

Part V: Tough Times for Tough Managers

As any manager can testify, management isn't all fun and games. In fact, managing can be downright difficult at times. In this part, we consider some of the toughest tasks of managing: risk management, ethics and office politics, managing change and disciplining and sacking employees.

Part VI: Tools and Techniques for Managing

Being a manager requires that you acquire and apply certain technical tools and skills. This part discusses guidelines for accounting and budgeting and working with today's technologies.

The most successful managers know that standing still in business is the same as falling behind. Good managers always look to the future and make plans accordingly. This part also covers developing and training employees, and creating a learning organisation.

Part VII: The Part of Tens

Finally, we include the Part of Tens: a quick-and-easy collection of chapters, each of which gives you ten (or so) pieces of information that every manager needs to know. Look to these chapters when you need a quick refresher on managing strategies and techniques.

Icons Used in This Book

To guide you along the way and draw your attention to particular bits of information, this book uses icons in its left margins. You'll see the following icons in this book:

The pearl points out wise sayings and other kernels of wisdom that you can take with you on your journey to becoming a better manager.

Remember these important points of information, and you'll be a much better manager.

This icon highlights tips and tricks that make managing easier.

These anecdotes from Bob, Peter, Richard and other real-life managers show you the right – and sometimes wrong – way to be a manager.

If you don't heed the advice next to these icons, the situation may blow up in your face. Watch out!

Where Do I Go from Here?

If you're a new or aspiring manager, you may want to start at the beginning (isn't that a novel concept?) and work your way through to the end. Simply turn the page and take your first step into the world of management.

If you're already a manager and are short of time (and what manager isn't?), you may want to turn to a particular topic to address a specific need or question. The Table of Contents gives a chapter-by-chapter description of the topics in this book. You can also find specific topics in the index.

Enjoy your journey!

Part I
So You Want to Be a Manager

'I'm getting worried about the boss.'

In this part . . .

Before you can become an effective manager, you
need to master some basic skills. In this part, you
find out what management is, the vital skills involved, the
most important tasks that you have to carry out and how
you become a leader.

Chapter 1

You're a Manager – Now What?

In This Chapter

▶ Working out what management is

▶ Moving from being a doer to becoming a manager of doers

▶ Understanding the changing workforce

▶ Defining the key functions of management

▶ Taking the first steps towards becoming a manager

Congratulations! You're reading this book, so you're probably

✔ A manager

✔ A manager-to-be

✔ Someone who's not sure about management or being a manager, but who'd like to know what all the fuss is about

Of course, if you're simply curious and want to discover the intimate details about the kinds of management techniques that can help you get the best from your employees every day of the week, you're equally welcome!

Managing is truly a calling – one that, as managers, the authors of this book are proud to have answered. *We're the few. The proud. The managers.* In the world of business, no other position allows you to have such a direct, dramatic and positive impact on the lives of others and on the ultimate success of your enterprise.

Identifying the Different Styles of Management

Managing is about:

- ✔ Getting things done through others
- ✔ Using scarce resources to best advantage
- ✔ Coping with change and uncertainty
- ✔ Achieving and delivering results

Seems simple enough. But why do so many bright, industrious people have trouble managing well? And why do so many companies today seem to offer flavour-of-the-month training programmes? How often have you been introduced to some hot new management concept – guaranteed to turn your organisation around in no time flat – only to watch it fade away within a few months, if not sooner? Of course, as soon as one management fad disappears, another is waiting in the wings to replace it.

> 'What? You didn't catch onto that concept of Six Sigma? That's okay – we decided that it doesn't really work anyway. Now, we want you to pay close attention to this DVD on Armadillo Management (hard on the outside, soft on the inside!) – this is the latest thing. The managing director read an article about it in the *Financial Times* and wants us to implement it throughout our UK operations right away!'

Unfortunately, good management is a scarce commodity – at once precious and fleeting. Despite years of evolution in management theory and the comings and goings of countless management fads, many workers – and managers, for that matter – have developed a distorted view of management and its practice, with managers often not knowing the right approach to take, or exactly what to do. And if managers don't know what to do, employees certainly won't either.

Do you ever hear any of the following statements at your office or place of work?

- ✔ We don't have the authority to make that decision.
- ✔ She's in charge of the department – fixing the problem is her responsibility, not ours.
- ✔ Why do they keep asking us what we think when they never use anything we say?

✔ I'm sorry, but that's our policy. We're not allowed to make exceptions.

✔ If my manager doesn't care, I don't either.

✔ It doesn't matter how hard you work; no one's going to notice in any case.

✔ You can't trust employees anyway.

When you hear statements like these at work, red lights should be flashing before your eyes and alarm bells should be ringing in your ears. Such statements indicate that managers and employees aren't communicating effectively – that managers don't trust their employees, and that employees lack confidence in their managers. If you're lucky, you can find out about these kinds of problems while you still have a chance to do something about them. If you're not so lucky and you miss the clues, you may be stuck making the same mistakes again and again.

The expectations and commitments that employees carry with them on the job are in large part a product of the way in which their managers treat them. Following are the most commonly adopted styles of management. Do you recognise your management style?

Macho management

Okay. Here's the $64,000 question: what's the best way to make something you've planned happen? Everyone seems to have a different answer. Some people see management as something you do *to* people, not *with* them. Does this type of manager sound familiar? 'We're going to do it my way. Understand?' Or perhaps the ever-popular threat: 'It had better be on my desk by the end of the day – or else!' If worst comes to worst, a manager can unveil the ultimate weapon: 'Mess up one more time, and you're sacked!'

This type of management is often known as *Theory X management*, which assumes that people are inherently lazy and you need to drive them to perform. Managing by fear and intimidation is always guaranteed to get a response. The question is: do you get the kind of response that you really want? When you closely monitor your employees' work, you usually end up with only short-term compliance. In other words, you never get the best from others by building a fire under them – you have to find a way to build a fire within them.

Sometimes managers have to take command of the situation. If you have to deliver a proposal in an hour and your customer just sent you some important changes, take charge of the situation to ensure that the right people are on the task – that is, if you're serious about keeping your customer. When you have to act quickly with perhaps not as much discussion as you'd like, however, it's important to apologise in advance and let people know why you're doing things the way you are.

Participative management

At the other end of the spectrum, some people see management as participative. *Theory Y management* assumes that people basically want to do a good job. In the extreme interpretation of this theory, managers are supposed to be sensitive to their employees' feelings and be careful not to do anything that may disturb their employees' tranquillity and sense of self-worth.

> 'I found a problem with your report because none of the numbers are correct. We therefore need to consider our alternatives for taking a more careful look at these figures in the future.'

Again, managers may get a response with this approach (or they may choose to do the work themselves!), but are they likely to get the best possible response? Sometimes, yes; not always, however. In many cases, employees can, and do, take advantage of their managers. But you do get a better response if you're at least supportive at first.

The best way

Good managers realise that they don't have to be tough all the time – and that participation does work if you really mean it. If your employees are diligently performing their assigned tasks and no business emergency requires your immediate intervention, you can step back and let them do their jobs. Not only do your employees become more responsible, but you also can concentrate your efforts on what's most important to the bottom-line success of your organisation.

A manager's main job is to inspire employees to do their best and establish a working environment that allows them to reach their goals. The best managers make every possible effort to remove the organisational obstacles that prevent employees from doing their jobs and to obtain the resources and training that employees need to do their jobs effectively. All other goals – no matter how lofty or pressing – must take a back seat.

Bad systems, bad policies, bad procedures and poor treatment of other people are organisational weaknesses that managers must be skilled at identifying and repairing or replacing.

Build a strong organisational foundation for your employees. Support your people, and you find they support you. Time and time again, when given the opportunity to achieve, workers in all kinds of businesses, from factories to venture capital firms, have proved this rule to be true. If you haven't seen it at your place of business, you may be mistaking your employees for problems. Stop squeezing them and start squeezing your organisation. The result is employees who want to succeed and a business that flourishes along with them. Who knows, your employees may even stop hiding when they see you coming their way!

Squeezing employees may be easier than fighting the convoluted systems and cutting through the bureaucratic barnacles that have grown on your organisation. You may be tempted to yell, 'It's your fault that our department didn't achieve its goals!' Yes, it may be tempting to blame your employees for the organisation's problems, but doing so isn't going to solve them. Of course, you may get a quick, short-lived response when you push your people, but ultimately, you're failing to deal with the organisation's real problems.

Everyone wants to win. The challenge of management is to define winning in such a way that it feels like winning for everyone in the organisation. This, of course, is extremely difficult. People are often competing with colleagues for a piece of the pie rather than trying to make the pie bigger. Your job is to help make a bigger pie.

Recognising that Quick Fixes Don't Work

Despite what many people want you to believe, management isn't prone to simple solutions or quick fixes. Being a manager isn't simple. Yes, the best management solutions tend to be common sense; however, turning common sense into common practice is sometimes difficult.

Management is an attitude – a way of life. Management is a very real desire to work with people and help them succeed, as well as a desire to help your organisation succeed. Management is a life-long learning process that doesn't end when you walk out of a one-hour seminar or finish viewing a 25-minute DVD. Management is like the old story about the happy homeowner who was shocked to receive a bill for £100 to fix a leaking pipe. When asked to explain the basis for this seemingly high charge, the plumber said, 'Tightening the nut cost you £5. Knowing which nut to tighten cost you £95!'

Building a tasty, but useless, manager

Once, Peter went to one of those touchy-feely off-site management meetings meant to build teamwork and communication among the members of the group. Picture this: just after lunch, a big tray of leftover veggies, bagels, fruit and such was sitting on a table at the side of the room. The course leader rose from his chair, faced the group and said, 'Your next task is to split yourselves into four groups and construct a model of the perfect manager using only the items on that tray of leftovers.' A collective groan filled the room. 'I don't want to hear any complaints,' the trainer said. 'I just want to see happy people doing happy things for the next half-hour.'

The teams feverishly went about their task of building the perfect manager. With some managers barely throttling the temptation to engage each other in a massive food fight, the little figures began to take shape. A banana here, a carrot stick there . . . and voilà! After a brief competition for dominance, the winners got their crowns. The result follows.

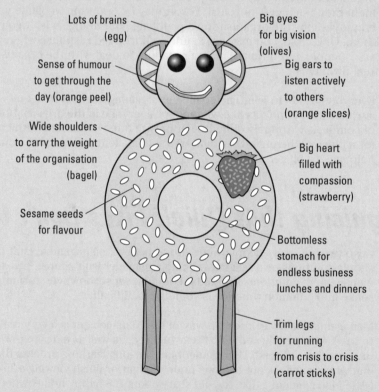

Lots of brains (egg)

Big eyes for big vision (olives)

Sense of humour to get through the day (orange peel)

Big ears to listen actively to others (orange slices)

Wide shoulders to carry the weight of the organisation (bagel)

Big heart filled with compassion (strawberry)

Sesame seeds for flavour

Bottomless stomach for endless business lunches and dinners

Trim legs for running from crisis to crisis (carrot sticks)

We have to admit that the result was kind of cute (and kind of tasty too), but did it really make a difference in the way these managers managed their employees when they returned to the office the next day? No. Was the seminar a nice break from the day-to-day office routine? Yes. Was it a meaningful teaching tool with lasting impact? No.

Management is a people job. If you're not up to the task of working with people – helping them, listening to them, encouraging them and guiding them – then you shouldn't be a manager.

Because management is such a challenge, an entire management training industry has sprung up, ready to help managers find out how to solve their problems. Unfortunately, trainers often focus on creating instant gratification among course attendees, many of whom have spent hundreds and even thousands of pounds to be there. 'Let's give them so much stuff to use that it's their fault if they never use any of it!'

Meeting the Management Challenge

When you're assigned a task in a non-management position, completing it by yourself is fairly simple and straightforward. Your immediate results are in direct response to your effort. To accomplish your task, you first review the task, you decide how best to accomplish it and then you set schedules and milestones for its successful completion. Assuming that you have access to the tools and resources necessary to accomplish your task, you can probably do it yourself quickly and easily. You're an expert doer – a bright, get-things-done type of person.

However, if you hold a management position, you probably got that job because you proved yourself to be very skilled in the areas that you're now responsible for managing.

Moving up and away

Peter's friend John was a member of a team of software programmers developing complex apps. When he was a team member, everything was fine. He came to work in a T-shirt and jeans – just like the rest of his teammates – and often spent time with his programmer friends after hours. The bond that they shared changed, however, when John was selected to manage the team.

In his new role of manager, John first shifted offices. Instead of sharing an open space with the other programmers, he moved into his own office – one with four walls and a window looking out over the car park. A secretary was assigned to guard his door. Of course, the jeans and T-shirt had to go – he replaced them with a suit and tie. Instead of having fun programming, John was now concerned with more serious topics such as cost overruns, schedule delays and returns on investments.

As John's role changed, so did he. And as John changed, so did his relationship with his team. He was no longer one of the crew; he was The Boss. To achieve his goals, John quickly had to make the transition from a doer to a manager of doers.

When you want to get a task done through someone else, you employ a different set of skills to when you do the task yourself. All of a sudden, because of this simple decision to pass the responsibility for completion of a task on to someone else, you introduce an interpersonal element into your equation. 'Oh, no! You mean I have to actually work with people?' Being technically good at your job isn't enough – no matter how good your technical skills are. Now you must have good planning, organisational, leadership and follow-up skills.

In other words, in addition to being a good doer, you have to be a good leader, director and organiser of doers.

The old rules don't work any more

If this challenge isn't already enough, managers today face yet another challenge – one that's shaken the foundations of modern business. The new reality is that managers and workers have a partnership in the workplace.

Originally, management was about dividing the company's work into discrete tasks, assigning the work to individual workers and then closely monitoring the workers' performance and steering them towards accomplishing their tasks on time and within budget. The old reality of management often relied on fear, intimidation and power over people to accomplish goals. If things weren't going according to management's plan, then management commanded its way out of the problem: 'I don't care what you have to do to get it done – just get it done. Now!' The line between managers and workers was drawn clearly and drawn often.

In the new business environment, what's going on inside the organisation is a reflection of what's going on outside the organisation. The following factors are creating rapid and constant change in today's new business environment:

- ✔ A surge of global competition and activity
- ✔ The global and international downturn leading to business difficulties
- ✔ The rise of global, commercial and organisational bases in China, India and elsewhere
- ✔ New technology and innovation
- ✔ The flattening of organisational hierarchies
- ✔ Widespread downsizing, re-engineering and lay-offs
- ✔ The rise of small businesses
- ✔ The changing values of today's workers
- ✔ The increasing demands for better customer service

The technology explosion is here!

Years ago, Charles Handy said of his old offices at Shell UK: 'In the future, we will not need these offices. Because of technology, people will be able to work wherever they need and wherever they want.' And – sure enough – he was right. Eighty per cent of Shell's old offices in London have been sold off and converted into apartments. And all because of technology! However, do note: managing people working away from the office brings all sorts of fresh challenges. And you can't insist that people come to work in the office just because you're not up to these challenges. The landscape of business worldwide has changed dramatically during the past couple of decades. If you don't change with it, you're going to be left far behind your competitors. You may think that you can get away with treating your employees like human assets or even like children, but you can't. You can't because your competitors are discovering how to unleash the hidden power of their employees. They're no longer just talking about it; they're doing it!

Of course, managers still have to divide and assign work, but workers are taking on more of that responsibility. Most importantly, managers are finding out that to get the best work, they can't command their employees – they have to create an environment that fosters their employees' desire to do their best work. This is the partnership between managers and workers in the workplace.

It's a new world

A few years ago, Bob made a presentation to a group of high-tech managers. As he was wrapping up his presentation, he opened the floor to questions. A hand shot up and the manager said, 'With all the downsizing and lay-offs that we've endured, people are lucky to get a salary, much less anything else. Why do we have to bother to empower and reward employees?' Before Bob had a chance to respond, another manager in the audience shot back, 'Because it's a new world.'

This response really sums it all up. In business, times are changing. Now that employees have tasted the sweet nectar of empowerment, you can't turn back. Companies that stick with the old way of doing business – the hierarchical, highly centralised model – are losing employees and customers to those companies that use the new ways of doing business and make them a part of their corporate culture. The best employees are leaving the old-model companies in droves, seeking employers who treat them with respect and who are willing to grant them greater autonomy and responsibility.

If you don't change, that leaves you with the employees who don't want to take risks or rock the boat. You get the yes-men and yes-women. No one challenges your ideas because they're afraid to. No one suggests better or more efficient ways to do business because they know that you don't listen or care anyway. Your employees don't bother to go out of their way to help a customer because you don't trust them to make the most basic decisions – the ones that can make the biggest difference to the satisfaction of your precious customers – or their lack of satisfaction.

Imagine the difference between an employee who tells your key customer, 'Sorry, my hands are tied. I'm not allowed to make any exceptions to our policies,' and the employee who tells that customer, 'I'll do everything in my power to get you your order by your deadline.' Who do you think your customers prefer to do business with? Who would you prefer to do business with? (**Hint:** Don't even think about the first alternative!)

Managers used to try to buy behaviour, commitment and loyalty; and some workers were even called *hired hands*. Today, hiring their hands isn't good enough on its own. You must find a way to engage their souls and get them to bring their best efforts to the workplace each and every day.

Trust isn't a four-letter word

Companies that provide exceptional customer service unleash their employees from the constraints of an overly controlling hierarchy and allow front-line workers to serve their customers directly and efficiently. For example, while many companies devote forests of paper to employee manuals, Nordstrom, an American department store chain, devotes exactly one page to its manual.

Figure 1-1 shows you what's on that page.

Figure 1-1:
Nordstrom's employee manual shows an exceptional amount of trust in employees.

> **We're glad to have you with our Company. Our number one goal is to provide outstanding customer service.**
>
> **Set both your personal and professional goals high.**
>
> **Nordstrom Rules:**
>
> **Rule #1: Use your good judgement in all situations.**
>
> **There will be no additional rules. Please feel free to ask your department manager, store manager, or division general manager any question at any time.**

(Source: *Business and Society Review*, Spring 1993, n85)

You may think that a small company with five or ten employees can get away with a policy like that, but certainly not a big company like yours. However, Nordstrom isn't a small business by any stretch of the imagination – unless you consider a company with 50,000 or so employees and more than $5 billion in annual sales small.

How does management at a large business like Nordstrom get away with such a policy? They do it through trust.

First, Nordstrom hires good people. Second, the company gives them the training and tools to do their jobs well. Then management gets out of the way and lets the employees do their work. Nordstrom knows that it can trust its employees to make the right decisions because the company knows that it has hired the right people for the job and has trained them well.

We're not saying that Nordstrom doesn't have problems – every company does. But Nordstrom has taken a proactive stance in creating the environment that employees most need and want.

Can you say the same for your organisation?

When you trust your employees, they respond by being trustworthy. When you recognise them for being independent and responsive to your customers, they continue to be independent and responsive to your customers. And when you give them the freedom to make their own decisions, they make their own decisions. With a little training and a lot of support, these decisions are in the best interests of the company because the right people at the right level of the organisation are making them.

Explaining the New Functions of Management

Remember the four classic functions of management – plan, organise, lead and control – that you learned at college? These management functions form the foundation from which every manager works. Although these basic functions are fine for taking care of most of your day-to-day management duties, they fail to reflect the new reality of the workplace and the new partnership of managers and workers. We need a new set of management functions that builds on the four classic functions of management. And you're in luck; we have them. The following sections describe the functions of the new manager in the twenty first-century workplace.

The ultimate employee letter

In his book *Please Don't Just Do What I Tell You! Do What Needs to Be Done* (Hyperion, 2002), Bob talks about the 'Ultimate Expectation' of every employer – for employees to do what needs to be done. In the following letter from manager to employee, Bob clearly outlines this expectation.

Dear Employee:

You've been hired to handle some pressing needs we have. If we could have managed by not hiring you, we would have. But we've determined that we needed someone with your skills and experience and that you were the best person to help us with our needs. We have offered you the position and you've accepted. Thanks!

During the course of your employment, you will be asked to do many things: general responsibilities, specific assignments, group and individual projects. You will have many chances to excel and to confirm that we made a good choice in hiring you.

However, there is one foremost responsibility that may never be specifically requested of you but that you need to always keep in mind through the duration of your employment. This is the Ultimate Expectation, and it is as follows:

ALWAYS DO WHAT MOST NEEDS TO BE DONE WITHOUT WAITING TO BE ASKED.

We've hired you to do a job, yes, but more importantly, we've hired you to think, to use your judgement and to act in the best interest of the organisation at all times.

If we never say this again, don't take it as an indication that it's no longer important or that we've changed our priorities. We are likely to get caught up in the daily press of business, the never-ending changes of the operation, and the ongoing rush of activities. Our day-to-day practices make it look like this principle no longer applies. Don't be deceived by this.

Please don't ever forget the Ultimate Expectation. Strive to have it always be a guiding principle in your employment with us, a philosophy that is always with you, one that is constantly driving your thoughts and actions.

As long as you are employed with us, you have our permission to act in our mutual best interests.

If at any time you do not feel we are doing the right thing – the thing you most believe would help us all – please say so. You have our permission to speak up when necessary to state what is unstated, to make a suggestion, or to question an action or decision.

This doesn't mean we will always agree with you, or that we will necessarily change what we are doing; but we always want to hear what you most believe would help us better achieve our goals and purpose and to create a mutually successful experience in the process.

You will need to seek to understand how (and why) things are done the way they are done before you seek to change existing work processes. Try to work with the systems that are in place first, but tell us if you think those systems need to be changed.

Discuss what is presented here with me, and others, in the organisation so that we might all become better at applying the Ultimate Expectation.

Sincerely,

Your Manager

Energise

Think of the best managers you know. What one quality sets them apart from the rest? Is it their organisational skills, their fairness or their technical ability? Perhaps their ability to delegate or the long hours they keep sets them apart.

Although all these traits may be important to a manager's success, we haven't yet named the unique quality that makes a good manager great. The most important management function is to get people excited and inspired – to *energise* them. You can't expect your people to be inspired, ambitious, enthusiastic or dedicated if you yourself aren't. Adopt the mantra: 'If it's to be, it's to begin with me.'

You can be the best analyst in the world, the most highly organised executive on the planet or fair beyond reproach, but if people can liken the level of excitement you generate more to a dishcloth than a spark plug, it handicaps your efforts to create a truly great organisation.

Great managers create far more energy than they consume. The best managers are organisational catalysts. Instead of taking energy from an organisation, they channel and amplify it. In every interaction, effective managers take the natural energy of their employees, add to it and leave the employees in a higher energy state than when they began. Management becomes a process of transmitting the excitement that you feel about your organisation and its goals to your employees in terms that they can understand and appreciate. Before you know it, your employees are as excited about the organisation as you are, and you can simply allow their energy to carry you forward.

A picture is worth a thousand words. This statement is as true for the pictures you paint in the minds of others as for the pictures people paint on canvas or print in magazines and books. Imagine taking a holiday with your family or friends. As the big day draws near, you keep the goal exciting and fresh in the minds of your family or friends by creating a vision of the journey that awaits you. Vivid descriptions of white sandy beaches, towering redwoods, glittering skylines, secluded lakes, hot food and indoor plumbing paint pictures in the minds of each of your fellow travellers. With this vision in mind, everyone works towards a common goal of having a successful holiday.

Successful managers bring everything to life. They create compelling visions – pictures of a future organisation that inspire and compel employees to bring out their best performance.

Empower

Have you ever worked for someone who didn't let you do your job without questioning your every decision? Maybe you spent all weekend working on a special project only to have it casually discarded by your boss. 'What were you thinking when you did this, Elizabeth? Our customers will never buy into that approach!' Or maybe you went out of your way to help a customer, accepting a return shipment of an item against company policy. 'Why do you think we have policies – because we enjoy killing trees for the paper to print them on? If we made exceptions for everyone, we'd go out of business!' How did it feel to have your sincere efforts at doing a great job disparaged? What was your reaction? Simple – you didn't bother making the extra effort again.

Despite rumours to the contrary, when you empower your employees, you don't stop managing. What changes is the way you manage. Managers still provide vision, establish organisational goals and determine shared values. However, they also have to establish a corporate infrastructure – skills training, teams and so on – that supports empowerment. And although all your employees may not want to be empowered, you still have to provide an environment that supports those employees who are eager for a taste of the freedom to apply their personal creativity and expertise to your organisation.

Great managers allow their employees to do great work. This role is the real and vital function of management, because even the greatest managers in the world can't succeed all by themselves.

To achieve the organisation's goals, managers depend on their employees' skills. Effective managers combine the efforts of every member of a work unit towards a common purpose. If you're constantly doing your employees' work for them, not only have you lost the advantage of the effectiveness that your employees can provide for you, you're also putting yourself on the path to stress, ulcers and worse.

When you don't empower employees, not only do you lose out, everyone in your organisation loses too. Your employees lose because you aren't allowing them to stretch themselves or to show creativity or initiative. Your organisation loses the insights that its creative workforce brings with it. Finally, your customers lose because your employees are afraid to provide them with exceptional service. Why should they if they're constantly worried about you punishing them for taking the initiative or for pushing the limits of the organisation to serve your customers better?

As William McKnight, former CEO of manufacturing giant 3M, put it, 'The mistakes people make are of much less importance than the mistakes management makes if it tells people exactly what to do.'

And as Phil McGovern, former General Manager of Panasonic UK, commented, 'Make mistakes? Of course we do. We make thousands of mistakes every day. I myself make mistakes. The important thing is that we learn from them. And we have to learn from them if we are to remain competitive.'

Support

A manager's job is no longer that of a watchdog, police officer or executioner. Increasingly, managers must be coaches, colleagues, cheerleaders and advocates for their staff. The main concern of today's managers needs to be shaping a more supportive work environment that enables each employee to feel valued and be more productive.

When the going gets tough, managers support their employees. This doesn't mean that you do everything for your employees or make their decisions for them. It does mean that you give your employees the training, resources and authority to do their jobs and then you get out of the way. You're always there for your employees to help pick up the pieces if they fall, but fall they must if they're going to learn. The idea is the same as learning to skate: if you're not falling, you're not learning.

The key to creating a supportive environment is establishing trust or openness throughout an organisation. In an open environment, employees can bring up questions and concerns. In fact, they're encouraged to do so. When the environment is truly open, an individual can express concerns without fear of retribution. Hidden agendas don't exist, and people feel free to say the same things in business meetings that they'd say after work. When employees see that their managers are receptive to new ideas, they're more likely to feel invested in the organisation, and to think of more and better ways to improve systems, to solve problems, to save money and to serve customers.

Managers also support each other. Personal fiefdoms, fighting between departments and withholding information have no place in the modern organisation; companies can't afford to support these dysfunctional behaviours. All members of the organisation – from the top to the bottom – must realise that they play on the same team. To win, team members support each other and keep their people up to date with the latest information. Which team are you on?

Communicate

Without a doubt, communication is the lifeblood of any organisation, and managers are the common element that connects different levels of employees with one another. We've seen at first hand the positive effects on a business and its employees of managers who communicate, and the negative effects on a business and its employees of managers who don't.

Managers who don't communicate effectively are missing out on a vital role of management.

Communication is a key function for managers today. Information is power, and as the speed of business accelerates, employees must get the information they need faster than ever. Continual change and increasing turbulence in the business environment necessitate more communication, not less. Who's going to be around in five years? The manager who's mastered this function or the one who hasn't?

With the proliferation of new means of communication, managers simply have no excuse not to communicate with their employees. You can even use the telephone or try a little old-fashioned face-to-face talk with your employees if you like!

To meet the expectations that you set for them, your employees have to be aware of those expectations. A goal is great on paper, but if you don't communicate it to employees and don't keep them up to date on their progress towards achieving that goal, how can you expect them to reach it? Simply, you can't. Such a goal would be like training for the Olympics but never being given feedback on how you're doing versus the competition.

Employees often appreciate the little things – an invitation to an upcoming meeting, praise for a job well done or an insight into the organisation's finances. Not only does sharing this kind of information make a business run better, it also creates tremendous goodwill and cements the trust that bonds your employees to the organisation and to the successful completion of its goals.

Taking the First Steps towards Becoming a Manager

Believe it or not, many managers never receive formal training in management (though thankfully this is changing). In many cases management is just something that's added to your job description. One day you may be a computer programmer working on a hot new app, and the next day you may be in charge of the new development team. Before, you were expected only to show up to work and create a product. Now, you're expected to lead and motivate a group of workers towards a common goal. You may get paid more to do the job, but the only training you may get for the task is in the school of hard knocks.

Managers (or managers-to-be) can easily discover how to become good managers by following the recommendations in the following sections. No one way is absolutely right or absolutely wrong; each has its pluses and minuses.

Look and listen

If you're fortunate enough to have had a skilled teacher or mentor during the course of your career, you're treated to an education in management that's equal to or better than any Master of Business Administration (MBA) programme. You get to know at first hand the right and wrong ways to manage people. You discover what it takes to get things done in your organisation, and you realise that customer satisfaction involves more than simply giving your customers lip service.

Unfortunately, any organisation with good management also has living, breathing examples of the wrong way to manage employees. You know the ones we're talking about: the manager who refuses to make decisions, leaving employees and customers hanging. Or the boss who refuses to delegate even the simplest decision to employees. Or the supervisor who insists on managing every single aspect of a department – no matter how small or inconsequential: 'No, no, no! The stamp goes on the envelope first, and then the address label, not the other way around!' Examples of the right way to manage employees are, regrettably, still few and far between.

You can benefit from the behaviours that poor managers model. When you find a manager who refuses to make decisions, for example, carefully note the impact their management style has on workers, other managers and customers. You can feel your own frustration. Make a mental note: 'I'll never, ever demotivate another person like that.' Indecision at the top inevitably leads to indecision at all ranks of an organisation – especially when people are punished for filling the vacuum that indecisive managers leave. Employees become confused, and customers become concerned as the organisation drifts aimlessly.

Observe the manager who depends on fear and intimidation to get results. What are the real results of this style of management? Do employees look forward to coming to the office every day? Are they all pulling for a common vision and goal? Are they extending themselves to bring innovation to work processes and procedures? Or are they more concerned with just getting through the day without being yelled at? Think about what you'd do differently to get the results you want.

You can always pick up something from other managers – whether they're good managers or bad ones.

A world-class teacher

By many measures, Jack Welch is considered to be one of the United States' top business leaders. Welch, who until recently was chairman of General Electric (GE), radically transformed his company's culture while dramatically improving its performance – and in the process created some $57 billion in value.

Although Welch did many different things to make the transformation a reality, one of the most telling was his takeover of GE's training facility in Ossining, New York. As he realised, designing a new culture is one thing, but getting the word out to employees and making it stick is another thing altogether. By directing the class curricula for all levels of workers, and by personally dropping into the training centre every two weeks or so to meet with students, Welch was able not only to determine what message would be communicated to GE employees, but also to ensure that they received the message

loudly and clearly. If the employees were confused, they had ample opportunity to ask him for clarification.

In a gesture that was at once symbolic and real, Welch directed the ceremonial burning of the old-school GE Blue Books. The Blue Books were a series of management training manuals that prescribed how GE managers were to get tasks done in the organisation. Despite the fact that the use of these books for training had been mothballed for some 15 years, they still exerted tremendous influence over the actions of GE managers. Citing the need for managers to write their own answers to day-to-day management challenges, Welch swept away the old order by removing the Blue Books from the organisation's culture once and for all. Now, GE managers are taught to find their own solutions rather than look them up in a dusty old book.

Do and learn

Perhaps you're familiar with this old saying (attributed to Lao Tze):

Give a man a fish, and he eats for a day,

Teach a man to fish, and he eats for a lifetime.

Such is the nature of managing employees. If you make all the decisions, do the work that your employees are able to do given the chance, and try to carry the entire organisation on your own shoulders, you're harming your employees and your organisation far more than you can imagine. Your employees never find out how to succeed on their own, and after a while they stop trying. In your sincere efforts to bring success to your organisation, you stunt the growth of your employees and make the organisation less effective and vital.

Top five management websites

Wondering where to find the best information about the topics we address in this chapter? Try some of our favourites:

✔ Chartered Management Institute: `www.managers.org.uk`

✔ Chartered Institute of Personnel and Development: `www.cipd.co.uk`

✔ ManagementFirst: `www.managementfirst.com`

✔ London Business School: `www.london.edu`

✔ Learning and Skills Council: `www.lsc.gov.uk`

Simply reading a book (even this one) or watching someone else manage – or fail to manage – isn't enough. To take advantage of lessons you learn, you have to put them into practice. Keep these key steps in mind:

1. **Take the time to assess your organisation's problems.**

   Which parts of your organisation work, and which don't? Why or why not? You can't focus on all your problems at one time. Concentrate and solve a few problems that are the most important before you move on to the rest.

2. **Take a close look at yourself.**

   What do you do to help or hinder your employees when they try to do their jobs? Do you give them the authority to make decisions? Just as important, do you support them when they go out on a limb for the organisation? Study your personal interactions throughout your business day. Do they result in positive or negative outcomes?

3. **Try out the techniques that you learn from your reading or from observing other managers at work.**

   Go ahead! Nothing changes if you don't change first. 'If it's to be, it's to begin with me.'

4. **Step back and watch what happens.**

   We promise that you can see a difference in the way you get tasks done and in the way your customers and employees respond to your organisation's needs and goals.

Chapter 2

Lead, Follow or Get Out of the Way

· ·

In This Chapter

▶ Comparing leadership and management

▶ Becoming a leader

▶ Zeroing in on key leadership traits

▶ Leading collaboratively

· ·

*W*hat makes a leader? Experts have written countless books, produced endless DVDs and taught innumerable seminars on the topic of leadership. But leadership is still a quality that eludes many who seek it.

Studies show that the two primary traits that all effective leaders have in common are a positive outlook and forward thinking. Effective managers are sure of themselves and their ability to inspire and influence others and to shape the future.

Everyone in an organisation wants to work for great leaders. Employees want the men and women they work for to exhibit leadership. 'I wish that my boss would just make a decision – I'm just marking time until she does. So I just wait until she lets me know what she does want me to do.' And wait employees do – until the boss finally notices that the project is two months behind. Top executives want the men and women who work for them to exhibit leadership. 'You need to take responsibility for your department and pull the numbers into the black before the end of the financial year!' And employees want their peers to show leadership. 'If she's not going to straighten out that invoicing process, then I'm just going to have to work around it myself!'

A leader is many things to many people. In this chapter, we discuss the key skills and attributes that make good managers into great leaders. Leadership requires the application of a wide variety of skills; no single trait, even when you've mastered it, suddenly makes you an effective leader. 'You mean I can't become a great leader just from watching that DVD?' However, you may notice that some leadership skills we describe in this chapter are also key functions of management – ones that we outline in Chapter 1. This similarity is no coincidence. Check out *Leadership For Dummies (2nd Edition)* by John Marrin (Wiley) for an in-depth look at leadership.

Understanding the Differences between Management and Leadership

Although similar, leadership and management are different: leadership goes above and beyond management. A manager can be organised and efficient at getting tasks done without being a leader – without being someone who inspires others to achieve their best. In short, managers *manage* processes and resources, and leaders *lead* people. According to management visionary Peter Drucker, leadership is the most basic and scarcest resource in any business enterprise. We concur wholeheartedly.

Being a good manager is quite an accomplishment. Management is by no means an easy task, and mastering the wide range of varied skills required can take many years. The best managers get their jobs done efficiently and effectively – with a minimum of fuss and bother. Like the people behind the scenes of a great performance in sports or the theatre, the best managers are often those you notice the least.

Great managers are experts at taking their current organisations and optimising them to accomplish their goals and get their jobs done. By necessity, they focus on the here and now – not on the tremendous potential of what the future can bring. Organisations expect managers to make things happen now – not at some hazy point in the future. 'Don't tell me what you're going to do for me next year or the year after that! I want results, and I want them now!' Having good managers in an organisation, however, isn't enough on its own.

Great organisations need great management. However, great management doesn't necessarily make a great organisation. For an organisation to be great, it must also have great leadership.

Leaders have vision. They look beyond the here and now to see the vast potential of their organisations. And although great leaders are also effective at getting things done in their organisations, they accomplish their goals in a different way to managers.

How is the leader's way different? Managers use values, policies, procedures, schedules, milestones, incentives, discipline and other mechanisms to push their employees to achieve the goals of the organisation. Leaders, on the other hand, challenge their employees to achieve the organisation's goals by creating a compelling vision of the future and then unlocking their employees' potential.

Think about some great leaders:

- ✔ In the darkest hours of the Second World War, Winston Churchill challenged the British people to stand alone and to fight for what was right. They did.

- ✔ Anita Roddick challenged the management and staff of The Body Shop to inspire and excite customers, not just to sell cosmetics to them. They did.

- ✔ Michael O'Leary of Ryanair challenged – and continues to challenge – his staff to improve everything they can, including turnaround times, speed of service, cleaning the aircraft cabins and keeping to schedule. They did – and they still do.

All these leaders share a common trait. They all painted compelling visions that grabbed the imagination of their followers and then challenged them to achieve these visions. Without the vision that leaders provide and without the contributions of their followers' hard work, energy and innovation, Great Britain would have fallen to the Nazis, The Body Shop would be just another company and Ryanair wouldn't be the second largest airline by passenger numbers carried in the European Union.

Looking at What Leaders Do

The skills required to be a leader are no secret. Some managers have worked out how to use the skills and others haven't. And although some people seem to be born leaders, anyone can discover what leaders do and how to apply these skills themselves.

Inspire action

Despite what some managers believe, most workers want to feel pride in their organisation and, when given the chance, would give their all to a cause they believe in. A tremendous well of creativity and energy is just waiting to be tapped in every organisation. Leaders use this knowledge to inspire their employees to take action and to achieve great things.

Leaders know the value of employees and their critical place in achieving the company's goals. Do the managers in your company know the importance of their employees? Have a look at what these managers had to say in Bob Nelson's *1001 Ways to Reward Employees* (Workman Publishing, 2005):

✔ Former chairman and CEO of the Ford Motor Company, Harold A. Poling, says, 'One of the stepping stones to a world-class operation is to tap into the creative and intellectual power of each and every employee.'

✔ Richard Branson, founder and CEO of the Virgin Group, states: 'The staff come first. Only by having expert, highly committed, and well rewarded staff can the Virgin Organisation hope to succeed through creating and delivering top quality products and services, and the best possible customer satisfaction.'

✔ Michael Marks, former chief executive of Marks and Spencer, used to say: 'Everyone who works for Marks and Spencer wants to do a good job. Without them we have no company. They are proud to work for this company; and I am very proud to have them working for me.'

Unfortunately, few managers reward their employees for being creative or for going beyond the boundaries set by their job descriptions. Too many managers search for workers who do exactly what they're told – and little else. This practice is a tremendous waste of workers' creativity, ideas, talent and commitment.

Use your influence as a manager to help your employees create energy in their jobs instead of draining it from them with bureaucracy, red tape, policies and an emphasis on avoiding mistakes.

Leaders are different. Instead of draining energy from their employees, leaders unleash the natural energy within all employees. They do so by clearing the roadblocks to creativity and pride from the paths of their workers and by creating a compelling vision for their employees to strive for. Leaders help employees to tap into energy and initiative that the employees didn't know they had.

Create a compelling vision for your employees and then clear away the roadblocks to creativity and pride. Your vision must be a stretch to achieve, but not so much of a stretch that the vision is impossible to achieve.

Communicate

Leadership takes place *among* people. Leaders therefore make a commitment to communicate with their employees and to keep them fully informed about every aspect of the organisation. Employees want to be an integral part of the organisation and want their opinions and suggestions to be heard and valued. Great leaders earn the commitment of their workers by building communication links throughout the organisation – from the top to the bottom, from the bottom to the top and from side to side.

So how do you build communication links in your organisation? Consider the experiences of the following business leaders, as listed in Bob's *1001 Ways to Reward Employees*:

✔ According to Donald Petersen, former president and CEO of Ford Motor Company, 'When I started visiting the plants and meeting with employees, what was reassuring was the tremendous, positive energy in our conversations. One man said he'd been with Ford for 25 years and hated every minute of it – until he was asked for his opinion. He said that question transformed his job.'

✔ Andrea Nieman, administrative assistant with the Rolm Corporation, a computer company now part of the IBM Corporation, summarises her company's commitment to communication like this: 'Rolm recognises that people are the greatest asset. There is no "us" and "them" attitude here; everyone is important. Upper management is visible and accessible. There is always time to talk, to find solutions, and to implement changes.'

✔ Says Robert Hauptfuhrer, former chairman and CEO of Oryx Energy, 'Give people a chance not just to do a job but to have some impact, and they'll really respond, get on their roller skates, and race around to make sure it happens.'

When Bob became a departmental manager at Blanchard Training and Development, he made a commitment to his team of employees to communicate with them. To make his commitment real, Bob added a specific promise: he promised that he would report the results of every executive team meeting within 24 hours. Bob's department valued his team briefings, because through this communication he treated all individuals as colleagues – not as underlings.

Great leaders know that leadership isn't a one-way street. Leadership today is a two-way interchange of ideas where leaders create a vision and workers throughout an organisation develop and communicate ideas of how best to reach the vision. The old one-way, command-and-control model of management doesn't work any more. Ordering people about may have worked satisfactorily once. As a daily means of managing a company today, it doesn't work well at all. Most employees aren't willing simply to take orders and be directed all day long; if treated this way, expert and otherwise committed employees merely take their talents elsewhere. And if you think your employees want to be ordered around, you're only fooling yourself.

Support and facilitate

Great leaders create environments in which employees are safe to speak up, to tell the truth and to take risks. An incredible number of managers punish their employees for pointing out problems that they encounter, for disagreeing with the conventional wisdom of management or for merely saying what's on their minds. Even more incredibly, many managers punish their employees for taking risks and losing, instead of helping their employees win the next time around.

Great leaders support their employees and facilitate those employees' abilities to reach their goals. The head of an organisation where Peter once worked did just the opposite. Instead of leading his employees with vision and inspiration, he pushed them with the twin cattle prods (120 volts!) of fear and intimidation. The management team members lived in constant fear of his temper, which could explode without warning and seemingly without reason. More than a few managers wore the psychological bruises and scars of his often-public outbursts. Instead of contributing to the good of the organisation, some managers simply withdrew into their shells and said as little as possible in this leader's presence. Consider these managers' statements in *1001 Ways to Reward Employees*:

- Catherine Meek, when president of compensation consulting firm Meek and Associates, said, 'In the 20 years I have been doing this and the thousands of employees I have interviewed in hundreds of companies, if I had to pick one thing that comes through loud and clear it is that organisations do a lousy job of recognising people's contributions. That is the number one thing employees say to us. "We don't even care about the money; if my boss would just acknowledge that I exist. The only time I ever hear anything is when I screw up. I never hear when I do a good job."'

- According to Lonnie Blittle, an assembly-line worker for Nissan Motor Manufacturing Corporation USA, 'There was none of the hush-hush atmosphere with management behind closed doors and everybody else waiting until they drop the bomb on us. They are right down pitching in, not standing around with their hands on their hips.'

- James Berdahl, vice-president of marketing for Business Incentives, says, 'People want to feel empowered to find better ways to do things and to take responsibility for their own environment. Allowing them to do this has had a big impact on how they do their jobs, as well as on their satisfaction with the company.'

Instead of abandoning their employees to the sharks, great leaders throw their followers life-jackets when the going gets particularly rough. Although leaders allow their employees free rein in how they achieve the organisation's goals, leaders are always there in the background – ready to assist and support workers whenever necessary. With the added security of this safety net, employees are more willing to stretch themselves and to take chances that can create enormous rewards for their organisations.

Surveying Leading Leadership Traits

Today's new business environment is unrelenting change. About the only constant you can be sure of any more is that everything will change. And after it changes, it changes again and again.

Get used to it now, because business will continue to transform in the foreseeable future. Although so much in business is shifting, great leadership remains steadfast – like a sturdy rock standing up to the storms of change. Numerous traits of great leaders have remained the same over the years and are still highly valued today. The following sections discuss the leading leadership traits.

Optimism

Great leaders always see the future as a wonderful place. Although they may encounter much adversity and hard work on the way to achieving their goals, leaders always look forward to the future with great optimism. This optimism becomes a glow that radiates from all great leaders and touches all those employees who come into contact with them.

Key business trends to watch out for

According to Stanley Bing, an incredibly insightful columnist for *Fortune* magazine, many trends are sweeping the business landscape. One major trend is the necessity for managers to *talk the talk* and *walk the walk.* Talking the talk means sounding like you know what you're doing, and walking the walk takes this idea a step further and requires that you also look like you know what you're doing – whether you do know or not.

The percentage of executives who can talk the talk and those executives who can walk the walk has been increasing since 1970. However, the ability of managers to talk the talk and walk the walk at the same time has steadily declined from its peak some 20 years ago. Here's some advice from Bing regarding these critical leadership skills:

✔ 'First, always talk the talk, even when others don't seem to understand what you're saying. It's all about consistency and perception – so keep it up!

✔ Second, if you're not in a position to talk the talk, either because someone superior is doing so or because you've got your mouth full, default to walking the walk exclusively, thereby projecting the necessary executive qualities in dignity and silence.

✔ Third, don't try doing both together until you're very good at it. There's nothing more pathetic than somebody attempting to walk/talk concurrently and getting his ankles all bollixed up while irreverent employees stand around chortling. So practice!'

People want to feel good about themselves and their futures, and they want to work for winners. Workers are therefore naturally attracted to people who are optimistic rather than pessimistic. Who wants to work for someone who enjoys nothing more than spouting doom and gloom about the future of a business? Negative managers only demotivate their employees and colleagues, which leads everyone to spend more time polishing up their CVs than concentrating on doing their work to the best of their ability and improving their organisations.

Optimism is infectious. Before long, a great leader can turn an organisation full of doom merchants into one that's overflowing with positive excitement for the future. This excitement results in greater worker productivity and an improved organisational environment. Morale increases, and so does the organisation's bottom line.

Be an optimist. Let your excitement rub off on those people around you.

Confidence

Great leaders have no doubt – at least not in public – that they can accomplish any task that they set their minds to.

'What? A 10,000-foot mountain is in the way? No problem – we'll climb it. You say that a vast ocean is separating us from our goal? No sweat – we'll swim it. Hmmm . . . a bottomless crevasse is blocking our path? Fine – we'll leap it. Whatever the challenge may be, we'll find a way to surmount it.'

Confident leaders make for confident followers, which is why organisations led by confident leaders are unstoppable. An organisation's employees mirror the behaviour of their leaders. When leaders are negative, tentative and unsure of themselves, so are workers (and the bottom-line results of the organisation). When leaders display self-confidence, workers follow suit, and the results can be astounding.

Be a confident leader. You inspire the best performance from your employees at the same time as you help them to become more confident in their abilities.

Integrity

One trait that sets great leaders apart from the rest of the pack is *integrity*: ethical behaviour, values and a sense of fair play. Honest people want to follow honest leaders. Integrity means establishing the standards by which you're determined to operate, and then never compromising on them. You make an absolute commitment to work on the basis of fairness, equality, honesty and trust, and then you deliver – always! You never succumb to pressure, you never compromise on fairness, you never tell lies – whatever the circumstances or adversity with which you're faced. And you can develop all this; you can choose to do things in these ways, or you can choose not to. Which are you going to choose?

In a recent survey, integrity was the trait employees most wanted from their leaders. When an organisation's leaders conduct themselves with integrity, the organisation can make a very real and positive difference in the lives of its employees, its customers and others who come in contact with it. This, in turn, results in positive feelings from employees about the organisation.

People working in the UK devote up to a third (or more) of their waking hours to their jobs. Whether the organisation makes light fittings, disposes of toxic waste, develops virtual reality software or delivers pizzas, people want to be part of an organisation that makes a positive difference in the lives of others. Of course money is important – people have to pay their bills and buy clothes for their children – but unless wages are very low, few people count *external* rewards as a primary consideration over the *internal* rewards that they themselves derive from their work.

Decisiveness

The best leaders are decisive. All employees' main complaint is that their bosses won't make decisions – and they say this over and over again. Despite the fact that making decisions is one of the key reasons that people are hired to be managers, too few are willing to risk the possibility of making a wrong decision. So instead of making wrong decisions – and having to face the consequences – many so-called leaders prefer to postpone making a decision indefinitely, instead continually seeking more information, alternatives and opinions from others. They hope that, eventually, events may overtake the need to make the decision, or perhaps that someone else will take the platform and make the decision for them.

Great leaders make decisions. Now, this statement doesn't mean that great leaders make decisions in a shoot-from-the-hip, cavalier, guess-at-the-right-answer fashion. No, great leaders take whatever time is necessary to gather whatever information, people or resources they need to make an informed decision within a reasonable time frame. If the data is immediately available, so be it. If not, then a leader carefully weighs the available data versus the relative need for the decision and acts accordingly.

Be decisive. Don't wait for the course of events to make decisions for you. Sometimes making a decision – even if you make the wrong one – is better than making no decision at all.

Fostering Collaborative Leadership

A new kind of leadership is gaining strength in an increasing number of organisations: *collaborative leadership*. When leaders lead collaboratively, they share leadership with others in the organisation. And not just with other managers and supervisors, but with employees at all levels – from the shop floor to the front line and everywhere else.

So, what exactly does collaborative leadership look like in the workplace? Here are a few examples:

- To encourage collaborative leadership, banking powerhouse JP Morgan Chase maintains a flat organisation with only four levels of employees worldwide – managing director, vice-president, associate and analyst. With fewer lines of reporting, every employee has the opportunity – and the responsibility – to play a much greater role in leading and in making decisions.

- Harvester, the pub/restaurant chain, did away with three levels of management – restaurant manager, office manager and head waiter. Chefs became responsible for planning the menus and ordering the food. Waiting staff collectively became responsible for taking and accepting bookings, showing guests to their tables and cashing up at the end of each working day. This is truly collaborative: the staff are responsible and accountable only to a regional manager.

- Colman's Foods makes mustards, sauces, herbs and spices for the retail grocery sector. While off duty, one employee had occasion to visit his local supermarket. To his horror, he saw that the whole stack of Colman's mustard had been badly labelled – the labels were either not straight or were scuffed or dirty. Accordingly, he bought the whole stock, took it back to the factory and presented it to his manager. And the company even refunded him his money!

- Dutton Engineering makes steel and aluminium furniture for industrial, commercial and office premises. In order to tackle the problem of ever-rising costs, Ken Lewis, the company's chief executive, organised every-one into self-managing teams. These teams recruit and select employees; set their own performance schedules (subject only to customer dead-lines); and establish their own pay, reward and bonus levels. Lewis has one assistant, but the teams now carry out all the work themselves; and he no longer has an office – the employees decided collectively that this space can be better used in a directly productive capacity.

In his book *Leadership Ensemble: Lessons in Collaborative Management from the World's Only Conductorless Orchestra* (Times Books, 2001), Peter (one of your authors) takes a very close look at the unique brand of collaborative leadership practised by New York City's Orpheus Chamber Orchestra.

Orpheus is one of the world's truly great orchestras, and it's one of very few to perform without a conductor. The vast majority of orchestras are noted not because of the musicians who play the music but because of their conductors, who are often visionary, charismatic (and autocratic) leaders. The conductor calls all the shots when it comes to the notes that an orchestra's musicians play, and how and when they play them.

By forgoing the traditional model of a conducted orchestra – with one leader and many followers – Orpheus fosters a culture of collaboration where every musician can be a leader, and all are expected to play an active role in shaping the group's final product – its music. Does this system work? Yes. Orpheus's performances have been acclaimed throughout the world, and the group has numerous Grammy-winning albums and other awards to its credit.

At the heart of the Orpheus process – the system of collaborative leadership that has brought the group great success over its three-decade history – are eight principles. These principles are:

- ✔ **Put power in the hands of the people doing the work.** Those employees closest to the customers are in the best position to know the customers' needs, and they're in the best position to make decisions that directly affect their customers.

- ✔ **Encourage individual responsibility for product and quality.** The flip side of putting power in the hands of the people doing the work is requiring employees to take responsibility for the quality of their work. When employees are trusted to play an active role in their organisation's leadership, they naturally respond by taking a personal interest in the quality of their work.

- ✔ **Create clarity of roles.** Before employees can be comfortable and effectively share leadership duties with others, they first have to have clearly defined roles so that they know exactly what they're responsible for, as well as what others are responsible for.

- ✔ **Foster horizontal teamwork.** Because no one person has all the answers to every question, effective organisations rely on horizontal teams – both formal and informal – that reach across departmental and other organisational boundaries. These teams obtain input, solve problems, act on opportunities and make decisions.

- ✔ **Share and rotate leadership.** By moving people in and out of positions of leadership – depending on an individual's particular talents and interests – organisations can tap the leadership potential that resides within every employee, even those employees who aren't part of the formal leadership hierarchy.

- ✔ **Discover how to listen, discover how to talk.** Effective leaders don't just listen: effective leaders talk – and they know the right times (and the wrong times) to make their views known. Effective organisations encourage employees to speak their minds and to contribute their ideas and opinions – whether or not others agree with what they have to say.

- ✔ **Seek consensus (and build creative systems that favour consensus).** One of the best ways to involve others in the leadership process is to invite them to play a real and important role in the discussions and debates that lead to making important organisational decisions. Seeking consensus requires a high level of participation and trust, and it results in more democratic organisations.

- ✔ **Dedicate passionately to your mission.** When people feel passion for the organisations in which they work, they care more about them and about their performance. This caring is expressed in the form of increased employee participation and leadership.

Collaborative leadership is growing in popularity in all kinds of organisations in all kinds of places. Why? Collaborative leadership is growing because organisations today can't afford to limit leadership to just a few individuals at the top. To survive and prosper, today's organisations need to get the most out of every employee. Every employee needs to take a leadership role in her organisation, to make decisions, to serve customers, to support colleagues and to improve systems and procedures. Employees – and leaders – who can't meet this challenge may soon find that they're left behind by others who can.

Top five leadership websites

Wondering where to find the best information on the web about the topics we address in this chapter? Well, you've come to the right place! Here are our top five favourites:

- ✔ *Management Today* **magazine:** www.managementtoday.com

- ✔ **London Business School Executive Programme:** www.london.edu/programmes/executiveeducation.html

- ✔ **Judge Business School, University of Cambridge:** www.jbs.cam.ac.uk/execed/

- ✔ **Said Business School, University of Oxford:** www.sbs.oxford.edu/

- ✔ **Institute of Directors:** www.iod.org.uk/executivedevelopment

Part II
Managing People

'Well, for a start, it's your spelling . . . .'

In this part . . .

If nothing else, managing is a people job. The best managers work well with all people. In this part, we show you how to hire great employees, inspire employees to achieve their best performance and coach and develop employees.

Chapter 3

Making the Million-Pound Decision: Recruitment and Selection

In This Chapter

▶ Determining your needs

▶ Recruiting new employees

▶ Interviewing do's and don'ts

▶ Evaluating your candidates

▶ Making the big decision

*G*ood employees are hard to find. If you've had the recent privilege of advertising for a job opening, you know that good employees aren't easy to come by. Here's the scenario: you place the advertisement and then wait for the applications to come flooding in. In just a day or two, you're pleased beyond your wildest dreams as you see the stack of applications awaiting your attention. How many are there – 100? 200? Well done indeed, what a response!

Your glee quickly turns to disappointment, however, as you begin your review. 'Why did this guy apply? He doesn't have half the required experience!' 'What? She's never even done this kind of work before.' 'Is this man joking? He must have responded to the wrong advertisement!'

Finding and hiring the best candidates for a job has never been easy. Unfortunately, with all the streamlining, downsizing and rightsizing going on in business nowadays, a lot of people are looking for work – and the chances are that very few of them have the exact qualifications that you're looking for. Your challenge is to work out how to pluck the best candidates out of the sea strewn with the wreckage of corporate cast-offs. The lifetime earnings of the average British worker can be as high as £1,000,000. Recruitment and selection really is, therefore, a million-pound decision!

Asking for the Right Stuff

Your mission is to locate the most highly qualified suitable candidates for your job opening. When you locate your candidates, your task is to narrow your selection down to one person and to ensure that recruitment leads to his successful entry into the organisation. This process isn't always as easy or as straightforward as it sounds.

Some years ago, the Ministry of Defence (MOD) advertised for a civilian quartermaster and stores manager. The post was to be based at a large army barracks in south-east England, and would additionally require work at other barracks nearby.

The MOD advertised the post, received numerous applications and drew up a shortlist. Finally, the organisation took on a candidate. The new employee, a man in his early forties, was pleasant, cheerful and polite. He made a good start to his work, and everybody liked him. At the end of his first week, his manager asked him to go off to one of the other barracks to collect some things. The conversation went like this:

> 'How do I get there?' asked the new employee.
>
> 'Take your car and claim the mileage – that's usual and that will be fine,' came the reply.
>
> 'But I don't drive.'

Because the MOD hadn't specified the need for a driving licence, and because this is something that 'everybody has', nobody had thought to check up on this small, but vital factor. As a consequence the MOD found itself forking out for a driver whenever the new employee had to go elsewhere as part of his duties. The MOD additionally paid for driving lessons; and when the new person had passed his test, they provided a loan at favourable rates for him to buy a car.

Employers look for many qualities in candidates. What do you look for when you interview? The following list gives you an idea of the qualities that employers consider most important when hiring new employees. Other characteristics may be particularly important to you.

- ✔ **Hard working:** Hard work can often overcome a lack of experience or training. You want to take on people who are willing to do whatever it takes to get the job done. Conversely, no amount of skill can make up for a lack of initiative or work ethic. Although you don't know for sure until you make your choice, careful questioning of candidates can give you some idea of their work ethic (or, at least, what they want you to believe about their work ethic).

✔ **Good attitude:** Although what constitutes a 'good' attitude is different for different people, a positive, friendly, willing-to-help perspective makes life at work much more enjoyable and makes everyone's job easier. When you interview candidates, consider what they'll be like to work with for the next five or ten years. Skills are important, but attitude is vital. 'Hire for attitude, train for success' is the mantra of US low-cost airline Southwest Airlines – apply it to your own organisation.

✔ **Experienced:** If you're asking for experience, be specific. In many cases, someone with 20 years' experience has in fact only had one year's experience – 20 times. So specify the things that you want the person to have done; and if you ask for '5/10/15 years' experience', spell out what you expect the candidate to have done during that period of employment. Make it clear that you're not seeking people of a particular age – age discrimination is illegal, and you can be prosecuted for unlawful discrimination. So be careful!

✔ **Initiative:** Everyone prefers somebody who takes the initiative to get work done. You're not going to get anything – from the new employee or from existing staff – if you take people on who are going to sit around waiting until you allocate tasks to them.

✔ **Team player:** Teamwork is critical to the success of today's organisations, which must do far more with far fewer resources than their predecessors. The ability to work with others effectively is a definite must for employees today.

✔ **Smart:** Smart people can often find better and quicker solutions to the problems that confront them. You need people who are going to do things for you, not say things to you.

✔ **Responsible:** You want to recruit people who are willing to take on the responsibilities of their positions. Questions about the kinds of projects that your candidates have been responsible for, and the exact roles they played in their success, can help you determine this important quality. Little factors, like showing up for the interview and remembering the name of the company they're applying to, can also be key indicators of your candidates' sense of responsibility.

✔ **Stable:** You don't want to hire someone today and then find out that he's already looking for his next position tomorrow. You can get some indication of a person's potential stability (or lack of) by asking how long he worked with his previous employer and why he left. Not only that, you can also enjoy listening to your candidates explain how they're ready to settle down.

Hiring the right people is one of the most important tasks that managers face. You can't have a great organisation without great people. Unfortunately, managers traditionally give short shrift to this task – devoting as little time as possible to preparation and to the actual interview process. As in much of the rest of your life, the results that you get from the hiring process are usually in direct proportion to the amount of time that you devote to it. If you commit yourself to finding the best candidates for a position, you're much more likely to find them. If you rely on chance to bring them to you, you may be disappointed by what and who you find.

Defining the Job and the Person

Whether the position is new, or you're filling an existing post, before you start the recruiting process you need to know exactly what standards you're going to use to measure your candidates. The clearer you are about what you need, the easier and less arbitrary your selection process becomes.

Draft a job description and person specification that fully describes all the tasks, responsibilities and characteristics of the position, and the minimum necessary qualifications and experience. And if the job requires a driving licence, for example, then say so! Otherwise, you start making mistakes right from the start.

If you're filling an existing position, review the current job description closely and make changes where necessary. This is a good opportunity to rearrange workloads and make changes if you need to. Again, make the job description reflect exactly the tasks and requirements of the position. When you hire someone new to fill an existing position, you start with a clean slate. For example, you may have had a difficult time getting a former employee to accept certain new tasks – say, taking minutes at staff meetings or filing travel vouchers. By adding these new duties to the job description before you begin recruitment, you make the expectations clear, and you don't have to struggle to get your new employee to do the job.

Finally, before you start recruiting, get the desired qualities and characteristics into a priority order. If necessary, consult with colleagues to make sure that you give yourself the best possible chance of getting the right candidate for the job.

Additionally, when you come to interviewing, by law you have to give everybody the same chance. So use the characteristics in their priority order as the basis for your interviewing and selection methods. If you fail to do this, unsuccessful candidates can question the basis on which you turned them down for the job, and if any doubt at all exists that they were given fair treatment, they can (and in many cases, do) make representations to employment tribunals. So get this right – now!

Finding Good People

People are the heart of every business. The better the people running your business, the better your business.

Some people are just meant to be in their jobs. You may know such individuals – someone who thrives as a receptionist or someone who lives to sell. Think about how great your organisation would be if you staffed every position with people who lived for their jobs.

Likewise, bad staff can make working for an organisation an incredibly miserable experience. The negative impacts of hiring the wrong candidate can reverberate throughout an organisation for years. If you, as a manager, ignore the problem, you put yourself in danger of losing your good employees. We can't overemphasise the importance of recruiting and retaining the right people. Do you want to spend a few extra hours up front to find the best candidates, or do you want to devote countless hours later trying to straighten out a problem employee? And if you still need convincing, a recent survey by the Chartered Institute of Personnel and Development estimates that replacing an employee costs up to twice their annual salary.

Of course, as important as the interview process is to selecting the best candidates for your jobs, you don't have anyone to interview if you don't have a good system for finding good candidates. So where can you find the best candidates for your jobs?

The simple answer is everywhere. Certainly, some places are better than others – you probably won't find someone to run your lab's fusion reactor project by advertising on the backs of matchboxes – but you never know where you can find your next star programmer or award-winning advertising copywriter. Who knows, he may be working for your competitors right now!

As you maximise your chances of success, you also minimise your chances of failure. The most effective recruitment and selection processes take place when you have plenty of time to evaluate all the candidates; and when you're not pressed to take on someone if you haven't so far attracted anyone of the calibre you want.

Ideally, you can involve other employees in the recruitment and selection process as well, especially if they're going to be working with the new candidate. So do at least consider any particular demands that other employees may have before you finalise your candidate list.

The following list presents some of the best ways to find candidates for your positions. Your job is to develop a recruitment campaign that can find the kinds of people that you want to take on. Don't rely solely on your human resources (HR) department to develop this campaign; you probably have a better understanding of where to find the people you need than they do, so work with HR to best advantage. And make sure that your contribution is noted.

- ✔ **Taking a close look within:** In most organisations, the first place to look for candidates is within the organisation. If you do your job in training and developing employees, then you probably have plenty of candidates to consider for your job openings. Only after you exhaust your internal candidates should you look outside your organisation. Not only is taking on people from within less expensive and easier, but you also get happier employees, improved morale and a steady stream of people who are already familiar with your organisation.

- ✔ **Personal referrals:** Whether from existing work groups, professional colleagues, friends, relatives or neighbours, you can find great candidates by referrals. Who better to present a candidate than someone whose opinion you already value and trust? You get far more insight about the candidates' strengths and weaknesses from the people who refer them than you get from applications alone. Also, research shows that people hired through current employees tend to work better, stay with the company longer and are happier. When you're getting ready to fill a position, make sure that you let people know about it.

- ✔ **Temporary agencies:** Taking on *temps*, or temporary employees, has become routine for many companies. When you simply have to fill a critical position for a short period of time, temporary agencies are the way to go. And the best part is that when you hire temps, you get the opportunity to try out employees before you take them on. If you don't like the temps you get, no problem. Simply call the agency, and they send replacements before you know it. But if you like your temps, most agencies allow you to employ them at a nominal fee or after a minimum time commitment. Either way, you win.

- ✔ **Professional associations:** Most professions have their accompanying associations that look out for their interests. Whether you're a doctor (and belong to the British Medical Association), or a lorry driver (and belong to the Transport and General Workers' Union), you can probably find an affiliated association for whatever you do for a living. Association newsletters, journals and magazines are great places to advertise your openings when you're looking for specific expertise, because your audience is already pre-screened for you.

- ✔ **Employment agencies:** If you're filling a particularly specialised position, are recruiting in a small market or simply prefer to have someone else take care of recruiting and screening your applicants, employment agencies are a good, albeit pricey alternative (with a cost of up to one-third of the employee's first-year salary, or more). Although employment agencies can usually locate qualified candidates in lower-level or administrative positions, you may need help from an executive search firm or *headhunter* (someone who specialises in recruiting key employees away from one firm to place in a client's firm) for your higher-level positions.

✔ **The Internet:** Every day, more and more companies discover the benefits of using the Internet as a hiring tool. Although academics and scientists have long used Internet newsgroups to advertise and seek positions within their fields, corporations are now following suit. The proliferation of corporate web pages and online employment agencies and job banks has brought about an entirely new dimension in recruiting. Web pages let you present almost unlimited amounts and kinds of information about your firm and about your job openings – in text, audio, graphic and video formats. Your pages work for you 24 hours a day, 7 days a week.

For an example of a particularly effective recruiting website, point your browser to www.qualcomm.com and click on the Careers button.

✔ **Recruitment advertising:** Recruitment advertising can be relatively expensive, but it's an easy way to get your message across. You can choose to advertise in your local paper or in nationally distributed publications such as the *Financial Times*. On the downside, you may find yourself sorting through hundreds or even thousands of unqualified candidates to find a few great ones. But that's what your HR department's for, right?

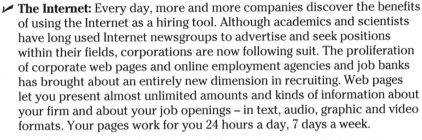

You have to consider whether or not you proceed if you don't find the right candidate. It's a real testament to your values and preliminary work to stick with your plan and extend the candidate recruiting period to allow for additional candidates, or delay the recruitment for another time.

Being the Greatest Interviewer in the World

After you narrow the field down to the top three or five applicants, you need to start interviewing. What kind of interviewer are you? Do you spend several hours preparing for interviews – reviewing applications, looking over job descriptions, writing and rewriting questions until each one is as finely honed as a razor blade? Or are you the kind of interviewer who, busy as you already are, starts preparing for the interview when you get the call from your receptionist that your candidate has arrived?

Spending some serious time preparing for your interviews is the secret to becoming the Greatest Interviewer in the World. Remember how much time you spent preparing to be interviewed for your current job? You didn't just walk in the door, sit down and get offered the job, did you? You probably spent hours researching the company, its products and services, its financial position, its market and other business information. You probably brushed up on your interviewing skills and may have even done some role-playing with a friend or in front of a mirror. Don't you think that you should spend at least as much time getting ready for the interview as do the people you're going to put through their paces?

Asking the right questions

More than anything else, the heart of the interview process is the questions that you ask and the answers that you receive in response. You get the best answers when you ask the best questions and actively listen to the answers. Lousy questions often result in lousy answers – answers that don't really tell you whether the candidate is going to be right for the job.

A great interviewer asks great questions. 'How do I ask great questions?' you may want to know. According to Richard Nelson Bolles, author of the perennially popular job-hunting guide *What Color Is Your Parachute?* (Ten Speed Press, 2010), you can categorise all interview questions under one of the following four headings:

- ✔ **Why are you here?** Really. Why is the person sitting across from you going to the trouble of interviewing with you today? You have just one way to find out – ask. You may assume that the answer is because he wants a job with your firm, but you may be surprised at what you discover.

  One of the candidates on the TV programme *The Apprentice*, who'd reached the later stages and was well in contention for the final, ruined his chances because he hadn't bothered to find out the exact nature of products made by Amstrad, the company that he'd be working for.

- ✔ **What can you do for us?** Always an important consideration. Of course, your candidates are all going to dazzle you with their incredible personality, experience, work ethic and love of teamwork – that almost goes without saying. However, despite what many job seekers seem to believe, the question isn't 'What can your firm do for me?' – at least not from your perspective. The question that you want an answer to is: 'What can you do for us?'

  One manager tells a story about the job applicant who slammed his hand on her desk and demanded a signing bonus. And this was before the interview had even started! We're not surprised that this particular candidate landed neither the job nor the bonus.

- ✔ **What kind of person are you?** Few candidates are going to be absolute angels or demons, but don't forget that you spend a lot of time with the person you hire. You want to take on someone you enjoy being with during the many work hours, weeks and years that stretch before you. (or at least someone you can tolerate being with for a few hours every once in a while). You also want to confirm a few other issues: are your candidates honest and ethical? Do they share your views in regard to work hours, responsibility and so forth? Are they responsible and dependable? Of course, all your candidates answer in the affirmative to bland questions like these. So, how do you find the real answers?

When Bob used to recruit, he'd try to 'project' applicants into a typical, real-life scenario and then see how they thought it through. This way, no right answer exists and the applicants are forced to expose their thinking process, for example the questions they'd ask, strategies they'd consider, people they'd involve and so forth. Ask open-ended questions and let your candidates do most of the talking. Your candidate should talk for at least 70 per cent of the interview.

✔ **Can we afford you?** It does you no good if you find the perfect candidate, but at the end of the interview, you bring up the topic of pay and find out that you're so far apart that you're actually in a different country. Keep in mind that the actual wage you pay to workers is only part of an overall compensation package. Although you may not be able to pull together more money for wages for particularly good candidates, you may be able to offer them better benefits, longer holidays, more development opportunities or, ultimately, a faster career track.

Interviewing do's

So what can you do to prepare for your interviews? The following handy checklist gives you ideas on where to start:

✔ **Review the applications of each interviewee the morning before interviews start.** Reading your interviewees' applications during the actual interview is not only poor form; it also means you miss out on the opportunity to tailor your questions to those little surprises that you invariably discover (such as gaps in employment).

✔ **Become completely familiar with the job description.** Are you familiar with all the duties and requirements of the job? Really? Telling interviewees that the position requires duties that it really doesn't is poor form. Surprising new staff with duties that you didn't tell them about – especially when they're major tasks – is definitely not good practice.

✔ **Draft your questions before the interview.** Make a checklist of the key experience, skills and qualities that you seek in your candidates and use it to guide your questions. Of course, one of your questions may trigger other questions that you didn't anticipate. Go ahead with such questions as long as they provide you with additional insights regarding your candidate and help to illuminate the information that you've outlined on your checklist. And remember, equality of treatment and employment law demand that you give all candidates the same opportunities to shine at interview.

✔ **Select a comfortable environment for both of you.** Your interviewee is likely to be uncomfortable regardless of what you do. You don't need to be uncomfortable too. Make sure that the interview environment is well-ventilated, private and protected from interruptions. You definitely don't want your phone ringing or employees barging in during your interviews. You get the best performance from your interviewees when they aren't thrown off track by distractions.

✔ **Avoid playing power games during the course of the interview.** Forget asking trick questions, turning up the heat or cutting the legs off their chairs (yes, some managers still do this game playing) to gain an artificial advantage over your candidates. Get real – you're in the twenty-first century, for heaven's sake!

✔ **Take lots of notes.** Write down the key points of your candidates' responses and their reactions to your questions. For example, if you ask why your candidate left his previous job, and he starts getting really nervous, make a note about this reaction. Finally, note your own impressions of the candidates; and make sure that you have a form to work on with columns allocated to each candidate. And when you write anything down about the candidates, make sure that you stick to the professional and occupational issues. If you then use phrases such as the following, make sure you can say why:

- 'Top-notch performer – the star of her class.'

- 'Fantastic experience with developing applications in a client-server environment. The best candidate yet.'

- 'Not right for this job.'

If you write anything disparaging or overtly disrespectful about a candidate, you *have* to be able to say why. If an unsuccessful candidate decides to take you to an employment tribunal, you don't want your notes coming back to haunt you. So avoid one-word statements such as 'Hopeless'; if someone isn't right for the job, briefly note why and move on. Your candidates have the right to see any notes that you may have made, so always write them as if you were going to share them anyway.

✔ **Don't rely on your memory when it comes to interviewing candidates.** If you interview more than a couple of people, you can easily forget who said exactly what and what your impressions were of their performances. Not only are your written notes a great way to remember who's who, they're also an important tool to have when you're evaluating your candidates. And if there's any comeback (see the previous bullet point), you have your notes to refer to.

As you've no doubt gathered by now, interview questions are one of your best tools for determining whether a candidate is right for your company. Although some amount of small talk is appropriate to help relax your candidates (*as sweat poured down the candidate's face, the interviewer asked the opening question with razor-like sharpness: 'Hot enough for you?'*), the heart of your interviews should focus on answering the questions just listed. Above all, don't give up. Keep asking questions until you're satisfied that you have all the information you need to make your decision.

TIP

Six steps to better interviewing

Every interview consists of six key steps. They are

1. **Welcome the applicant.**

   Greet your candidates warmly and chat with them informally to help loosen them up. Questions about the weather, the difficulty of finding your offices or how they found out about your position are old stand-bys.

2. **Summarise the position.**

   Briefly describe the job, the kind of person you're looking for and the interview process that you use.

3. **Ask your questions (and then listen!).**

   Questions should be relevant to the position and should cover the applicant's work experience, education and other related topics. Limit the amount of talking you do as an interviewer. Many interviewers end up trying to sell the job to an applicant instead of probing whether or not she's a good fit.

4. **Probe experience and find out the candidates' strengths and weaknesses.**

   Past behaviour is the best predictor of future behaviour, which is why exploring

applicants' past experience can be so helpful to see what they did and how they did it. Although asking your candidates to name their strengths and weaknesses may seem clichéd, the answers can be very revealing. So ask the applicants – and then listen carefully to the answers.

5. **Get candidates to ask questions of you.**

   Good candidates always want to know something further than they've gained either from your website or the job information. So make sure that you set some time aside towards the end of the interview to enable them to ask questions.

6. **Conclude the interview.**

   Allow your candidates the opportunity to offer any further information that they feel is necessary for you to make a decision and to ask any outstanding questions. Thank them for their interest and let them know when they can expect your firm to contact them.

Interviewing don'ts

Interviewing don'ts could probably fill a whole chapter. If you've been a manager for any time at all, you know that you can run into tricky situations during an interview and that certain questions can land you in major hot water if you make the mistake of asking them.

Some interviewing don'ts are merely good business practice. For example, accepting an applicant's invitation for a date probably isn't a good idea. After a particularly drawn-out interview at a well-known high-tech manufacturer, a male candidate asked out a female interviewer. The interviewer considered her options and declined the date; she also declined to make Prince Charming a job offer.

Then you have the blunders of the major legal type – the kind that can land you and your firm in court. Interviewing is one area of particular concern in the hiring process because it pertains to the possibility of discrimination. For example, although you can ask applicants whether they're able to fulfil job functions, you can't ask them whether they're disabled.

Always ask whether the organisation needs to make any adjustments or provisions in order for a candidate to gain an equal opportunity in their application. This includes access to your place of work, application forms and directions in Braille, and any other specific issues.

Because of the critical nature of the interview process, you must know the questions that you should absolutely never ask a job candidate. Here's a brief summary of the kinds of topics that may, depending on the exact circumstances, get you and your firm into trouble:

- ✔ Applicant's ethnicity or skin colour
- ✔ Applicant's national origin
- ✔ Applicant's gender
- ✔ Applicant's sexual orientation
- ✔ Applicant's marital status
- ✔ Applicant's religion (or lack of)
- ✔ Applicant's height and weight
- ✔ Applicant's debts
- ✔ Applicant's disability
- ✔ Applicant's age
- ✔ Applicant's arrest and conviction record (with statutory exceptions)

    You can take into account offences involving money, theft, fraud, physical and psychological abuse, violence, vandalism and damage to property – even if the convictions are spent (or, in other words, the person has served their time). In the case of other spent convictions, you need to be prepared to justify why you have taken them into account, whether or not you do make someone a job offer.

Legal or illegal, the point is that none of the preceding topics is necessary to determine the applicants' ability to perform their jobs. So, ask questions that directly relate to the candidates' ability to perform the tasks required. To do otherwise puts you at risk. In other words, what *do* count are job-related criteria; that is, information that's directly pertinent to the candidate's ability to do the job (you clearly need to decide this *prior* to interviewing).

Evaluating Your Candidates

Now comes the tricky part of the recruitment process – evaluating your candidates. If you've done your homework, then you already have a good selection of candidates to choose from, you've narrowed your search down to the ones showing the best potential to excel in your position and you've interviewed them to see whether they can live up to the promises that they've made in their applications. Before you make your final decision, you need a little bit more information.

Checking references

You've just interviewed the best candidate on Earth. What an application! What an interview! What a candidate! Now, would you be surprised to find that this shining employee-to-be didn't really go to Oxford? Or that he really wasn't the account manager on that nationwide marketing campaign? Or that his last supervisor wasn't particularly impressed with his analytical skills?

Applications, curricula vitae and interviews are great tools, but you do need references. However, getting references can be tricky – for although you're entitled to ask previous employers specific questions about the candidate's performance, they may choose whether or not to answer them.

The primary purpose of checking references is to verify the information that your candidates provide. If you want further insights into how your candidates really performed in previous jobs, then you need to ask specific questions about absence records, achievements and jobs or positions held.

When you contact a candidate's referees, limit your questions to those related to the work to be done. As in the interview process, asking questions that can be considered discriminatory to your candidates isn't appropriate.

Here are some of the best places to do your reference checking:

- **Check academic references.** A surprising number of people exaggerate or tell lies when reporting their educational experience. Start your reference check here. If your candidates didn't tell the truth about their education, you can bet that the rest of their experience is suspect too, and you can toss the candidate into the discard pile before you proceed.

- **Call current and former supervisors.** Getting information from employers is increasingly difficult. Many businesspeople are rightfully concerned that they may be sued for libel or defamation of character if they say anything negative about current or former employees. Still, it doesn't hurt to try. You get a better picture of your candidates if you speak directly to their current and former supervisors instead of to their firms' HR department, especially if the supervisors you speak to have left their firms. The most you're likely to get from HR is a confirmation that the candidate worked at the firm during a specific period of time.

✔ **Check your network of associates.** If you belong to a professional association, union or similar group of like-minded careerists, you have the opportunity to tap into the rest of the membership to get the word on your candidates. For example, if you're a member of the Chartered Institute of Personnel and Development (MCIPD) and want to find out about a few candidates for a position in HR, you can check with the members of your professional association to see whether anyone knows anything about them.

✔ **Surf the web.** Especially for top, senior and specialist positions, type your candidate's name into a search engine such as Google (www.google.co.uk), along with the name of the company where he last worked or the city in which he lives. You never know what can turn up!

What a reference won't do is tell you how a candidate will perform in the future if you appoint him. However good he's been in the past, this doesn't mean that he'll make an excellent employee in the future. By the same token, if he receives a bad or average reference from a previous employer, you need to find out why, so that you have the fullest information before deciding whether to accept or reject him. You do have to be careful with references!

Reviewing your notes

You did take interview notes, didn't you? Now's the time to drag them back out and look them over. Review the information package for each candidate – one by one – and compare your findings against your pre-determined criteria. Take a look at the candidates' applications, your notes and the results of your reference checks, such as they are. How do the candidates stack up against the standards that you set for the position? Do you see any clear winners at this point? Any clear losers? Organise your candidate packages into the following piles:

✔ **Winners:** These candidates are clearly the best choices for the position. You have no hesitation in hiring any one of them.

✔ **Potential winners:** These candidates are questionable for one reason or another. Maybe their experience isn't as strong as that of other candidates, or perhaps you weren't impressed with their presentation skills. Neither clear winners nor clear losers, you hire these candidates only after further investigation, or if you can't hire anyone from your pool of winners.

✔ **Losers:** These candidates are clearly unacceptable for the position. You simply don't consider hiring any of them.

Make sure that you can justify your choice for each pile on the basis of capability, willingness and availability to do the job alone.

Conducting second (or third) interviews

When you're a busy manager, you're under pressure to get things done as quickly as possible, and you're tempted to take shortcuts to achieving your goals. It seems that everything has to be done yesterday – or maybe the day before. When do you have the opportunity to really spend as much time as you want to complete a task or project? Time is precious when you have ten other projects crying out for your attention. Time is even more valuable when you're hiring for a vacant position that's critical to your organisation and needs to be filled right now.

Recruitment is one area of business where you can't take shortcuts. Finding the best candidates for your vacancies requires a very real investment of time and resources to be successful. Your company's future depends on it.

Depending on your organisation's policies or culture, or because you're undecided as to the best candidate, you may decide to bring candidates in for several rounds of interviews. In this kind of system, lower-level supervisors, managers or interview panels conduct initial screening interviews. Candidates who pass this round are invited back for another interview with a higher-level manager. Finally, the best two or three candidates interview with the organisation's top manager.

But keep in mind that the timescale for an offer is very different depending on the job you're interviewing for. Lower-level job hunters can't afford to be unemployed (if they are) for long, and they often get and accept job offers quickly. A higher-level position – say, a general manager – gives you more time.

The ultimate decision on how many rounds and levels of interviews to conduct depends on the nature of the job itself, the size of your company and your policies and procedures. If the job is simple or at a relatively low level in the company, a single phone interview may be sufficient to determine the best candidate for a job. However, you may need several rounds of testing and personal interviews if the job is complex or at a relatively high level in the organisation.

Engaging the Best (and Leaving the Rest)

Ranking your candidates within the groups of winners and potential winners that you established during the evaluation phase of the process is the first step in making a recruitment decision. You don't need to bother ranking the losers because you wouldn't take them on anyway – no matter what. The best candidate in your group of winners is first, the next best is second and so on. If you've done your job thoroughly and well, the best candidates for the job should be readily apparent at this point.

Getting on the phone and offering your first choice the job is the next step. Don't waste any time – you never know whether your candidate has had interviews with other employers. Investing all this time in the recruitment process is wasted if you find out that he just accepted a job with one of your competitors. If you can't reach an agreement with your first choice within a reasonable amount of time, then go on to your second choice. Keep going through your pool of winners until you take someone on, or exhaust the list of candidates.

The following sections give you a few tips to keep in mind as you rank your candidates and make your final decision.

Being objective

In some cases, you may prefer certain candidates because of their personality or personal charisma – regardless of their ability or work experience. Sometimes the desire to like these candidates can obscure their shortcomings, while a better qualified, albeit less socially adept, candidate may fade in your estimation.

Be objective. Consider the job to be done and consider the skills and qualifications that being successful requires. Do your candidates have these skills and qualifications? What would it take for your candidates to be considered fully qualified for the position?

Don't allow yourself to be unduly influenced by your candidates' looks, champagne-like personalities, expensive haircuts or dangerously named colognes. None of these characteristics can tell you how well your candidates can perform the job. The facts are present for you to see in your candidates' applications, interview notes and reference checks. If you stick to the facts, you can still go wrong, but the chances are diminished.

And one more thing: diversity in all staffing practices is positive for any organisation – both for the business and for society in general. Leave your bias at the door!

Trusting your instincts

Sometimes you're faced with a choice between two equally qualified candidates, or with a decision about a candidate who's marginal but shows promise. In such cases, you've weighed all the objective data and you've given the analytical side of your being free rein, but you still have no clear winner. What do you do in this kind of situation?

Listen to yourself. Unlock your heart, your feelings and your intuition. What do you feel in your gut? What do your instincts tell you? Although two candidates may seem equal in skills and abilities, do you have a feeling that one is better suited to the job than the other? If so, go with it. As much as you may want your hiring decision to be as objective as possible, whenever you introduce the human element into the decision-making process, a certain amount of subjectivity is naturally present.

In reality, rarely are two candidates equally qualified, although often one or more people seem to have more to bring to the job than anticipated (for example, industry focus, fresh ideas, previous contacts and so forth). Your preliminary work can be invaluable here in keeping you focused. Can they both do the job? If so, the bonus traits can tip the scale.

Other options:

- Take one or the other (or both) on for a trial period.
- Have them both back for a round of interviews (and if this seems expensive, remember the consequences of a bad decision).

A further review of two more or less equally qualified candidates may draw you to the conclusion that, in fact, neither is good enough; in that case, advertise again.

A civil engineering company based in London was having great difficulty attracting and retaining reception staff. They were constantly asking West End employment agencies to send candidates. Each person the company took on was capable and competent to do the work; however, they always moved on within six months. When asked why they were moving on, the standard response was: 'Not very glamorous, civil engineering, is it?' The company solved the problem by hiring a man in his early forties. An ex-soldier, this man had broken his back on a mountaineering expedition and now used a wheel-chair. He's held the post of receptionist for nearly nine years now; and, to date, has never had a day off sick.

One more thing: be sure to keep in touch with other top candidates as additional needs arise in case your first choice doesn't work out.

Adjusting after the offer

What do you do if, heaven forbid, you can't hire anyone from your group of winners? This does happen; but no one said that management is easy. Take a look at your stack of potential winners. What would it take to make your top potential winners into winners? If the answer is as simple as a training course or two, then give these candidates serious consideration – with the agreement that they take the necessary training soon after engagement. Perhaps they just need a little more experience before you can put them in the ranks of the winners. You can make a judgement call as to whether you feel that their current experience is sufficient to carry them through until they gain the experience you're looking for. If not, you may want to keep looking for the right candidate. After all, this person may be working with you for a long time – waiting for the best candidate only makes sense.

If you're forced to go to your group of almost winners, and no candidate really seems up to the task, don't hire someone simply to fill the position. If you do, you're probably making a big mistake. Taking people on is far easier than getting rid of them. The damage a bad choice can cause for colleagues, customers and your organisation (not to mention the person you hire) can take years and a considerable amount of money to undo. Such a situation is also extremely stressful. You can also consider whether to redefine the job, re-evaluate other current employees or give someone a temporary contract to see whether a potentially risky candidate really works out.

Top five hiring websites

Here are our top five favourite recruitment advice websites:

- ✔ *Financial Times:* www.ft.com/recruitment

- ✔ *The Times:* http://jobs.thetimes.co.uk/employers

- ✔ *The Daily Telegraph:* http://jobs.telegraph.co.uk

- ✔ **Advisory, Conciliation and Arbitration Service (ACAS):** www.acas.org.uk

- ✔ **Chartered Institute of Personnel and Development (CIPD):** www.cipd.co.uk/recruitment

Chapter 4

Inspiring Employees to Better Performance

In This Chapter
▶ Introducing the Greatest Management Principle in the World
▶ Finding out what motivates employees
▶ Deciding what behaviours to reward
▶ Starting with the positive
▶ Rewarding the little things
▶ Using non-monetary rewards

*T*he question of how to motivate employees has loomed large over managers ever since management was first invented. Most of management comes down to mastering skills and techniques for motivating people – to make them better, more productive employees who love their jobs more than anything else in the world. Well, perhaps not quite that much; but you do want them to turn up and be as happy, effective and productive as possible.

You have two ways to motivate employees – rewards and punishments. If employees do what you want them to do, reward them with incentives that they desire – awards, recognition, important titles, money and so on. We often call these *positive consequences*. Alternatively, if employees don't do what you want, punish them with what they don't desire – warnings, reprimands, demotions, firings and so on – often known as *negative consequences*. By nature, employees are drawn towards positive consequences and shy away from negative consequences.

Increasingly, however, with today's employees, to be an effective manager you have to work harder at providing a greater number of positive consequences on an ongoing basis when employees perform well (they expect it). And you have to be *much* more selective as to when and how you use negative consequences. Firing people is much harder than in previous times, and wrongful and unfair dismissals get you into trouble with the law.

This chapter deals with the positive side of employee motivation – positive consequences, especially recognition and rewards. (We're sorry if you're eager to read about the punishment side, but we cover that in Chapter 16.) Besides, 100 years of research in behavioural science and continuing extensive studies at all of the world's major business schools show that you have a much greater impact on getting the performance you want from your employees when you use positive consequences rather than negative ones.

We aren't saying that negative consequences don't have a place; sometimes you have no choice but to punish, reprimand or even dismiss employees. However, first give your employees the benefit of the doubt that they do want to do a good job and acknowledge them when they do so. Make every effort to use positive recognition, praise and rewards to encourage the behaviours you seek, and catch people doing things right. If you follow this approach, your employees are more motivated to want to excel in their jobs, performance and morale improve and employees consider your company a much better place to work.

By leading with positive reinforcements, not only can you inspire your employees to do what you want, but you can also develop happier, more productive employees in the process – and that combination is tough to beat.

The Greatest Management Principle in the World

We're about to let you in on the Greatest Management Principle in the World. This simple rule can save you countless hours of frustration and extra work, and it can save your company many thousands or perhaps even millions of pounds. Sounds pretty awe-inspiring, doesn't it? Are you ready? Okay, the statement is:

> You get what you reward.

Don't let the seeming simplicity of the statement fool you – read on to explore it.

Recognition isn't as simple as it looks

You may think that you're rewarding your employees to do what you want them to do, but are you really?

Consider the following example. You have two employees: Employee A is incredibly talented and Employee B is a marginal performer. You give similar assignments to both employees. Employee A completes the assignment before the due date and hands it in with no errors. Because Employee A is already done, you give her two additional assignments. Meanwhile, Employee B is not only late, but when she finally hands in the report you requested, it's full of errors. Because you're now under a time crunch, you accept Employee B's report and then correct it yourself.

What's wrong with this picture? Who's actually being rewarded: Employee A or Employee B?

If you answered Employee B, you're right. This employee has discovered that submitting work that's substandard and late is okay. Furthermore, she also sees that you personally fix her mistakes. That's quite a nice reward for an employee who clearly doesn't deserve one. (Another way to put it is that Employee B certainly has you well trained!)

On the other hand, by giving Employee A more work for being a diligent, outstanding worker, you're actually punishing her. Even though you may think nothing of assigning more work to Employee A, she knows the score. When Employee A sees that all she gets for being an outstanding performer is more work (while you let Employee B get away with doing less work), she's not going to like it one little bit. And if you end up giving both employees basically the same pay rise (and don't think that they won't find out), you make the problem even worse. You lose Employee A, either literally, because she takes another job, or in spirit, because she stops working so hard.

If you let the situation continue, all your top performers eventually realise that doing their best work isn't in their best interest. As a result, they leave their position to find an organisation that values their contribution, or they simply sit back and forget about doing their best work. Why bother? No one (that means you, the manager) seems to care anyway.

Biscuit motivation

Giving everyone the same incentive – the same salary increase, equal recognition or even equal amounts of your time – we call *biscuit motivation*. Although this treatment may initially sound fair, it isn't.

Nothing is as unfair at work as the equal treatment of unequal performers. You need to assess the performance of everyone. You then make clear to all people why they've received rewards and bonuses, or why they haven't. You must evenly and honestly distribute these rewards. And if everyone meets the standards demanded, then reward them all as you've promised.

Thinking through your rewards

Richard tells the story of the City of London branch of an international bank that was having problems with sickness absence. Staff were phoning in sick for all kinds of reasons, and collective absenteeism was in the order of 7 per cent (it was taking 107 people to do the work of 100 at any given time).

Being a concerned employer, the bank decided to reward positive behaviour rather than punishing bad or negative behaviour. Consequently, a note went round to all staff informing them that anyone who hadn't taken any self-certificated sickness absence was entitled to an extra week's holiday the following year.

Needless to say, the plan misfired. Genuine hardworking employees who'd had a day or two off as the result of real illnesses and injuries now found themselves slighted – tarred with the same brush as malingerers. Having had a day or two off with genuine ailments, good staff now used holiday entitlement rather than sickness days so as not to miss out on the additional week's holiday that everyone else was getting.

The bank's human resources department met to review the policy. Acknowledging the weakness of the plan, another note informed staff that they would still get their extra week's holiday provided that all absences were covered by a doctor's certificate. In no time at all, HR became swamped with doctors' certificates, and had to take on another member of staff just to deal with them. Those with genuine illnesses and injuries complained about having to visit a doctor – and often paying for a certificate – to prove that their condition was real. For the malingerers, payment for a doctor's certificate simply validated a false position.

The bank reviewed the policy again. The suggestion was raised (seriously) that all those who'd had fewer than five days self-certificated absence should be entitled to an extra two weeks' holiday the following year. Only at this point did the HR director take matters into her own hands; at last, she cancelled the policy and concentrated efforts on the malingerers rather than the genuine, committed and hardworking staff.

If people aren't performing to standard, then take the particular individuals aside and tell them why. Tell them what they need to do to make the grade, and how they can go about it. Doing so is much better than letting people go about things without your active involvement and interest. You want everyone working as well as possible, and your job is to sort out those who aren't up to scratch.

Don't forget the Greatest Management Principle in the World – you get what you reward.

Before you set up a system to reward your employees, make sure that you know exactly what behaviours you want to reward and then align the rewards with those behaviours.

After you put your employee reward system in place, check periodically to see that the system is getting the results that you want. Check with those you're trying to motivate and see whether the programme is still working. If it isn't, change it!

Discovering What Employees Want

In today's tight, stressful, changing times, what things are most important to employees? Bob conducted a survey of about 1,500 employees from across seven industries to answer that question. We list the top ten items that employees said were most important, along with some thoughts on how you can better provide each of these elements for your own employees:

- ✔ **A learning activity (No. 1) and choice of assignment (No. 9):** Today's employees most value opportunities in which they gain skills that can enhance their worth and marketability in their current job as well as future positions. Discover what your employees want to find out, how they want to grow and develop, and where they want to be in five years. Give them opportunities as they arise and the ability to choose work assignments whenever possible. When you give employees the choice, more often than not they rise to meet or exceed your expectations.

- ✔ **Flexible working hours (No. 2) and time off from work (No. 7):** Today's employees value their time – and their time off. Be sensitive to their needs outside work, whether they involve family or friends, charity or church, education or hobbies. Provide flexibility whenever you can so that employees can meet their obligations. Time off may range from an occasional afternoon to attend a child's play at school or the ability to start the work day an hour early so the employee can leave an hour early. By allowing work to fit best with employees' life schedules, you increase the chances that they're motivated to work harder while they're at work, and do their best to make their schedules work. And from a managerial standpoint, as long as the job gets done, what difference does it make what hours someone works? Bear in mind that employees now have a legal right to request flexible working hours, and you have a legal obligation to consider their request.

- ✔ **Personal praise – verbal (No. 3), public (No. 8) or written (No. 10):** Although you can thank someone in 10 to 15 seconds, most employees report that they're never thanked for the job they do – especially not by their manager. Systematically start to thank your employees when they do good work, in person, in the hallway, in a group meeting, on voice-mail, in a written thank-you note, in an email or at the end of each day at work. Better yet, go out of your way to act on and share and amplify good news when it occurs – even if it means interrupting someone to thank her for a great job she's done. By taking the time to say you noticed and appreciate her efforts, you help those efforts – and results – to continue. And bring her efforts to your manager's attention; doing so reinforces your own integrity as well as ensures full credit goes where it's due.

✓ **Increased autonomy (No. 5) and authority (No. 4) in their job:** The ultimate form of recognition for many employees is to have increased autonomy and authority to get their job done, including the ability to spend or allocate resources, make decisions or manage others. Greater autonomy and authority says, 'I trust you to act in the best interests of the company, to do so independently and without the approval of myself or others.' Award employees with increased autonomy and authority as a form of recognition for their past results. Autonomy and authority are privileges, not rights, which you should grant to those employees who've most earned them, based on past performance, and not based on tenure or seniority.

✓ **Time with their manager (No. 6):** In today's fast-paced world of work in which everyone is expected to get more done faster, personal time with your manager is in itself also a form of recognition. Because managers are busier, taking time with employees is even more important. The action says, 'Of all the things I have to do, one of the most important is to take time to be with you, the person or people I most depend on for us to be successful.' Especially for younger employees, time spent with a manager is a valued form of validation and inspiration, as well as serving a practical purpose of learning, communicating, answering questions, discussing possibilities or just listening to an employee's ideas, concerns and opinions.

By the way, you may wonder where money ranked in importance in this survey. A 'cash reward' ranked 13th in importance to employees. (We say more about the topic of money as a motivator later in this chapter.) Everyone needs money to live, but work today involves more than what anyone gets paid.

Employees report that the most important aspects at work today are primarily the intangible aspects of the job that any manager can easily provide – if she makes it a priority to do so. Now we're going to tell you a big secret. This secret is the key to motivating your employees. You don't need to attend an all-day seminar or join the management-DVD-of-the-week club to discover this secret: we're letting you in on it right here and right now at no extra charge:

Ask your employees what they want.

This statement may sound silly, but you can take a lot of the guesswork out of your job by simply being clear about what your employees most value in their jobs. It may be one or more of the items we mention earlier in this section, or it may be something entirely different. The simplest way to find out how to motivate your employees is to ask them. Often managers assume that their employees want only money. These same managers are surprised when their employees tell them that other things – such as being recognised for doing a good job, being allowed greater autonomy in decision making or having a more flexible work schedule – may be much more motivating than cash. Regardless of what preferences your employees have, you're much better off knowing those preferences explicitly rather than guessing or ignoring them. So:

✔ **Plan to provide employees with more of what they value.** Look for opportunities to recognise employees for having done good work and act on those opportunities as they arise, realising that what motivates some employees doesn't motivate others.

✔ **Stick with it over time.** Motivation is a moving target and you need to constantly be looking to meet your employees' needs in order to keep them motivated to help you meet your needs.

Consider the following as you begin setting the stage for your efforts:

1. **Create a supportive environment for your employees by first finding out what they most value.**

2. **Design ways to implement recognition to thank and acknowledge employees when they do good work.**

3. **Be prepared to make changes to your plan, based on what works and what doesn't.**

Creating a supportive environment

Today's new business realities bring a need to find different ways to motivate employees. Motivation is no longer an absolute, my-way-or-the-highway prop- osition. The incredible acceleration of change in business and technology is coupled with greatly expanded global competitive forces. With these forces pressing in from all sides, managers can have difficulty keeping up with what employees need to do, much less figure out what to tell them to do. In fact, a growing trend is for managers to manage individuals who are doing work that the managers themselves have never done. (Fortunately, given a little time and a little trust, most employees can work out what needs to be done by themselves.)

Inspiring managers must embrace these changing business forces and man- agement trends. Instead of using the power of their position to motivate workers, managers must use the power of their ideas. Instead of using threats and intimidation to get things done, managers must create environments that support their employees and allow creativity to flourish.

You, as a manager, can create a supportive workplace in the following ways:

- ✔ **Build and maintain trust and respect.** Employees whose managers trust and respect them are motivated to perform at their best. By including employees in the decision-making process, today's managers get better ideas (that are easier to implement), and at the same time they improve employees' morale, loyalty and commitment.

- ✔ **Removing the barriers to getting to work.** If you ask your employees what are the biggest hurdles they face in coming to work, you get a huge range of answers – rush-hour traffic, getting the kids to school, having to use public transport and so on. By allowing them to choose their hours of work, you give your staff the opportunity to work around these barriers. You're also entitled to expect that, having chosen their hours of work, they then show up and do a good job. You can't do this for every eventuality, and crises always happen. However, as long as the employee is prepared to give you a reasonable and regular pattern of hours, you should at least consider being flexible.

- ✔ **Open the channels of communication.** The ability of all your employees to communicate openly and honestly with one another is critical to the ultimate success of your organisation and plays a major role in employee motivation. Today, quick and efficient communication of information throughout your organisation can be what differentiates you from your competition. Encourage your employees to speak up, to make suggestions and to break down the organisational barriers – the rampant departmentalisation, turf protection and similar roadblocks – that separate them from one another, where and whenever they find them.

- ✔ **Make your employees feel safe.** Are your employees as comfortable telling you the bad news as they are telling you the good news? If the answer is no, you haven't created a safe environment for your employees. Everyone makes mistakes; people discover valuable lessons from their mistakes. If you want employees who are motivated, make it safe for them to take chances and to let you know the bad along with the good. And use mistakes and errors as opportunities for growth and development; never punish mistakes and errors except those generated as the result of negligence or incompetence.

- ✔ **Develop your greatest asset – your employees.** By meeting your employees' needs, you also respond to your organisation's needs. Challenge your employees to improve their skills and knowledge and provide them with the support and training that they need to do so. Concentrate on the positive progress they make and recognise and reward such success whenever possible.

Having a good game plan

Motivated employees don't happen by accident. You must have a plan to reinforce the behaviour you want. In general, employees are more strongly motivated by the potential to earn rewards than they are by the fear of punishment. Clearly, a well thought out and planned motivation, incentive and rewards system is important to creating a committed, effective workforce. Here are some simple guidelines for setting up a system of low-cost rewards in your organisation:

- **Link rewards to organisational goals.** To be effective, rewards need to reinforce the behaviour that leads to achieving an organisation's goals. Use rewards to increase the frequency of desired behaviour and decrease the frequency of undesired behaviour.

- **Define parameters and mechanics.** After you identify the behaviours you want to reinforce, develop the specifics of your reward system. Create rules that are clear and easily understood by all employees. Make sure that goals are attainable and that all employees have a chance to obtain rewards, whatever their job and occupation.

- **Obtain commitment and support.** Of course, communicate your new rewards programme to your employees. Many organisations publicise their programmes at group meetings. They present the programmes as positive and fun activities that benefit both the employees and the company. To get the best results, plan and implement your rewards programme with your employees' direct involvement.

- **Monitor effectiveness.** Is your rewards system getting the results you want? If not, take another look at the behaviours you want to reinforce and make sure that your rewards are closely linked to them. Even the most successful reward programmes tend to lose their effectiveness over time as employees begin to take them for granted. Keep your programme fresh by discontinuing rewards that have lost their lustre and bringing in new ones from time to time.

Deciding What to Reward

Most organisations and managers reward the wrong things, if they reward their employees at all. This tendency has led to a crisis of epic proportions in the traditional system of incentives and motivation in business. For example:

- A major London commodity market gave bonuses of 6 per cent of salary to outstanding employees and 3 per cent of salary to everyone else. Average and adequate performers were therefore receiving exactly the same reward.

✔ A top professional footballer on many thousands of pounds a week joined one of the very top football clubs, only to find himself playing in the reserve team at exactly the time when he was trying to develop his career and reputation through playing regularly. He was therefore receiving a very good reward, but not the one that he wanted.

✔ A council employee rated 'exceptional' was told by her manager that she had to be downgraded to 'average' because her department had no money to pay her bonus.

If workers aren't being rewarded for doing outstanding work, what are they being rewarded for? As we point out in the 'Biscuit motivation' section, earlier in the chapter, organisations often reward employees just for showing up for work.

For an incentive programme to have meaningful and lasting effects, it must be contingent; that is, it must focus on performance – nothing less and nothing more.

'But wait a second,' you may say, 'that isn't fair to the employees who aren't as talented as my top performers.' If that's what you think, we can straighten out that particular misunderstanding right now. Everyone, regardless of how smart, talented or productive they are, has the potential to be a top performer.

Suppose that Employee A produces 100 widgets an hour and stays at that level of performance day in and day out. On the other hand, Employee B produces 75 widgets an hour but improves output to 85 widgets an hour. Who should you reward? Employee B! This example embodies what you want to reward: the efforts that your employees make to improve their performance, not just to maintain a certain level (no matter how good that level is).

The following are examples of *performance-based measures* that any manager must recognise and reward. Consider what measures you should be monitoring, measuring and rewarding in your organisation. Don't forget, just showing up for work doesn't count.

✔ Defects decrease from 25 per 1,000 to 10 per 1,000.

✔ Annual sales increase by 20 per cent.

✔ The department records system is reorganised and colour-coded to make filing and retrieval more efficient.

✔ Administrative expenses are held to 90 per cent of the authorised budget.

✔ The organisation's mail is distributed in 1 hour instead of 1½ hours.

Praising guidelines

A basic foundation for a positive relationship is the ability to praise well. To offer effective praise, Bob uses a system called 'ASAP-cubed', which means:

✔ **As soon:** Timing is very important when using positive reinforcement. Give praise as soon as the person displays the desired behaviour.

✔ **As sincere:** Words alone can fall flat if you're not sincere in why you're praising someone. Praise someone because you're truly appreciative and excited about the other person's success. Otherwise, the praise may come across as a manipulative tactic or simply patronising.

✔ **As specific:** Avoid generalities in favour of details of the achievement. For example, 'You really turned that angry customer around by focusing on what you could do for him, not on what you couldn't do for him.'

✔ **As personal:** A key to conveying your message is praising in person, face to face. This shows that the activity is important enough to you to put aside everything else you have to do and just focus on the other person.

✔ **As positive:** Too many managers undercut praise with a concluding note of criticism. When you say something like 'You did a great job on this report, but you made quite a few typos', the *but* becomes a verbal erasure of all that came before.

✔ **As proactive:** Lead with praise and catch people doing things right. Otherwise, you tend to be reactive – typically about mistakes – in your interactions with others.

You can give praise directly to the employee, in front of another person (in public) or when the person isn't around (via letter, email, voice-mail and so forth). Praising employees only takes a moment, but the benefits – to your employees and to your organisation – last for years.

Some managers break incentives into two categories – *results measures*, where measures are linked to the bottom line, and *process measures*, where the link to the bottom line isn't as clear. You need to recognise achievement in both categories.

Starting with the Positive

You're more likely to lead your employees to great results by focusing on their positive accomplishments rather than by finding fault with and punishing their negative outcomes. Despite this fact, many managers' primary mode of operation is correcting their employees' mistakes instead of complimenting their successes.

In a recent study, 58 per cent of employees reported that they seldom received a personal thank you from their manager for doing a good job even though they ranked such recognition as their most motivating incentive. They ranked a written thank you for doing a good job as motivating incentive No. 2, but 76 per cent said that they seldom received thanks from their managers. Perhaps these statistics show why a lack of praise and recognition is one of the leading reasons people leave their jobs.

Years of psychological research clearly shows that positive reinforcement works better than negative reinforcement for several reasons. Without getting too technical, the reasons are that positive reinforcement:

- ✔ Increases the frequency of the desired behaviour
- ✔ Creates good feelings within employees

On the other hand, negative reinforcement may decrease the frequency of undesired behaviour, but doesn't necessarily result in the expression of desired behaviour. Instead of being motivated to do better, employees who receive only criticism from their managers eventually come to avoid their managers whenever possible. Furthermore, negative reinforcement (particularly when manifested in ways that degrade employees and their sense of self-worth) can create tremendously bad feelings in employees. And employees who are unhappy with their employers have a much more difficult time doing a good job than employees who are happy with their employers.

The following ideas can help you seek out the positive in your employees and reinforce the behaviours you want:

- ✔ **Have high expectations for your employees' abilities.** If you believe that your employees can be outstanding, soon they believe it too. When Peter was growing up, his parents rarely needed to punish him when he did something wrong; he needed only the words 'we know that you can do better' to get him back on course.

- ✔ **Recognise that your employees are doing their best.** If a shortfall in performance occurs, then support and encourage; punishing people for things that they can't do is pointless.

- ✔ **Give your employees the benefit of the doubt.** Do you really think that your employees want to do a bad job? No one wants to do a bad job; so your job is to work out everything you can do to help employees do a good job. Additional training, encouragement and support should be among your first choices – not reprimands and punishment.

> ✔ **Catch your employees doing things right.** Most employees do a good job in most of their work, so instead of constantly catching your employees doing things wrong, catch them doing things right. Not only can you reinforce the behaviours that you want, but you can also make your employees feel good about working for you and for your organisation.

Making a Big Deal about Something Little

Okay, here's a question for you: should you reward your employees for their little day-to-day successes, or should you save up rewards for when they accomplish something really major? The answer to this question lies in the way that most people get their work done on a daily basis.

The simple fact is that, for most people in business, work isn't a string of dazzling successes that come one after another without fail. Instead, most work consists of routine, daily activities; employees perform most of these duties quietly and with little fanfare. A manager's typical workday, for example, may consist of an hour or two reading memos and emails, listening to voice-mail messages and talking to other people on the phone. The manager spends another couple of hours in meetings and perhaps another hour having one-to-one discussions with staff members and colleagues, much of which involves dealing with problems as they occur. With additional time spent on preparing reports or filling out forms, the manager actually devotes precious little time to decision making – the activity that has the greatest impact on an organisation.

For a line worker, this dearth of opportunities for dazzling success is even more pronounced. If the employee's job is assembling lawnmower engines all day (and he does a good, steady job), when does he have an opportunity to be outstanding in the eyes of his supervisor?

Saga recognises – everyone!

Saga, a specialist holiday, travel and financial services company for the over-fifties, had just completed its best ever year. Profits rose by 25 per cent; turnover by 40 per cent. The company was set to be listed on the London Stock Exchange.

Sydney De Haan, the company's founder, considered how best to reward everyone involved in this success. He instituted a scheme of annual bonuses, based on both individual and collective performance. At the end of the bumper year, he also paid for a holiday for all staff and their families.

We've taken the long way around to say that major accomplishments are usually few and far between, regardless of your place in the organisational chart. Work is a series of small accomplishments that eventually add up to big ones. If you wait to reward your employees for their big successes, you may be waiting a long time.

Reward your employees for their small successes as well as their big ones. You may set a lofty goal for your employees to achieve – one that stretches their abilities and tests their resolve – but remember that praising your employees' progress towards the goal is perhaps even more important than praising them when they finally reach it.

Money and Motivation

You may think that money is the ultimate incentive for your employees. After all, who isn't excited when they receive a cash bonus or pay rise? *As visions of riches beyond his wildest dreams danced through his head, he pledged his eternal devotion to the firm.* The problem is that money really isn't the top motivator for employees – at least not in the way that most managers think. And money can be a huge demotivator if you manage it badly.

Compensating with wages and salaries

Money is clearly important to your employees. They need money to pay bills, buy food and clothes, put petrol in their cars and afford the other necessities of life.

Most employees consider the money they receive to be a fair exchange for the work they put in. Payment for work carried out is a legal right. Recognition, on the other hand, is a gift. Using recognition, however, helps you get the best effort from each employee.

Realising when incentives become entitlements

In particular, employees who receive annual bonuses and other periodic, money-based rewards quickly come to consider them part of their basic pay.

The problem arises when achieving bonuses and incentives is easy or straightforward. Productivity and output begin to flatten out; and the incentive effect of the payments themselves begins to diminish. People work on the basis that the incentives and bonuses are forthcoming anyway.

Incentives work best when they're related to direct goals or targets and short-term performance. In particular, incentives don't make a bad or boring job more interesting – they make it more bearable, and only in the short term.

So the issue becomes again: what are you rewarding? You need to work out what the goals are, what rewards people expect for achieving them and the best way of delivering these rewards. Consolidating incentives into standard pay and reward packages simply puts up the payroll costs without any tangible returns.

Management expert Peter Drucker hit the nail on the head when he pointed out in his book *Management: Tasks, Responsibilities, Practices* (Butterworth-Heinemann, 2007):

> *Economic incentives are becoming rights rather than rewards. Merit raises are always introduced as rewards for exceptional performance. In no time at all, they become a right. To deny a merit raise or to grant only a small one becomes punishment. The increasing demand for material rewards is rapidly destroying their usefulness as incentives and managerial tools.*

In other words, money becomes an expectation, then an entitlement, for many if not most workers.

The ineffectiveness of money as a motivator for employees is a good news/bad news kind of thing. We start with the bad news. Many managers have thrown lots of money into cash-reward programmes, and for the most part these programmes haven't really had the positive effect on motivation that the managers expected. Although we don't want to say that you waste your money on these programmes, you can use it more effectively.

Now you get the good news: because you know that money isn't the most effective motivation tool, you can focus on using tools that are more effective – and the best forms of recognition cost little or no money!

Working out what motivates your staff

If you're a busy manager, cash rewards are convenient because you simply fill out a single request to take care of all your motivation for the year. By contrast, the manager-initiated, based-on-performance stuff seems like a lot of work. To be frank, running an effective rewards programme does take more work on your part than running a simple but ineffective one. But as we show you, the best rewards can be quite simple. After you get the hang of using them, you can easily integrate these rewards into your daily routine. Doing so is part of managing today.

To achieve the best results:

- ✔ Concentrate on what the employees need, want and expect. The only way to be absolutely sure is to ask them.

- ✔ Concentrate rewards on the things you really want done. And keep in mind that what gets rewarded gets done.

Don't save up recognition for special occasions only – and don't just use them with the top performers. You need to recognise all employees when they do good work in their job. Your employees are doing good things – things that you want them to do – every day. Catch them doing something right and recognise their successes regularly and often.

The following incentives are simple to execute, take little time and are the most motivating for employees:

- ✔ Personal or written congratulations from you for a job well done

- ✔ Public recognition, given visibly by you for good job performance

- ✔ Morale-building meetings to celebrate successes

- ✔ Time off or flexibility in working hours

- ✔ Asking employees their opinions and involving them in decision making

For unbelievably comprehensive listings of incentive ideas that really work, check out Bob's best-selling books *1001 Ways to Reward Employees*, *1001 Ways to Energize Employees* and *The 1001 Rewards & Recognition Fieldbook* (all Workman Publishing); and Richard's *Managing the Flexible Workforce* (Capstone, 2002).

Realising that you hold the key to your employees' motivation

In our experience, most managers believe that their employees determine how motivated they choose to be. Managers tend to think that some employees naturally have good attitudes, that others naturally have bad attitudes and that managers can't do much to change these attitudes. 'If only we could unleash the same passion and energy people have for their families and hobbies,' these managers think, 'then we could really get something done around here.'

As convenient as blaming your employees for their bad attitudes may be, looking in a mirror may be a more honest approach. Managers need to

- ✔ Recognise their employees for doing a good job
- ✔ Provide a pleasant and supportive working environment
- ✔ Create a sense of joint mission and teamwork in the organisation
- ✔ Treat their employees as equals
- ✔ Avoid favouritism
- ✔ Make time to listen when employees need to talk

Ten ways to motivate employees

Here are some easy, no-cost things you can do to create a motivating workplace:

- ✔ Personally thank employees for doing a good job – one-to-one, in writing or both. Do it timely, often and sincerely.

- ✔ Take the time to meet with and listen to employees – as much as they need or want.

- ✔ Provide employees with specific and frequent feedback about their performance. Support them in improving performance.

- ✔ Recognise, reward and promote high performers; deal with low and marginal performers so that they improve.

- ✔ Provide information on how the company makes and loses money, upcoming products and services and strategies for competing. Explain the employee's role in the overall plan.

- ✔ Involve employees in decisions, especially those that affect them. Involvement equals commitment.

- ✔ Give employees a chance to grow and develop new skills; encourage them to be their best. Show them how you can help them meet their goals while achieving the organisation's goals. Create a partnership with each employee.

- ✔ Provide employees with a sense of ownership in their work and their work environment. This ownership can be symbolic (for example, business cards for all employees, whether they need them to do their jobs or not).

- ✔ Strive to create a work environment that's open, trusting and fun. Encourage new ideas, suggestions and initiative. Learn from, rather than punish for, mistakes.

- ✔ Celebrate successes – of the company, of the department and of individuals. Take time for team- and morale-building meetings and activities. Be creative and fresh.

Top five motivation websites

Wondering where to find the best information on the web about the topics we address in this chapter? Well, you've come to the right place! Here are our top five favourites:

- ✔ **Trades Union Congress:** `www.tuc.org.uk`

- ✔ **Confederation of British Industry:** `www.cbi.org.uk`

- ✔ **Green Templeton College, Oxford:** `www.gtc.ox.ac.uk`

- ✔ **Chartered Institute of Personnel and Development (CIPD):** `www.cipd.co.uk`

- ✔ **Tesco:** `www.tesco-careers.com`

For the most part, you determine how motivated (and demotivated) your employees are. Managers create a motivating environment that makes it easier for employees to be motivated. When the time comes, recognise and reward them fairly and equitably for the work they do well.

When you give out rewards, keep in mind that employees don't want hand-outs, and they hate favouritism. Provide rewards for the performance that helps you be mutually successful. Don't give recognition when none is warranted. Don't give it just to be nice, or with the hope that people will like you better. Doing so not only cheapens the value of the incentive for the employee who received it, but makes you lose credibility in the eyes of your other employees. Trust and credibility are two of the most important qualities that you can build in your relationship with your employees; if you lose these qualities, you risk losing the employee.

Chapter 5

Coaching, Mentoring and Development

In This Chapter

▶ Understanding what a coach is

▶ Developing basic coaching skills

▶ Recognising the development needs of your employees

▶ Creating the conditions for successful and enduring development

▶ Becoming an effective mentor

*O*ne recurring theme throughout this book is the role of managers as people who support and encourage their employees, instead of telling them what to do (or worse, simply expecting them to perform). The best managers are *coaches* – that is, individuals who guide, talk with and encourage others on their journey. With the help of coaches, employees can achieve outstanding results, organisations can perform better than ever and you can sleep well at night, knowing that everything is just fine.

Coaching plays a critical part in the learning process for employees who are developing their skills, knowledge and self-confidence. Your employees don't learn effectively when you simply tell them what to do. In fact, they usually don't learn at all.

As the maxim goes:

Tell me . . . I forget.

Show me . . . I remember.

Involve me . . . I learn.

Nor do your employees learn effectively when you throw a new task at them with no instruction or support whatsoever. Of course, good employees can, and do, eventually work things out for themselves, but they waste a lot of time and energy in the process. 'What on earth am I supposed to be doing? Let's have a go anyway and see what happens!'

Between these two extremes – being told what to do and being given no support whatsoever – is a happy medium where employees can thrive and the organisation can prosper. This is the happy land where everyone lives in peace, harmony, prosperity and achievement – and this happy medium starts and finishes with coaching.

Playing a Coach's Role

Even if you have a pretty good sense of what it means to be a manager, do you really know what it means to be a coach? A coach is a colleague, counsellor and cheerleader, all rolled into one. Based on that definition, are you a coach? How about your boss? Or your boss's boss? Why or why not?

We bet that you're familiar with the role of coaches in other non-business activities. A drama coach, for example, is almost always an accomplished actor. The drama coach's job is to conduct auditions for parts, assign roles, schedule rehearsals, train and direct cast members throughout rehearsals and support and encourage the actors during the final stage production. These roles aren't all that different from the roles that managers perform in a business, are they?

Coaching a team of individuals isn't easy, and certain characteristics make some coaches better than others. Fortunately, as with most other business skills, you can discover, practise and improve your grasp of the traits of good coaches. You can always find room for improvement, a fact that good coaches are the first to admit. The following list highlights some important characteristics of coaching:

> ✔ **Coaches set goals.** Whether an organisation's vision is to become the leading provider of global positioning systems in the world, to increase revenues by 20 per cent a year or simply to get the staffroom walls

painted this year, coaches work with their employees to set goals and deadlines for completion. Coaches then withdraw, to allow their employees time to work out how to achieve the goals.

✔ **Coaches support and encourage.** Employees – even the best and most experienced – can easily become discouraged from time to time. When employees are learning new tasks, when a long-term account is lost or when business is down, coaches are there, ready to step in and help the team members through the worst of it. 'That's okay, Kim. You've learned from your mistake, and I know that you can get it right next time!'

✔ **Coaches emphasise both team success and individual success.** The team's overall performance, not the stellar abilities of a particular team member, is the most important concern. Of course, you need everyone's contribution; but coaches know that no one person can carry an entire team to success. Winning takes the combined efforts of everyone. The development of teamwork skills is a vital step in an employee's progress in an organisation.

✔ **Coaches can quickly assess the talents and shortfalls of team members.** The most successful coaches can quickly determine their team members' strengths and weaknesses and, as a result, tailor their approach accordingly. For example, if one team member has strong analytical skills but poor presentation skills, a coach can concentrate on providing support to help the employee develop better presentation skills. 'You know, Mark, I want to spend some time with you to work on making your sales presentations more effective.'

✔ **Coaches inspire their team members.** Through their support and guidance, coaches are skilled at inspiring their team members to the highest levels of human performance. Teams of inspired individuals are willing to do whatever it takes to achieve their organisation's goals.

✔ **Coaches create environments that allow individuals to be successful.** Great coaches ensure that their workplaces are structured to let team members take risks and stretch their limits without fear of retribution if they fail.

✔ **Coaches provide feedback.** Communication and feedback between coach and employee form a critical element of the coaching process. Employees must know where they stand in the organisation – what they're doing right, and what they're doing wrong. Equally important, employees must let their coaches know when they need help or assistance. And this must be a continuous process for both parties. Otherwise problems get raised only at performance reviews and appraisals, or, worse still, get lost altogether.

Coaches are available to advise their employees or just to listen to their problems if need be, whether the issue is work related or personal.

Firing someone doesn't constitute effective feedback. Unless an employee has engaged in some sort of intolerable offence (such as physical violence, theft or intoxication on the job; see Chapter 16 for more details), a manager needs to give the employee plenty of verbal and written feedback before even considering termination. With employees who simply can't see what they're doing wrong, your coaching either makes or breaks. If you simply fire someone, you never know whether the problem was his – or yours.

Coaching: A Rough Guide

Besides the obvious coaching roles of supporting and encouraging employees in their quest to achieve an organisation's goals, coaches also teach their employees *how* to achieve those goals. Drawing from their experience, coaches lead their workers step by step through work processes or procedures. After the workers discover how to perform a task, the coach delegates full authority and responsibility for its performance to them.

For the transfer of specific skills, you can find no better way of teaching – and learning – than the *show-and-tell* method. If you need to get people up to speed on workplace skills, knowledge and understanding, then do it on the job. There's simply no better place. And – if you need to – you can get people working fully productively very quickly.

Show-and-tell or on-the-job coaching has three steps:

1. *You do, you say.* **Sit down with your employees and explain the procedure in general terms while you perform the task.**

   All businesses now use computers as a critical tool for getting work done. If you're coaching a new employee in the use of an obscure word processing or spreadsheet program, the first thing you need to do is to explain the technique to the employee while you demonstrate it. 'I click my left mouse button on the Insert command on the toolbar and pull down the menu. Then I point the arrow to Symbol and click again. I choose the symbol I want from the menu, point my arrow to it and click to select it. I then point my arrow to Insert and click to place the symbol in the document; then I point my arrow to Close and click again to finish the job.'

2. *They do, you say.* **Next get the employee to do the same procedure as you explain each step.** '

   Click your left mouse button on the Insert command on the toolbar and pull down the menu. Okay, good. Now point your arrow to Symbol and click again. Excellent! Choose the symbol you want from the menu and point your arrow to it. Now click to select it. All right – point your arrow to Insert and click to place the symbol in the document. Okay, you're almost done now. Point your arrow to Close and click again to finish the job. There you are!'

3. *They do, they say.* **Finally, as you observe, get your employee to perform the task again as he explains to you what he's doing.**

'Okay, Miles, now it's your turn. I want you to insert a symbol in your document and tell me what you're doing.'

'All right, Senti. First, I click my left mouse button on the Insert command on the toolbar and pull down the menu. Then I point the arrow to Symbol and click again. I decide the symbol I want from the menu, point my arrow to it and click to select it. Next, I point the arrow to Insert and click to place the symbol in the document. Finally, I point my arrow to Close and click again to finish the job. I did it!'

Get employees to create a 'crib sheet' of the new steps to refer to until they become habit.

Coaching Metaphors for Success in Business

In business, when it comes to coaching and teamwork, the metaphor of a company as a winning sports team is often applied. In many organisations chief executives hire professional athletes and coaches to lecture their employees on the importance of team play and winning. Managers are labelled *coaches* or *team leaders*, and workers are labelled *players* or *team members*.

This being the case, ignoring the obvious parallels between coaching in sports and in business is difficult. So we're going to get this out of our system once and for all and refrain from linking coaching in sports and business anywhere else in this book after the following list of examples:

✔ Terry Venables, legendary football coach, on his appointment to Barcelona FC: 'The first thing that I had to do was to get this group of highly talented individuals playing as a team.'

✔ Clive Woodward, England World Cup-winning rugby coach: 'To build a team, you have to coach people as a team. Of course, you work on individual strengths and weaknesses; in the end, however, it is how they perform together, not how they perform individually, that determines your success.'

✔ Arsene Wenger, manager and head coach at Arsenal FC: 'One of the most important things that I have to do is to maintain the players' belief in themselves. This is easy when you are winning – sometimes you have to rein them in. But when you are losing – this is the most important part of the job. And if you simply shout at people or threaten them – you will always fail.'

✔ José Mourinho, legendary (some would say controversial) football coach who's produced winning teams in three different countries and cultures already: 'If the players do not want to do things my way, I do not want them. Good players who will work as team members will always do better than brilliant individuals working in isolation.'

✔ Alf Ramsey, World Cup-winning England football manager and coach: 'The best teams are not necessarily made up of the best individuals. When one player thanked me for picking him, I replied: "I don't pick individuals, I pick teams."'

One last point: in sports, as in business, *everybody* needs a coach. Who's the greatest tennis player of all time? Pete Sampras? Probably. But most people don't realise that all the time he was playing, even Pete Sampras had a coach to help him stay sharp and to improve.

Tapping into the Coach's Expertise

Coaching isn't a one-dimensional activity. Because every person is different, the best coaches tailor their approach to their team members' specific, individualised needs. If one team member is independent and needs only occasional guidance, recognise where the employee stands and provide that level of support. This support may consist of an occasional, informal progress check while making the rounds of the office. If, on the other hand, another team member is insecure and needs more guidance, the coach recognises this employee's position and assists as required. In this case, support may consist of frequent, formal meetings with the employee to assess progress and to provide advice and direction as needed.

Although every coach has an individual style, the best coaches employ certain techniques to elicit the greatest performance from their team members:

✔ **Meet and make time for team members.** Managing is primarily a people job. Part of being a good manager and coach is being available to your employees when they need your help. If you're not available, your employees may seek out other avenues to meet their needs – or simply stop trying to work with you. Always keep your door open to your employees and remember that they're your Number 1 priority. Manage by walking around. Regularly get out of your office and visit your employees at their workstations. 'Do I have a minute, Elaine? Of course, I always have time for you and the other members of my staff.'

✔ **Provide context and vision.** Instead of simply telling employees what to do, effective coaches explain *why*. Coaches provide their employees with context and a big-picture perspective. Instead of spouting long lists of do's and don'ts, they explain how a system or procedure works and then define their employees' parts in the scheme of things. 'Sanjeev, you have a very important part in the financial health and vitality of our company. By ensuring that our customers pay their invoices within 30 days after we ship their products, we're able to keep our cash flow on the plus side, and we can meet our obligations such as rent, electricity and your salary on time.'

✔ **Transfer knowledge and perspective.** A great benefit of having a good coach is the opportunity to discover information and know-how from someone who has more experience than you do. In response to the unique needs of each team member, coaches transfer their personal knowledge and perspective. 'We faced the exact situation about five years ago, Hayden. I'm going to tell you what we did then, and I want you to tell me whether you think that it still makes sense today or if you have a better idea that we could try.'

✔ **Be a sounding board.** Coaches talk through new ideas and approaches to solving problems with their employees. Coaches and employees can consider the implications of different approaches to solving a problem and role-play customer or client reactions before trying them out for real. By using active listening skills, coaches can often help their employees work through issues and come up with the best solutions themselves. 'Okay, David, you've told me that you don't think your customer will buy from us if we put the prices up by 20 per cent. What options do we have with price increases, and are some better than others?'

✔ **Obtain necessary resources.** Sometimes coaches can help their employees make the jump from marginal to outstanding performance simply by providing the resources that their employees need. These resources can take many forms – money, time, staff, equipment or other tangible assets. 'So, Kathleen, you're confident that we can improve our cash flow if we put two more staff on to invoicing? Okay, let's give it a try.'

✔ **Offer a helping hand.** For an employee who's learning a new job and is still responsible for performing her current job, the total workload can be overwhelming. Coaches can help workers through this transitional phase by reassigning current duties to other employees, authorising overtime or taking other measures to relieve the pressure. 'Jill, while you're learning how to de-bug the new software, I'm going to assign the rest of your workload to Rachel. We can get back together at the end of the week to see how you're doing.'

Developing and Mentoring Employees

Developing your employees is the other side of coaching. You have to have employees who can and are willing to be developed. Taking people on in isolation from what you expect of them is useless; they must always be prepared to do things your way, making their expertise work for the good of everyone.

So, it's time for a quick look in the mirror. What kind of manager are you? Do you take on new employees and then just let them go on their merry way? Or do you stay actively involved in the progress and development of your employees, helping to guide them along the way? If you're a manager-to-be, do you know what having a mentor is like, someone who takes a personal interest in your career development? Mentoring is vitally important because as well as needing to make your own mistakes (and you will!), you also need someone to guide you, act as a sounding board, strengthen and test your determination and indicate areas where you could improve.

Employee development is the process by which you make everyone (including yourself) better at their jobs and improve their willingness to carry them out to the best of their abilities. Employee development is also concerned with the development of skills, knowledge, attitudes and behaviour; building experience and achievements into expertise. Employee development concentrates on the key areas of workplace development, professional and occupational priorities, and personal choices, so that everyone benefits and individuals take active responsibility for their own future.

The best employee development is continuous and requires that you support and encourage your employees' initiative. Recognise, however, that all development is self-development; you can really only develop yourself. You can't force your employees to develop; they have to want to for themselves. You can, however, help create an environment that makes it more likely that they want to develop, grow and succeed.

Explaining How Employee Development Helps

Development boils down to one important point: as a manager, you're in the best position to provide your employees with the support they need to advance in your organisation. Not only can you provide them with the time and money required for training, you can also offer unique on-the-job learning opportunities and assignments, mentoring, team participation and more. Besides, someone's got to be there to take your place when you get promoted.

Employee development involves a lot more than just going to a training class or two. In fact, approximately 90 per cent of development occurs on the job.

Training, learning and development are all different aspects of the same process:

- ✔ **Training** is the most straightforward – you tell people how to do something that's either more or less standard; or you take a step-by-step approach to something more complex.

- ✔ **Learning** requires you to create the conditions, environment and context – and employee confidence – in which development is most effective.

- ✔ **Development** is what goes on with everyone in all aspects of their lives, including work. From a manager's point of view, you should see employee development as a combination of personal, professional, occupational and career advancement and enhancement; and the improvement of knowledge, attitudes, behaviour and experience, as well as skills and expertise.

Now, have you ever wondered why your employees continue to mess up assignments that you know they can perform? In case you don't have any inkling whatsoever why developing your employees is a good idea, the following list provides the full justification:

- ✔ Development assures that your employees have the knowledge they need.

- ✔ Employees who work effectively are better employees.

- ✔ Someone has to be prepared to step into your shoes; for example, when you go on holiday, or in case you yourself move on.

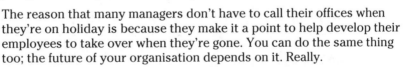

  The reason that many managers don't have to call their offices when they're on holiday is because they make it a point to help develop their employees to take over when they're gone. You can do the same thing too; the future of your organisation depends on it. Really.

- ✔ Your employee wins, and so does your organisation; and most important, you prepare your employees to fulfil the roles that your organisation needs them to fulfil in the future.

Your employees are worth your time and money. And if this sounds almost too obvious to state at all, remember that employees take anything up to three-quarters of the fixed costs of any organisation. So make sure that you make them as capable and as willing to work for you as you possibly can. Constantly offer new challenges and opportunities for all your employees; and make sure that they respond by stretching themselves to the limit.

Working in the factory: Not what it used to be

Many jobs that people with a relatively low level of education used to carry out have been transformed out of all recognition. For example, the factories in the United States and Western Europe that Japanese car and electrical goods companies established during the 1970s revolutionised both factory work and manufacturing.

Companies such as Sharp, Sony, Nissan and Toyota set out to change their reputation for producing cheap, low-quality and often shoddy goods. In the new locations, they paid above the market and industry rate in return for what they called conformity and commitment. These

Japanese companies spent millions training production staff to be fully skilled and totally flexible, able to do any job demanded, both before and after the production lines were switched on.

The results transformed manufacturing; and ruined British car and electrical goods companies in many cases. Employee development – a demonstrable commitment to staff and their future – drove everything the Japanese companies did. As employees' capabilities increased so did their enthusiasm, ambition and aspirations, which multiplied the beneficial effect.

Creating Career Development Plans

The career development plan is the heart and soul of your efforts to develop your employees. Unfortunately, many managers don't take the time to create development plans with their employees, instead trusting that when a need arises, they can find training to accommodate that need. This kind of reactive thinking ensures that you're always playing catch up to the challenges that your organisation faces.

Why wait for the future to arrive before you prepare to deal with it? Are you really so busy that you can't spend a little of your precious time planting the seeds that your organisation can harvest years from now? No! Although you do have to take care of the seemingly endless crises that arise in the here and now, you also have to prepare yourself and your employees to meet the challenges of the future. To do otherwise is an incredibly short-sighted and ineffective way to run your organisation.

All career development plans must contain as a minimum the following key elements:

✔ **Specific learning goals, supported by milestones along the way:** Each and every employee in your organisation benefits from having learning goals; and you need to set individual goals for each person. For example, say that your employee's career path starts at the position of junior buyer and works up to manager of purchasing. The key learning goals for this employee may be learning the stocks and supplies, training how to plan for stock replacement, spreadsheet analyses and introduction to management.

✔ **Resources required to achieve the designated learning goals:** Make sure you can resource everything that's needed.

✔ **Employee responsibilities and resources:** Career development is the joint responsibility of an employee and his manager. A business can and does pay for things, but so can employees (as any employee who's paid out of his own pocket to get a university degree can testify). A good career development plan should include what the employee is doing in his own time.

✔ **Required date of completion for each learning goal:** Make sure that employees stick to these dates, or else that they can give a clear explanation for failure to meet the dates for completion.

✔ **Standards for measuring the accomplishment of learning goals:** Assess these at each milestone.

Helping Employees to Develop

Employee development takes the deliberate and continuous efforts of employees with the support of their managers. If employees or managers lose heart, commitment or faith, then employees don't develop, and the organisation suffers the consequences of not having the employees it needs to meet the challenges it faces. This outcome definitely isn't good. As a manager, you want your organisation to be ready for the future, not always trying to catch up with it.

The employee's role is to identify the areas where development can help to make him a better and more productive worker, and then to relay this information to his manager. After the employee identifies further development opportunities, the manager and employee work together to schedule and implement them.

As a manager, your role is to be alert to the development needs of your employees and to keep an eye out for potential development opportunities. Managers in smaller organisations may be assigned to determine where the organisation will be in the next few years. Armed with that information, you're responsible for finding ways to ensure that employees are available to meet the needs of the future organisation. Your job is then to provide the resources and support required to develop employees so that they're able to fulfil the organisation's needs.

To develop your employees to meet the coming challenges within your organisation, follow these steps:

1. **Meet with each employee about his career.**

   Meet with individuals to discuss where you see them in the organisation and also to find out where in the organisation they want to go.

   This effort has to be a joint one! Having elaborate plans for an employee to rise up the company ladder in sales management isn't going to do you any good if your employee hates the idea of leaving actual sales to become a manager of other salespeople.

2. **Discuss your employee's strengths and weaknesses.**

   Have a frank discussion regarding the employee's strengths and areas for development. Your main goal here is to identify the areas that the employee is interested in and good at – that is, strengths that your employee can develop to allow his continued progress in the organisation and to meet the future challenges that your business faces. Focus the majority of your development efforts and resources on these opportunities.

   Spend time developing strengths as well as improving weaknesses. Improving and enhancing a skill that your employee finds easy and enjoyable is more valuable for you and your organisation than forcing the employee to be merely adequate at things others excel in. However, everyone needs to be proficient in essential tasks, even if they don't like them.

3. **Assess where the employee is now.**

   Determine the current state of your employee's skills and talents. Doing an assessment provides you with an overall road map to guide your development efforts.

4. **Create a career development plan.**

   A *career development plan* is an agreement between you and your employee that spells out exactly what formal support (tuition, time off, travel expenses and so on) your employee may receive to develop his skills, and when he may receive it. Career development plans have review and evaluation points, assessments of progress and agreements on the next step.

5. **Follow through on your agreements, and make sure that the employee follows through on his.**

   Don't break the development plan agreement. Make sure that you provide the support that you agreed to provide. Make sure that your employee upholds his end of the bargain too! Check on his progress regularly. If he misses schedules because of other priorities, reassign his work as necessary to ensure that he has time to focus on his career development plans.

Top ten ways to develop employees

The basics for developing employees are:

✔ Provide employees with opportunities to learn and grow.

✔ Be a mentor to an employee.

✔ Let an employee fill in for you in staff meetings.

✔ Give employees secondment and project work opportunities.

✔ Allow employees to pursue and develop any ideas they have.

✔ Provide employees with a choice of assignments.

✔ Send an employee to a seminar on a new topic.

✔ Take an employee along with you when you call on customers.

✔ Introduce your employees to top managers in your organisation and arrange to have them perform special assignments for senior people.

✔ Allow an employee to shadow you during your workday.

So when is the best time to sit down with your employees to discuss career planning and development? The sooner the better! Conducting a career development discussion twice a year with each of your employees isn't too often. Quarterly is even better; and a brief chat once a month is best of all. And make sure that you commit to the discussion – it represents time, money and effort well spent! Include a brief assessment in each discussion of the employee's development needs. Ask your employee what he can do to fulfil these needs. If he requires additional support, determine what form of support the employee needs and when you should schedule the support. Adjust career development plans and redirect resources as necessary.

Finding a Mentor, Being a Mentor

When you're an inexperienced employee working your way up an organisation's hierarchy, having someone with more experience to help guide you along the way is invaluable. Someone who's already seen what it takes to get to the top can advise you about the things that you must do and the things that you shouldn't do as you work your way up. This someone is called a *mentor*.

A mentor is typically an individual elsewhere or higher up in the organisation who isn't your boss. A manager's job is clearly to coach and help guide employees. Although managers certainly can act as mentors for their own employees, mentors most often act as confidential advisers and sounding boards for their chosen employees and therefore aren't typically in the employee's direct chain of command. Anyone can be a mentor; but doing so takes both capability and commitment. You can be a mentor to staff within your department, but if you do this, beware of accusations of patronage or favouritism.

The day that a mentor finds you and takes you under her wing is a day for you to celebrate because not everyone is lucky enough to one. And don't forget that some day you may be in a position to be a mentor to someone else. When that day comes, don't be so caught up in your busy business life that you neglect to reach out and help someone else find her way up the organisation.

Effective mentors are worth their weight in gold to any organisation; and they make a crucial contribution to the next generation as follows:

- ✔ Explain how the organisation really works, and make sure that new staff know their way through it.
- ✔ Lead by example, making sure that the conduct and behaviour of new starters is as effective as their performance.
- ✔ Provide development, growth, learning and training opportunities and experiences; and as well as formal opportunities, good mentors provide introductions to all kinds of other activities and organisations.
- ✔ Provide career guidance and direction; and this is worked out on a joint basis, exactly the same as effective performance management and appraisal.

The mentoring process often happens when a more experienced employee takes a professional interest in a new or inexperienced employee. Employees can also initiate the mentoring process by engaging the interest of potential mentors while seeking advice or working on projects together. However, recognising the potential benefits for the development of their employees, many organisations have formalised the mentoring process and made it available to a wider range of employees than the old, informal process ever could. If a formal mentoring programme isn't already in place in your organisation, why don't you recommend starting one?

Balancing Development and Downsizing

You've seen the stories: a thousand employees laid off at Barclays Bank, thousands more employees laid off at Vauxhall Motors and even more in the National Health Service. Most companies aren't immune when the economy downturns. Maybe your organisation has felt the sharp knife of re-engineering, downsizing or reductions. If so, you may ask, 'Isn't employee development too difficult to perform when everything is changing so fast around me? My employees may not even have careers next year, much less the need to plan for developing them.'

Actually, nothing can be farther from the truth. Although businesses are going through rapid change, employee development is more important than ever. As departments are combined, dissolved or reorganised, employees have to be ready to take on new roles and duties that they may never have performed before. In some cases, employees may have to compete internally for positions or sell themselves to other departments to ensure that they retain their employment with the organisation. In this time of great uncertainty, many employees feel that they may have lost control of their careers and even their lives.

Career planning and development provide employees in organisations undergoing rapid change with the tools that they need to regain control of their careers. The following list describes what some of the largest and most high-profile companies have done to help get their employees through redundancies and reorganisations:

✔ British Airways has undergone major reorganisations over the past decade in pursuit of reducing staff costs and managerial and administrative overheads. BA offers all staff at risk of redundancy opportunities for retraining and redeployment; and they're in a 'staff pool' for a period of up to 12 months before the organisation finally releases them. During this period the staff have access, within reason, to any training and development that may enhance their future employment prospects.

✔ Computer giant IBM overhauled the career plans of thousands of employees who transitioned from staff positions to sales positions as a result of a massive corporate reorganisation.

✔ Most famous of all, Mitsubishi, a Japanese manufacturing corporation, transformed itself from producing aircraft and ships into a major car manufacturer without any job losses whatsoever. Staff were simply told what was going to happen, and then retrained as car workers. This was effected through a £42 million investment in training, technology and re-equipment.

Despite the obvious negative effects of downsizing on employee morale and trust, times of change provide managers with a unique opportunity to shape the future of their organisations. For many managers, this is the first time that they've had such an opportunity to help remake the organisation. And each of the stories in the preceding list shows that alternatives exist to simply laying people off.

Employee development is more important than ever as employees are called upon to take on new and often more responsible roles in your organisation. Your employees need your support now. Make sure that you're there to provide it. This help just may be one of the most valuable gifts that you can give to your employees.

Top five mentoring and development websites

The following websites provide the best information on the web about the topics we address in this chapter:

✔ **The Business Mentor:** www.thebusiness mentor.net

✔ **University College London (UCL Advances):** www.ucl.ac.uk/advances

✔ **Deloitte:** www.deloitte.co.uk

✔ **Chartered Management Institute:** www.managers.org.uk

✔ **e-skills UK:** www.e-skills.com/professional-development/

Part III
Making Things Happen

'I like a young man who knows where he's going.
If you'll just go through that door while
my directors & I discuss your promotion
application...'

In this part . . .

Employees without goals are employees without direction. And after you set goals with employees, you have to measure employees' progress towards their goals. In this part, we address setting goals with employees, measuring employee performance and conducting performance evaluations the right way.

Chapter 6

Setting Goals and Targets

· ·

In This Chapter

▶ Linking goals to your vision

▶ Creating SMART goals

▶ Concentrating on fewer goals

▶ Publicising your goals

▶ Following through with your employees

▶ Determining sources of power

· ·

Ask any group of workers, 'What's the primary duty of management?' The answer 'setting goals' is likely to be near the top of the list. If setting goals appears near the bottom of the list, you know you've got a problem! In most companies, top management sets the overall purpose – the vision – of the organisation. Middle managers then have the job of developing goals and plans for achieving the vision that top management has established. Managers and employees work together to set goals and develop schedules for attaining them.

As a manager, you're probably immersed in goals – not only for yourself but also for your employees, your department and your organisation. This flood of goals can overwhelm you as you try to balance the relative importance of each one.

Should I tackle my department's goal of improving turnaround time first, or should I get to work on my boss's goal of finishing the budget? Or maybe the company's goal of improving customer service is more important. Well, I think I may just try to achieve my own personal goal of setting aside some time to eat lunch today.

So when you're faced with this kind of confusion, you first need to be absolutely sure where your priorities truly lie. And although you need goals in order to prioritise, as you discover in this chapter, having too many goals and too many divergent demands can be as bad as not having any goals at all.

Goals provide direction and purpose. Don't forget: if you can see it, you can achieve it. Goals help you see where you're going and how you can get there. And the *way* that you set goals can influence how motivating they are to others.

If You Don't Know Where You're Going, How Do You Know When You Get There?

Did you realise that Lewis Carroll's classic book *Alice in Wonderland* offers lessons that can enhance your business life? Consider the following passage from Carroll's book, in which Alice asks the Cheshire Cat for advice on which direction to go:

> *'Would you tell me please, which way I ought to go from here?'*
>
> *'That depends a good deal on where you want to go,' said the Cat.*
>
> *'I don't much care where . . .' said Alice.*
>
> *'Then it doesn't matter which way you go,' said the Cat.*
>
> *'. . . so long as I get somewhere,' Alice added as an explanation.*
>
> *'Oh, you're sure to do that,' said the Cat, 'if you only walk long enough.'*

Getting *somewhere* takes no effort at all. Just do nothing, and you're there. (In fact, everywhere you go, there you are!) However, if you want to get somewhere meaningful, you first have to know where you want to go. And after you decide where you want to go, you need to make plans on how to get there. This practice is as true in business as in your everyday life.

For example, suppose you have a vision of starting up a new sales office in Prague so that you can better service your Eastern European accounts. How do you go about achieving this vision? You have four choices:

- ✔ An unplanned, non-goal-oriented approach
- ✔ A set of bland statements masquerading as goals
- ✔ A planned, goal-oriented approach
- ✔ A hope and a prayer

The choice is yours! Do note, however, the difference between setting real goals and making statements that pretend to be goals. For example:

✔ When asked what his goal was, Sir John French, the allied military commander on the Western Front during the First World War, stated: 'Why, to advance and win the war.'

✔ When asked what they intended to achieve by opening up a large call centre facility in Bombay, India, a large financial services company replied: 'We do not know, but we are confident of success anyway.'

Make up your mind now to choose the planned, goal-oriented approach. Following are the main reasons to set goals whenever you want to accomplish something valuable or worthwhile:

✔ **Goals provide direction.** In the example of starting up a new sales office in Prague, you can probably find a million different ways to service your Eastern European business accounts more effectively. However, to get something done, you have to set a definite vision – a target to aim for and to guide your and your organisation's efforts. You can then translate this vision into goals that take you where you want to go. Without goals, you're doomed to waste countless hours going nowhere. With goals, you can focus both your and your staff's efforts specifically on the activities that move you towards where you're going – in this case, opening a new sales office.

✔ **Goals tell you how far you've travelled.** Goals provide milestones along the road to accomplishing your vision. If you determine that you must accomplish several specific milestones to reach your final destination and complete a few of them, you know exactly how many remain. That is, you know exactly where you stand and how far you have yet to go.

✔ **Goals help to make your overall vision attainable.** You can't reach your vision in one big step – you need many small steps to get there. If, again, your vision is to open a new sales office in Prague, you can't expect to proclaim your vision on Friday and walk into a fully staffed and functioning office on Monday. You must accomplish many goals – from shopping for office space, to hiring and relocating staff, to printing stationery and business cards – before you can attain your vision. Goals enable you to achieve your overall vision by dividing your efforts into smaller pieces that, when accomplished individually, add up to big results.

✔ **Goals clarify everyone's role.** When you discuss your vision with your employees, they may have some idea of where you want to go but no idea of how to approach the process of getting there. As your well-intentioned employees head off to help you achieve your vision, some employees may duplicate the efforts of others, some may ignore some tasks and some may simply do something else altogether (and hope that you don't notice the difference). Setting goals with employees clarifies what the tasks are, who does which tasks and what you expect from each employee.

✔ **Goals give people something to strive for.** People are typically more motivated when you challenge them to attain a goal that's beyond their normal level of performance – this is what's known as a *stretch goal*. Not only do goals give people a sense of purpose, they can also relieve the potential boredom created by performing a routine job day after day. Be sure to discuss the goal with your employees and gain their commitment.

✔ **Goals move everyone and everything on.** Achieving one set of goals provides the foundation for establishing and determining the next set of goals.

For goals to be useful, they have to link directly to the final vision. To stay ahead of the competition, or simply to remain in business, organisations create compelling visions and then management and employees work together to set and achieve the goals to reach those visions. Look over these examples of compelling visions that drive the development of goals at several successful enterprises:

✔ Swatch, the company created by Nicolas Hayek to revitalise the declining Swiss watch industry, set the goal of creating the best component-manufacturing processes in the world. And not only were they to be the best, they were to be the most cost effective. This meant creating factory, manufacturing and production facilities in Switzerland more cost effective than those in China and Japan.

✔ Motorola, long known for its obsession with quality, has set a truly incredible vision for where it wants to be. Motorola has set a target of no more than two manufacturing defects per billion units.

✔ Anita Roddick set out to create The Body Shop as an ethical company in terms of the ways in which it dealt with its suppliers and customers. She did this at exactly the time that Western economies were moving into recession; therefore, the last thing that the commercial world needed was a new cosmetics company; and anyone creating companies at that time sought to minimise, rather than optimise, start-up costs. However, by setting distinctive standards and reinforcing these with a commitment to dedicating the business 'to the pursuit of social and environmental change', she was able to establish clear goals and direction for the company in spite of the otherwise adverse trading conditions.

When it comes to goals, the best ones

✔ Are few in number, specific in purpose

✔ Are stretch goals – not too easy, not too hard

✔ Involve people – when you involve others, your goal becomes their goal

Identifying SMART Goals

You can find all kinds of goals in all types of organisations. Some goals are short term and specific ('starting next month, we'll increase production by two units per employee per hour'), and others are long term and nebulous ('within the next five years, we'll become a learning organisation'). Employees easily understand some goals ('line employees will have no more than 20 rejects per month'), but others can be difficult to fathom and subject to much interpretation ('all employees are expected to show more respect to each other in the next financial year'). Still others can be accomplished relatively easily ('reception staff will always answer the phone by the third ring'), but others are virtually impossible to attain ('all employees will master the five languages that our customers speak before the end of the financial year').

How do you know what kind of goals to set? The whole point of setting goals, after all, is to achieve them. Going to the trouble of calling meetings, hacking through the needs of your organisation and burning up precious time is pointless if you end up with goals that employees don't act on or complete. Unfortunately, this scenario describes what far too many managers do with their time.

The best goals are SMART. SMART refers to a handy checklist for the five characteristics of well-designed goals, as follows:

- ✔ **Specific:** Goals must be clear and unambiguous; broad and fuzzy thinking has no place in goal setting. When goals are specific, they tell employees exactly what you expect, when and how much. Because the goals are specific, you can easily measure your employees' progress towards their completion.

- ✔ **Measurable:** What good is a goal that you can't measure? If your goals aren't measurable, you never know whether your employees are making progress towards their successful completion. Not only that, but your employees may have a tough time staying motivated to complete their goals if they have no milestones to indicate their progress. Ultimately, you can only measure anything against what you set out to achieve.

- ✔ **Attainable:** Goals must be realistic and attainable by average employees. The best goals require employees to stretch a bit to achieve them, but they aren't extreme. That is, the goals are neither out of reach nor below standard performance. Goals that are set too high or too low become meaningless, and employees naturally come to ignore them.

- ✔ **Relevant:** Goals must be an important tool in the grand scheme of reaching your company's vision and mission. The Pareto principle when applied to productivity states that 80 per cent of workers' productivity comes from only 20 per cent of their activities. Relevant goals address the

20 per cent of workers' activities that have such a great impact on performance and bring your organisation closer to its vision; as well as try to make better use of the 80 per cent of time that's otherwise unproductive.

✔ **Time-bound:** Goals must have starting points, ending points and fixed durations. Commitment to deadlines helps employees to focus their efforts on completion of the goal on or before the due date. Goals without deadlines or schedules for completion tend to be overtaken by the day-to-day crises that invariably arise in an organisation.

SMART goals make for smart organisations. In our experience, many supervisors and managers don't work with their employees to set goals together. And even in the organisations where they do work in that way, goals are often unclear, ambiguous, unrealistic, unmeasurable, demotivating and unrelated to the organisation's vision. By developing SMART goals with your employees, you can avoid these traps while ensuring the progress of your organisation and its employees.

Although the SMART system of goal setting provides guidelines to help you frame effective goals, you have additional considerations to keep in mind. These considerations help you ensure that anyone in your organisation can easily understand and act on the goals that you and your employees agree, as explained in the following list:

✔ **Ensure that goals are related to your employees' role in the organisation.** Pursuing an organisation's goals is far easier for employees when those goals are a regular part of their jobs. For example, suppose you set a goal for employees who solder circuit boards to 'Raise production by 2 per cent per quarter'. These employees spend almost every working moment pursuing this goal, because the goal is an integral part of their job. If, however, you give the same employees a goal of 'Improving the diversity of the organisation', they wonder exactly what that has to do with their role. Nothing. The goal may sound lofty and may be important to your organisation, but because your line employees don't make the hiring decisions, you're wasting both your time and theirs with that particular goal.

✔ **Whenever possible, use values to guide behaviour.** What's the most important value in your organisation? Honesty? Fairness? Respect? These values translate into specific goals, as follows:

• To be honest in all our dealings with customers and suppliers

• To be fair in all staff management practices

• To be respectful to the environment and everything that we do that affects it

In this way, you're stating a direct relationship between what you do and how you do it – and both are vital.

✔ **Simple goals are better goals.** The easier your goals are to understand, the more likely the employees are to work to achieve them. Goals should be no longer than one sentence; make them concise, compelling and easy to read and understand.

Goals that take more than a sentence to describe are actually multiple goals. When you find multiple-goal statements, break them into single, one-sentence goals. Goals that take a page or more to describe aren't really goals; they're books. File them away and try again.

Setting Goals: Less Is More

Years ago, Richard worked for an industrial training board. This organisation was a subdivision of a much larger government department, the Manpower Services Commission (MSC). The board's purpose was to provide facilities, resources, expertise and development for the building materials, pottery and glass industries.

Because the organisation was a government department, everything was planned, right down to the last detail. The organisation employed a planning director, together with expert economists, statisticians and manpower experts. The job of the planning director and his people was to give absolute assurances, both to the government and to the industries served, on the following issues:

✔ Why the board existed

✔ What services it provided

✔ How the industries acquired and used these services

✔ The number of training and development activities to be carried out

✔ The nature of training and development activities to be carried out

✔ The number of research activities to be carried out

✔ The nature of research activities to be carried out

The board employed training officers, training advisers and researchers. When companies in the relevant industries called in training officers and training advisers to help them, they first had to check whether or not these activities had been planned for and scheduled. When researchers (such as Richard) were asked to conduct analyses for particular companies, they had to make sure that the activities had indeed been planned for, and that sufficient resources were allocated to enable the work to be done fully and effectively.

The result was that the board spent all of its time planning, and not enough time doing. On an individual basis, staff gained a reputation for being cheerful and knowledgeable, but totally unresponsive. The fact that the planning processes and the board's constitution tied staff's hands was of no concern to the industries – all they wanted was to get the work done.

Following government reforms, the MSC and most of the training boards were disbanded in 1982. This didn't prevent the board's planning division from producing a strategic and operational plan until 1985 – as required by the board's constitution and MSC regulations.

Don't let all your hard work end in nothing. When you go through the trouble of setting goals, keep them to a manageable number that you can realistically follow up. And when you finish one goal, move on to the next.

When it comes to goal setting, less is more. So prioritise!

The following guidelines can help you select the right goals – and the right number of goals – for your organisation:

- ✔ **Pick two to three goals to focus on.** You can't do everything at once, and you can't expect your employees to either. A few goals are the most you should attempt to conquer at any one time. Picking too many goals dilutes the efforts of you and your staff and can result in a complete breakdown in the goal-setting process.

- ✔ **Pick the goals with the greatest relevance.** Certain goals take you a lot farther down the road to attaining your vision than do other goals. Because you have only so many hours in your work day, concentrating your efforts on a few goals that have the biggest pay-off – rather than on a boatload of goals with a relatively lower pay-off – clearly makes sense.

- ✔ **Focus on the goals that tie most closely to your organisation's mission.** You can be tempted to take on goals that are challenging, interesting and fun to accomplish but that are far removed from your organisation's mission. Don't.

- ✔ **Periodically revisit the goals and update them as necessary.** Business is anything but static, and periodically assessing your goals is important to making sure that they're still relevant to the vision you want to achieve. If so, great – carry on. If not, meet with your employees to revise the goals and the schedules for attaining them.

Avoid taking on too many goals in your zeal to get as many things done as quickly as you can. Too many goals can overwhelm you – and your employees. Set a few, significant goals and then concentrate your efforts on attaining them. Don't forget that management isn't a game of huge success after huge success. Instead, it's a game of meeting challenges and opportunities every day – gradually, but inevitably, improving the organisation in the process.

Communicating Your Goals to Your Team

Having goals is great, but how do you get the word out to your employees? As you know, goals grow out of an organisation's vision. Establishing goals helps you ensure that employees focus on achieving the vision in the desired time frame. You have many possible ways to communicate goals to your employees, but some ways are better than others. In every case, you must communicate goals clearly, the receiver must understand the goals and everyone involved must follow through the goals.

Goals in the NHS

The British National Health Service went through a period of radical reform. Mantras such as the 'agenda for change', 'patient choice' and 'purchasing options' abounded. Some years on, waiting lists are allegedly now structured so that everyone is seen within a certain period of time, subject only to medical need; targets for the treatment of high-profile diseases, especially cancer, are clearly established. At the top of the organisation, and in political circles and directorates, 'transformation' is the goal, the target – the absolute priority.

Or not. The problem is translating all these ideals into specific goals that those who work in the service can identify with. To many people, no relevant goal setting seems to be taking place. The basic proposal of 'We have to change' isn't then followed up with a clear statement of 'Change from what? To what? When? Where? How? Why?'

The result is that the staff don't know what they need, want or have to do. 'Goals' therefore become simply meeting today's problems. This means:

✔ For managers: Responding to the latest edict; providing data on request; closing wards and laying off staff to save money.

✔ For medical staff: Treating the patients in front of them; and where this is not possible, doing their best to make appointments to see the patients again at some indeterminate time in the future, without (hopefully) breaking the waiting list and waiting time targets.

The clear, predictable and assured results are as follows – and they apply to any organisation that doesn't set clear targets, goals and priorities:

✔ A division bordering on conflict exists between management and medical staff whose 'goals', such as they are, rarely coincide in practice.

✔ Anything that gets done is being achieved more slowly, for fewer people, more expensively and with greater margins for error.

And yet the remit – the goal or target – of any hospital, doctor's surgery or other medical facility ought to be clear and simple: to provide the necessary analysis, diagnosis and treatment for all patients on request.

Communicating your organisation's vision is as important as communicating specific goals. You can communicate the vision in every way possible, as often as possible, throughout your organisation and to significant others such as clients, customers, suppliers and so forth. And you need to be aware of possible obstacles: often an organisation's vision is pounded out in a series of gruelling management meetings that leave the participants (you, the managers) beaten and tired. By the time the managers reach their final goal of developing a company's vision, they're sick of the process and ready to go on to the next challenge.

Many organisations and managers like the idea of cascading the vision, goals and targets down through different layers of management. The concept is neat and tidy; and the image of pouring champagne into a stack of glasses and watching it cascade from the top to the bottom is pretty glamorous. Unfortunately, by the time the champagne reaches the glasses at the bottom, it's warm, flat and lifeless. Communication cascades have exactly the same effect – so don't use them unless you have to!

When you communicate vision and goals, do it with energy and with a sense of urgency and importance. You're talking about the future of your organisation and your employees – not about chopped liver. If your employees think that you don't care about the vision, why should they care? Simply put, they won't.

Companies usually announce their visions with much pomp and fanfare. The following are different ways in which companies commonly announce and communicate their vision:

- ✔ By conducting huge employee rallies where they unveil the vision in inspirational presentations

- ✔ By printing their vision on anything possible – business cards, letter-heads, massive posters, newsletters, employee name badges and more

- ✔ By encouraging managers to 'talk up' the vision in staff meetings and when they're having discussions with employees

To avoid a cynical 'oh no, another fad' reaction from employees suspicious of management's motives when unveiling a new initiative, make consistent, casual references to the vision – this approach is much more effective than a huge, impersonal event. Again, in this case, less is often better.

Goals, on the other hand, are much more personal, and the methods you use to communicate them must be much more formal and direct. The following guidelines can help you out:

✔ **Make sure that each employee has a written copy of the goals.**

That way, you remove the chance of any misunderstandings.

✔ **Always conduct one-to-one, face-to-face meetings with your employees to introduce, discuss and assign individual goals.**

If physical distance or any other reason prevents you from conducting a face-to-face meeting, have your meeting over the phone. The point is to make sure that your employees receive the goals, understand them and have the opportunity to ask for clarification.

✔ **Call your team together to introduce team-related goals.**

You can assign goals to teams instead of to individuals. If this is the case, get the team together and explain the role of the team and each individual in the successful completion of the goal. Make sure that all team members understand exactly what they're to do. Get them fired up and then let them loose. We discuss the function of teams in more detail in Chapter 11.

✔ **Gain the commitment of your employees.**

Whether individually or in teams, inspire your employees to commit to the successful accomplishment of their goals.

Ask your employees to prepare and present plans and milestone schedules explaining how they can accomplish the assigned goals by the deadlines that you agree. After your employees begin working towards their goals, regularly monitor their progress to ensure that they're on track and meet with them to help them overcome any problems.

Juggling Priorities

When you've decided on the goals that are important to you and to your organisation, you come to the difficult part. How do you maintain your employees' focus – and your own focus, for that matter – on achieving the goals that you've set?

The process of goal setting often generates a lot of excitement and energy within employees – whether the goals are set in large group meetings or in one-to-one encounters. This excitement and energy can quickly dissipate as soon as everyone gets back to their desk. You, the manager, must take steps to ensure that the organisation's focus remains centred on the goals and not on other matters (which are less important but momentarily more pressing). Of course, this task is much easier said than done.

Implementing goals at Pret A Manger

Up-market sandwich retailer Pret A Manger produces good-quality snacks and sandwiches at premium prices. The company buys all the ingredients it uses fresh on the day it uses them. Employees cook and bake each of the products – sandwiches, bagels, pasta mixes, croissants and doughnuts – on the premises for immediate consumption. Pret A Manger gives anything not consumed by the end of the day to charity.

In order to deliver this level of quality and service, the company has specific goals and targets that it communicates regularly to all staff, and displays on the walls of both the retail and staff areas. These are as follows.

- ✔ Customers must not have to wait for more than three minutes before being served; longer than that and they begin to feel slighted, and this leads to loss of reputation.

- ✔ Customers are not to wait for more than 90 seconds while they're being served; longer than that and they begin to feel unvalued, and again this leads to loss of reputation.

- ✔ Customers don't expect to have to queue for more than 30 seconds to pay for their products if they've picked them off the shelf themselves.

Managing the overarching goals of quality, value, service and convenience has meant that the company has had to pay attention to these specific details in order to ensure that it maximises business opportunities whenever customers come in through the door.

In order to fulfil these goals, Pret A Manger and its managers have additionally to address the following priorities:

- ✔ Assessing the peaks and troughs of demand throughout the day and scheduling staff accordingly

- ✔ Ensuring that all staff who are working (even during busy periods) have access to tea- and coffee-making facilities and tills

- ✔ Ensuring that all staff can recognise each of the products on offer

- ✔ Ensuring that all staff are friendly, pleasant and polite

A lack of attention to any of these goals and targets reduces the real and perceived distinctive quality and style of Pret A Manger, which would result in customers seeing the company as a largely unbranded, undifferentiated, standard convenience food chain. So that this doesn't happen, the staff know and understand clearly what they have to do, why and how, and what the results are.

Staying focused on goals can be extremely difficult – particularly when you're a busy person and the goals are on top of your regular responsibilities. Think about situations that fight for your attention during a typical day at work:

- ✔ How often do you sit down at your desk in the morning to plot out your priorities for the day, only to have them pushed aside five minutes later when you get a call from your boss?

Maria, I need you to drop everything and get to work on a report for the general manager right away! She has to have it on her desk by 3 p.m. today.

✔ How many times has an employee come to you with a problem?

Sorry, Maria, but I think you'd better hear about this problem before it gets any worse. Jenny and Tony just had a heated argument and Jenny says she's leaving. We can't afford to lose Jenny – especially not right now. She's the key to the development project. What are we going to do?

✔ How often do you get caught in a 15-minute meeting that actually drags on for several hours?

Are there any questions on steps 1 to 14 of the new recruitment process? Fine, now let's get started on steps 15 to 35.

In unlimited ways, anyone can lose sight of what they need to be doing in order to get the organisation's goals accomplished. One of the biggest problems employees face is confusing activity with results. Do you know anyone who works incredibly long hours – late into the night and on weekends – but never seems to get anything done? Although this employee always seems to be busy, the problem is that she's working on the wrong things. This scenario is called *presenteeism* or the *activity trap*, and anyone can fall into it if they're not careful.

In the 'Identifying SMART Goals' section, earlier in this chapter, we mention the Pareto rule stating that 80 per cent of workers' productivity is generated by 20 per cent of their activity. The flip side of this rule is that only 20 per cent of workers' productivity comes from 80 per cent of their activity. This statistic illustrates the activity trap at work. What do you do in an average day? More important, what do you do with the 80 per cent of your time that produces so few results? You can get out of the activity trap and take control of your schedules and priorities. However, you have to be tough, and you have to be single-minded in pursuit of your goals. And you have to take your employees with you.

Achieving your goals is all up to you. No one, not even your boss (perhaps especially not your boss), can make it any easier for you to concentrate on achieving your goals. You have to take charge – now! If you aren't controlling your own schedule, you're simply letting everyone else control your schedule for you.

Following are some tips to help you and your employees get out of the activity trap:

✔ **Do your Number 1 priority first!** With all the distractions that compete for your attention, with the constant temptation to work on the easy stuff first and save the tough stuff for last, and with people dropping into your office just to chat or to unload their problems on you, concentrating on your Number 1 priority is always a challenge. However, if you don't do your Number 1 priority first, you're almost guaranteed to find yourself in the activity trap. That is, you'll find the same priorities on your list of tasks to do day after day, week after week and month after month. If your Number 1 priority is too big, divide it into smaller chunks and focus on the most important one of those.

✔ **Do your Number 2 priority second!** This has the advantage of keeping you concentrated on what's truly important and making sure that you don't get sidetracked by the hustle and bustle of daily life. Additionally, you need to focus on priority Number 2 until it's done – the same as everything else.

✔ **Get organised!** Getting organised and managing your time effectively are incredibly important pursuits for anyone in business. If you're organised, you can spend less time trying to figure out what you should be doing and more time *doing* what you should be doing.

✔ **Just say no!** If someone tries to make his problems your problems, just say no. If you're a manager, you probably like nothing more than taking on new challenges and solving problems. The conflict arises when solving somebody else's problems interferes with solving your own. You have to constantly be on guard and fight the temptation to fritter your day away with meaningless activities. Always ask yourself, 'How does this help me achieve my goals?' Focus on your own goals and refuse to let others make their problems yours.

Using Your Power for Good: Making Your Goals Happen

After you create a wonderful set of goals with your employees, how do you make sure that the goals happen? How do you turn your priorities into your employees' priorities? If people don't achieve them, the best goals in the world mean nothing. You can choose to leave this critical step in the process to chance, or you can choose to get involved.

You have the power to make your goals happen.

Power isn't inherently wrong provided you use it responsibly. Everyone has many sources of power within them. Not only do you have power, but you also exercise power to control or influence people and events around you on a daily basis. So power is a positive thing; it's only negative when abused. Bullying, victimisation, manipulation, exploitation and coercion have no place in the modern workplace. You can use the positive power within you to your advantage – and to the advantage of the people around you – by tapping into it to help achieve your organisation's goals. People and systems often fall into ruts or non-productive patterns of behaviour that are hard to break. Power properly applied can kick-start these people and systems and move them in the right direction – the direction that leads to the accomplishment of their goals.

Everyone has five primary sources of power, and everyone has specific strengths and weaknesses related to these sources. Recognise your own strengths and weaknesses and use them to your advantage. As you review the five sources of power in the following list, consider your own personal strengths and weaknesses:

- ✔ **Personal power:** This comes from within your character. Your passion for greatness, the strength of your convictions, your ability to communicate and inspire, your personal charisma and your leadership skills all add up to personal power.

- ✔ **Relationship power:** Everyone has relationships with others at work. These interactions contribute to the relationship power that you wield in your workplace. Sources of relationship power include close friendships with top executives, partners or owners, people who owe you favours and colleagues who provide you with information and insights that you normally don't get through your formal business relationships.

- ✔ **Knowledge power:** To see knowledge power in action, just watch what happens the next time your organisation's computer network goes down! Then you see who really has the power in an organisation (in this case, your computer network administrator). Knowledge power comes from the special expertise and knowledge that you've gained during the course of your career. Knowledge power also comes from obtaining academic degrees (think MBA) or special training.

- ✔ **Task power:** This comes from the job or process you perform at work. As you've undoubtedly witnessed on many occasions, people can facilitate or impede the efforts of their colleagues and others through the application of task power. For example, when you submit a claim for payment to your insurance company and months pass with no action ('We don't seem to have your claim in our computer – are you sure you submitted one? Maybe you should send us another one just to be sure'), you're on the receiving end of task power.

- ✔ **Position power:** This kind of power derives strictly from your rank or title in the organisation and is a function of the authority that you wield to command human and financial resources. Although the position power of the receptionist in your organisation is probably quite low, the position power of the president or owner is at the top of the chart. The best leaders seldom rely on position power to get things done.

Top five goal websites

Wondering where to find the best information on the web about the topics we address in this chapter? Well, you've come to the right place! Here are our top five favourites:

✔ **Mind ools for personal goal setting:** www.mindtools.com/page6.html

✔ **Goals-2-Go for setting business and management goals:** www.goals2go.com

✔ **The awesome power of goal setting for human resources:** www.humanresources.about.com/library/weekly/aa121000a.htm

✔ **Advanced Performance Institute:** www.ap-institute.com

✔ **myGoals.com for setting personal development goals:** www.mygoals.com

If you're weak in certain sources of power, you can work on increasing your power in those areas. For example, work on your weakness in relationship power by making a concerted effort to know your colleagues better and to cultivate relationships with higher-ranking managers or executives. Instead of declining invitations to get together with your colleagues after work, join them – have fun and strengthen your relationship power at the same time.

Be aware of the sources of your power and use your power in a positive way to help you and your employees accomplish the goals of your organisation. In getting things done, a little power can go a long way.

Chapter 7

Being an Expert at Performance Appraisal and Management

In This Chapter

▶ Quantifying and qualifying your goals

▶ Developing a performance management and appraisal system

▶ Putting your system into practice

▶ Making sure your system works

▶ Avoiding the pitfalls of systems

Setting goals – for individuals, for teams and for the overall organisation – is extremely important. (Chapter 6 addresses the whys and wherefores of setting goals.) However, ensuring that the organisation is making progress towards the successful completion of its goals (in the manner and time frames agreed to) is equally important. The organisation's performance depends on each individual who works within it. Achieving goals is what this chapter is all about.

Measuring and monitoring the performance of individuals in your organisation is like walking a tightrope: you don't want to over-measure or over-monitor your employees. Doing so only leads to needless bureaucracy and red tape, which can negatively affect your employees' ability to perform their tasks. Neither do you want to under-measure or under-monitor your employees. Such a lack of watchfulness can lead to nasty surprises when a task is completed late, over budget or not at all. 'What? The customer database conversion isn't completed yet? I promised the sales director that we'd have that job done two weeks ago!'

Please keep in mind that, as a manager, your primary goal in measuring and monitoring your employees' performance isn't to punish them for making a mistake or missing a milestone. Instead, you help your employees stay on track and find out whether they need additional assistance or resources to do so. Few employees like to admit that they need help getting an assignment done – whatever the reason. Because of their reluctance, you must systematically check on the progress of your employees and regularly give them feedback on how they're doing.

If you don't monitor desired performance, you won't achieve desired performance. Don't leave achieving your goals to chance; develop systems to monitor progress and ensure that employees achieve your goals. And you can't measure anything except against what you set out to achieve.

Taking the First Steps

The first step in checking your employees' progress is to determine the key indicators of a goal's success. If you follow the advice in Chapter 6, you set goals with your employees that are few in number and *SMART* (specific, measurable, attainable, relevant and time-bound).

When you quantify a goal in precise numerical terms, your employees have no confusion over how their performance is measured and when their job performance is adequate (or less than adequate). For example, if the goal is to produce 100 sprockets per hour, with a reject rate of 1 or lower, your employees clearly understand that producing only 75 sprockets per hour with 10 rejects is unacceptable performance. You leave nothing to the imagination, and the goals aren't subject to individual interpretation or to the whims of individual supervisors or managers.

How you measure and monitor the progress of your employees towards completion of their goals depends on the nature of the goals. You can measure goals in terms of time, units of production or delivery of a particular work product (such as a report or a sales proposal), for example.

Table 7-1 offers examples of different goals and ways to measure them.

Table 7-1	Sample Goals and Measurements
Goal	**Measurement**
Plan and implement a company news-letter before the end of the second quarter of the current fiscal year	The specific date (for example 30 June) that the newsletter is sent out *(time)*
Increase the number of mountain bike frames produced by each employee from 20 to 25 per day	The exact number of mountain bike frames produced by the employee each day *(quantity)*
Increase profit on the project by 20 per cent in financial year 2012	The total percentage increase in profit in the year to 31 December 2012 *(percentage increase)*

Although noting when your employees attain their goals is obviously important, recognising your employees' *incremental* progress towards attaining their goals is just as important. For example:

✔ The goal for your drivers is to maintain an accident-free record. This goal is continuous – no deadline exists. To encourage drivers in their efforts, you can prominently post a huge banner in the middle of the garage that reads '153 Accident-free Days'. Increase the number for each day of accident-free driving.

✔ The goal of your accounts clerks is to increase the average number of transactions from 150 per day to 175 per day. To track their progress, you can publicly post a summary of the daily production count at the end of each week. As production increases, praise the progress of your employees towards the final goal.

✔ The goal set for your production staff is to turn customer orders around within 24 hours, without errors. You can publicly post the results for all to see; and in this case, when orders are either not turned around within 24 hours or when errors occur, you have a very quick, public and agreed point for investigation.

The secret to performance measuring and monitoring is the power of positive feedback. When you give positive feedback (increased number of units produced, percentage increase in sales and so on), you encourage the behaviour that you want. However, when you give negative feedback (number of errors, number of work days lost and so on), you aren't encouraging the behaviour you want; you're only discouraging the behaviour that you don't want. Consider the following examples:

✔ **Instead of measuring this:** Number of defective cartridges

✔ **Measure this:** Number of correctly assembled cartridges

✔ **Instead of measuring this:** Number of days late

✔ **Measure this:** Number of days on time

✔ **Instead of measuring this:** Quantity of late transactions

✔ **Measure this:** Quantity of completed transactions

From our experience as managers, we find that you're much more likely to get the results you want when you put group performance measures (total revenues, average days sick and so on) out in the open for everyone to see, but keep individual performance measures (sales performance by employee, absence rankings by employee and so on) private. The intention is to get a team to work *together* to improve its performance – tracking and publicising group measures and then rewarding improvement in them can lead to dramatic advances in the performance you seek. What you do *not* want to do is embarrass your employees or subject them to ridicule by other employees when their individual performance isn't up to par. Instead, deal with these employees privately, and coach them (and provide additional training and support, as necessary) to improve performance.

Developing a System for Providing Immediate Performance Feedback

You can measure an infinite number of behaviours or performance characteristics. What you measure and the values you measure against are up to you and your employees. In any case, keep certain points in mind when you design a system for measuring and monitoring your employees' performance. Build your system on the *MARS – milestones, actions, relationships* and *schedules* – system. We describe each element of the MARS system in the following sections.

Application of each characteristic – milestones, actions, relationships and schedules – results in goals that you can measure and monitor. If you can't measure and monitor your goals, chances are that your employees never achieve them and you don't know the difference. And wouldn't that be a shame?

Setting your checkpoints: The milestones

Every goal needs a starting point, an ending point and points in between to measure progress along the way. *Milestones* are the checkpoints, events and markers that tell you and your employees how far along you are on the road to reaching the goals you've set together.

For example, suppose that you establish a goal of finalising corporate budgets in three months' time. The third milestone along the way to your ultimate goal is that draft department budgets are submitted to division managers no later than 1 June. If you check with the division managers on 1 June and your employees haven't submitted the draft budgets, you quickly and unambiguously know that the project is behind schedule. If, however, all the budgets are in on 15 May, you know that the project is ahead of schedule and that you may reach the final goal of completing the corporate budgets sooner than you originally estimated.

Reaching your checkpoints: The actions

Actions are the individual activities your employees perform to get from one milestone to the next. To reach the third milestone in your budgeting project –

submitting draft department budgets to division managers by 1 June – your employees must undertake and complete several actions after they reach the second milestone in the project. In this example, these actions may include the following:

- ✔ Review prior-year expenditure reports and determine the relationship, if any, to current activities.
- ✔ Review current-year expenditure reports and project and forecast final results.
- ✔ Meet with department staff to determine their training, travel and capital equipment requirements for the new financial year.
- ✔ Review the possibilities of new staff, lay-offs, redundancies and pay rises to determine the impact on payroll costs.
- ✔ Put everything onto a computerised draft budget spreadsheet using the figures from the actions already taken.
- ✔ Print off the draft budget and double-check the results, correcting them if necessary.
- ✔ Submit the draft budget to your own manager before forwarding it to the division manager.

Each action gets your employees a little farther along the way towards reaching the third milestone in the project and is therefore a critical element in their performance.

When developing a plan for completion of any activity or project, note each action in writing. By taking notes, you make concentration easier for your employees because they know exactly what they must do to reach a milestone, how far they've gone and how much farther they have to go. And each time they do reach a milestone, record it.

Acting in sequence: The relationships

Relationships are how milestones and actions interact with one another. Relationships shape the proper sequencing of activities that lead you to the successful, effective accomplishment of your goals. Although sequences don't always matter, it's often more effective to perform certain actions before others and to attain certain milestones before others.

For example, in the list of actions needed to achieve the third project milestone, covered in the preceding section, trying to perform the fifth action before the first, second, third or fourth isn't going to work! If you don't work out the right numbers to put into your spreadsheet before you fill in the blanks, your results are meaningless.

Measuring instead of counting

According to management guru Peter Drucker, most business people spend too much time counting and too little time actually measuring the performance of their organisations.

Drucker likens counting to a doctor using an X-ray machine to diagnose an ill patient. Although some ailments – broken bones, pneumonia and so on – do show up on an X-ray, other, more life-threatening illnesses such as leukaemia, hypertension and AIDS don't. Similarly, most managers use accounting systems to X-ray their organisation's financial performance. However, accounting systems don't measure a catastrophic loss of market share or a failure of the firm to innovate until the problem has already gone on too long and the 'patient' is damaged – perhaps irretrievably.

Keep in mind that you may have more than one way to reach a milestone and give your employees the scope to find their own ways to reach their goals. Doing so empowers your employees to take responsibility for their work and to benefit from both their mistakes and their successes. The results are successful performance and happy, productive employees.

Establishing your timeframe: The schedules

How do you determine how far apart your milestones should be and how long project completion should take? You can plan better by estimating the *schedule* of each individual action in your project plan.

Using your experience and training to develop schedules that are realistic and useful is important. For example, if you give someone a deadline of two years' time, they won't take any notice of it until two or three months before the actual date. If you do need to set long-term deadlines, then make sure that you break the activities up into milestones and points of reference that you can realistically measure along the way.

Reducing shrinkage

Shrinkage refers to the amount of products, equipment and supplies lost through wastage, theft, damage or breakage. Shrinkage is therefore a euphemism for sloppiness, lack of attention and, above all, an inability to set standards of performance that stick.

Many organisations are complacent about shrinkage. According to Lawrence King, managing director of the ORIS Group, a consultancy that monitors the efficiency and effectiveness of resource utilisation for its customers,

> *Some retailers especially do not even know what their shrinkage numbers are. I know of two major businesses, one in pharmaceuticals and the other in fashion, neither of which want to know how bad the problem is, because they know that they would have to do something about it if they did know. They have therefore put this problem into the 'too hard to cope with' basket. The trouble is, it does cost money to find out what the losses are. And then once you know what the losses are, you clearly have to do something about it.*

In the past, organisations thought that shoplifting and petty pilfering were the only real sources and causes of shrinkage, and so considered they had little to worry about. Shrinkage, however, occurs through staff dishonesty and information systems failure as well as through theft by customers. Part of the problem is a result of changing patterns of employment. King states:

> *Not that long ago, most retail staff were full-time. It was a career, and they worked until they drew their pensions. Now, retailers have cut their costs, there are far more part-time staff, so the manager in a typical retail outlet may be the only full-time member of staff. That may not be quite true in bigger stores of course; but the general trend is the same. There is consequently a lot less loyalty and a lot less commitment than there used to be. In addition, the pay is almost invariably lower. Retail has never been the best pay in the world, so maybe people feel that there is an opportunity to supplement low rates of pay by helping themselves a bit.*

Any organisation faced with a serious shrinkage problem has to be able to establish absolute standards – standards below which it doesn't slip, nor allow employees to slip. You can only address shrinkage problems under the following conditions:

- ✔ **Recognising the issue at all levels.** Recognition must be underpinned by a determination at board level to deal fully and effectively with the problem.

- ✔ **Enforcing zero tolerance for theft or fraud among staff.** No matter how senior, experienced or valued the colleague is, he must be dismissed if he's caught stealing from the business. This is the *only* way to deal with pilfering.

- ✔ **Making shrinkage culturally unacceptable.** Make it clear that shrinkage is an enemy of the business. Relate shrinkage rates to turnover and profitability in all staff briefings.

✔ **Rewarding the desired behaviour.** The desired behaviour is established through a combination of policies and practice. The policies very clearly state both what's required and how people are to behave and not behave. In particular, you need to focus on the conduct of everyone from the point of view of ensuring that

- Everyone knows and understands that stealing, lying and cheating are an affront to everyone.

- You monitor all aspects of shrinkage that concern you, and make sure that you also involve all the staff.

- Shrinkage is treated from the point of view that, by stealing or lying, individuals affect not just themselves but also everyone else.

Making sure that you reward honest employees adequately for their work, so that you remove their temptation to steal, is the key to this problem. An open and honest culture needs to underpin the organisation; ensuring that employees are honest is impossible if those further up the organisation aren't. Paying attention to matters such as punctuality, commitment and enthusiasm helps to generate loyalty and engagement; and the more loyal and engaged employees are, the less likely they are to steal from their employer.

Reading the Results

You establish your goals, you set performance measures and you obtain pages of data for each of your employees and activities. Now what? Now you determine whether your employees achieved the expected results, as follows:

✔ **Compare results to expectations.** Did your employees achieve the expected goal? Suppose that the goal is to complete the budget by 1 June. When did your employees complete the budget? It was completed on 17 May – well ahead of the deadline. Brilliant! The employees accomplished the mission with time to spare.

✔ **Record the results.** Make note of the results – perhaps put them in the files that you maintain for each employee or print them out on your computer and post them in the work area.

✔ **Praise, coach or counsel your employees.** If they did the job right, on time and within budget, congratulate your employees for a job well done and reward them appropriately: a written note of appreciation, a day off with pay, a formal awards presentation – whatever you decide.

However, if employees didn't achieve the expected results, find out why and what you can do to ensure that they are successful next time. If employees need only additional support or encouragement, coach them for a better performance. Listen to your employees, clarify their difficulties and then formulate a response; consider referring them to other employees for advice or providing your own personal examples that may be applicable to their situation. If the poor results stem from a more serious shortcoming, then retrain, or discipline, your employees. (See Chapter 16 for the lowdown on disciplining staff.)

Appraising Performance: Why It Matters

You can find many good reasons for conducting regular formal performance appraisals with your employees and of your activities. Formal performance appraisals are just one part of an organisation's system of delegation, goal setting, coaching, motivating and ongoing informal and formal feedback on employee performance. If you don't believe us, try a few of these positive elements of performance appraisals on for size:

✔ **A chance to meet regularly:** Meeting regularly means that you know what your employees are doing and they know you're available for support when needed. When you establish regular informal meetings, you also have a much better basis for effective regular formal reviews when they happen.

✔ **A chance to summarise past performance and establish new performance goals:** All employees want to know whether they're doing a good job. Formal performance appraisals force managers to communicate performance results – both good and bad – to their employees and to set new goals. In many organisations, the annual performance appraisal is the only occasion when supervisors and managers speak to their employees about performance expectations and the results of employee efforts for the preceding appraisal period.

✔ **An opportunity for clarification and communication:** You need to continually compare expectations. Try this exercise with your manager. List your ten most important activities. Then ask your manager to list what she considers to be your ten most important activities. Surprise – the chances are that your lists are quite different. On average, businesspeople who do this exercise find that their lists overlap by only 40 per cent at best. Performance appraisals help the employer and employee to compare notes and make sure that assignments and priorities are in sync.

✔ **A forum for learning goals and career development:** In many organisations, career development takes place as a part of the formal performance appraisal process. Managers and employees are all very busy and often have difficulty setting aside the time to sit down and chart out the steps that they must take to progress in an organisation or career. Although career development discussions should generally take place in a forum separate from the performance appraisal process, combining the activities does afford the opportunity to kill both birds with the same stone . . . or something like that.

✔ **A formal documentation to promote advancement or dismissal:** Most employees get plenty of informal performance feedback – at least of the negative kind along the lines of: 'You did what? Are you nuts?' Most informal feedback is verbal and, as such, undocumented. If you're trying to build a case to give your employee a promotion, you can support it more easily if you have plenty of written documentation (including formal performance appraisals) to justify your decision. And if you're coming to the conclusion that you need to dismiss someone for poor performance, then you must have written evidence, including performance appraisals, that you've tried to address this performance before.

So, the preceding list gives very important reasons for conducting regular, formal performance appraisals. However, consider this statement: many companies have paid a lot of money to employees and former employees who've successfully sued them for wrongful or unfair dismissal, or for other biased and prejudicial employment decisions. Imagine how lonely you'd feel on the witness stand in the following scene, a scene that's replayed for real in courts of law and employment tribunals the length and breadth of the country:

Lawyer: So, Manager-on-the-spot, would you please tell the court exactly why you terminated Employee X?

Manager-on-the-spot: Certainly, I'll be glad to. Employee X was a very poor performer – clearly the worst in my department.

Lawyer: During the five years that my client was with your firm, did you ever conduct formal performance appraisals with her?

Manager-on-the-spot: Er . . . well, no. I meant to, but I'm a very busy person. I was never quite able to get around to it.

Lawyer: Manager-on-the-spot, do you mean to say that, in all the time with your firm, Employee X never received a formal performance appraisal? Exactly how was my client supposed to correct the alleged poor performance when you failed to provide her with the feedback needed to do so?

Manager-on-the-spot: Hmmm . . .

Spelling Out the Performance Appraisal Process

Believe it or not, one of the most important things you can do as a manager is to conduct accurate and timely performance appraisals of your employees. As the saying goes, feedback is the breakfast of champions – make it a regular part of your management diet!

Many managers, however, tend to see the performance appraisal process in very narrow terms: how can I get this thing done as quickly as possible so I can get back to my real job? (Whatever their 'real' job is as managers.) In their haste to get the appraisal done and behind them, many managers merely consider a few examples of recent performance and base their entire appraisal on them. And because few managers give their employees the kind of meaningful, ongoing performance feedback that they need to do their jobs better, the performance appraisal can become a dreaded event – full of surprises and dismay. Or it can be so sugar-coated that it becomes a meaningless exercise in management. Neither scenario is the right way to evaluate your employees.

Have separate discussions for each of the following:

- ✔ Pay rises and bonuses
- ✔ Promotions
- ✔ Career development
- ✔ Ways to improve present performance and develop future performance
- ✔ Poor performance

Of course, in practice you can't possibly keep each of the topics totally separate from the rest. But you can prioritise; and you need to spell out to the employee the specific purpose of the present discussion.

The performance appraisal process begins on the day that your employees are hired, continues each and every day that they report to you and doesn't end until, through transfer, promotion, dismissal or resignation, they move out of your sphere of responsibility.

The performance appraisal process is much broader than just the formal, written part of it. The following steps help you encompass the broader scope of the process. Follow them when you evaluate your employees' performance:

1. **Set goals, expectations and standards – together.**

   Before your employees can achieve your goals, or perform to your expectations, you have to set goals and expectations with them and develop standards to measure their performance. And after you've done all this, you have to communicate the goals and expectations *before* you evaluate your employees – not after. In fact, the performance review really starts on the first day of work. Tell your employees immediately how you evaluate them, show them the forms to be used and explain the process.

   Make sure that job descriptions, tasks and priorities are clear and unambiguous, and that you and your employees understand and agree to the standards set for them. This is a two-way process. Make sure that employees have a voice in setting their goals and standards and that you have their agreement. Refer to Chapter 6 for more on setting goals.

2. **Give continuous and specific feedback.**

   Catch your employees doing things right – every day of the week – and tell them about it then and there. And if you catch them doing wrong (nobody's perfect!), then let them know about that too. Feedback is much more effective when you give it regularly and often than when you save it up for a special occasion (which can become victimisation if the feedback is constantly negative). The best formal performance appraisals contain the fewest surprises.

   Constantly bombarding your employees with negative feedback has little to do with getting the performance that you want from them and costs you their respect.

3. **Prepare a formal, written performance appraisal with your employee.**

   Every organisation has different requirements for the formal performance appraisal. Some appraisals are simple, one-page forms that require you to tick a few boxes; others are multi-page extravaganzas that require extensive narrative support. The form often varies by organisation, and by the level of the employee being evaluated. Regardless of the requirements of your particular organisation, the formal performance appraisal should be a summary of the goals and expectations for the appraisal period – events that you've discussed previously (and frequently) with your employees. Support your words with examples and make appraisals meaningful to your employees by keeping your discussion relevant to the goals, expectations and standards that you developed in Step 1.

   As a collaborative process, have the employee complete his own performance appraisal. Then compare your (the manager's) comments with the employee's comments; the differences that you find become topics of discussion and mutual goal setting.

4. **Meet personally with your employees to discuss the performance appraisal.**

Most employees appreciate the personal touch when you give the appraisal. Set aside some quality time to meet with them to discuss their performance appraisal. This doesn't mean five or ten minutes, but at least an hour or maybe more. When you plan performance appraisal meetings, less is definitely not more. Pick a place that's comfortable and free from distractions. Make the meeting positive and upbeat. Even when you have to discuss performance problems, centre discussions on ways that you and your employees can work together to solve them.

The tone of performance appraisals and discussions can often become defensive as you raise negative elements and the employee starts to feel that he'll get a small, or no, pay rise. Start with letting the employee share how his job is going, what's working – and what's not – then share your assessment, starting with the positive.

5. **Set new goals, expectations and standards.**

The performance appraisal meeting gives you and your employee the opportunity to step back from the inevitable daily issues for a moment and take a look at the big picture. You both have an opportunity to review and discuss the things that worked well and those that, perhaps, didn't work so well. Based on this assessment, you can then set new goals, expectations and standards for the next review period. The last step of the performance appraisal process becomes the first step, and you start all over again.

The entire performance appraisal process consists of setting goals with your employees, monitoring their performance, coaching them, supporting them, counselling and guiding them, and providing continuous feedback on their performance – both good and bad. If you do these things before you sit down for your annual or semi-annual performance appraisal sessions with your employees, reviews will be a pleasant and positive experience, looking at past accomplishments, instead of a disappointment for both you and them.

When it comes to conducting performance appraisals, managers have plenty of things to remember. Here are a few more:

✔ Communication with employees should be frequent so that no surprises occur (okay, *fewer* surprises). Give your employees informal feedback on their performance early and often.

✔ The primary focus of performance appraisals should be on going forward – setting new goals, improving future performance – rather than on looking back.

✔ Learning and development should always be included as a part of the performance appraisal process (although sometimes a discussion about pay rises can be separate).

✔ You need to make performance appraisal a priority yourself – a part of your 'real' job – you are, after all, dependent on the performance of your employees for your own success and effectiveness.

Turning the tables: Upward and 360-degree evaluations

Recently a new kind of performance appraisal has emerged. Instead of the typical downward appraisal where managers review their workers' performance, the upward appraisal process stands this convention on its head by requiring workers to evaluate their managers' performance. If you think that getting a performance appraisal from your manager is uncomfortable, you haven't seen anything yet. Nothing's quite like the feeling you get when a group of your employees appraise you, giving you direct and honest feedback about the things you do that make it hard for them to do a good job. Ouch!

However, despite the discomfort that you may feel, the upward appraisal is invaluable – who better to assess your real impact on the organisation than your employees? The system works so well that companies such as Federal Express and others have institutionalised the upward appraisal and made it part of their corporate culture. Recent surveys show that many of the world's top companies are using some form of the upward performance appraisal to assess the performance of their managers.

Also popular is the 360-degree evaluation. The *360-degree evaluation process* is when you're appraised from all sides – superiors, subordinates, colleagues and anyone from other departments with whom you happen to be working at the time. Levi Strauss & Co, for example, dictates that all employees are evaluated by their supervisors and by their underlings and peers.

The results can be quite a surprise to the lucky manager who's the subject of the appraisal, who may find that other employees see him as less caring and visionary than he thought. A study by Charles Handy many years ago found the same thing – that 70 per cent of managers and supervisors who rated themselves as caring and concerned were rated in turn as autocratic and distant by their employees.

Preparing for the No-Surprises Appraisal

If you're doing your job as a manager, the appraisal holds no surprises for your employees. Follow the lead of the best managers: keep in touch with your employees and give them continuous feedback on their progress. Then, when you do sit down with them for their formal performance appraisal, the session is a recap of the things that you've already discussed during the appraisal period, instead of an ambush. Keeping up a continuous dialogue lets you use the formal appraisal to focus on the positive things that you and your employees can work on together to get the best possible performance.

Above all, be *prepared* for your appraisals!

Anecdotal evidence

The following stories illustrate and reinforce the need to conduct performance appraisals thoroughly and effectively, the results that accrue from doing so and the consequences if performance appraisal isn't adequate or targeted effectively.

✔ Arnold Weinstock, former chief executive of GEC, built the electrical conglomerate into the most valuable British organisation in great part on the basis of weekly performance appraisals and reviews with all of his top, senior and general managers and divisional directors. Often conducted late at night or over the weekend, these performance reviews normally consisted of a one-hour telephone conversation in which Arnold Weinstock would question each top manager closely on the following areas: performance, performance targets and revenues; reasons for achievement or non-achievement; proposals for the following week; review and commentary on longer-term plans and issues. As one manager said: 'Arnold knew the stuff, and you needed to know it. If you couldn't answer his questions in detail, or if you tried to flannel your way out of things – you didn't last.'

✔ Mark McCormack, founder and chief executive of sports representation agency IMG until his death in 2004, used to manage-by-walking-about (MBWA) as far as possible. He tried to meet up with every top and senior manager, as well as other employees in the organisation; and anyone he couldn't meet, he phoned, just as Arnold Weinstock did. Again, the purpose was to get to the detail of performance and progress, and to hammer out any problems or issues. Mark McCormack stated: 'The reason for this is quite simple. We represent the interests of some of the most famous and high-profile people in the world. If we do a bad job for them, they will simply go elsewhere; and that means we are doing a bad job for us, and for those clients and connections with whom we seek to develop business. Only by attending to performance review in this way, and in this detail, can we hope to keep everybody happy and satisfied.'

✔ The strategic human resources unit of a large UK local authority devised a system of merit pay. Merit was decided by a rigorous system of performance appraisal; and anyone meeting the merit criteria received a merit pay award. Cometh the hour, cometh the system – and after working through the performance appraisal exercise with all 53,000 staff employed by the local authority, 30 merit awards were allocated. Of the 30, almost half went to the 14 members of the strategic human resources unit that had dreamed up the system in the first place! If you're determined to introduce merit pay, do at least put the ideas out to full consultation before you go live – it will save you a fortune, and moreover, you'll get a reputation for being completely fair and transparent.

Like interviews, many managers leave their preparation for performance appraisal meetings to the last possible minute – often just before the employee is scheduled to meet with them. 'Oh, no. Cathy is going to be here in five minutes. Now, what did I do with her file? I know it's here somewhere!' The average manager spends about one hour preparing for an employee review covering a whole year of performance.

To avoid this unprofessional and unproductive situation, follow these tips:

- ✓ Set time aside, make a proper appointment with the employee and stick to it.

- ✓ Make a clear statement to the employee: 'The purpose of this performance appraisal is as follows . . .' and stick to it.

Performance appraisal is a year-round job. Whenever you recognise a problem with your employees' performance, mention it to them, make a note of it and drop it in your their files. And do the same whenever your employees do something great. Then, when you're ready to do your employees' periodic performance appraisals, you can pull out their files and have plenty of documentation available on which to base them. Not only does this practice make the process easier for you, it also makes the appraisal much more meaningful and productive for your employees.

Top five performance appraisal websites

The best online information about the topics we address in this chapter is on these websites:

- ✓ **Balanced Scorecard Institute for Performance Management:** www.balancedscorecard.org

- ✓ **Chartered Institute of Personnel and Development:** www.cipd.co.uk/performancemanagement

- ✓ **Accenture:** www.accenture.com/

- ✓ **Introduction to Performance Appraisal:** www.performance-appraisal.com/intro.htm

- ✓ **Work911:** www.work911.com/performance

Chapter 8

Being an Expert Manager within Your Environment

In This Chapter

▶ Recognising the forces and influences operating at work

▶ Understanding how to analyse your environment

▶ Taking responsibility

▶ Addressing green issues

All managers have to work in the context of the environment in which they find themselves. To do so, they first need to recognise the difference between the forces in the environment that they can control and influence, and those they can't. For example, oil prices, property values and availability of bank credit may all act as constraints on a business. Acknowledging their influence, managers then need to find ways to work around them.

This chapter covers how to take a detailed look at your business environment and work out which elements you can influence to make them work for you.

Scrutinising Your Environment

To develop a sound basis for knowing and understanding your business environment, you need to analyse it. You can apply various methods of analysis, including PESTEL and SWOT, to help you really take a hard look at the influences on your business. When you recognise these influences, you can then work out how to deal with them. The following sections cover a selection of tools and methods to apply to your business environment; use them alone, in succession or a few points from each – whatever you feel works for your business.

Conducting a PESTEL analysis

PESTEL stands for *political, economic, social, technological, environmental and legal* and refers to the factors affecting your business. First you apply a PESTEL analysis to factors within your own business, as follows:

- **Political:** Internal political systems, sources of power and influence, key groups of workers, key departments, and key managers and executives.

- **Economic:** Financial structure, objectives and constraints in the workplace.

- **Social:** Social systems in the workplace, departmental and functional structures, and work organisation and methods.

- **Technological:** The effects of the organisation's technology, the uses to which you put the technology and the technology that may become available in the future.

- **Environmental:** The effects of the organisation's activities on staff behaviour and activities, including waste disposal, health and safety management, specific training and development needs, specialist equipment and technology.

- **Legal:** The effects on your activities of the law and any regulatory or statutory demands that you have to comply with, including employment law, product and service regulations, advertising and marketing. compliance – and, of course, presenting your accounts when required!

Next, you consider forces outside the control of the organisation, or of particular managers, as follows:

- **Political:** Legal and statutory changes that may take place, such as legislation that limits the ways in which companies can advise, or legal changes to maximum and minimum work hours.

- **Economic:** The effects that prosperity and hardship have on your activities.

- **Social:** How people's habits and customs change, and how these changes may affect your business or your ability to employ staff.

- **Technological:** Technological changes and advances that are being developed, whether your company needs them and the effects of other companies acquiring and using them.

- **Environmental:** How the activities and operations of the company affect the 'green' environment, both short and longer term; and how changes in environmental attitudes change prevailing business practices.

✔ **Legal:** The fundamental shifts in the legal sphere as these affect businesses. These include new and more stringent provisions against price collusion and bribery, and new corporate governance statutes and regulations introduced in the UK, EU and US over the past few years.

Although outside your control, these factors nevertheless constitute the boundaries within which your business operates and you need to understand them in full.

To conduct a PESTEL analysis, follow these steps:

1. **Gather together your team or department.**

2. **Brainstorm a list of all the factors that you recognise under each of the PESTEL headings.**

3. **Use your findings to start a discussion about how each factor may affect your company.**

4. **Work out ways in which to deal with, influence or work around each factor, to the benefit of your organisation.**

For example, if you recognise reductions in consumer spending as an economic factor, you can investigate ways to make your product appealing to people on a limited budget. Or if you spot that a new technological innovation will make your own equipment obsolete, you can plan how to budget for new machinery over the next couple of years.

Doing a SWOT analysis

SWOT stands for *strengths*, *weaknesses*, *opportunities* and *threats*. A SWOT analysis looks at things a business does well and can capitalise on, things it struggles with and needs to improve, and outside factors that affect the success or failure of its products or services. SWOT is broken down as follows:

✔ **Strengths:** Things that the organisation and its staff are good at, and for which they have a good reputation.

✔ **Weaknesses:** Things that the organisation and its staff are bad at, or for which they have a poor reputation.

✔ **Opportunities:** Potentially profitable directions that may be worth exploring in the future.

✔ **Threats:** Potential problems facing the organisation, such as new competitors, strikes or resource or revenue constraints.

In practical application, a persistent limitation of SWOT is lack of insight, foresight and objective breadth. For example, many middle managers fearful of offending top management daren't suggest that their product is viewed as second-rate by customers, even when that's exactly the case!

Make sure that you understand the likely reception of your SWOT analysis. If sensitive issues are revealed, such as the CEO's pet project going wrong or an IT system that's plainly not working, make sure you have clear evidence to back up your findings.

To do a SWOT analysis, get your team together and generate a list of everything that comes to mind regarding the company and its products or services. Then place each item under one of the four SWOT headings listed above. Discuss and plan how to:

- ✔ Build on strengths
- ✔ Eliminate weaknesses
- ✔ Recognise and take advantage of opportunities
- ✔ Minimise or eliminate threats

Test your results on trusted colleagues, key customers and clients, and other stakeholders. Doing so enables you to gain valuable insights into what everyone else thinks about the state of your business. And most importantly, you can discover *why* they think that particular things are strengths, weaknesses, opportunities or threats.

Also consider carrying out a SWOT analysis on one of your competitors – ideally the industry leader, or else one of the fastest growing firms in your sector. Concentrate on their strengths as well as their weaknesses, so that you see for yourself what you have to compete with, as well as the opportunities presented by what they don't do so well.

SWOT analysis is particularly useful for understanding and addressing your weaknesses. For example, if one of your identified weaknesses is slow invoicing, which in turn negatively affects your cash flow, you can turn immediately to working out how to speed up this process.

So a SWOT analysis is easy, right? All you have to do is identify factors within the organisation, list them under relevant headings – and you suddenly achieve full understanding! Actually, no. Although you do (hopefully) identify lots of strengths and opportunities, you're also revealing to everyone where the organisation's difficulties truly lie. After you identify your problems and everyone knows that you do indeed have them, you need to move on to the truly challenging job of tackling and resolving them.

Putting on your analysis SPECTACLES

In his book *Mastering the Organisation in its Environment* (Macmillan Masters, 2000), Roger Cartwright takes a very detailed approach to environmental analysis. He identifies a ten-point approach, summarised with the acronym SPECTACLES, as follows:

✔ **Social:** Changes in society and societal trends; demographic trends and influences.

✔ **Political:** Political processes and structures; lobbying of political institutions (within the country and larger governing bodies); political pressures brought about by market regulations.

✔ **Economic:** Sources of finance; stock markets; inflation; interest rates; local, regional, national and global economies.

✔ **Cultural:** International and national cultures; regional cultures; organisational cultures; cultural clashes; culture changes; cultural pressures on business and organisational activities.

✔ **Technological:** Understanding the technological needs of a business; technological pressures; relationship between technology and work patterns; communications; e-commerce; technology and manufacturing; technology and bio-engineering.

✔ **Aesthetic:** Communications; marketing and promotion; image; fashion; organisational body language; public relations.

✔ **Customer:** Consumerism; importance of analysing customer bases; customer needs and wants; customer care; anticipating future customer requirements; customer behaviour.

✔ **Legal:** Sources of law; codes of practice; legal pressures; product liability; health and safety; employment law; competition legislation; European law; whistle-blowing.

✔ **Environmental:** Responsibilities to the planet; pollution; waste management; farming activities; genetic engineering; cost–benefit analyses; legal pressures.

✔ **Sectoral:** Competition; cartels and monopolies; competitive forces; co-operation within sectors; differentiation; segmentation.

SPECTACLES analysis requires managers to take a detailed look at each key aspect of their operation within its particular environment.

Any analysis technique can yield difficult truths and questions, but SPECTACLES analysis is likely to raise precise and sometimes uncomfortable questions that many managers (especially senior managers) may rather not address. For example, after considering cultural factors in great detail, an organisation may have to face the fact that it doesn't actually understand the effects of particular customs on buying patterns or on its ability to recruit staff.

SWOT analysis is also not simple because you must be able to say *why* the things that you list as strengths, weaknesses, opportunities and threats are indeed so. You can justify your categorisations by

✔ Explaining how political, economic, social, technological, legal and ethical forces will affect your business.

✔ Describing the threat created by potential new competitors and market entrants.

✔ Estimating the strength of forces that drive your business and restrain any changes you may implement.

✔ Prioritising and justifying your findings and conclusions so that you can argue your points credibly with top and senior managers.

✔ Constructing ways forward to address and resolve the issues that you've identified. For example, if your company produces retail products and you lack a channel to convenience stores, make sure that you have credible and practical suggestions for opening channels of distribution to these outlets; don't just leave it as a statement of weakness.

Knowing your market

Analysing the environment, or *environmental scanning*, involves looking at it from different perspectives. Combining multiple points of view builds your knowledge of your environment, highlights where different pressures are likely to come from and gives you a clearer understanding of how different bits of information are important to different people, institutions and groups. One key output of environmental scanning is that you come to know and understand each of your markets in detail, including:

✔ Economic, social and legal pressures

✔ The behaviour patterns of consumers within the market

✔ The behaviour of competitors and alternatives within the competitive environment

✔ Changes in customer and client attitudes

Keep your knowledge and understanding of your existing markets up to date by reading the business and trade press on a regular basis. But even more critically, go out and see for yourself what's happening in your sector and with commercial activities as a whole.

Be wary of what might at first glance appear to be industry news but is instead deftly-worded commercial propaganda put out by a company's public relations department. For example, a bold description of a novel initiative that lacks any evidence of value or success is little more than media image-building, even if the 'story' appears in the business news section.

You also need to become an expert in any new markets that you're considering entering *before* you open for business. For new markets, you specifically need to know:

- Customers' buying habits – and things that cause these habits to change.

- Why customers are loyal to their present suppliers – and what may cause them to change their loyalties. (**Hint:** you must deliver more than just lower prices; you also need to provide positive benefits!)

Identifying other issues and dealing with them

In addition to all the pressures that become apparent when you do the analyses we outline in the preceding sections, be aware of the following:

- **'Everyone else is doing it':** For example, outsourcing, using external consultants, expanding overseas and branching out into exciting new ventures. Don't conform for the sake of it.

- **'We must save money':** This statement often leads to job losses or the closure of factories, plants or premises, whether or not this is actually right.

- **Shareholder influence:** Shareholders interested in their dividends may try to enforce ways of working to create (possible) short-term share price advantages.

- **Revaluation or devaluation of assets:** Organisations do this to make their balance sheets look better.

- **Removing particular ventures and expenditures from balance sheets:** Organisations do this to create an enhanced impression of organisational financial strength.

- **Reorganisations leading to turmoil and uncertainty:** These are especially difficult at times when you need staff commitment founded on certainty.

- **Rushing at things:** Bear in mind Roman Emperor Marcus Aurelius's response to this situation: 'We never had time to do anything properly. So we always had to find time to do everything twice.'

From time to time all managers get tempted, forced or pressurised into doing these often superficially very attractive things, simply because they make you appear to be busy. (Doing so often means that you don't have time to confront the real issues because you *are* so busy!) However, these actions are invariably destructive, and they always delay rather than remove the evil day when you have to address the real problems and issues.

> # How The Body Shop conducted – and conducts – itself
>
> How your organisation conducts itself has a major effect on its success or failure. If the organisation is known, believed or perceived to be cavalier, dishonest or sloppy, people will conduct their business elsewhere. Consider The Body Shop.
>
> For the first 27 years of its existence, The Body Shop had the longest staff waiting list in the UK as a percentage of numbers employed. This situation was in large part because it set clearly understood standards of conduct, behaviour and performance. It was also clearly identified as having a very distinctive ethical approach to business.
>
> The company's major growth phase occurred during the late 1980s, in the midst of a global recession. Although people tend to spend on needs rather than wants in times of economic hardship, nevertheless The Body Shop thrived because consumers knew, understood and supported the company's ethical stance and standards.

Considering your company's reputation

Above all, the business environment is the place where you work and your organisation conducts its business. Your behaviour and that of your organisation needs to be above reproach.

This point is often lost on organisations and their managers – everyone has a very strong need to be recognised, accepted, respected and valued (see Chapters 4 and 24). Unfortunately, we often create organisations and perform activities that are unacceptable in terms of conduct, behaviour, performance or reputation. View your organisation as a *corporate citizen* – a member of the community in which it exists – and let this view guide what you do and how you do it. Always consider the impact that your organisation also has on its environment; it's a two-way process.

Reaching a conclusion

Recognising that it's complex is the main knowledge to gain from scanning and analysing your business environment! You can't be certain how the environment will behave or react to the things that you want to do. Change and uncertainty are universal factors affecting the business environment and you need to be able to cope with them (see Chapters 1, 2 and 15 for more on dealing with change). When considering your environment, always take into account:

- ✔ The laws that you have to comply with

- ✔ The volumes of money and other resources available

- ✔ The nature of your market and customer base from the perspective of their size, duration and spending power

- ✔ The economic and social pressures that you have to be aware of and work under

You need to create an environment in which your organisation has the best possible chance of conducting successful, effective and profitable business, whatever constraints you have to work within.

Recognising and Accepting Your Responsibilities

As a manager, your responsibility is to decide how you and your employees can work effectively in light of various environmental factors. Of course, you can abdicate responsibility; and many have done so in the past. Consider the following statements:

- ✔ 'The time for contrition is over. It is time to respect bankers and every-thing that they do' (Bob Diamond, CEO of Barclays Bank, January 2011 – defending high levels of remuneration for bankers following criticism from political sources and the media).

- ✔ 'We would have made a huge profit if it hadn't been for unusually hot/cold/wet/dry weather, or swine flu/bird flu/war in Iraq' (perennial state-ments in company annual reports to explain away poor results – in spite of the fact that the organisations knew that these things could, would and indeed had happened).

So you recognise that one of your key responsibilities is being able to operate within the most adverse of trading conditions and to respond as these condi-tions change. In the current climate, such responsibility also means:

- ✔ Accepting your obligations and being accountable for your actions

- ✔ Considering the environment

Facing up to your obligations and actions

So what exactly are your obligations? You can't wash your hands of them (the Pontius Pilate school of management), but you can decide what your obligations are. If you say, 'What could I do? The shareholders made me do it, so effectively I had no choice', you're actively taking the decision to go along with whatever it was that the shareholders wanted.

Of course, if you're ordered to do things by someone more senior or more influential than you, in practice you often have little choice but to comply. You should, however, have the moral courage, professional knowledge and expertise to argue the alternative point of view. If you're still required to go ahead, then at least know and understand the implications.

If you do take the Pontius Pilate approach and try to wash away your obligations, you'll be seen as an abdicator. Not a nice reputation.

Facing up to your obligations and being accountable for your actions are increasingly important. Gone are the days when companies could act as laws unto themselves. In particular, people are no longer ready to let organisations and their managers blame 'circumstances', 'the environment' or 'difficult trading conditions' – rather, they observe the decision-making processes of organisations and how managers actively meet and discharge their responsibilities and obligations.

Being, and going, green

Being as environmentally friendly as possible is another management responsibility. This responsibility is in any case driven by adverse and difficult trading conditions; that is, ensuring that you conduct your business as cost effectively as possible, producing as little waste and effluent as possible and disposing of waste in ways that don't further harm the environment makes sense (as well as being morally right).

Managing resources

Your obligation is to get the most out of what you have. You also need to look for continued improvements in things that you can affect, especially:

- Energy and fuel efficiency and water consumption
- Transport and distribution management
- Use of hazardous and toxic substances
- Packaging
- Disposal of waste

Put this way, managing resources is a very straightforward proposition – looking after the environment and looking after yourself are directly linked. Yet not everyone sees things so clearly. For example:

TRUE STORIES

✔ South West Water was fined £13 million for dumping chemical effluent into the river Camel in Cornwall. The company was supposed to be managing this waterway yet it found it *cheaper* to dispose of waste in it.

✔ Ciba-Geigy dumped effluent from its chemical processing plant at Basle, Switzerland, into the river Rhine because it knew that paying the maximum fine of £500,000 would be *cheaper* than spending millions on disposing of the waste properly.

Yet ultimately both companies lost out as the result of their actions. Legal and regulatory authorities now scrutinise them far more closely and they've lost credibility in the eyes of the wider public.

Take the broadest possible view of optimising your resource utilisation where you can, get the maximum from the resources that you do have and look to technological advances and best management practices to ensure that you always improve everything you do.

Dealing with waste

Obviously you need to minimise waste wherever you can as you go about getting the best from your resources. Nevertheless, everyone produces waste and has to dispose it. What you do with your waste is subject to regulatory and social scrutiny the same as everyone else.

You face both a cost decision and an ethical dilemma. For example, how do you respond:

✔ If you produce a large amount of rubbish that a refuse collecting company then takes away and dumps in a landfill site?

✔ If the company says that it will get the rubbish recycled and you subsequently discover that it's being dumped in a landfill anyway?

✔ If the company says that the fee it charges you for collecting and disposing of the rubbish will go down, and you then find that it's dumping the rubbish in places such as South-east Asia and West Africa?

On the one hand, you're meeting your cost obligations to your organisation; on the other, are you meeting your obligations to the world by giving your contracts to companies such as these? The perfect answer is that you never trade with such companies; in practice, life isn't always so simple.

Repeating the mantra: green is profitable, waste is not

If you push the green issue to its logical conclusion, it stands to reason that the fewer the resources you consume, and the greater the effectiveness and efficiency with which you use them, the less waste and effluent you produce. And less waste means greater cost effectiveness and a firmer foundation for your long-term sustainability, viability and profitability.

Top five environmental management websites

Here are the five best websites for supporting your dealings with the environment:

✔ **Environment Agency:** www.environment-agency.gov.uk

✔ **Department for Environment, Food and Rural Affairs (Defra):** www.defra.gov.uk

✔ **Bank of England:** www.bankofengland.co.uk

✔ **Department for Transport:** www.dft.gov.uk

✔ **Global Issues:** www.globalissues.org/issue/168/environmental-issues

---

The reverse is also true. If you're profligate or if you waste resources unnecessarily, you quickly become perceived as wasteful and slapdash. This attitude – and even reputation – then spills over into all that you do.

Additionally, in the effective management of resources you have to make sure that you concentrate them where they're most needed. For example:

✔ Having very cost-effective and efficient administrative and support functions is no use if they add nothing to the central business of producing and selling excellent goods and services.

✔ Having effectively produced packaging is no use if it adds little or nothing to the actual value of the products.

So resource management isn't an end in itself. You need to directly relate the effectiveness of your resource management to the needs, wants and priorities of the business.

According to Michael O'Leary, Ryanair's chief executive, in relation to the company's constant quest for resource maximisation and cost effectiveness: 'I never exclude any idea which is sincerely offered. And every time someone says to me "I can save you money" I am interested. I always listen. And it doesn't matter who says it – we get suggestions from our customers, suppliers, from people in bars. Most of the time of course – they cannot save us money. But only by following up every idea and by constantly listening do we get to the gems that really do work out.'

Your attention to resources creates an image in terms of your relationship with the environment. If you're effective and efficient at resource and waste management, you gain the reputation of being effective and efficient in everything that you do. If you're profligate and produce a lot of waste, you create the impression of being wasteful in everything that you do.

Part IV
Working with (Other) People

'If you want to be part of our management team, you've got to be able to do this.'

In this part . . .

No manager is an island. Managers work with other people – clients, suppliers, shareholders, teams, co-workers and their own managers, to name a few – all the time. In this part, we introduce some key skills for communicating effectively with others, working with teams and managing flexible employees.

Chapter 9

Knowing and Understanding Your Stakeholders

In This Chapter

▶ Doing your best to keep everyone happy

▶ Inspiring confidence in people

▶ Understanding the different demands of your stakeholders

▶ Recognising different ways to handle and manage people

▶ Responding to particular problems

*S*takeholders are all of those people or organisations who have a vested interest in or are affected by your company. If a big part of management is about working with *other* people, then you need to know who the *other* people are, what they expect from you, what will keep them happy and engaged with you – and what won't!

Some common denominators exist: everyone expects to be treated with respect, honesty, openness and integrity. Everyone expects fair dealing and to be treated with courtesy and understanding. And everyone gets upset when they aren't treated well. This chapter ensures that you know and understand – and can do – everything that it takes to get on with all the other people with whom you come into contact.

Getting On with People

Have you ever come across managers who are thoroughly pleasant in their private life but ogres at work? Make sure that you're not one of these people! You can be assertive, authoritative, firm, open and straight with people without losing the fundamental pleasantries. Can't you?

Pleasing who you can, when you can

Keeping everyone happy is one of the biggest challenges managers face.

You can please all of the people some of the time; you can please some of the people all of the time; but you can't please all of the people all of the time. The best organisations and managers recognise this reality of business life. They decide upon their standards, communicate them effectively to everyone in their business environment – and stick to them.

You need to be straight with all of your stakeholders – staff, customers, clients, backers and suppliers. They expect you to communicate with them honestly and openly on a regular basis. They also expect you to tell them when problems arise or issues need to be dealt with and what you propose to do to resolve them.

Your good relations also need to apply to the community in which you conduct your business. This community expects you to be a good corporate citizen, making a social as well as economic contribution.

Keep in mind that effective communications don't always cast companies in the best light. Credibility rapidly shrinks to zero when management is secretive and insists that it can do no wrong. People are more inclined to react favourably to an honest and frank communication, regardless of whether the content is positive or negative. For example, in 2010 when BP created an oil disaster in the Gulf of Mexico, the company at first tried to block information or take responsibility. The universal outcry against both BP and its management forced the CEO to step down. The new management at BP then made sure that communication was direct and open, acknowledging their mistakes and the steps they were taking to put the situation right. Such frankness ultimately played a pivotal role in ensuring that BP was not subsequently excluded from American markets.

Inspiring confidence

The consistency with which you treat people is the basis for their confidence in you. Be consistent in your dealings with all of your stakeholders. You can build confidence both immediately and over extended periods of time.

Immediate confidence is inspired by how you're perceived in people's initial dealings with you. If you come across as friendly, positive, expert and committed, you form the immediate basis for confidence. If you seem diffident or uncertain, then no matter how good you actually are at your job, you have to work harder to inspire confidence in subsequent meetings.

You can develop communication skills. Chapter 10 has the lowdown on making yourself a positive and assertive communicator – the results are priceless.

Over longer periods of time you constantly reinforce and enhance people's confidence in you by the quality of your work and your integrity. Stakeholders want to know where you're coming from. If they trust your judgement, they come to appreciate that if you raise an issue with them it's important and they then treat it as such.

Handling discomfort

Making clear the basis upon which you conduct your business, and the standards you apply, means that all of your stakeholders begin to identify your organisation with a set of expectations. Knowing where they stand makes people comfortable and assured in their dealings with you; and provides a sound basis for any business or employment relationship.

However expert a manager you are, though, and however good you generally are at dealing with your stakeholders, sometimes you have to deal with uncomfortable situations. For example:

✔ Nobody likes dealing with unpleasant, cold or distant people. Yet everyone has to do so occasionally. When the time comes, your heart sinks – you prevaricate and find other things to do. But dealing with the person as soon as possible is the best approach. As a manager, you need to rise above people's personalities and focus on their role in the organisation. If, however, their behaviour is affecting other members of staff, then you need to address it.

✔ No one likes being in awkward situations, including facing up to mistakes, but sometimes they must. However uncomfortable you are dealing with your own or someone else's errors, that is your role as a manager.

If you can deal with discomfort and take it in your stride, you greatly strengthen your managerial abilities. We don't mean that you rejoice in trouble or indeed seek it; rather, you develop a reputation for being cool under fire and unafraid to deal with difficult or confrontational situations. Nobody dies from embarrassment; not you or the person you're dealing with.

Recognising Your Stakeholders

What do your stakeholders expect from you? Regardless of whether the stakeholders are financial backers, customers, suppliers or your own staff, they expect consistency, integrity and a fundamental honesty in all of your dealings with them. The following sections consider all of the stakeholder groups in some detail.

Financial backers

Nothing destroys confidence in a managerial relationship faster than dishonesty over money. Your financial backers have put money and resources into your company or venture because they expect to see it flourish and prosper. As a result, they're entitled to be informed of:

✔ Progress

✔ Returns and results

✔ Hold-ups and glitches

✔ Problems and issues that have arisen or that might arise

✔ Changes in financial condition, solvency and stability

✔ Thoughts about new possible directions and activities for the company

You need to be absolutely committed to keeping backers informed of how things are going. Schedule a regular series of meetings with your backers or set up a more general (and again, regular) reporting mechanism, or use a combination of the two.

Always ensure that you have a two-way mechanism for contacting and being contacted by your backers, in case of crises or emergencies.

If this complete honesty sounds a bit utopian, bear in mind that you cannot be 'a bit' dishonest or duplicitous in relation to money. Everyone's tempted from time to time to stretch the truth over financial performance or returns. You need to resist that temptation! Any backer of substance already has a pretty good idea of how things are going. If you start spinning yarns to backers, they simply investigate further. Not only can they pull the plug on their financial backing of your company, if they discover dishonest practice you could be prosecuted or disqualified from operating.

Always keep your backers informed of progress, and ensure that they know and understand their returns; how much they are, and why. If you do have financial problems, open up discussion with your backers as soon as possible with a view to getting them sorted out.

Customers and clients

Tom Peters, the management guru, stated: 'If you make good products and services, and service them well, you will make your fortune.' In a nutshell, this statement is the key to understanding your customers and clients. You need to be clear about what they want and expect from you, and what they don't. Ensure that you deliver to the standards that they require, at the very least. Doing so means that your products, services and service arrangements must be available in the quantities and locations requested, to the quality required and at prices that your customers and clients are willing to pay.

You can conduct customer and client analyses to find out:

- ✔ Why they come to you; and why others don't come to you.
- ✔ What keeps them coming to you; and what would drive them away.
- ✔ What would cause them to come to you more, or less, often.
- ✔ What would get them to change their buying and spending habits with you.

You also need to have a clear view of where customer service lies in your own order of priorities.

A bit of empathy goes a very long way! For example, how do you feel when you try to speak to someone about a customer service issue, only to be put on hold or told that the person you need is on holiday or unavailable? Discontented, we imagine.

If you outsource customer service to another organisation, make sure it adheres to your own high standards.

Customer and client types

One way of looking at your customers and clients is as follows:

- ✔ **Apostles:** Those who think that you're the most wonderful organisation (and manager) in the world; and who'll hear no evil and speak no evil of you under any circumstances.

- ✔ **Loyalists:** People who have a strong affinity and feel a sense of identity with you and your products and services, and who'll continue to do business with you as long as you maintain and support that loyalty.

- ✔ **Mercenaries:** Those who'll do business with you purely on an economic basis – either your quality is excellent or your prices are low.

- ✔ **Browsers and passing trade:** People who'll call in on you out of interest or because they happen to be looking at things that you sell; you need to turn them into loyalists.

- ✔ **Terrorists:** Customers who understand and perceive themselves to have been badly served by you; they seek compensation or do their best to tarnish you with a bad reputation by covering your misdeeds in the media.

Make sure that you know and understand what category your customers fall into, and therefore how to manage them! If terrorists are evident, address their concerns before they sully your reputation. Also bear in mind that you need a great number of loyalists to make your company economically viable and sustainable.

Staff

'Our staff are our most valuable asset.' How often have you seen this line in annual company reports? For many organisations and their managers, of course, this statement is clearly true. Sadly, for many others, it isn't.

You cannot maximise and optimise the potential of your organisation, or produce the best possible range of returns on investment, if you don't understand and respect your staff. You need to:

- Understand their hopes, fears and aspirations
- Recognise their priorities
- Know what they expect from you in terms of equality and fairness of treatment
- Set targets
- Conduct performance appraisals
- Handle problems, including disciplinary procedures and grievances
- Provide promotion, training and development opportunities

Compare what your staff expect from you in each of these areas with your expectations of them, then make sure they match. Always be open and honest with your staff and let them know that you expect the same in return.

On staff management, Tom Peters stated: 'If you don't like people, leave now. You cannot be a good manager unless you like and trust people; and are prepared to treat them with respect.'

At work, you need to be accessible at all times, at the very least by mobile phone or email. Set aside regular times to walk around the company and be available to staff; make clear that they can approach you on any matter at all.

Treat all issues raised by your staff as important, because:

- The issue was important enough to the individual to have raised it with you.
- Raising the issue may be an opening for the individual to go on to discuss other, more serious matters.
- Even if the issue turns out to be trivial, you've actually wasted nothing and gained a lot by treating the person's concern with respect.

Being brusquely dismissive of staff concerns risks creating a permanent divide between staff and management ('them' and 'us'), which will make future communications difficult, if not impossible.

Your staff expect fair dealing from you. By being fair and understanding their concerns, you in turn provide a strong foundation for what you expect them to deliver.

If your staff have confidence in you and know that you treat everyone fairly and deal with matters whenever they're brought to your attention, you gain a reputation for being open, approachable – and effective. If people don't feel that they can come to you, you may discover problems only when they become crises; or worse, when someone from another team or even company brings them to your attention.

Your staff are key stakeholders in your business; hang on to them.

Suppliers

Of all stakeholders in a business, suppliers are often at the mercy of managers and organisations who think that they can take advantage of them. Below are some common tactics:

- ✔ Delaying payments to suppliers
- ✔ Imposing your own credit terms on suppliers
- ✔ Imposing your own prices and charges on suppliers
- ✔ Setting deadlines and delivery schedules that are impossible to meet
- ✔ Arranging a multiplicity of suppliers and sources so that you keep everyone on their toes

Now, which of these is the basis for a long-term, enduringly mutually beneficial, commercial and working relationship? Obviously – none! These tactics provide the basis for doing business only for reasons of expediency. Ultimately, the suppliers will seek to reduce their dependency on you and eventually may refuse to do business with you at all.

Treating suppliers badly can seriously damage your reputation. Alternatively, supplier practices can reflect on you. Consider these examples:

- ✔ Marks & Spencer cancelled contracts with some of their Scottish clothing suppliers with a mere 24 hours' notice. News coverage concentrated on Marks & Spencer's business practices; and it was widely felt that they were simply behaving like corporate bullies.
- ✔ Nike, Gap, Puma and Adidas were revealed as sourcing from suppliers in Asia and Central America who use child labour, enforce unpaid overtime and abuse workers' rights.

Frozen fish

Helmont Ltd is a fish-processing and cannery company located in the West Midlands. The company sources fresh and frozen fish from Ocean-Going Trawlers Ltd, a fishing fleet based in Liverpool. Helmont is a very successful and profitable company, supplying to all of the main fish brands, including John West, Birds Eye and Ross. Helmont also supplies fresh, frozen, canned and processed fish products to the supermarket chains for sale under their own brand names.

Following new quota arrangements introduced by the EU, the price of landed fish catches in the UK rose by 10 per cent. Accordingly, Helmont decided to look around for an alternative supplier. After extensive research, the company found that a fishing fleet in Cadiz, Spain was prepared to supply Helmont with the volumes of fish and the regularity of deliveries required.

Helmont unilaterally cancelled the contract with Ocean-Going Trawlers and took up with Cadiz. The fish prices in Cadiz were 53 per cent lower than in Liverpool; and the full cost, including transport, worked out at 38 per cent cheaper than the Liverpool supplies. Clearly, a cost advantage existed. However, Helmont's previous suppliers were barely 100 miles away, and thus any problems were easily sorted. The new suppliers were over a thousand miles away, and consequently there was a much greater likelihood of things going wrong.

And they did; from refrigeration lorries breaking down, to strikes at the various ports, to roadworks and traffic congestion on UK motorways. Even the fish was problematic; although of equally good quality, it was unlike what the brand companies and supermarkets were used to. Ultimately, the new cheap suppliers turned out to be very expensive indeed. Eventually, Helmont had to go back to the Liverpool fishing fleet and reinstate the contract. And of course they did so – but with additional insurances, penalty clauses and deposits up front!

Treat your suppliers with respect and integrity. And make sure that their business practices are in line with your own. Cleaning up a tarnished reputation is extremely difficult.

Communities

The communities in which you work expect you to provide jobs, conduct yourself well, keep waste and pollution to a minimum and make a wider contribution to the life of the area. Sounds simple? Unfortunately, many organisations and their managers exploit the locations in which they're based. They choose certain places because they offer a large supply of cheap labour, or relaxed employment, environment and pollution laws apply there.

> # Good practice from the nuclear industry
>
> The Sellafield nuclear power station in Cumbria has always had a bad reputation. It is perceived as having caused extensive nuclear pollution in its immediate environment and in the Irish Sea. Environmental pressure groups have long sought to have the plant closed down. To the locals, however, Sellafield is a pillar of the community, providing several hundred jobs in an area that desperately needs them, support for the local schools and sponsorship for social groups in the area. It also sponsors Christmas festivities, sports teams and events such as firework displays.
>
> Why is Sellafield so active in its local area? For commercial and public relations reasons, of course. But everyone wins!

Nobody expects an organisation or manager to increase their overheads as a result of behaving ethically. What is expected, however, is that a company acts in the best interests of the community in which it's situated and considers it when making decisions. For example, you may decide to increase your deliveries and run a fleet of lorries at night. What about the housing estate situated near your premises? Will you disturb the residents' sleep?

Companies don't exist in isolation. Always behave considerately and, where appropriate, consult the locals.

Taking Everyone Else into Account

Knowing and understanding your main stakeholders is crucial to being an expert manager. However, you're certain to also come across others who need treating with respect, honesty and integrity. Of particular importance are the media, the government, regulatory bodies and pressure groups.

The media

Everyone likes media coverage – when it provides them with free publicity and enhances their reputation. Unfortunately, not all media coverage is friendly. You may get attention when you're doing things well – but you're *certain* to get it when things go wrong or when you're at the centre of a crisis or scandal. How you conduct yourself in the face of such difficulties is what people judge you by.

The financial crisis – again!

The 2008 financial crisis was inevitable. However, it was accelerated by the run on the Northern Rock building society, when customers heard rumours that the institution was about to collapse and rushed to withdraw their savings. This run forced Northern Rock's directors and the UK government to step in and deny that anything was wrong.

This denial led to further investigations; one journalist in particular began to scrutinise the value of assets held by other banks, including HBOS. When he realised that HBOS assets were vastly over-stated, the bank responded by attacking the journalist's private life and character. According to HBOS, the journalist visited strip clubs, used cocaine and had once spent thousands of pounds on a financial sector corporate celebration. Now the press knew they had a story!

Rubbishing the source of stories simply adds fuel to the investigative fire. If you're faced with awkward or unpleasant truths, be prepared to face them and respond to people's legitimate concerns.

Let 'First tell no lies; then do no harm' be your guide in business dealings.

If you're suddenly faced with a crisis, you need to understand three things:

- ✔ The media have a legitimate interest in covering it.
- ✔ They'll want to find out what you and your colleagues are doing.
- ✔ They'll criticise you if they possibly can.

Be very careful when dealing with the media. A single false word or action can have devastating effects. If you say something off the cuff and strike a wrong note, you're likely to compound rather than resolve the problem. Devise a structured response to a crisis so that you're not caught on the hoof; for example, write a press release providing the bare facts of the situation and follow it up with regular reports on what you're doing to put things right. Always be truthful. And never engage in verbal sparring with the media – you'll always lose!

If you get caught lying to the media, they'll pursue the story until they get the full truth from other sources. However well you think you've covered your tracks, misdeeds generally come to light eventually.

Government and regulators

You have to comply with the law, and other statutory and regulatory demands relevant to your business. This sounds so simple! But in practice things can and do go wrong. Conduct your dealings with legislative bodies on the same basis as other stakeholders. Like your staff, suppliers and local community, they too have a legitimate interest in what you do and how you do it.

Be especially aware of the legitimate role and function of:

- Company and sectoral regulatory bodies
- Universal, statutory and regulatory bodies, such as the Health and Safety Executive, the Advertising Standards Authority, Trading Standards institutions and consumer protection groups
- The Advisory, Conciliation and Arbitration Service (ACAS)
- The police
- The taxation and revenue authorities
- Your auditors

In your dealings with these bodies, you need to instil confidence in your honesty and ethical behaviour. Do so by complying fully with their demands and expectations, and being transparent in all your actions.

Huntington Life Sciences

Huntington Life Sciences is a pharmaceutical research organisation based in Cambridge. For many years it has worked at the cutting edge, providing data for many very advanced medical and surgical treatments. In order to provide this information, Huntington Life Sciences has to experiment on, and with, live animals. These practices have led to sustained protests from animal rights' groups, which have taken the legitimate view that the scientists shouldn't treat animals with cruelty. The more extreme animal rights' campaigners have threatened some of the company staff with violence and damage to their own homes. Campaigners have also raided and torched company premises. An effective media campaign conducted over many years meant that the company was widely vilified for the work it carried out and the ways in which it worked.

Huntington Life Sciences' first response was to step up its security. It protected its premises, provided staff with secure access to and egress from work, and kept personnel data extremely secret. However, Huntington Life Sciences' biggest step towards protecting its position was to engage in an active, high profile PR and media campaign to promote the other side of the story – its own legitimate and regulated work, the results that it had achieved, and the benefits to society at large and to the patients for whom its treatments and inventions were intended.

As an expert manager you need to devise strategies for dealing with these kinds of pressures. You have to be able to assert your own legitimate position. If you can reconcile your position with that of the pressure group, so much the better. If you can't, at least you can assert your own position with integrity.

Failure to comply with statutory and regulatory demands always results in loss of reputation. If a misunderstanding exists in your dealings with official bodies, immediately take steps to put it right. Never ignore legitimate requests for information or clarity from a governmental and regulatory body.

Pressure groups, lobbies and vested interests

Many people may have an interest in your business and its activities. They too are stakeholders and you have to deal with the issues they raise as well as defend or preserve your own legitimate position.

Recognise that such groups may have legitimate concerns about:

- ✔ The environment
- ✔ Employment practices
- ✔ Use of resources
- ✔ The profits that you make and what you do with them
- ✔ Waste management practices and their impact
- ✔ Noise and light pollution
- ✔ Healthy and safe working practices

If you determine to deal with all such groups and interests on the basis of their legitimacy, and treat their concerns with respect, you do nothing but good for your organisation. View such diplomacy as a vital part of your ability to work effectively with (all other) people.

Top five stakeholder management websites

Here are the five best websites for improving your stakeholder management practice:

- ✔ **Trading Standards:** www.trading standards.gov.uk

- ✔ **Consumer Direct:** www.consumer direct.gov.uk

- ✔ **UK Advice Guide:** www.adviceguide. org.uk

- ✔ **Financial Services Authority:** www.fsa. gov.uk

- ✔ **Reuters:** www.reuters.com

Chapter 10

Communicating Effectively

In This Chapter

▶ Looking at new ways to communicate

▶ Dealing with barriers to communication

▶ Listening effectively

▶ Communicating your thoughts in writing

*H*ow important is getting your message across to your employees, peers, boss, suppliers, clients and customers? Very! Your roles as cheerleader, advocate, negotiator, coach, setter of standards and role model all demand that you're an expert and effective communicator. So commit yourself to becoming an expert and effective communicator. You can't be a good manager otherwise.

You have more sources of information and more ways to communicate than ever before, and more are on the way. And you need to be an expert performer whichever methods you use. If you deliver a presentation, you need to know in advance what you want people to remember from it. If you send an email, you want the recipient to read it and respond. If you participate in a meeting, you want the other participants to respect, value and act on your contributions.

This chapter covers how to make all of your communications – regardless of channel – effective.

Viewing Communication as the Cornerstone of Your Business

Communication is all-important for the growth and survival of today's organisations. How big or small your organisation is doesn't matter – communication must be its cornerstone. In order of significance, most business communication occurs in the form of:

- Listening
- Speaking
- Writing
- Reading

Interestingly, we are taught how to communicate via these media in the following order:

- Reading – at age four
- Writing – at age five
- Speaking – seldom
- Listening – almost never

So how we're trained to communicate bears no relation to how people actually do so. Many managers fail because they don't understand this critical point. The occasional speeches you make, the beautifully crafted memos you write and the many articles on chaos theory that you read have no effect on how you really communicate with your employees. You can make a difference when you talk to your employees one to one, face to face, day in and day out. Listening to them and really hearing what they have to say are vital.

Compared to the spoken word, most other means of communication are relatively ineffective, especially when taken in isolation.

Table 10-1 shows that the best means of communication are face to face, individually or with small groups. Techniques such as briefing groups, though they're comfortable for managers and have a neat and tidy look, aren't effective means of communication.

Table 10-1	Channels of Communication		
Communication Method	*How Information is Imparted*	*Result*	*Effect on Performance*
Simple centralised	Information flows to central person	Central person can perform task alone	Good performance
Simple decentralised	Information flows all around the network	No one person has all the required information	Grapevine, leading to poor performance and infighting
Complex centralised	Information flows to and from central person	Central person becomes saturated	Poor performance, lobbying, distortion
Complex decentralised	Depends on quality and completeness of information for effective flows all around the network	No one person becomes saturated	Good performance, provided that information is openly available
Hierarchical	Information flows up and down	No one person has all the required information	Poor performance in long/ large hierarchies
Briefing	Information flows from briefer to group	Depends on quality of briefer	Depends on quality of briefer
Hourglass	Key figure is at 'neck'	Filtration and limitation	Leads to performance required by the 'neck'
Chains	Information flows along chain	Distortions at links	Poor understanding likely; poor motivation and morale; slow movement of information
Cascade	Information cascade (for example, briefing groups)	Dilution at every stage	Loss of quality, leading to poor performance

Obviously a need does exist for formal and written communication at certain times. Documentation is still essential for contracts, invoices and deliveries; for maintaining staff records; and for noting organisational, industry, government and European Union directives.

Being at the Cutting Edge of Information and Communication Technology

The explosion in information technology has brought with it numerous, often surprising and powerful new ways to communicate. Whether you like them or not, they're here to stay. And more are on the way. You can opt to ignore them and be left behind, or you can choose to use these new technologies to your advantage. (See Chapter 19 on ways to harness the power of technology.)

Today's manager no longer needs to be in an office to communicate with clients and colleagues. You can get in touch from anywhere – all it takes is the right tools. With a laptop, mobile phone and Blackberry you can be in touch with anyone, at any time, in any location.

Taking advantage of email, voice-mail, fax machines, mobile phones, pagers and overnight air delivery services, business is now a 24-hours-a-day, 7-days-a-week affair. You can leave a message at any time of the day or night at almost any business. Using voice-mail, you can access your date- and time-stamped messages remotely from anywhere in the world that has access to phone technology. You can reply to these messages, forward them to colleagues or save them for future reference.

Additionally, employers know that employees who have such equipment spend more of their personal time doing work. A study of individuals whose company provides them with telecommunications equipment indicates that these individuals work an additional 20 to 25 per cent more hours in their own time (though whether or not this is a good thing for overworked employees is a different matter altogether).

 Whatever the organisation or situation, you need to be able to communicate effectively. Talk to your staff, colleagues, peers and superiors. And get in the habit of sending emails or other communications that have a purpose – giving information or asking for something to be acted on. People will assume you have nothing to say if they never hear from you.

Speed and flexibility

Whatever your choice of communication equipment, only invest in it if it makes you and your organisation faster, more flexible, more competitive, more effective – and more profitable. If you kit people out with the equipment they need, everyone benefits.

According to the Chartered Management Institute, technological innovation, effectively used, gives any business the edge over less flexible competitors. Advantages arise as the direct result of firms' ability to harness technology in order to work faster, and more responsively to customer needs.

Consider these advantages of information and communication technology (ICT):

✔ New production and service technologies can be utilised rapidly.

✔ As companies become electronically linked, outsourcing of functions, from accounting to product development, creates many opportunities for highly skilled subcontractors.

✔ Electronic bulletin boards and online data services give everyone access to more market data and business opportunities than ever before, allowing them to discover and respond to new opportunities quickly.

✔ Cheap computer-aided design and manufacturing software, together with flexible working practices, allow anyone to develop new products and present them to the market quickly and effectively.

✔ Groups of companies increasingly use information links to form networks and alliances, and engage in partnerships as much as in direct competition.

✔ Mobile computing lets you compete anywhere in the world without the necessity of setting up expensive regional offices.

Use the latest advances in ICT to make your organisation faster and more flexible. The faster people distribute and act on information within your organisation, the more competitive and successful your business is likely to be.

Gadgets and gizmos

Organisations and their staff can be swamped by technology. New gadgets and gizmos constantly hit the market and many managers feel they have to have them.

A word of caution: make sure you buy new technology because it makes your business more effective and profitable, not as a fashion item or status symbol. Technological wizards in your organisation may be experts at making overtly reasoned and substantive cases for new gadgets, when in fact they're just after the latest 'must have'.

Make sure that any upgrade is compatible with your existing technology. Otherwise, you may have to invest in a complete technological refurbishment – which is expensive.

Any technology still has to deliver messages in ways the recipients can access, understand and act on. A message beautifully presented on-screen, on a website or via a computer link is useless if people don't know where to look for it, or can't access or download it.

Videoconferencing

Not too many years ago, if you wanted to have a meeting with your design team members in London, production engineers in Nottingham and sales staff scattered all over the countryside, you had to all gather in a central location. Hours of travel and thousands of pounds later, you all gathered in the same place at the same time. Heaven help you if you left something important back at the office!

Now, you can link together large groups of individuals into virtual meetings, where everyone can see and speak to each other through videoconferencing. Videoconferencing is rapidly becoming more common as computers and telecommunications systems become ever-more powerful. Use it to set up meetings of employees at different locations, whether across the country or around the world – and save substantial amounts of both time and money.

Everyone who wants to take part needs access to a computer with an appropriate software package, a webcam and a fast broadband connection; that's it. And on an individual basis, videoconferencing can be useful to see what your client is trying to describe to you; and forming relationships with people is easier when you can picture them. Thus the miracle of videoconferencing.

Which do you prefer, Option A or Option B?

> ✔ **Option A:** 'I just made the changes to the sales figures and printed out a new graph. Now, sales rose 39.5 per cent in 209 to £45.5 million. Our north-western sales office led the surge. In the first quarter of 2010 we saw a decline to an annualised figure of £39.1 million in sales, primarily due to weak sales out of the south central and north central sales offices that were off target by a combined total of £4.2 million. The

second quarter looks a lot better. It looks like we're back on track with an annualised figure of £44.7 million. Did you get all that?'

✔ **Option B:** 'I've just made the changes to the sales figures and entered them into the spreadsheet – you should be able to bring it up now. Do you have any questions?'

Now you need never again be stuck on the M25 waiting for the traffic to clear, or endure another night on a lumpy mattress in some nameless town in the middle of nowhere. Unless, of course, that's your idea of fun. Just turn on your computer, fire up your webcam and meet to your heart's content!

 Use technology – don't let it use you. Always consider which is the most appropriate method of communication: videoconferencing, teleconferencing (using the phone rather than video technology to conduct group meetings) or getting people together face to face.

Badmouthing Bad Communication

Effective communication isn't easy. The next sections cover the all-too-common problems you may encounter along the road to model communication.

Knowing what causes bad communication

However you communicate – whether face to face or through the use of technological wizardry – barriers to effective communication can exist, whether by accident, negligence or design.

✔ **Accident:** With the best will in the world, you may choose the wrong language or medium to get your message across. Address the situation as quickly as possible. If you keep delivering messages in the wrong way, you eventually put people's backs up, however well intentioned you may be.

✔ **Negligence:** Barriers can arise by default, usually as the result of managerial complacency. The organisation and its managers think that things are 'going along pretty well' or 'as well as can be expected' or at least 'not too badly'. Almost invariably, this complacency extends to communication. Poor communication is simply 'one of those things', which leads to managers facing communication problems with indifference or a shrug of the shoulders. Your peers and colleagues quickly get the message that the organisation doesn't care about them, what they're doing or what happens to them.

✔ **Design:** Barriers may be created by people in the organisation for their own ends. The huge range of technology available provides ample opportunity for those who need or want to manipulate systems and messages to do so. Consider the case of bad news – how many times have you received upsetting or provocative information late on a Friday afternoon, meaning you have the whole weekend to mull it over.

Jo Moore, an adviser at the Home Office, produced an immediate response to news of the 9/11 bombings in New York stating: 'This is an excellent day to bury bad news.' While Jo Moore lost her job as a result of this callous statement, this approach is commonplace in many organisations. Be careful if you try to manipulate information to serve a particular purpose; your efforts may well be counterproductive.

Looking at barriers to good communication

Barriers to effective communication include the following:

✔ **Physical distance:** Distance hinders communication simply because you can't see the other person's facial expression, what she's thinking or how she's receiving what you tell her. Especially if you have bad news to deliver, always do so face to face.

✔ **Psychological distance:** Psychological distance springs from reinforcing the gap between you and those you're communicating with through the use of status, rank, job title, dress and mannerisms. Managers also use psychological distance – not always honestly – to assert their position, as well as to reinforce their ability to get their own way.

✔ **Interest:** People respond to those things that they're interested in. So if you want a response, deliver your message in a way that's of interest to the receivers. Especially highlight opportunities that will arise as the result of whatever your message is announcing; emphasise the positives; and make sure that people know where they stand and what they have to do as the result of your communication. Otherwise be prepared for supreme indifference!

✔ **Withholding information:** Issuing different information to different individuals and groups on a need-to-know basis sets up barriers. Although on the surface doing so may appear to be sensible, you need to make sure that you're withholding information from the highest possible motives. If not, you appear to suggest:

- Contempt for your employees and colleagues, in that they're not capable of understanding all the information available.

- An implied lack of capability on the part of employees and colleagues to understand what's being done in their name.

- A difference in value placed on different groups of staff, colleagues and employees – especially those who aren't on the 'need-to-know' list.

- An inequality of access – in order to be privy to certain information, you must have reached a certain level or rank within the organisation.

- General disrespect – again, to those excluded from the 'need-to-know' list.

So unless a personal issue or trade secret is involved, at least start from the position that the more everyone knows, the better organisational life will be.

People dislike being treated with arrogance and disrespect. If you constantly adopt a superior attitude to your employees and colleagues, they lose their respect for you and for everything that you set out to do.

Poisoning the well of communication

A toxic organisational environment – one in which standards, quality of working life and overall integrity are greatly compromised – compounds problems created by communication barriers. In such a situation, many communications take the following form:

- **Blaming and scapegoating:** Managers find junior employees to carry the can for corporate failings. Accusation, counter-accusation, backbiting and backstabbing prevail. Individuals may be named and shamed openly; or, more insidiously, they may not be named officially, but their identity is allowed to leak out through the organisational grapevine.

- **Departmental feuding:** Departments are actively encouraged to go to war with each other in the always mistaken belief that putting departments at loggerheads promotes improved performance and output.

- **Meddling:** People or departments meddle outside their legitimate areas of concern or activity; or lobby to be included on projects that aren't otherwise within their normal remit. A not-uncommon example of meddling is when top managers promise favoured customers or staff that special activities and deals can be done on their behalf; they then interfere in the workloads of others in order to deliver the promised favours.

- **Keeping secrets:** Information becomes a commodity to be used as a source of influence and bargaining chip. Communication is then concerned with controlling, editing, filtering and presenting, rather than with disseminating information.

Toxic communicators issue toxic communications – whatever they produce is for their own advantage, rather than the good of the organisation, their colleagues and employees. Some individuals also introduce toxicity – gossip and rumour designed to have a particular effect. Toxic communicators misrepresent, lie and cheat, and manipulate information for their own particular ends.

As a manager, you need to be constantly aware of the aspects of communication that can go wrong, and the reasons why. Good managers address these problems as soon as they arise by making sure that everything is brought out into the open and fully debated. Rumours are addressed, and confirmed or squashed. Meddling, dishonesty and toxicity are dealt with by removing the rewards and advantages that others seek through behaving in these ways.

Hearing It For Listening

The communication equation has two sides. The preceding sections cover what most people think about when they hear the word *communication* – the doing side. However, just as important is the other side of the equation – the listening side.

You're a busy person. You probably have 10 million things on your mind at any given time: the proposal you have to get out before 5 p.m. today; the budget spreadsheets that don't seem to add up; lunch; and, if that isn't enough already, the latest office gossip. With all the distractions, you can easily appear rude and distant to other people if you're not careful.

When you don't give the person on the other side of your desk your full attention, you short-change both yourself and them. Not only do you miss out on the information they wish to impart, your inattention also sends its own special message: 'I don't really care what you have to say.' Is that the message you really want to convey? When you listen actively, you increase the likelihood that you understand what the other person is saying. Depending on what you're talking about, understanding can be quite important.

Don't leave listening to chance. Be an active listener. When someone has something to say to you, make a decision to participate in the communication, or to let the other person know that you're busy and have to get back to her later. 'Sorry, I've got to sort this lot out before lunch. Can we get together later this afternoon?' If you decide to communicate, then clear your mind of all its distractions. Forget for a moment the proposal that has to go out in a few hours, the spreadsheets and that growling in the pit of your stomach. Give the other person your full attention.

Of course, making an effort to give your full attention is easier said than done. How can you focus on the other person and not allow all the people and tasks vying for your attention to distract you? The following tips may help:

- ✔ **Express your interest.** One of the best listening techniques is to be interested in what your counterpart has to say. For example, give the person you're talking to your full attention and ask questions that clarify what she has to say. You can say, 'That's really interesting. What brought you to that conclusion?' The greatest turn-off to communication is for you to yawn, look around the room aimlessly or otherwise show that you're not interested in what your colleague is saying. The more interest you show, the more interesting the speaker becomes.

- ✔ **Maintain your focus.** People speak at the rate of approximately 150 words per minute, but think at approximately 500 words per minute. This gap leaves a lot of room for your mind to wander. Make a point of keeping your mind focused on listening to what the other person has to say. If your mind starts to wander, then rein it back in immediately.

- ✔ **Ask questions.** If something is unclear or doesn't make sense to you, then ask questions to clarify the issue. Not only does questioning make your communication efficient and accurate, it also demonstrates to the speaker that you're interested in what she has to say. *Reflective listening* – summarising what the speaker has said and repeating it back – is a particularly effective way of ensuring accuracy in communication and demonstrating your interest. For example, you can say, 'So you mean it's your belief that we can sell our excess capacity to other firms?'

- ✔ **Seek the key points.** Figure out what exactly your counterpart is trying to tell you. Anyone can easily get lost in the forest of details in a conversation and miss seeing the trees as a result. As you listen, make a point of categorising what your speaker has to say into information that is key to the discussion and information that isn't really relevant. If you need to ask questions to help you decide which is which, then don't be shy – ask away!

- ✔ **Avoid interruptions.** Although asking clarifying questions or employing reflective listening techniques is okay, continually interrupting the speaker or allowing others to do so isn't. When you're having a conversation with an employee, make her the most important thing in your life at that moment. If someone telephones you, don't answer the phone – that's what voice-mail is for, after all. If someone knocks on your door and asks whether he can interrupt, say no, but that you can talk after you finish your current conversation. If your building is on fire then you may interrupt the speaker.

✔ **Listen with more than your ears.** Communication involves a lot more than the obvious, verbal component. According to experts, up to 90 per cent of the communication in a typical conversation is non-verbal. Facial expressions, posture, position of arms and legs, and much more add up to the non-verbal component of communication. This being the case, you need to use all of your senses when you listen, not just your ears.

✔ **Take notes.** Remembering all the details of an important conversation hours, days or weeks after it took place can be quite difficult. Be sure to take notes when you need to remember something. Jotting down notes can be a terrific aid to listening and remembering what the person said. Plus, when you review your notes later, you can take the time to organise what the person said and make better sense of it.

By practising the listening habits we list here, you understand the message, and your colleagues appreciate the fact that you consider them important enough to give them your full attention. So listen early and listen often.

Harnessing the Power of the Written Word

At first thought, you may consider that the information revolution has made the written word less important. Nothing is farther from the truth. Actually, the variety of written media at your beck and call has increased and so has the speed at which the written word travels. Writing well in business is more important than ever – you need to write concisely and clearly.

Regardless of whether you're writing a one-paragraph email or a 100-page report, business writing shares common characteristics. Use the list of writing tips that follows and practise them at every opportunity. The more you write, the better you get at it. So write, write – and write again.

✔ **Get to the point.** Before you set pen to paper (or fingertip to keyboard), think about what you want to achieve. Determine what information you're trying to convey, and what you want the reader to do as a result. Think about who your audience is and how you can best reach that audience. Get into the habit of saying to yourself – or writing down on a notepad – 'The purpose of this email/report/memo is . . .'

✔ **Get organised.** Organise your thoughts before you write. Jotting down notes or creating a brief outline of your major points may be beneficial. Bounce your ideas off colleagues and business associates or find other ways to refine your thoughts.

- **Write the way you speak.** Written communication and spoken communication have a lot more in common than many people think. The best writing most closely resembles normal, everyday speech. Writing that's too formal or stilted is less accessible and harder to understand than conversational writing. Although writing as you speak doesn't mean that you can use slang like *gonna* and *ain't* in your reports and memos, it does mean that you can loosen up.

- **Make it brief and concise.** Write every word with a purpose. Make your point, support it and then move on to the next point. Don't fill your memos, letters and other correspondence with needless fluff simply to give them more weight or to make them seem more impressive. If you can make your point in three sentences, don't write three paragraphs or three pages to accomplish the same goal.

- **Keep it simple.** Simplicity is a virtue. Be alert to the tendency to use a complicated word when a simple one works. Avoid cryptic acronyms and jargon that mean nothing outside of a small circle of industry insiders and replace them with more common terminology whenever possible.

- **Write and then rewrite.** Few writers can get their thoughts into writing perfectly on the first try. Write a first draft without worrying too much about whether you've completed it perfectly. Then read through it and edit for content, flow, grammar and readability. Keep polishing your work until it shines.

- **Convey a positive attitude.** No one likes to read negative memos, letters, reports or other business writing. Instead of conveying the intended points to its intended targets, negative writing often only reflects poorly on its author, and the message is lost. Be active, committed and positive. Even when you convey bad news, your writing can indicate that a silver lining is inside even the blackest cloud.

If you want to develop better writing skills, plenty of books are available to help. However, Peter still swears by the timeworn 1971-vintage printing of *The Elements of Style*, by William Strunk, Jr. and E. B. White. The book's advice is timeless, the writing direct and compelling. Consider Rule 13:

> *Vigorous writing is concise. A sentence should contain no unnecessary words, a paragraph no unnecessary sentences, for the same reason that a drawing should have no unnecessary lines and a machine no unnecessary parts. This requires not that the writer make all his sentences short, or that he avoid all detail and treat his subjects only in outline, but that every word tells.*

A survey conducted by the employment agency Office Angels found that people working in organisations particularly dislike these phrases:

- Blue-sky thinking
- Thinking outside the box
- Hitting the ground running
- Work smarter, not harder

This type of language is known as *management speak* – and no manager worthy of the name should use it. These phrases are meaningless – especially to those who have to endure listening to them. Make up your mind never to use them.

Top five communication websites

Go to the following websites for excellent information on communicating effectively:

- **Communications Management Ltd:** `www.communicationsmanagement.co.uk`
- **ProjectSmart:** `www.projectsmart.co.uk`
- **Melcrum:** `www.melcrum.com/products/journals/scm.shtml`
- **Presentations.com:** `www.presentations.com`
- **University College London:** `www.ucl.ac.uk/advances`

Chapter 11

Working Together in Teams and Groups

In This Chapter

▶ Flattening the organisation

▶ Empowering employees

▶ Categorising teams

▶ Recognising the advantages of teams

▶ Managing new technology and teams

*I*n practice, few managers work in isolation, and most have responsibilities for teams and groups of staff. Teams and groups start out as disparate collections of individuals who are gathered together for a purpose, and whose remit is to deliver specific results, resolve problems, address particular issues and create ways of working that are suitable for the work in hand. A team is two or more people who work together to achieve a common goal.

Teams offer an easy way to tap into the knowledge and resources of all employees – not just supervisors and managers – to do the work of the organisation and deliver its goals. This in turn means having teams that produce and deliver products and services, enhance business performance, contribute their own expertise for the greater good and solve the organisation's problems. A well-structured team draws together employees with different skills and knowledge, often from different functions and levels of the organisation, to help find the best way to approach an issue. Smart companies have discovered (and not-so-smart companies are figuring out) that to remain competitive they can no longer rely solely on management to guide the development of work processes and the accomplishment of organisational goals. The companies need to involve those employees who are closer to both the problems and their customers. Guess who those employees are? The front-line workers!

Perhaps management expert Peter Drucker best answers the question 'Why use teams?' when he considers the importance of ranking knowledge over ego in the modern organisation. According to Drucker:

> *No knowledge ranks higher than another; each is judged by its contribution to the common task rather than by any inherent superiority or inferiority. Therefore, the modern organization cannot be an organization of boss and subordinate. It must be organized as a team.*

This chapter discusses the main kinds of teams and how they work, the impact of computer-based technology on teams and insights for conducting the best team meetings ever.

Phasing Out the Old Hierarchy

The last couple of decades have seen a fundamental shift in the distribution of power and authority in organisations. Until recently, most organisations were *vertical* – they had many layers of managers and supervisors between top management and front-line workers. The classic model of a vertical organisation is the traditional military organisation. In the army, privates report to corporals, who report to sergeants, who report to captains and so on, up to the top general. When a general gives an order, it passes down the line from person to person until it reaches the person who's expected to execute it.

Until relatively recently, large companies such as Ford, British Airways and British Telecom weren't that different from this rigid, hierarchical model; and this remains a serious problem in some public services. Employing hundreds of thousands of workers, these organisations depended – and in many cases still depend – on legions of supervisors and managers to control the work, the workers who did it and when and how they did it. (Okay, perhaps today's legions are smaller.) The primary goal of top management was to command and control workers' schedules, assignments and decision-making processes very closely to ensure that the company met its objectives (and to ensure that workers were actually doing something!). The result of this kind of organising is, without any exception, that less gets done, more slowly, more expensively, with more errors, for fewer people.

Downsizing organisations

The problems presented by a hierarchical model of organisation are compounded by the fact that, in many cases, supervisors and managers make little or no direct contribution to the production of a company's products or services. Instead of producing things, managers merely manage other managers or supervisors and serve as liaisons between levels, ultimately doing little more than pushing paper from one part of their desk to another. In the model's worst scenario, the levels of supervisors and managers actually impede their organisations' capability to get tasks done – dramatically adding to the cost of doing business and slowing down the response time of decision making. All those expense account lunches add up.

Although this problem was overlooked as the global economy continued to expand in the last half of the twentieth century, factors such as the economic slowdown in the late 1980s and the telecoms and dot-com crashes in the early 2000s made for quite a wake-up call for those companies with unproductive – or worse, counterproductive – middle management.

John Tusa, former deputy director general of the BBC, stated: 'If many large organisations entered the University Boat Race, the cox would be doing all the rowing, while each of the eight crew shouted contrary orders.'

Although downsizing workforces after economic downturns has obvious negative effects on the employees who lose their jobs – and in many cases, their hopes for a comfortable retirement – this dark cloud has a silver lining. In flatter organisations a new life (and a quicker pace) comes to the following important areas:

- **Decision making:** Decisions, which may have taken weeks or even months to make in the old, bloated bureaucracy, are made in hours or minutes.

- **Communicating:** Instead of being intercepted and possibly distorted by middle managers at numerous points along its path, communication now travels a more direct – and much speedier – route from front-line workers to top management and vice versa, or to whoever the person needs to get information from. There's nothing like cutting six layers of management out of an organisation to improve communication!

Also, this transformation from vertical to *horizontal* businesses (organisations with a minimum of levels of management) has a fundamental impact on financial and organisational elements:

- **Quantifiable benefits to the bottom line:** By cutting out entire layers of management employees, many companies save money by substantially reducing the costs of personnel, facilities and expense account lunches.

- **Movement of authority and power:** This move happens from the very top of the organisation down to the front-line employees who interact with customers on a day-to-day basis. With fewer middle managers to interfere, front-line employees naturally have more autonomy and authority.

Moving towards co-operation

More than ever before, businesses worldwide are rewarding employees for co-operating with each other instead of competing against one another. Organisations are no longer measuring employees only by their individual contributions, but also by how effective they are as contributing members of their work teams.

Coupled with this shift of authority is a fundamental change in the way that many businesses structure their work. Of course, most businesses still organise their operations by departments, divisions and so forth, but smart managers now encourage, rather than discourage, their employees to cross formal organisational lines, and set up teams made up of employees from different departments whose members work together to perform tasks and achieve common goals.

Following are benefits that your organisation can reap from promoting co-operation:

- ✔ **Reducing unproductive competition:** Promoting a co-operative, team-oriented work environment reduces the chance of your employees becoming over-competitive with each other.

  If allowed to continue unabated, over-competitiveness results in the shutdown of communication between employees and, ultimately, reduces organisational effectiveness (because over-competitive employees build and defend private fiefdoms). Besides, over-competition between employees invariably leads to backbiting, in-fighting and denigration of other people; and it can lead to bullying, victimisation and harassment.

- ✔ **Sharing knowledge:** Knowledge is power. If you're in the know, you have a clear advantage over someone who's been left in the dark – especially if your finger is on the light switch. In a co-operative work environment, team members work together and thereby share their areas of knowledge and expertise, using it to the best advantage of everyone – they don't defend it or use it as a bargaining chip.

- ✔ **Fostering communication:** Using teams helps to break down the walls between an organisation's departments, divisions and other formal structures to foster communication between organisational units.

- ✔ **Achieving common goals:** Developing teams with members from various departments encourages workers from all levels and all parts of a company to work together to achieve common goals.

Empowering Your Teams

So if organisational structures are flatter (see the preceding section), employees gain more authority and autonomy from top management. The result: employees are more responsive to customers' needs and resolve problems at the lowest possible level in the organisation. The transfer of power, responsibility and authority from higher-level to lower-level employees is called *empowerment*.

By empowering workers, managers place the responsibility for decision making with the employees in the best position to make the decision. In the past, many managers felt that *they* were in the best position to make decisions that affected a company's products or customers. How wrong they were. Although they may have been right in some cases, their driving need to control workers and processes at all costs often blinded managers – so much so that control became more important than encouraging employee initiative.

If, in addition to creating effective teams, your staff spend a lot of time away from the office or place of work, you *have* to empower people! Otherwise, they simply sit at their remote location, waiting for you to tell them what to do; and then at each stage of their activities they ask you to check up on things. So concentrate on results – leave the process to your staff.

Recognising the value of an empowered workforce

Effective managers know the value of empowering their workers. Not only can employees serve customers better, but also by delegating more responsibility and authority to front-line workers, managers are free to pursue other important tasks that only they can do, such as coaching, 'big-picture' communicating, long-range planning, and production and service scheduling. The result is a much more efficient, more effective organisation all round. For example:

> ✔ Nissan UK runs the most productive car factory in the world, measured in terms of output per member of staff. One of the keys to this impressive outcome is that the company has given full responsibility and autonomy to the production crews (the teams) for all aspects of each car they produce. In particular, the company refers complaints from distributors and customers directly back to the crew who made the car. No quality assurance hierarchy exists; everything is the responsibility of the particular crew.

✔ British Airways' cabin crew staff deliver a top-quality service on long haul flights around the world. When they meet up, each team has only one hour to mould themselves into an effective crew for the particular flight. Crew members are individually rostered, which means that they seldom, if ever, work with the same people more than once. The cohesion required of the crews is founded on extensive training, clear team rules, the authority of the cabin services director and the total commitment of every member of the team (many of whom have wanted to be cabin crew staff from an early age). Within these rules, every member of the crew is then expected to do whatever is right in the particular set of circumstances to keep the travelling public happy.

Empowerment is also a great morale booster in an organisation. Managers who empower their workers show that they trust them to make decisions that are important to the company's success.

Managing your teams

If you want productive, effective and profitable groups working in harmony together, then concentrate on the following:

✔ Managing the task, ensuring that everybody knows what the purpose of the group is and what they're supposed to be contributing to it.

✔ Managing the people, ensuring that you have effective, productive and positive working relationships between everyone involved, whatever their profession, occupation or expertise.

✔ Managing communications between everyone involved; and managing communication between different work groups, disciplines and occupations.

✔ Managing individuals, to ensure that everyone gets the best possible opportunity to make the contribution required.

✔ Clarity of purpose and common aims and objectives, to which everyone has agreed and to which they can contribute.

✔ Group and team spirit, a combination of shared values, together with specific ways of working, a helpful attitude and a positive atmosphere within the group.

✔ Managing conflict, ensuring that you assess openly and honestly the potential for conflict within all groups. You need to pay particular attention to the nature and mix of personalities involved, the nature and mix of expertise and talent involved, and any divergence of objectives between group members, individuals and the overall objectives of the group.

Finally – finally – do make sure that the style of management and leadership is itself participative, positive and supportive! No point lies in creating work groups and expecting them to succeed if the organisation is constantly restraining and restricting the capability of those groups to operate to their full potential.

Identifying the Advantages of Teams

Teams not only have the potential to make better decisions, they can make faster decisions too. Because team members are closest to the problems and to one another, fewer delays occur because of the need to communicate with or get approval from others in the organisation.

Teams used to be considered beneficial only for projects of short duration. However, many companies no longer follow this line of thinking. According to Peter Drucker, 'Whereas team design has traditionally been considered applicable only to short-lived, transitory, exceptional task-force assignments, it is equally applicable to some permanent needs, especially to the top-management and innovating tasks.' Indeed, the team concept has proved itself to be a workable long-term solution to the needs of many organisations.

Smaller and nimbler

Large organisations often have a hard time competing in the marketplace against smaller, more nimble competitors. Smaller units within a large organisation – such as teams – are better able to compete. The rate and scope of change in the global business environment has led to increased competitive pressure on organisations in almost every business sector, so the importance of speed and responsiveness also increases.

As customers can get products and services faster, their expectations are constantly rising; and so organisations have to be able to meet these expectations. As they can buy products more cheaply as a result of technology improvements or global competition, they expect lower prices as well. And the expectation of quality in relation to price has dramatically increased over the years – especially with consumers' experience in obtaining more advanced electronics and computer technology for progressively lower prices. In short, customer values are changing so that they now want products and services 'any time, any place, anywhere'.

Innovative and adaptable

Teams are more adaptive to the external environment as it quickly or constantly changes. Thus, a team's size and flexibility give it a distinct advantage over competing organisations structured in a more traditional way. At Xerox and Hewlett-Packard, for example, design, engineering and manufacturing functions are closely intertwined in the development of new products – dramatically shortening the time from concept to production compared with their previous, more hierarchical structure. Indeed, Hewlett-Packard now only manufactures to order; and this decision is becoming more commonplace in other organisations and industry sectors.

Setting Up and Supporting Your Teams

When setting up a team, the first point you need to consider is what kind of team is appropriate for the situation. Three main kinds of teams exist: *formal*, *informal* and *self-managed*. Each type of team offers advantages and disadvantages depending on the specific situation, timing and the organisation's needs.

Whatever kind of team you're setting up, you need a good mix of characteristics. You need people with creative bursts of energy; people who'll question everything; and people who'll do the painstaking bits – the attention to detail, progress chasing and checking, and making sure that the team does everything on time. And you need effective team leadership!

Meredith Belbin produced a structure for the composition of effective teams, which is shown in Table 11-1.

Table 11-1	Members of Effective Teams	
Type	*Typical features*	*Positive qualities*
Company Worker	Conservative, dutiful, practicable	Organising ability, practical common sense, hard working
Chair	Calm, self-confident, controlled	A capacity for treating and welcoming all potential contributors on their merits and without prejudice
		A strong sense of objectives
Shaper	Highly strung, outgoing, dynamic	Drive and readiness to challenge inertia, ineffectiveness, complacency or self-deception

Type	Typical features	Positive qualities
Plant (Questioner)	Individualistic, serious minded, unorthodox	Genius, imagination, intellect, knowledge
Resource Investigator	Extroverted, enthusiastic, curious, communicative	A capacity for contacting people and exploring anything new An ability to respond to challenge
Monitor-Evaluator	Sober, unemotional, prudent	Judgement, discretion, hard-headedness
Team Worker	Socially oriented, rather mild, sensitive	An ability to respond to people and to situations, and to promote team spirit
Completer-Finisher	Painstaking, orderly, conscientious, anxious	A capacity to follow through Perfectionism

Source: Belbin (1986)

In teams of only five or six members, clearly some people have to be prepared to carry out more than one role. A certain amount of discipline and commitment to the group also needs to exist, requiring members, in many cases, to do things in ways that they're not normally comfortable or familiar with.

These points apply to any team, whatever its purpose.

Formal teams

A *formal team* is set up for a particular purpose and has specific goals to achieve. These goals can range from developing a new product line, determining the system for processing customer invoices or planning a company picnic. Types of formal teams include:

- **Quality improvement group and work improvement group:** A formal team assembled in order to tackle specific problems and issues relating to product and service innovation and development; specific problems and issues concerning quality, durability and accessibility; and managing customer complaints.

- **Project team:** A team drawn together for a specific purpose, and assembled for the duration of the particular project. Successful and effective project teams are crucial to the success of civil engineering and other engineering projects, the design and installation of information systems, and the development of new products and services.

✔ **Task force:** A formal team assembled on a job and finish basis to address specific problems or issues, very often at strategy or policy level. For example, a task force may be assembled to determine why a particular strategic initiative isn't delivering the intended results. Task forces are also a well-known and understood approach to addressing the detail required to implement new strategy and policy initiatives. A task force usually has a deadline for solving the issue and reporting the findings to top and senior management.

✔ **Committee:** A long-term or permanent team created to perform an ongoing, specific organisational task. For example, some companies have committees that select employees to receive awards for performance or that make recommendations to management for safety improvements. Although committee membership may change from year to year, the committees continue their work regardless of who belongs to them.

✔ **Command team:** Made up of a manager or supervisor and all the employees who report directly to that person. Such teams are by nature hierarchical and represent the traditional way that managers communicate tasks to workers. Examples of command teams include company sales teams, management teams and executive teams.

Formal teams are important to most organisations because much of the communication within the company traditionally occurs within the team. News, goals and information pass from employee to employee via formal teams. And they provide the structure for assigning tasks and soliciting feedback from team members on accomplishments, performance data and so on.

Informal teams

Informal teams are casual associations of employees that spontaneously develop within an organisation's formal structure. Such teams include groups of employees who eat lunch together every day, form bowling teams or simply like to hang out together – both during and after work. The membership of informal teams is in a constant state of flux as members come and go and friendships and other associations between employees change over time.

Although informal teams have no specific tasks or goals that management has assigned, they're very important to organisations for the following reasons:

✔ Informal teams provide a way for employees to get information outside of formal, management-sanctioned communication channels.

✔ Informal teams provide a (relatively) safe outlet for employees to let off steam about issues that concern them and to find solutions to problems by discussing them with employees from other parts of the organisation – unimpeded by the walls (actual and metaphorical) of the formal organisation.

For example, although they're not formally constituted, dozens of informal work improvement groups (WIGS) exist at GlaxoSmithKline. The purpose of these groups is simply to enable people to get together, share information and ask for and offer solutions to problems that have occurred. Some of the groups have a regular membership; others are constituted to confront one particular problem and are then dissolved after they've addressed the matter.

Ad hoc groups are informal teams of employees assembled to solve a problem, with only those who are most likely to contribute invited. For example, you may form an ad hoc team when you select employees from your human resources and accounting departments to solve a problem with the system for tracking and recording pay changes in the company's payroll system. You don't invite participants from shipping to join this informal team because they probably can't provide meaningful input to solving the problem.

Self-managed teams

Self-managed teams combine the attributes of both formal and informal teams. Normally established by management, self-managed teams often quickly adopt lives of their own as members take over responsibility for the day-to-day workings of the team. Self-managed teams usually contain from three to 30 employees whose job is to get together to find solutions to common worker problems. Self-managed teams are also known as *high-performance teams*, *cross-functional teams* or *super-teams*.

To save time and gain benefits, an organisation's self-managing teams must be:

✔ Made up of people from different parts of the organisation

✔ Small, because large groups create communication problems

✔ Self-managing and empowered to act, because referring decisions back up the line wastes time and often leads to poorer decisions

✔ Multi-functional, because that's the best – if not the only – way to keep the actual product and its essential delivery system clearly visible and foremost in everyone's mind

Self-managed teams of workers at Batchelor's Foods increased productivity by 25 per cent every year for ten years. This success was partly driven by investment in production technology; however, that the work teams were able to operate to maximum efficiency and effectiveness was an essential component of the improvement. Teams of six were allowed to divide up the work as they saw fit; and when they additionally became responsible for handling production and output defects, rejects from end of production and packaging functions, and customer complaints, rejection rates fell to negligible levels. And another by-product was that production crew absenteeism fell from 7 per cent to almost zero!

Oticon, a hearing technology specialist, organises all its staff into self-managed project teams. The additional difference at Oticon is that the company expects staff to find projects to work on, as well as receiving assignments. Under this structure the company has developed revolutionary mainstream hearing technology, using such different sources of information and expertise as the mobile phone industry, television and radio, and the music recording industry. Lars Kolind, a former managing director at Oticon, stated: 'I want people to do what they do best. I want people to enjoy themselves – to have fun. Only by doing this will we get the best products and work out of them.'

Where management is willing to let go of the reins of absolute authority and turn them over to workers, self-managing teams are increasingly rising to the challenge and making major contributions to the success of their firms. Indeed, the future success of many businesses lies in the successful implementation of self-managed teams.

The real world

Empowerment is a beautiful thing when it flourishes in an organisation. However, real empowerment is still rare. Many false substitutes are out there masquerading as empowerment! Although many managers tell a good story about how they empower their employees, few actually do it. When they're real and not pale imitations, empowered teams typically

- ✔ Make the most of the decisions that influence team success
- ✔ Choose their leaders
- ✔ Add or remove team members
- ✔ Set their goals and commitments
- ✔ Define and perform much of their training
- ✔ Receive rewards as a team

Unfortunately, employee empowerment, for the most part, may be only an illusion. A survey of team members showed that plenty of room for change and improvement in the working of teams still exists. Survey respondents clearly felt that intra-group trust, group effectiveness, agenda setting, meeting content and idea conformity could do with some improvement.

A great deal of research has investigated what makes effective teams. And in the overwhelming majority of cases, teams aren't fully empowered – top management is still making the strategic decisions. The studies all find that you can give much greater autonomy to teams by:

- ✔ **Making your teams empowered, not merely participative.** Instead of just inviting employees to participate in teams, grant team members the authority and power to make independent decisions.

- ✔ **Removing the source of conflicts.** Despite their attempts to empower employees, managers are often unwilling to live with the results. Be willing to start up a team, and then be prepared to accept the outcome.

- ✔ **Changing other significant factors that influence team effectiveness.** Each of these factors indicates that an organisation hasn't yet brought true empowerment to its employees. You have the power to change this situation. Do it!

Although clear examples of companies where management has truly empowered its teams do exist (they're out there somewhere), team empowerment doesn't just happen. Supervisors and managers must make concerted and ongoing efforts to ensure that authority and autonomy pass from management to teams. You can too!

New technology and teams

In a team environment *process management information* moves precisely to where the team needs it, unfiltered by a hierarchy. Raw numbers go straight to those who need them in their jobs because front-line workers, such as salespeople and machinists, are trained in how to use that information. By letting information flow to wherever the team needs it, a horizontal self-managed company isn't only possible, it's also inevitable. Information technology-enabled team support systems include email, computer conferencing and videoconferencing, which co-ordinate geographically, as well as across time zones, more easily than ever before. The development and use of computer software to support teams is growing also. An example is the expanding body of software called *groupware*. Groupware consists of computer programs specifically designed to support collaborative work groups and processes, both in a single location and anywhere in the world.

As organisations make better use of information technology, they don't need middle managers to make decisions as often. The result? Organisations can dramatically reduce the number of management levels and the number of managers. Jobs, careers and knowledge shift constantly. Typical management career paths are eliminated, and workers advance by learning more skills, making them more valuable to the organisation.

Top five teams websites

Wondering where to find the best information on the Internet about the topics we address in this chapter? Well, you've come to the right place! Here are our top five favourites:

- **Meredith Belbin's team roles:** `www.belbin.com`

- **MotivAction:** `www.motivaction.co.uk`

- **Teambuildinginc.com:** `www.teambuildinginc.com`

- **NASA's Teams and Teamwork:** `www.hq.nasa.gov/office/hqlibrary/ppm/ppm5.htm`

- **Fast Company:** `www.fastcompany.com/online/resources/teamwork.html`

Those managers who remain need to take on new skills and attitudes to be more like coaches, supporters and facilitators to front-line employees. Supervisors and managers no longer have the luxury of spending time trying to control the organisation – instead, they change it. Their job is to seek out new customers at the same time as they respond to the latest needs of their established customers. Managers still have considerable authority, but instead of commanding workers, their job is to inspire them.

Chapter 12

Managing Flexible Workers

In This Chapter
▶ Managing new types of employees
▶ Monitoring remote and off-site working
▶ Managing different work patterns
▶ Looking at the future of telecommuting

*N*owadays, workplaces are often more worker-friendly and working arrangements more flexible than in the past. Legislation now requires companies to consider making flexible working available to employees who request it; and denial has to be on the grounds of operational considerations only. Everyone is entitled to apply to work on a flexible basis, be they full or part time, and regardless of length of service, occupation or hours worked.

Of course, these patterns of work have long been established in the transport, telecommunications, healthcare and electricity, gas and water supply sectors. Commercial considerations, the availability of technology and changes in working demands have all driven organisations to consider how best to optimise their resources, the ways in which work is carried out and how, when and where best to engage their staff. Consequently, today's managers need to be much more willing to work with the different requirements of their employees than ever before. Whether employees need to drop off their children at school in the morning, work only on certain days of the week or take time off to care for ill relatives and dependants, managers have to be flexible and willing to accommodate these needs. In return, managers know that with a little consideration they can get – and are entitled to expect – much more from their staff.

These changes in the law and shifts in attitudes (as well as changes in the nature of work, technological advances and reductions in layers of management in many organisations) have led to flexible staff spending the majority of their working time away from the office; employees managed from a distance; employees who work a variety of patterns of hours, shifts and starting and finishing times; annualised and compressed hours; nine-day fortnights/15-day months; and employees who work from home.

Managers don't always find these changes easy to get used to. For managers who are accustomed to having their staff close by – ready to respond instantly to the needs of customers and clients – managing flexible workers can be disconcerting.

In this chapter, we consider flexible workers, and how to get the best out of them. We explore strategies for managing those who work away from the office, as well as those who work different shifts; and we look at the future of telecommuting.

Making Room for a New Kind of Employee

New kinds of employees are already out there – flexible workers. *Flexible workers* are those who work elsewhere besides the regular and familiar offices of the organisation; and those who've accepted (often having asked for) a variety of alternative working arrangements, including flexi-time, hours to suit and term-time working agreements, to name but three.

Providing flexible working opportunities is a legal obligation if no reason exists why an organisation cannot do so. Alternative working arrangements can range from allowing employees to start and end their working days at times that suit them to working full time from home.

Managing people you don't see very often can be challenging, and you need to approach it differently to managing those who work in the same place as you.

Perhaps your employees are always on the road, located at different premises or even at the other end of the country; or maybe they work evenings only or from home. Regardless of the reason for the separation, distance makes it much harder to identify and enforce standards of behaviour and performance. As a manager, you have to be absolutely certain that those following non-standard patterns of work and located elsewhere are performing to the same levels of output and quality as those in the office.

Preparing to be flexible

Is your organisation ready for flexible working? And are *you*? Here's a quick and easy checklist to determine your organisation's readiness to embrace new working patterns:

✔ Your company sets and enforces clear output and quality standards.

✔ Potential flexible workers have the equipment they need to work effectively away from the office.

✔ The work can be performed – and performed better – away from the office.

✔ The work can be performed without continuous interaction with other employees.

✔ Potential flexible workers have demonstrated that they can work effectively without constant supervision.

✔ Supervisors can manage and monitor employees by results rather than by direct observation.

✔ Non-standard places of work have been assessed to ensure that they're adequately equipped.

✔ Non-standard places and patterns of work conform to health and safety standards.

If you tick several points, then your organisation is probably ready, willing and able to implement alternative working arrangements. If hardly any of these points apply to your organisation, you have lots to do before you can reasonably expect flexible working to be a viable option.

Whatever the present state of affairs, you need to be clear about why your organisation has chosen to go down the flexible route – whether to maximise the opportunities of technology, cost cutting or dealing with customers on the other side of the world.

As a first move, you need to assess the corporate and collective attitude to flexible working. Everyone needs to know and understand why some people follow different patterns of work and have different demands on their time.

In all cases, you need to establish collective and individual performance indicators and targets, and make clear how you'll monitor and supervise those on non-standard patterns of work. Consider how to measure volume, quality and reliability of work; and how to observe and keep on top of deadlines. You may need to devise specific ways of working for flexible workers.

A full risk assessment is also necessary when considering changing people's work patterns. Look at technological security; staff reliability, security and well-being; product, service and output delivery viability; and problem identification and resolution capability.

Prepare the groundwork for flexible working and you create the conditions whereby people can have a much greater say in their own work–life balance. As a result, you improve staff morale. Sanctioning flexible working doesn't mean that you become sloppy over deadlines or demands; it does mean that within these constraints, employees can work when they choose.

Anticipating changes to the organisation's culture

When an increasing number of people work flexibly – often outside the office or outside regular hours – company culture and staff performance may be affected. A company's culture is, after all, mostly defined by the daily interactions of staff. Those who work outside the mainstream and aren't involved in the everyday office environment may have little or no grounding in the organisational culture, values and goals, and little identity with other employees. Making everyone feel included is essential, whatever their hours of attendance or location or pattern of work. Fortunately, you can take a number of steps to help your flexible workers plug into your company's culture, become team players and gain a stake in the organisation's goals in the process. Consider the following ideas:

- ✔ Schedule regular meetings that everyone attends, in person if possible, or conference call if necessary. Discuss current company events and set aside time for the group to tackle and solve at least one major or pressing problem (more if time permits).

- ✔ Create effective communication channels that everyone can access. Make sure that everyone gets to know about important or urgent issues within the company – as well as all the gossip.

- ✔ Schedule periodic team-building events for everyone, both flexible and standard workers, to build working relationships and trust.

- ✔ Initiate a programme of regular and inexpensive group events that draw people together. Picnic lunches, helping local charities, holding games afternoons – the possibilities are endless.

As a manager, you need to consider that flexible workers face issues that normal employees don't, including:

✔ They may find that they're not fairly compensated for using home resources (space, computers, electricity, furniture and so on) that they contribute to the job.

✔ They may feel that their privacy is being invaded if management efforts are intrusive. Remember that flexible workers aren't available 24/7. Respect their working hours and use work phone numbers and email addresses – not their home ones – when you want to communicate.

✔ They may find that family pressures intrude on work duties much more than they do for office-based staff. Be very clear that 'working from home' means just that. Wherever and whenever they work, you need to ensure that you get the required level of output from all of your staff.

Regular employees may become resentful of what they perceive to be the 'special privileges' given to flexible workers. Ensure that everyone knows and understands why all of their colleagues work in particular ways, and what their contribution to overall performance is.

The issues associated with flexible working don't mean that you just forget about offering alternative working arrangements; you have to be prepared to make such arrangements by law, after all. But bear them in mind, and work to ensure that they don't cause problems for anyone, flexible or otherwise.

If it does become clear to you that resentment exists because some people are granted flexible working but not others, confront the issue. Seek out those who feel that they have a cause for concern, and discuss their views with them. And if they themselves wish to try flexible working, either give them the opportunity to do so or else make it very clear why this isn't possible at present.

Managing from a Distance

Flexible working is increasingly commonplace, and if people request it you have to be prepared to offer it, or else give sound operational and managerial reasons why you can't do so. With the changing nature of work today, managers have to adapt to new circumstances. How can you keep up with an employee's performance when you may not have physical contact with them for weeks or even months at a time? Basic human interaction, of course. Consider the following ideas:

✔ **Make time for people.** Nothing beats face-to-face meetings in building lasting, trusting relationships. Managing is a people job. Schedule in time to either meet up with or talk to employees who may work odd hours.

✔ **Increase communication as you increase distance.** The greater the distance, the greater the effort all parties need to make to keep in touch. Although some employees want to be as autonomous as possible, minimising their day-to-day contact with you, others quickly feel neglected, isolated or ignored if you don't make the effort to keep in touch. So increase phone and email communication, send frequent organisational updates and schedule regular meetings and visits. Also encourage your employees to contact you (communication is a two-way process, after all). You need to go out of your way to provide the same access to communication, information and meetings for all of your employees, regardless of when and how they work; so arrange meetings that everyone can get to – and make sure that they attend!

✔ **Use technology; don't let technology use you.** Use technology as an active means of communication, not just for giving out information. Promote the exchange of ideas, encourage questions and make sure that you always reply. Set up chat rooms, and create bulletin boards to encourage your employees to interact and exchange information.

Today's managers have to work harder to manage all the different patterns of work and ways of working. If you value strong working relationships and clear communication, you need to talk to people to make sure that adequate communication is taking place.

Managing Different Shifts and Patterns of Work

Managing people is hard enough, and changing work patterns make it harder still. Employers have had to develop new approaches to organising work, so that tasks get done at all hours of the day, and staff can be employed for hours that suit them. Managing employees who work different hours and shift patterns is a critical issue.

Make things easier for employees who work shifts or non-standard hours by providing:

✔ **Effective induction:** All new employees need to get their bearings, and those on shifts are often at a disadvantage because they work outside normal hours. Make sure that new employees know exactly what their job entails and that the organisational rules, procedures and regulations are explained. Help them get to know everyone and to get settled in quickly.

✔ **Adequate resources:** Giving your employees what they need to be productive encompasses everything from providing the right equipment to making sure they know where to go to ask questions. It also means providing training, if necessary.

Long-distance recognition

Everyone needs recognition for their sense of self-worth – including managerial acknowledgement of a job well done. Because some people are out of sight doesn't mean they should be out of mind. Use the following tips to make sure that your flexible staff feel just as valued and appreciated as everyone else:

✔ Provide flexible staff with opportunities to tell their manager and everyone else about their achievements.

✔ Schedule regular meetings between flexible workers and both managers and colleagues – just because they're flexible and working in remote locations for much of the time doesn't mean that you can't call these staff in when necessary or desirable.

✔ Regularly review the achievements of flexible staff so that you don't forget them and they remain integrated with everyone else.

✔ Ensure that flexible staff get the same opportunities for recognition, promotion, progress and variety of work as everyone else.

✔ Include flexible staff in all workplace celebrations and social events.

✔ Thank flexible staff when appropriate, exactly the same as everyone else.

✔ **Continuous communication:** You can't underestimate the value of communication. Some employees may be labelled as difficult to work with when in fact they're given poor instructions and struggle to follow them rather than risk appearing slow to understand an assignment. Constantly check that staff who work shifts or non-standard hours are able to ask questions, and are given help if they need it. Make every contact count. Some managers make themselves available at shift changeovers to facilitate contact with two shifts at once.

✔ **Inclusive recognition:** Publicly acknowledge everyone, whatever their hours or patterns of work. Recognition and appreciation go a long way towards building loyalty and commitment, and getting that little bit extra out of people when you need it.

✔ **Equal treatment:** Treat everyone the way you want them to act. If you want people to take a long-term perspective, involve them in the company's long-term plans. Get them involved. Make flexible workers part of the team, and make them *feel* part of the team.

Supporting flexible working and being seen as treating all employees in the same way enhances your organisation's reputation. You may well find that these qualities are appealing to new people, making it easier to recruit staff in the future.

Taking up Telecommuting

Telecommuting is a work arrangement in which employees enjoy flexibility in working location and hours; the daily commute to a central place of work is replaced by telecommunication links. Broadband connections, laptops, Blackberries, videoconferencing – technology really does mean that people can work anywhere. The question for a manager is no longer *can* my employees telecommute and work from home but, rather, is do I let them?

In an old-style office, employees are often no more than a few feet away from you, their manager. If you need them, you can get hold of them. If they're away from their desks or workstations, no problem, you can catch them later.

Telecommuting changes this picture. You can't get hold of people immediately (and they can't always get hold of you). Communication can become a series of voice-mail messages, emails and faxes. You may come to feel disconnected from your staff – and vice versa.

However, telecommuting offers lots of benefits. Staff productivity and output can increase by up to 30 per cent. People don't lose time travelling to and from work. Staff are more satisfied with their jobs. And society benefits from fewer cars on the road during rush hour periods.

When he worked normal hours, John Holland, a systems analyst at DigitalCompaq, didn't see his children from first thing on Monday morning till Friday night. When DigitalCompaq allowed John to choose his own hours and location of work, he set up an office at home. Doing so enabled him to save nearly three hours' commuting per day. He got more work done, more quickly and to a higher standard; and the family had their evening meal together every day. John subsequently moved his family from a London suburb to a rural town in northern England, some 300 miles from the office. DigitalCompaq was happy with this arrangement because John's output continued to rise, and his loyalty and commitment were assured.

Consider the pros and cons of telecommuting. The advantages are:

- ✔ Depending only on specific deadlines being met, staff can set their own schedules and hours of work.
- ✔ Because they're never interrupted, staff have more time for customers.
- ✔ Your business saves money by downsizing facilities and premises, and on the cost of electricity, heating and other overheads.
- ✔ Staff morale is boosted.

And the disadvantages are:

- ✔ Monitoring performance is harder.

- ✔ Scheduling meetings and get-togethers is more difficult.

- ✔ You may have to buy your staff the equipment they need to be flexible and telecommute.

- ✔ Employees can become disconnected and alienated from the organisation.

- ✔ Managers have to reorder their own priorities and daily schedules to include specific attention to those following non-standard patterns of work.

- ✔ Managers have to be more precise in setting work and assignments.

Ian Baines works for one of the world's best-known airlines near Heathrow airport. With the agreement of the airline, he now works one day per week at home. On this day, Ian manages to get done in a matter of hours what otherwise takes full days because of constant interruptions. His staff can get hold of him at home if they need to; and if he does have to go into work for meetings on this day, he travels later, which means that he completes his journey in 20 minutes rather than the two hours it takes during the rush hour. Clearing paperwork during his one day at home, leaves Ian free to deal with institutional problems and his other responsibilities fully and effectively during the rest of the week.

Top five virtual management websites

Here's the best of the web for the topics we discuss in this chapter:

- ✔ **Chartered Institute of Personnel and Development:** www.cipd.co.uk

- ✔ **Department of Trade and Industry:** www.dti.gov.uk

- ✔ **Advisory, Conciliation and Arbitration Service (ACAS):** www.acas.org.uk

- ✔ **Chartered Management Institute:** www.managers.org.uk

- ✔ **Trades Union Congress:** www.tuc.org.uk

Part V
Tough Times for Tough Managers

'Look, Filligrew, this company has always
insisted its employees leave their private
lives at home.'

In this part . . .

No one ever said that being a manager is easy. Rewarding? Yes. Easy? No. In this part, we present the issues surrounding ethics and office politics, risk, managing change in the workplace, disciplining employees easily and effectively and conducting dismissals and layoffs.

Chapter 13

Understanding and Managing Risk

● ●

In This Chapter

▶ Understanding what risk is

▶ Taking steps to identify risks

▶ Employing effective techniques for managing risk

▶ Becoming risk aware

● ●

*A*wareness of risk and how to manage it come very high on the list of managerial responsibilities. You need to know and understand everything that can possibly and conceivably go wrong within your business and its wider environment, why, what the consequences are – and what, if anything, you can do about it.

You start by acknowledging Murphy's Law: anything that can go wrong, will go wrong. You can't trust to luck or fortune. Risk stems from the way in which the organisation is run, the decisions taken at the top and overall organisational strategy.

When the Lockheed Martin aerospace company collapsed in 1983, the top managers met up to find out why, to review what they'd done wrong and to determine where mistakes had been made. They concluded that nobody had done anything wrong! The world's third-largest aerospace and defence company had collapsed – and it was just 'one of those things'! And yet Lockheed Martin continued to build turbo-prop aircraft when everyone was demanding jets; they built sturdy cumbersome helicopters when everyone wanted fast and flexible helicopters; and they were late with their deliveries. So actually plenty of risk was attached to that company in that situation! And, of course, finding fault with the staff or the products was pointless – it was the decisions to build these products in the first place that were the source of the company's downfall.

You need to make sure that everyone in your organisation recognises that things can go wrong, which processes and systems are most vulnerable, what they can and can't control and influence and what to do when they hit difficulties. Railing against the state of the world is pointless! You have to exist within the world as it is, not as you'd like it to be.

This chapter covers how to approach everything you're up against in the real world in such a way that you maximise your chances of doing things right – and take the correct steps to tackle things when they do go wrong.

Defining Risk

Risk simply means the possibility of experiencing misfortune, loss, accident, injury or some type of failure. Managers need to be able to assess the likelihood of such events happening in their organisations and take steps to avoid them or device strategies for dealing with them. Always consider:

- ✔ Whether the risk of something happening is worth accepting or not (probability × consequences)
- ✔ What the consequences of (and in some cases, opportunities created by) something occurring are
- ✔ The likely and possible effects on the company or organisation, and its business
- ✔ Whether the risk can be measured and quantified
- ✔ The range of possible alternative actions for dealing with the risk

If you know and understand the risk involved in an action or situation, you can choose to accept that risk or take steps to avoid it. You can also insure against the likelihood of particular events occurring; the greater your knowledge and understanding of the wider situation as well as the detail, the greater your ability to insure accurately and/or take effective risk management actions.

When he was US Secretary of Defense, at the height of the military activities in Iraq, Donald Rumsfeld was asked what the risks were. He replied: 'The risks are based on what we know. We know what we know; and we know what we think we know. Additionally, there are things that we know that we don't know; and there are things that we don't know that we don't know.' Unsurprisingly, this statement was ridiculed. However, what Rumsfeld was actually saying was: the greater your knowledge and understanding, the lower the risks. And that statement applies to everything!

Volcanic ash

The volcanic ash cloud that disrupted air travel in the spring of 2010 was seen by many first as a nuisance and then as an opportunity for an extended holiday. That ash cloud, however, had serious consequences for organisations all over the world. Many of them didn't immediately recognise that a volcano in Iceland would have knock-on effects on their business; for example:

✔ Producers of organic vegetables in Africa were unable to fly their products to their European and North American markets.

✔ The plane maker Airbus couldn't move components between its manufacturing bases in the UK, France and Germany.

✔ Businesspeople were unable to travel between Hong Kong and Australia because their planes were grounded in European and North American airports.

✔ And, of course, people stuck waiting for flights couldn't get back to work.

Airlines were required to incur the expense of accommodating stranded passengers. And they couldn't maintain their planes because they were in the wrong place; neither could they pick up passengers because they were stranded elsewhere.

Recognise that your organisation is vulnerable to events in the wider environment and take the widest view possible of the effects on your business.

Your company and risk

You need to apply Murphy's Law – anything that can go wrong, will go wrong – to your own company and everything that it does. Consider the internal workings of the organisation and what's likely to happen if:

✔ Your IT systems crash.

✔ An extended power cut occurs.

✔ You suddenly lose three members of your team.

✔ The staff go on strike.

✔ A train strike stops staff getting to work on the day you need to process a major order.

Then take a look at wider issues within your organisation, such as:

✔ What if a security breach occurs?

✔ What if your boss suddenly announces that he's leaving?

✔ What if the CEO suddenly leaves?

✔ What if your technology suddenly fails to function?

Thinking about these possibilities helps you recognise that anything can happen at any time. Your job is to be prepared for such eventualities and to formulate plans for dealing with them.

Allowing yourself to drift along, refusing to face reality and failing to plan for all eventualities means that at some point you'll be in the midst of a crisis and unable to deal with it. We've all seen CEOs and top managers floundering on the television when faced with questions about things that they could, and should, have foreseen. Don't be one of them

The business environment and risk

Your organisation doesn't operate in a vacuum; it's also vulnerable to events occurring in the wider business environment and in the markets in which you operate. You need to evaluate your environment and market by asking questions such as:

✔ What if the price of components, data, energy or raw materials suddenly trebles?

✔ What if the price of fuel doubles?

✔ What if public transport costs suddenly shoot up and staff seek jobs nearer home?

✔ What if a competitor sets up nearby and pays higher wages than you do?

✔ What if traffic jams delay our supplies?

✔ What if road works slow down our deliveries?

✔ What if everything comes to a standstill because of strikes, disputes or environmental disasters over which we have no control?

Knowing What Can Go Wrong, and Why

The most expert of managers encounter delays, breakdowns and mistakes. Managing risk thus means that, first and foremost, you pay constant attention to the work of your department and team; second, your relationships with other stakeholders – staff, suppliers, other departments and managers, customers and clients; and third, the wider economic environment. Never become complacent.

Joe Telfer, business development manager at Westwoodnine, a property company based in the City of London, states:

> *The main reason why things go wrong here is that people fill up their lives with the good bits of their job. These get done well. It is the bad bits that you have to pay attention to – the bits that people dislike or – most of all – never quite get around to, or cannot be bothered to do at all.*

Thanks to your excellent managerial skills, your staff are all busy, happy, active, committed and productive. Yet things still go wrong – why? The answer lies in managing the work as people should do it, not as they are doing it.

Tom Peters, the great management guru, once stated of Walmart's top managers: 'You will see top executives earning £250,000 a year sharing cheap desks at the company's headquarters. And the reason is simple – Walmart want their executives out and about with clients and suppliers, not cosily snuggled up in the office.'

Losses

Any organisation, product, service or project can make a loss: the key is working out why. If something is running inefficiently or making a loss, you can look at:

- ✔ The product, service or project itself – the problem is at the grassroots level.

- ✔ Whether being inefficient is what customers expect from you – and so staff don't push themselves to improve.

- ✔ Bureaucratic overload – you spend too much time and money on processes and administration and not enough on products, services and sales.

- ✔ Company imbalance – you spend too much money on offices and not enough on active product, service and project delivery.

The UK's National Health Service (NHS) is the largest civilian organisation in the world. It employs just over a million staff. But only just over half that number are medical professionals dealing with patients. The rest are in administration and management. In addition, between 2009–2010, the NHS spent over £300 million on externally appointed management consultants. So, in a nutshell, managers were appointing managers to tell them how to manage, while at the same time attempting to deliver the full range of health services. No organisation can sustain this kind of overload; you need to concentrate your resources at the frontline.

Taking heed of the warnings from disasters

When the *Herald of Free Enterprise*, a cross-channel ferry operating between Dover and Belgium, sank outside Zeebrugge harbour in 1987, the subsequent inquiry found that the operating company, Townsend Thoresen, was 'riddled with the disease of sloppiness'. The ship sailed before its bow doors closed, and as a result the water rushed in. When the ship then sank, 193 people lost their lives. No systems were in place to make sure that the doors were closed before the ship set sail, and nobody thought it important enough to check.

Not long after, P&O took over Townsend Thoresen. However, the losses incurred as the result of the disaster took years to recoup, requiring cuts and restructuring of the service. The company's position wasn't helped by the opening of the Channel Tunnel in 1994, and by the growth of low-cost air travel. By this point, the company had quite enough on its plate without adding to its own woes by allowing forms of

sloppiness and malpractice that were certain to end in disaster.

Similarly, the Paddington rail crash of 1996 revealed the parlous state of the UK rail infrastructure. Two trains collided and 39 people lost their lives. Railtrack, the Network Rail managing company, tried to blame the drivers for going through red signals. However, it quickly became clear that at least one signal was faulty. The problem was compounded by a senior manager at Railtrack, Richard Bowker, stating: 'People should stop worrying. We have had an accident, that is all. We need to move on.'

In both cases, court proceedings investigating who was at fault dragged on for many years, damaging the resources, morale and reputation of the companies involved. Finally, both Townsend Thoresen and Railtrack went broke! Take note of the warnings highlighted by disasters; accidents can be avoided and their results on your business can be catastrophic.

And in case you think that this scenario is purely a public service problem, the same applied to Marks & Spencer and Abbey (now part of Santander), both of which, when faced with losses, business uncertainties and declining sales, chose to spend upwards of £200 million on refurbishing their London headquarters.

To work out where your organisation is making losses, or where they might potentially occur, and to diagnose where root problems may lie, look out for:

- Rising costs and stable revenues
- Stable costs and falling revenues
- Stable revenues and declining product and service quality
- Rising costs and stable quality

Develop your own early warning system for risk based on this information and closely monitor business performance.

Accidents

Everyone has accidents. Keeping them to a minimum is what matters. The fewer accidents you have – involving people, products, services or systems – the more highly you and your company will be regarded.

And the converse is also true – the more accidents you have, the lower the regard in which people hold you, and the more customers, clients and suppliers turn elsewhere as their confidence in you declines.

Accident prevention is often common sense: keep the workplace clean and tidy; train people to use equipment correctly; provide suitable clothing, if necessary – and don't cut corners. And adopt an active approach to those who do cut corners, skip inspections or 'never quite get around' to putting things right.

Crime

Crime is a risk to everyone, of course! Recognise the types of crimes that can occur in your organisation or sector, and take active steps to prevent them.

In practice, very few people ever set out to break their own high standards. One of the problems is created by what Clayton Christensen, Professor of Business Administration at Harvard Business School, calls 'just this once'. According to him, everyone experiences pressure to do something they wouldn't normally do 'just this once'. 'Just this once' I'll take some money from the petty cash and no one will notice; 'just this once' I'll drive even though I probably had too much to drink at lunchtime; the boss did say the delivery was urgent – and so on. And then, of course, 'just this once' you either break the law or turn a blind eye to a crime; and the damage is done.

Crimes which may happen at work include:

- ✔ Financial crimes, including fraud, theft and fiddles
- ✔ Vandalism, including sabotage of production equipment and information technology
- ✔ Violence, especially of staff towards each other
- ✔ Bullying, victimisation, discrimination and harassment
- ✔ Corporate crime, including insider dealing in shares and commodities
- ✔ Security hacking into databases and systems

✔ Drug dealing

✔ Drug and alcohol misuse

✔ Breaches of employment health and safety legislation

Risks are associated with all of these crimes, but what the issue actually boils down to is this: would you want to be associated with an organisation that condones this sort of behaviour?

Would you beat a path to the door of a company like Enron (the world's largest-ever corporate fraudster) to be their next high value client. And if your own organisation was caught up in criminal activity, would you feel good about the company? Of course not – and neither will anyone else. As well as facing prosecution, you also lose reputation, customers, clients, profits and people's confidence in you.

Attitudes towards corporate crime vary from country to country and even from industry to industry. The USA, for example, inflicts long prison sentences on executives convicted of price-collusion; severe sentences like these are rare in the EU, where such cases occur less frequently. In the UK construction industry, more than a dozen builders were recently accused of bid rigging. The response of would-be defendants in several instances was that, while the action was regretted, it was nonetheless justified by the dire financial circumstances faced by the companies involved.

In the face of changing economic or social conditions, yesterday's serious crime may become tomorrow's mere incident to be sidestepped by capable legal advisors. For management of the company itself, an inner moral compass must exist that is not subject to being weakened in times of stress or unprofitability.

Realising What Can Really Go Wrong

The preceding sections cover what can go wrong; now we look at what can *really* go wrong. Why? Because everybody believes that none of the incidents or scenarios we outline earlier can possibly happen to them! So here we look at the sort of behaviour that really results in huge losses, disasters and the committing of crimes.

If top and senior managers take decisions, they don't want to hear that they've got things wrong; and if you're the one who tells them they've bungled, it may well be you who's fired. Bad decisions remain a huge risk for organisations. One approach to dealing with this problem is to set up a review system for all major decisions, just to check that before things are implemented they're re-examined briefly before getting the go-ahead.

Considering the truly wild and wacky

Some years ago, Richard asked some ridiculous questions:

✔ What if interest rates fall to 0.5 per cent?

✔ What if the value of the pound and euro reach parity?

✔ What if another oil crisis happens?

✔ What if the value of property starts to fall?

These questions no longer seem quite so wacky! Indeed, all of these scenarios have happened in recent years. So you need to constantly expand your vision. Wild questions to consider today are:

✔ What if the value of property halves?

✔ What if the stock market collapses?

✔ What if UK unemployment reaches 5 million?

✔ What if China unilaterally raises its minimum wage?

And then you need to work out the effect of each of these occurrences on your organisation. They're certain to have either a direct or indirect effect in terms of suppliers, customers and clients. Actively considering outrageous scenarios – and how you'd deal with them – is an excellent risk management discipline.

People criticise the review approach, especially on the grounds of it being yet another delay in the call to action. Yet the review shouldn't take long. If you have nothing to worry about, then a short delay won't matter. But if you *do* have something to worry about, then finding that out now rather than after you've committed yourself is so much better. Richard calls this 'wait a minute' – and a minute should be all the review takes. The review isn't a further examination of everything – just a final check.

Complacency is another cause of things going really wrong. Organisations and their managers, especially after a long run of successes, come to see themselves as invincible. People take decisions and enter into ventures without proper scrutiny. The result is that errors start to creep in.

Closely related to complacency is another key issue: assumption. In this context, assumption is a risk on the grounds that, because somebody at the top of the organisation or in a managerial position has decided something, it'll work out and everything will go according to plan. Whatever is decided and whoever decides it, you still have to look at the core issue of risk – that anything that can go wrong, will go wrong. For example:

✔ The financial crisis of 2008 and beyond was brought about as the result of assumptions that assets and investments being traded would continue to rise and not fall in value.

✔ The 2009 political crisis created by expense account fraud came about as the result of the assumption that politicians wouldn't fiddle their expenses.

Risks are inherent every time you don't fully address something or are complacent or make assumptions – anything rather than doing the hard work.

Knowing What You Can, and Must, Do

You need to get everyone involved in risk management. Encourage your employees to think about what could go wrong in your organisation and always be open to their concerns.

To minimise the risks within and facing your organisation, and to mitigate their effects, you need to:

- ✔ Make sure that everyone knows and understands what can possibly go wrong.
- ✔ Make sure that you use staff meetings and briefings to cover risks in full.
- ✔ Make sure that everyone knows and understands that risk management is a joint venture involving everyone in the organisation.
- ✔ Make sure you don't heap blame on the person who happens to bring the problem to light – 'shooting the messenger'.

The last point is especially important. If someone raises a concern with you, you need to treat that person with respect and take their concern seriously. Investigate the issue until you're satisfied that no danger exists. And if a problem does exist, deal with it immediately.

Above all, effective risk management is about developing your knowledge. You need to use real and potential risks to make sure that your department learns from its mistakes and never makes them again. Also ensure that you learn from the mistakes and shortcomings of others.

Andy Clarke, the CEO of Asda, inspired media attention by describing his company's value-line food and household products as poor quality. Unsurprisingly, a downturn in sales occurred; and it also called into question the quality of some of the company's other products. Andy Clarke could've learned from the experience of Gerald Ratner, who years ago described his company's products as 'rubbish' – and destroyed the whole organisation with that one unguarded phrase.

British Airways and Terminal 5

When British Airways opened its brand new Terminal 5 building at London's Heathrow airport, the company promised that everything would go smoothly and would be the beginning of a whole new travel experience for all of BA's passengers.

In the run-up to the opening, the ticketing, baggage handling and security technology were tested; and the company's top management looked upon the results and were truly delighted.

For the staff who were going to be working there, however, things weren't quite so clear. The staff asked for training and briefing in how to use the technology in an operational situation; and they warned that the baggage system wouldn't be able to cope with multiple arrivals. They also warned that the staff access security technology wouldn't be able to handle the volumes of people at shift changeovers.

The company didn't want to hear any of this. When the terminal opened, chaos ensued as systems first proved to be inadequate, and then crashed altogether. It took six months for British Airways to reposition the baggage, check-in and security systems in order to accommodate real workloads and staff volumes. To date, the security system can't accept passengers who arrive less than 40 minutes before their flight departure (even if they've actually been at the terminal in plenty of time and have got held up in queues).

Keep in mind the following as you move forward after a mistake:

- **Never make the same mistake twice.** Everyone makes mistakes – and will, of course, continue to make them. You can use the knowledge you gain from mistakes to improve your company's future performance. Always learn from things going wrong and put them right. And don't be afraid to acknowledge mistakes– people will have more confidence in your company if you do.

- **Never get caught by the same scam twice.** If you've been defrauded, bought substandard components on the Internet or arranged shipments that never arrived, don't get conned again! Once is acceptable; twice isn't.

The banking and financial crisis of 2008 revealed that many organisations from the UK and elsewhere had put money into high interest savings schemes in Iceland. It was clear to many that such schemes weren't viable because the Icelandic financial sector wasn't large enough to meet all its obligations. However, this didn't prevent organisations from using the schemes. The people that did this duly learned their lesson through the vast losses they incurred, so it would now be grossly negligent to do the same thing again. The financial world has been caught once by this and it needn't happen again.

If something is too good to be true, it generally isn't!

Remembering That Risk Management Is Profitable

If you follow the approach to risk management that we advocate in this chapter, you'll find that doing so is profitable. You, your company and your staff will be able to spot the pitfalls as well as the possibilities in everything you do. If this means taking a bit more time to get things right, or that you don't go blundering off into things that you know little about (however exciting that prospect may be), the payoffs in terms of stability, reputation and a more serene corporate life are worth it.

Top five risk assessment and management websites

Here are the five best websites to help you carry out risk assessment in your organisation:

✔ **Healthy Working Lives:** www.healthy workinglives.com

✔ **The Sarbanes-Oxley Act:** www.soxlaw. com/

✔ **PricewaterhouseCoopers:** www.pwc. com/ca/en/risk/financial-risk

✔ **Risk Assessment Templates:** www.risk-assessment-template.com

✔ **The Institute of Risk Management:** www. theirm.org

Chapter 14

Dealing with Ethics and Office Politics

. . . .

In This Chapter

▶ Doing what's right

▶ Assessing your political environment

▶ Identifying the real side of communication

▶ Discovering the unwritten rules of your organisation

▶ Defending your personal interests

. . . .

*E*thics and office politics are very powerful forces in any organisation. *Ethics* is the framework of values that employees use to guide their behaviour. You've seen the devastation that poor ethical standards can lead to – witness the string of business failures attributed to less than sterling ethics in more than a few large, seemingly upstanding businesses. Today, more than ever, managers are expected to model ethical behaviour and to ensure that their employees follow in their footsteps – and at the same time to purge the organisation of employees who refuse to align their own standards with those of their employer.

At its best, *office politics* means the relationships that you develop with your colleagues – both up and down the chain of command – that allow you to get tasks done, to be informed about the latest goings-on in the organisation and to form a personal network of business associates for support throughout your career. Office politics help to ensure that everyone works in the best interests of their colleagues and the organisation. At its worst, office politics can degenerate into a competition in which employees concentrate their efforts on trying to increase their personal power at the expense of other employees, and of their organisations.

This chapter is about building an ethical organisation, determining the nature and boundaries of your political environment, understanding the unspoken side of office communication, unearthing the unwritten rules of your organisation and, in the worst-case scenario, becoming adept at defending yourself against political attack.

Doing the Right Thing: Ethics and You

With an endless parade of business scandals regarding overstated revenues, mistaken earnings and misplaced decimals hitting the daily news, rocking the stock market and shaking the foundations of the global economic system, you may often wonder whether anyone in charge knows the difference between right and wrong. Or, if they know the difference, whether they really care.

Of course, the reality is that many business leaders do know the difference between right and wrong, despite appearances to the contrary. Now more than ever, businesses and the leaders who run them are trying to do the right thing, not just because the right thing is politically correct, but also because it's good for the bottom line.

Defining ethics

Do you know what ethics is? In case you're a bit rusty on the correct response, the long answer is that *ethics* is a set of standards, beliefs and values that guide conduct, behaviour and activities – in other words, a way of thinking that provides boundaries for action. The short answer is that ethics is simply doing the right thing. Not just talking about doing the right thing, but really doing it!

Although you come to a job with your own sense of ethical values, based on your upbringing, your beliefs and your life experiences, the organisations and leaders for which you work are responsible for setting clear ethical standards for you to operate within.

When you have high ethical standards on the job, you generally exhibit some or all of the following personal qualities and behaviours:

- Accountability
- Dedication
- Fairness
- Honesty
- Impartiality

- ✔ Integrity
- ✔ Loyalty
- ✔ Responsibility

Ethical behaviour starts with *you*. As a manager, you're a leader in your organisation, and you set an example – both for other managers and for the many workers watching your every move. When others see you behaving unethically, you're sending the message loud and clear that ethics doesn't matter. The result? Ethics doesn't matter to them, either.

However, when you behave ethically, others follow your example and behave ethically too. And if you practise ethical conduct, it also reinforces and perhaps improves your own ethical standards. As a manager, you have a responsibility to try to define, live up to and improve your own set of personal ethics.

Creating a code of ethics

Although most people have a pretty good idea about what kinds of behaviour are ethical and what kinds aren't, ethics are to some degree subjective, and a matter of interpretation to the individual employee. One worker may, for example, think that making unlimited personal phone calls from the office is okay, but another may consider that to be inappropriate.

Instead of leaving your employees' definition of ethics on the job to chance or their upbringing, you need to spell out clearly in a code of ethics that stealing, sharing trade secrets, sexual harassment and other unethical behaviour is unacceptable and may be grounds for dismissal.

A *code of ethics* spells out for all employees – from the very top to the very bottom of the organisation – your organisation's ethical expectations, clearly and unambiguously.

A code of ethics isn't a substitute for company policies and procedures; the code complements these guidelines.

Four key areas form the foundation of a good code of ethics:

- ✔ Compliance with internal policies and procedures
- ✔ Compliance with external laws and regulations
- ✔ Standards based on organisational values
- ✔ Standards based on individual values

Any code of ethics must cover rights, responsibilities, authority and account-ability; the work carried out and the ways in which work is carried out; matters of right and wrong; compliance with the law; and a reflection of social and cultural customs and values. Running through the code of ethics is a strong vein of honesty and integrity.

Of course, a code of ethics isn't worth the paper it's printed on if it doesn't address some very specific issues, as well as the more generic ones listed previously. The following list highlights some of the areas a code of ethics needs to address:

- Conflicts of interest, especially those that occur when managers are faced with the choice of courses of action that serve their own interests at the expense of those of the organisation.

- Gifts and gratuities that can be understood or perceived to be induce-ments to act in a particular way.

- Financial issues, including fraud, misuse of company funds, attitudes to expenses and bonuses, and other irregularities.

- Loyalty and dedication to the organisation; this is a two-way process – you can't expect loyalty and dedication from your employees if you don't provide loyalty in return.

- Compliance with the law as it stands; and commitment to deal with employees who break the law in accordance with statutory provisions.

- Conditions in which hard and effective work can be expected, required and carried out.

- Commitment to constant improvement of all aspects of the organisation – products and services; working practices; returns to shareholders; and dealings with all stakeholders.

- Commitment to avoiding favouritism and victimisation – remember, in cases of victimisation, law courts and tribunals normally hear an allega-tion provided that it can be substantiated. In recent years some who've proved or demonstrated victimisation or discrimination have gained huge settlements – so apart from not being right, victimisation or dis-crimination can also be very expensive!

- Prohibitions against disclosing trade secrets, product and service infor-mation, or anything concerning the internal workings of the organisation without specific permission to do so.

- Expectations of the highest standards of conduct in matters concern-ing employee health, safety and welfare. Make sure that this extends to anyone visiting the organisation. Expose vandalism, fraud, theft and dishonesty wherever they're found; if you don't, you may be cited as an accessory after the fact if and when such a case comes to light.

✔ Commitment to exposing sexual misconduct and harassment wherever it's found – remember that not doing so may render you liable to prosecution.

✔ Commitment to establishing and upholding the principles of equality of treatment for all, regardless of ethnic origin, gender, sexual orientation, age, disability, occupation or length of service. Ensure equality of treatment and opportunity for all in specific organisational matters, especially promotions; recruitment and selection; training and development opportunities; project work and secondments; and other specific organisational issues.

✔ Paying particular attention to how technology is used. Of especial concern here are matters to do with the nature of websites accessed (such as pornography, religious and political extremism), and the content of emails (especially those that are bullying or abusive). Also, clear collective commitment is required to ensure that the organisation confidentially maintains personal and financial data and supplier and client records.

All these areas of ethics are underpinned by the ways in which you conduct yourself. So make sure that you set the same standards for yourself in all things that you expect from everyone else. And especially never make promises to anyone that you can't keep – staff, suppliers, customers and clients, or shareholders.

The Freedom of Information Act specifies that anyone can request to know what's being said about them or done in their name, so make sure that you commit yourself to the highest possible standards of behaviour. Additionally, the Whistleblowers' Charter states that if someone exposes wrongdoing at your organisation, you can't discipline or victimise that person as a result. So be good and be careful!

In addition to working within an organisation, a well-crafted code of ethics can be a powerful tool for publicising your company's standards and values to people outside your organisation, including suppliers, clients, customers, investors, potential job applicants, the media and the public at large. Your code of ethics tells others that you value ethical behaviour and that it guides the way you and your employees do business.

Of course, simply having a code of ethics isn't enough. You and your employees must also live according to the code. Even the world's best code of ethics does you no good if you file it away and never use it. Require your employees to read and sign a copy acknowledging their acceptance of the code; that way everyone knows what you expect of them.

Citing the Ethics Resource Center's comprehensive code

According to the US-based Ethics Resource Center website (www.ethics.org), a comprehensive code of ethics has seven parts. These parts are:

✔ **A memorable title:** Examples include PricewaterhouseCooper's 'The Way We Do Business' and the World Bank Group's 'Living Our Values'.

✔ **A leadership letter:** A cover letter briefly outlining the content of the code of ethics and clearly demonstrating commitment from the very top of the organisation to ethical principles of behaviour.

✔ **A table of contents:** Listing the main parts within the code, by page number.

✔ **An introduction:** Explaining why the code is important, the scope of the code and which people the code applies to.

✔ **A statement of core values:** Listing and describing the organisation's primary values in detail. Organisations more or less universally describe themselves as equal opportunities employers that provide equality of treatment for all regardless of gender, ethnic origin, religion, age, occupation, length of service or hours worked.

✔ **Code provisions:** This part is the meat of the code, describing the organisation's position on a wide variety of issues, including such topics as sexual harassment, privacy, conflicts of interest, gratuities and so forth.

✔ **Information and resources:** Listing sources of further information or specific advice.

Living ethics

You may have a code of ethics, but if you don't behave ethically in your day-to-day business transactions and relationships, you call into question the purpose of having a code in the first place. Ethical challenges abound in business – some are spelled out in your company's code of ethics, or in its policies and procedures, and some aren't. What, for example, do you do if

✔ One of your favourite employees gives you tickets to a football match?

✔ An employee asks you not to discipline her for a moderate breach of company policies?

✔ You sold a product to a client that you later found out to be faulty, but your boss wants you to forget about it?

> ✔ Your department's financial results are actually lower than what appears in your boss's presentation to the board of directors?

> ✔ You find out that your star employee actually didn't graduate from university as she claimed in her job application?

> ✔ You know that a product you sell doesn't actually do everything your company claims it does?

You make ethical choices in your job every day, and the decisions you take have an impact on your business. Consider these six keys to making good ethical choices:

E: Evaluate circumstances through the appropriate filters. Filters include culture, laws, policies, circumstances, relationships, politics, perceptions, emotions, values, biases, prejudice and religion.

T: Treat people and issues fairly within the established boundaries. And remember that fair doesn't always mean equal.

H: Hesitate before making critical decisions. (Richard calls this 'wait-a-minute'.)

I: Inform those affected of the standard/decision that you've set/made.

C: Create an environment of consistency for yourself and your working group.

S: Seek guidance when you have any doubt. Make sure that the guidance comes from honest people who've earned your respect.

Evaluating Your Political Environment

How political is your office or workplace? As a manager, having your finger on the political pulse of the organisation is particularly important. Otherwise, the next time you're in a management meeting you may blurt out, 'Why is it so difficult to get an employment requisition through human resources? You'd think it was their money!' only to later discover that the CEO's daughter-in-law heads the HR department.

With just a little bit of advance information and forethought, you can approach this issue much more tactfully. Being aware of your political environment can help you be more effective, and help your department and your employees have a greater impact within the organisation.

Assessing your organisation's political environment

Asking your colleagues insightful questions is one of the best ways to assess your organisation's political environment. Such questions show you to be the polite, mature and ambitious employee that you are, and are a sure sign of your well-developed political instincts.

Give these questions, or something like them, a try:

- What's the best way to get a special item approved?
- How can I get a product from the warehouse that my client needs today when I don't have time to do the paperwork?
- Can I do anything else for you before I go home for the day?

Although asking politically pointed questions gives you an initial indication of the political lie of the land, you can do more to assess the political environment in your organisation. Watch out for the following signs while you're getting a sense of how your organisation really works:

- **Find out how others who seem to be effective get tasks done.** How much time do they spend preparing before sending through a formal request? Which items do they delegate and to which subordinates? When you find people who are particularly effective at getting tasks done in your organisation's political environment, emulate them, and apply their methods to your own goals.

- **Observe how the organisation rewards others for the jobs they do.** Do managers swiftly and enthusiastically give warm and personal rewards in a sincere manner to make it clear what behaviour they consider important? Do they give credit to everyone who helped make a project successful, or is the manager the only one singled out for praise? By observing your company's rewards, you can tell what behaviour your organisation expects of employees. Practise this behaviour.

- **Observe how the organisation disciplines others and for what.** Do your managers come down hard on employees for relatively small mistakes? Do they criticise employees in public or in front of colleagues? Do they hold everyone accountable for decisions, actions and mistakes even if someone had no prior involvement? Such behaviour on the part of management indicates that they don't encourage risk taking. If your management doesn't encourage risk taking, make your political style outwardly reserved as you work behind the scenes.

✔ **Consider how people behave towards each other, and how appropriate their conduct is.** For example, blurting out 'That's a stupid idea. Why would we even consider doing such a thing?' in a staff meeting is clearly unacceptable. Make sure that people conduct themselves professionally at all times. A more appropriate statement is: 'That's an interesting possibility. Can we explore the pros and cons of implementing such a plan?' Make mutual respect standard behaviour in your company.

Identifying key players

So now that you've discovered that you work in a political environment (did you really have any doubt?), you need to determine who the key players are. Why? Because these individuals can help make your department more effective and provide positive role models to you and your employees.

Key players are those politically astute individuals who make things happen in an organisation. You can identify them by their tendency to make instant decisions without having to refer to people 'upstairs', their use of the latest corporate slang and their tendency to always speak up in meetings, if only to ask, 'What's our objective here?'

Sometimes influential people don't hold influential positions. For example, Jack, as the department head's assistant, may initially appear to be nothing more than a clerk. However, you may find out that Jack is responsible for scheduling all his boss's appointments, setting agendas for departmental meetings and vetoing actions on his own authority. Jack is an informal leader in the organisation and, because you can't get to the department head without going through Jack, you know that he has much more power than his title may indicate. You need to be able to influence those who act as gatekeepers to top and senior managers.

Use the following questions to identify the key players in your organisation:

✔ Which employees do others go to for advice?

✔ Which employees do others consider to be indispensable?

✔ Whose office is located closest to those of the organisation's top management and whose is farthest away? Evidence shows that the farther away you work from head office, the less influence you have.

✔ Who are the members of the inner circle? Who eats lunch with top and senior management?

As you work out who the key players in your organisation are, you start to notice that they have different office personalities. Use the following categories to help you figure out how to work with the different personality types of your organisation's key players:

- **Movers and shakers:** These individuals usually far exceed the boundaries of their office positions. For example, you may find a mover and shaker who's in charge of purchasing helping to negotiate a merger. Someone in charge of the physical plant may have the power to designate a wing of the building to the group of her choosing. Non-political individuals, on the other hand, tend to be bogged down by responsibilities – such as getting their own work done.

- **Corporate citizens:** These employees are diligent, hardworking, company-loving individuals who seek slow but steady, long-term advancement through dedication and hard work. Corporate citizens are great sources of information and advice. You can count on them for help and support, especially if your ideas seem to be in the best interest of the organisation.

- **Town gossips:** These employees always seem to know what's going on in the organisation – usually before those individuals who are actually affected by the news know it. Always assume that anything you say to a gossip will get back to the person your commenting on.

- **Firefighters:** These individuals relish rushing in at the last possible moment to save a project, client, deadline or whatever. High drama and great fanfare precede their arrival. Keep a firefighter well informed of your progress so that you aren't the subject of the next 'fire'.

- **Vetoers:** These people have the authority to kill your best ideas with a simple comment such as, 'We tried that and it didn't work.' Keeping them away from you is the best way to deal with vetoers. Try to find other individuals who can get your idea approved or rework it until you hit on an approach that satisfies the vetoer.

- **Techies:** Every organisation has technically competent workers who legitimately have a high value of their own opinions. Experts can take charge of a situation without taking over. Get to know your experts well – you can trust their judgements and opinions.

- **Moaners and whiners:** A few employees are never satisfied with whatever you do for them. Associating with them inevitably leads to a pessimistic outlook, which you can't easily turn around. Or worse, your boss may think that you're a whiner too. In addition, pessimistic people tend to get promoted less often than optimists. Be an optimist: your upbeat outlook can make a big difference to your career.

Redrawing your organisation chart

Your company's organisation chart may be useful for determining who's who in the formal organisation, but it really has no bearing on who's who in the informal political organisation. What you need is the real organisation chart. Figure 14-1 illustrates a typical official organisation chart.

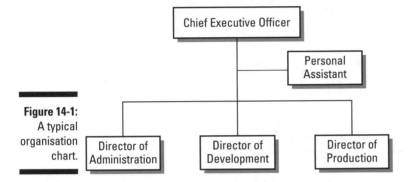

Figure 14-1:
A typical
organisation
chart.

Start by finding your organisation's official organisation chart – the one that looks like a big pyramid. Throw it away. Now, from your impressions and observations, start outlining the *real* relationships in your organisation in your mind. (But be careful! You don't always want people to know what you're up to.) Begin with the key players you've already identified. Indicate their relative power by level and relationships. Use the following questions as a guideline:

✔ **Who associates with these influential people?** Draw the associations on your chart and connect them with solid lines. Also connect friends and relatives, other clear associates and anyone who you know enjoys particular patronage or favour.

✔ **Who makes up the office cliques?** Be sure that all members are connected, because talking to one is like talking to them all.

✔ **Who are the office gossips?** Use dotted lines to represent communication without influence and solid lines for communication with influence.

✔ **Who's your competition?** Circle those employees that managers are likely to consider for the next promotion. Target them for special attention.

✔ **Who's left off the chart?** Don't forget about these individuals. The speed at which organisations change nowadays means that someone who's not featured on the chart on Friday may be on it by Monday. Always maintain positive relationships with all of your colleagues and never burn bridges between you and others throughout the company, whatever their position. Otherwise, you may find yourself omitted from the chart at some point.

The result of this exercise is a chart of who really has political power in your organisation and who doesn't. Figure 14-2 shows how the organisation really works. Update your organisation chart as you find out more information about people. Take note of any behaviour that gives away a relationship – such as your boss cutting off a colleague in mid-sentence – and factor this observation into your overall political analysis. Of course, understand that you may be wrong. You can't possibly know the inner power relationships of every department. Sometimes individuals who seem to have power may have far less of it than people who've discovered how to use their power more quietly.

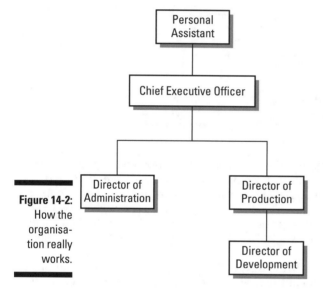

Figure 14-2:
How the organisation really works.

Scrutinising Communication: What's Real and What's Not?

One of the best ways to determine how well you fit into an organisation is to see how well you communicate. But deciphering the real meaning of communication in an organisation takes some practice. So how do you determine the underlying meaning of words in your organisation? By observing behaviour, reading between the lines and, when necessary, knowing how to obtain sensitive information – that's how.

Believing actions, not words

One way to decipher the real meaning of communication is to pay close attention to the corresponding behaviour of the communicator. People's values and priorities (that is, their ethics) tend to be revealed more clearly in what they do than what they say.

So, for example, if your manager repeatedly says she's trying to get approval for a pay rise for you, look at what actions she's taken towards that end. Did she make a call to her boss or hold a meeting? Did she submit the necessary paperwork or establish a deadline to accomplish this goal? If the answers to these questions are no, or if she's continually 'waiting to hear', the action is probably going nowhere fast. To counter this situation, try to get higher up on your boss's list of priorities by suggesting actions that she can take to get you your pay rise. You may find that you need to do some or all of the footwork yourself. Alternatively, your manager's actions may indicate that she doesn't wield much power in the organisation. If that's the case, then try to attract the attention of the power players who can help you get the pay rise you deserve.

Reading between the lines

In business, don't take the written word at face value. Probe to discover the real reasons behind written communications. For example, a typical notice in a company newsletter announcing the reorganisation of several departments may read like this:

> With the departure of JR McNeil, the Marketing Support and Customer Service Department will now be a part of the Sales and Administration Division under Elizabeth Olsen, acting divisional director. The unit will eventually be moved under the direct supervision of the sales director, Tom Hutton.

Such an announcement appears straightforward on the surface, but if you read between the lines, you may be able to conclude:

> JR McNeil, who never did seem to get along with the director of sales, finally did something bad enough to justify getting fired. Tom Hutton apparently made a successful bid with the board of directors to add the area to his empire, probably because his sales were up 30 per cent from last year. Elizabeth Olsen will be appointed as acting divisional director for an interim period to do some of Tom's dirty work by clearing out the dead wood. Tom thus starts with a clean slate, 20 per cent lower overheads and an almost guaranteed increase in profits for his first year in

the job. This all fits very nicely with Tom's personal strategy for advancement – both the organisation's and his own. (*PS: A nice congratulatory call to Tom may be in order.*)

Announcements like these have been written dozens of times by so many people that they appear to be logical and valid when you initially read them. By reading between the lines, however, you can often determine what's really going on. Of course, you have to be careful not to jump to the wrong conclusions. JR McNeil may have simply gone on to better opportunities and the company has taken advantage of that event to reorganise. Make sure to validate your conclusions with others in the company to get the real story.

Note the people who always seem to stay in a job for just two to three years. Do your best to check up on what they really achieve in each of these periods before moving on. Of course, many who do this do have a good track record of achievement behind them. But many others don't; and they always move on just before the mess that they've made becomes apparent. Richard calls these 'Errol Flynn managers' – like the great movie star, they're always just the right side of the drawbridge when it comes up!

Probing for information

In general, you can get excellent information about your organisation by being a trusted listener to as many people as possible. Show sincere interest in the affairs of others, and they may talk about themselves more openly. After they begin talking, you can shift the topic to work, work problems and eventually more sensitive topics. Ask encouraging questions and volunteer information as necessary to keep the exchange equitable.

Even after you've developed such trusted relationships, you need to know how to probe to uncover the facts about rumours, decisions and hidden agendas. Start by adhering to the following guidelines:

- ✔ Have at least three ways of obtaining the information.
- ✔ Check the information through two sources.
- ✔ Promise anonymity whenever possible.
- ✔ Generally, know the answers to the questions you ask.
- ✔ Be casual and non-threatening in your approach.
- ✔ Assume that the initial answer is superficial.
- ✔ Ask the same question in different ways.
- ✔ Be receptive to whatever information people give you.

Interpreting the company policy manual

Even when written in black and white, an organisation's policies are rarely what they appear to be. Most policies come about as a directive from the top to solve a particular problem. For example, if an employee wears gaudy jewellery to work, the individual can be asked to tone down her appearance in a two- to three-minute discussion. Often, however, managers respond to such a situation by appointing a task force to draw up a policy for dealing with it. For example, it may be tasked with developing a dress code and company plan for personal hygiene. Even after the policy is in place, the targeted individual may well be oblivious to any perceived problem and may even wholeheartedly endorse the new code 'for all those who need it'; that is, seemingly, everyone except the actual target. You can explain many policies in the same way.

Be alert to the following ways in which some employees try to shirk their responsibilities in relation to company policies:

✔ Referring to the policy only when it clearly supports exactly what they want to do.

✔ Assuming that a policy that doesn't support what they want is intended for others.

✔ Claiming an inability to equitably enforce policies they don't like by citing a rumoured abuse or possible misinterpretation.

✔ Arguing that a policy is too specific (for general application) or too general (for specific circumstances).

✔ Stating that all policies should be considered as flexible guidelines.

Some policies just don't work – and it's your job to recognise them and change or abandon them. For example, if you want to give your employees the flexibility to set their own work schedules, but company policy prohibits it, do whatever you can to enact a new policy that accomplishes your goal.

One more thing: if you find yourself in an organisation that's rife with political intrigue, where you're always looking over your shoulder and are wondering whether the next rumour will concern you, seriously consider changing jobs! Every organisation has its share of politics, but spending too much time worrying about it is certainly counterproductive, and it can't be good for your well-being.

Uncovering the Unwritten Rules of Organisational Politics

Every organisation has rules that are never written down and seldom discussed. Such unwritten rules pertaining to the expectations and behaviour of employees in the organisation can play a major role in your success or failure.

Because unwritten rules aren't explicit, you have to piece them together by observation, insightful questioning or simply through trial and error.

Never underestimate the power of the unwritten rules of organisational politics. In many companies the unwritten rules carry just as much importance, if not more, than the written rules contained in the company's policy manual.

Be friendly with all

The more individuals you have as friends in an organisation, the better. If you haven't already done so, start cultivating friends in your immediate work group and then extend your efforts to making contacts in other parts of the organisation. The more favourably your colleagues view you, the greater your chances of becoming their manager in the future. Cultivate your colleagues' support by seeking advice or by offering assistance.

You never know who you'll report to in the future. As one saying goes, 'Be nice to people on the way up because you may meet them on the way down.' And as an Arab proverb goes, 'Keep your friends close and hold your enemies closer.'

Build a network by routinely helping new employees who enter your organisation. As they join, be the person who takes them aside to explain how the organisation really works. As the new employees establish themselves and move on to other jobs in other parts of the organisation, you have a well-entrenched network for obtaining information and assistance.

Knowing people throughout the organisation can be invaluable for clarifying rumours, obtaining information and indirectly feeding information back to others. An astute manager maintains a large number of diverse contacts throughout the organisation, all on friendly terms. The following are excellent ways to enlarge your network:

- **Walk around.** Those managers who walk the floor tend to be better known than those who don't. Return telephone and email messages in person whenever possible. Not only do you have the opportunity for one-to-one communication with the individual who left you the message, but also you can stop by to see everyone else you know along the way.

- **Get involved.** You need to meet superiors, peers and colleagues from a wide range of functions, departments, divisions and locations, so take every opportunity that presents itself to do so. Attend meetings, discussion groups, professional gatherings and problem-solving forums; and always support social and informal events.

✔ **Join committees.** Whether the committee forms to address employee security or simply to determine who cleans out the refrigerator in the employee lounge, take part. You get to meet new people in an informal and relaxed setting.

Help others get what they want

A fundamental, unwritten rule of office politics is that getting what you want is easier when you give others what they want. Win the assistance of others by showing them what they stand to gain by helping you. When a benefit isn't readily apparent, create or allude to one that may occur if they offer to help. Such benefits can include:

✔ **A favour returned in kind:** Surely you can provide some kind of favour to your counterparts in exchange for their assistance. Lunch or the temporary secondment of an employee to their department is always a popular option.

✔ **Information:** Don't forget: information is power. Everyone desperately wants to know the latest and greatest information and gossip in an organisation – and your colleagues are no different. Be the one to give them information if you can.

✔ **Money:** Perhaps you have a little extra money in your equipment budget that you can allocate to someone's project in exchange for that person's help.

✔ **A recommendation:** Top and senior managers trust your judgement. Your willingness to recommend colleagues for promotion to a higher position or for recognition because of their extraordinary performance is a valuable commodity. The right words to the right people can make all the difference to someone's success in an organisation.

We're not suggesting that you do anything unethical or illegal. Don't violate your personal set of ethics or company policy to get ahead. When you provide these kinds of benefits to others in your organisation, make sure that you're within your company's rules and policies. And as a side benefit, you may actually find satisfaction in giving to others.

Don't party at company parties

Social affairs are a serious time for those employees seeking to advance within a company. Social events offer one of the few times when everyone in the company is supposed to be on an equal footing. Don't believe it, though.

Although social functions provide managers at the top with a chance to show that they're normal people and give employees below a chance to ask questions and laugh at their bosses' jokes, parties are also a time to be extremely cautious.

Beware of who you talk to and, of course, what you say. Social functions, such as Christmas parties and company picnics, aren't the time or the place to sink your career by making some injudicious comment or by making a fool of yourself. Managing most social encounters involves art and skill, especially those encounters that involve colleagues. If you have to attend such functions, then make them work to your advantage. Use these techniques at your next company party:

- Use the middle of the room to intercept individuals you especially want to speak to. As an alternative strategy for getting their attention, watch the buffet table or the punch bowl. Go for refills when the person you're seeking does so.

- Drink orange juice or mineral water. Never ever get drunk on the organisation's premises, in the organisation's time or at an organisational social function.

- Keep discussion loose and light and avoid talking about work topics with anyone other than your boss. Try to move on before the person you're speaking to runs out of topics to discuss and has a blank expression. Don't fawn or use flattery. These behaviours are more likely to lose respect for you than to gain it.

- Leave the social function only after the departure of the highest-ranking company official. If you have to leave before, let that person know why.

Manage your manager

Successful managers know the importance of managing not just their employees, but their manager as well. The idea is to encourage your manager to do what most directly benefits you and your staff. The following tried-and-tested techniques for manager management have evolved through the ages:

- **Keep your manager informed of your successes:** 'That last sale puts me over quota for the month.'

- **Support your manager in meetings:** 'Gadsby is right on this. We really do have to consider the implications of this change for our customers.'

- **Praise your manager publicly:** 'Mr Gadsby is probably the best manager I've ever worked for.'

Although a well-controlled relationship with your manager is important, you need connections to those above your manager too. A key relationship to develop is with your manager's manager – an individual who's likely to have a very big influence on your future career.

Volunteer for an assignment that happens to be one of your manager's boss's pet projects. If you do a good job, the senior boss may well ask you to carry out another project. Failing such an opportunity, try to find an area of common interest with your manager's boss. Bring up the topic in casual conversation and agree to meet later to discuss it in more detail. But do make sure that you maintain your own sense and appearance of integrity; don't create the impression that you're cavalier with the organisation's ranks, hierarchies and ways of working.

Move ahead with your mentors

Having a mentor is almost essential for ensuring any long-term success within an organisation. A *mentor* is an individual – usually someone higher up in the organisation – who provides advice and helps to guide your progress. (Chapter 5 has the lowdown on mentors.) Mentors are necessary because they can offer you important career advice, as well as becoming your advocate to higher levels of the organisation – the levels that you don't have direct access to.

Make sure the person you select as your mentor (or who selects you, as is more often the case) has organisational clout and is vocal about touting your merits. If possible, get the support of several powerful people throughout the organisation. *Sponsorships* (your relationships with your mentors) develop informally over an extended period of time.

Seek out a mentor by finding an occasion to ask for advice. If you find the advice extremely helpful, frequently seek more advice from the same person. Initially, ask for guidance related to your work, but as time goes on, you can ask for advice about business in general and your career advancement specifically. Proceed slowly, or your intentions may be suspect. Always display tact and discretion in your approach to your mentor:

- **The wrong approach:** 'Mr Fairmont, I've been thinking. In the marketing department, a lot of bad rumours have been going around about you and Suzy. I could try to squash some of them if I see something in it for me. You know: you take care of me, and I take care of you. What do you say?'

- **The right approach:** 'Here's that special report you asked for, Ms Smith. Correlating customer colour preferences with the size of orders in the Eastern region was fascinating. You seem to be one of the most forward-looking people in this organisation.'

Be trustworthy

Similar to having a mentor is being a loyal follower of an exceptional performer within the organisation. Finding good people to trust can be difficult, so if you're trustworthy, you're likely to become a valued associate of a bright peer. As that person rises quickly through the organisation, she can bring you along. However, whenever possible, make sure that you have many connections – when people fall, they fall very quickly and you don't want to go with them.

Protecting Yourself

Inevitably, you may find yourself on the receiving end of someone else's political aspirations. Astute managers take precautions to protect themselves – and their employees – against the political manoeuvrings of others. These precautions can also help if your own strategies go wrong. What can you do to protect yourself?

Document for protection

Document the progress of your department's projects and activities, especially when expected changes in plans or temporary setbacks affect them. Documenting the changes or setbacks gives you an accurate record of your projects' history and ensures that individuals who don't have your best interests at heart don't forget what happened (or inappropriately use what happened against you). The form of the documentation can vary, but the following are most common:

- Confirmation memos
- Activity reports
- Project folders
- Correspondence files
- Notes

Don't make promises you can't keep

Avoid making promises or firm commitments when you don't want to or can't follow them through. Don't offer a deadline, final price or guarantee of action or quality unless you're sure you can meet it. When you make promises that you can't fulfil, you risk injuring your own reputation when deliveries are late, or costs are higher than expected.

If you find yourself forced to make promises when you aren't certain you can meet them, consider taking one of the following actions:

✔ **Hedge.** If you have to make a firm commitment to an action that you're not sure you can meet, hedge your promise as much as possible by building in extra time, staff, money or some other qualifier.

✔ **Extend time estimates.** If you have to make a time commitment that may be unrealistic, extend the estimate (add extra time to what you think you really need) to give yourself room to manoeuvre. If your employees deliver early, they're heroes.

✔ **Extend deadlines.** As deadlines approach, bring any problems you or your staff encounter – even the most basic ones – to the attention of the person who requested that you do the project. Keeping people informed prevents them from being surprised if you need to extend your deadlines.

Be visible

To get the maximum credit for the efforts of you and your staff, be sure to publicise your department's successes. To ensure that credit goes where credit is due, do the following:

✔ **Advertise your department's successes.** Routinely send reports about successfully completed projects and letters of praise for every member of your staff to your manager and to your manager's boss.

✔ **Use surrogates.** Call on your friends in the organisation to help publicise your achievements and those of your employees. Be generous in highlighting your employees' achievements. If you highlight your own achievements at the expense of your hard-working staff, you appear tactless and boastful – and dishonest.

✔ **Be visible.** Make a name for yourself in the organisation. And performing at a level that separates you from the rest of the pack is the best way to do it. Work harder, work smarter and respond better to the needs of the organisation and your customers, and you get noticed!

Top five ethics and office politics websites

Wondering where to find the best information on the web about the topics we address in this chapter? Well, you've come to the right place! Here are our top five favourites:

✔ **Business for Social Responsibility:** www. bsr.org

✔ **Ethics Resource Center:** www.ethics. org

✔ **Office Politics:** www.officepolitics. co.uk

✔ **Corporate Social Responsibility:** www. csrnetwork.com/csr.asp

✔ **Corporate responsibility guide:** www. csr.gov.uk

Chapter 15

Managing Change at Work

In This Chapter

▶ Dealing with crises

▶ Processing change

▶ Helping others through change

▶ Inspiring initiative in others

▶ Moving on with your life

*N*othing stays the same, in business or in life. Change is all around us – it always has been, and it always will be. But although many people consider change something to fear and avoid at any cost, the reality is that change brings with it excitement, new opportunities and growth.

So what does change mean to you as a manager? The world of business is constantly changing, and the pressures on managers to perform are greater than they've ever been before. In addition, most organisations have gone from being bastions of stability and status quo in the stormy seas of change to being agile ships, navigating the fluid and ever-changing waters in which they float. 'Heywood, we've decided to reorganise the division. Starting tomorrow, you're in charge of our new factory in Singapore. I hope you like spicy food!'

The words *business* and *change* are quickly becoming synonymous. And the more things change, the more everyone in an organisation is affected. This chapter is about managing and thriving on change. It also covers helping your employees find ways to take advantage of change (instead of change taking advantage of them).

Peter Drucker stated: 'One does not manage change. One leads and directs change.' So *you* have to take the initiative!

Keeping Pace

What's your typical working day like? You get into the office, grab a cup of coffee and scan your appointment diary. Looks like a light day for meetings – two in the morning and only one in the afternoon. Maybe you can finally get a chance to work on the budget goal you've been meaning to complete for the past few months, plus have some extra time to go for a walk at lunch to unwind. (Wouldn't that be nice.) Next, you pick up your telephone to check your voice-mail. Of the 25 messages, ten are urgent. When you check your email, you find much the same ratio.

As you begin to formulate responses to these urgent messages, an employee arrives and tells you that the computer network has broken down, and until someone fixes it, the entire corporate financial system is inaccessible. While you're talking to your employee, your boss calls to tell you to drop everything because he's selected you to write a report for the chief executive that you absolutely have to do by the close of business today.

So much for working on your budget goal. And you can forget that relaxing walk at lunch. This day is turning out to be just another fun day in management!

Choosing between legitimate urgency and crisis management

Urgency has its place in an organisation. The rate of change in the global business environment demands it. The revolutions in computer use, telecommunications systems and information technology demand it. The necessity to be more responsive to customers than ever before demands it. And companies that provide the best solutions faster than anyone else are the winners. The losers are the companies that wonder what happened as they watch their competitors streak by.

However, an organisation has a real problem when its managers manage by crisis and fall into the trap of reacting to change instead of leading change. When every problem in an organisation becomes a drop-everything-else-you're-doing crisis, the organisation isn't showing signs of responsiveness to its business environment. Instead, it's showing signs of poor planning and lousy execution. Someone (perhaps a manager?) isn't doing their job.

Recognising and dealing with crises

Sometimes forces beyond your control as a manager cause crises. For example, suppose that a vital customer requests that you submit all project designs by this Friday instead of next Wednesday. Or perhaps the local council informs you that your plant will have no electricity for three days when maintenance is carried out on the underground cables. Or bad weather makes all flights into and out of the UK impossible for the rest of the week.

On the other hand, many crises occur because someone in your organisation makes a mistake, and now you (the manager) have to fix everything. The following are avoidable crisis situations:

- ✔ Hoping that a problem will go away, a manager avoids making a necessary decision. Surprise! The problem didn't solve itself, and now you have a crisis to deal with.

- ✔ An employee forgets to relay an important message from your customer, and you're about to lose the account as a result. Another crisis. (See Chapter 16 for how to discipline employees.)

- ✔ A colleague decides that informing you about a major change to a manufacturing process isn't important. As a result of your experience, you'd have quickly seen that the change was likely to lead to quality problems in the finished product. When manufacturing grinds to a halt, you come in after the fact to clean up the mess. One more crisis to add to your list.

You need to be prepared to deal with externally generated crises. You have to be flexible, you have to know your stuff and you need to know what can go wrong. But your organisation can't afford to become a slave to internally generated crises. Managing by crisis forgoes one of the most important elements in business management. That element is *planning*.

You establish plans and goals for a reason – to make your company as successful as possible. However, if you continually set your plans and goals on the back-burner because of today's crisis, why waste your time making plans in the first place? And where does your organisation go then? (Chapter 6 covers the importance of having plans and goals.)

When you, as a manager, allow everything to become a crisis through your own inaction or failure to anticipate change, not only do you sap the energy of your employees, eventually they also lose the ability to recognise when a real crisis exists. After responding to several manufactured crises, your employees begin to see these situations as routine, and they may not be there for you when you really need them.

Embracing Change

Change happens, and you can't do anything about it. You can try to ignore change, but does that stop it? No, you only blind yourself to what's really happening in your organisation. You can try to stop change, but does that keep it from happening? No, you're only fooling yourself if you think that you can stop change – even for a moment. You can try to insulate yourself and those employees around you from the effects of change, but can you really afford to ignore it? No, to ignore change is to sign a death warrant for your organisation and, quite possibly, for your career.

Unfortunately, our personal observations tell us that most managers seem to spend their entire careers trying to fight change – to predict and control it and its effects on the organisation. But why? Change is what allows organisations to progress, products and services to get better and people to advance, both personally and in their careers.

If you're in charge of leading, directing and managing change, you give yourself the best possible chance of success by breaking down what needs to be done into the following components: change from what, to what, when, where, how and why.

Identifying the four stages of change

Change isn't a picnic. Despite the excitement that change can bring to your working life – both good and bad – you've probably had just about all the change you can handle right now, thank you. But as change continues, you go through four distinct phases in response:

1. **Deny change.**

   When change happens, your first response (if you're like most people) is immediate denial. 'Whose stupid idea was that? That idea is never going to work here. Don't worry, they'll see their mistake and go back to the old way of doing things!' This attitude resembles an ostrich sticking its head in the sand: if you can't see the change, it goes away. You wish!

2. **Resist change.**

   At some point, you realise that the change isn't just a clerical error; however, this realisation doesn't mean that you have to accept the change lying down. Resistance is a normal response to change – everyone goes through it. The key is to not let your resistance hold you back. The quicker you accept the change, the better for both your organisation and your career.

3. **Explore change.**

   By now, you know that further resistance is futile and the new way just may have some pluses. 'Well, maybe that change actually does make sense. And I can see opportunities for making the change work for me instead of against me.' During this stage, you examine both the positive and negative implications of the change, and decide on a strategy for managing them.

4. **Accept change.**

   The final stage of change is acceptance. At this point you've successfully integrated the change into your routine. Now the change that you so vigorously denied and resisted is part of your everyday routine; the change is now the status quo.

At the end of your change responses, you come full circle, and you're ready to face your next change.

When you ask people to face up to great changes, describe them within a personal context. Ask employees to think about changes in their personal lives, such as moving house, getting married or divorced, having children or changing career. You go through exactly the same cycle of emotions when you have to face changes at work.

Figuring out whether you're fighting change

You may be fighting change and not even know it. Besides watching the number of grey hairs on your head multiply, how can you tell? Look out for these seven deadly warning signs of resistance to change:

- ✔ **You're still using the old rules to play a new game.** Sorry to be the ones to bring you this bad news, but the old game is gone; lost forever. The pressures of global competition have created a brand new game with a brand new set of rules. For example, if you're one of those increasingly rare managers who refuses to find out how to use a computer (don't laugh, they do exist!), you're playing by the old rules. Information and communications technology (ICT) literacy forms the new rule. If you're not playing by the new rules, not only is this a warning sign that you're resisting change, but you can bet on being left behind as the rest of your organisation moves along to the future.

- ✔ **You're dodging new assignments.** You may behave in this way for one of two reasons. One, your current job may be overwhelming you and you can't imagine taking on any more duties. If you're in this situation, try to remember that new ways often make your work more efficient or even wipe out many old things that you do. Two, you may simply be uneasy with the unknown, and so you resist change.

Dodging new assignments to resist change is an old game. One very common practice is for those who are resisting change to create present crises, and then to fill their entire working lives clearing up the mess – the mess that they themselves have made.

- ✔ **You're trying to slow things down.** Trying to slow down is a normal reaction for most people. When something new comes along – a new way of doing business, a new assignment or a new approach to the marketplace – most people tend to want to slow down, to give themselves time to examine and analyse the facts, and then decide how to react.

As a manager, you want to remain competitive in the future. You don't have the luxury of slowing down every time something new comes along. From now on, the amount of new stuff that you have to deal with is going to greatly outweigh the old. Instead of resisting the new by slowing down (and risking making your organisation uncompetitive and obsolete), you need to keep up your pace. How? When you're forced to do more with less, focus on less.

✔ **You're working hard to control the uncontrollable.** Have you ever tried to keep the sun from rising in the morning; or clouds from dropping rain on your head? How about trying to remain 29 years old forever? Face it: you just can't control many things in life – and you're wasting your time if you try.

Are you resisting change by trying to control the uncontrollable at work? Perhaps you want to try to delay a planned corporate reorganisation, or block your foreign competitors from having access to your domestic markets, or stop a much larger company acquiring your firm. The world of business is changing all around you, and you can't do anything about it. You have a choice: you can continue to resist change by pretending that you're controlling it (believe us, you can't), or you can concentrate your efforts on working out how to respond to change most effectively in order to ensure that everything works to your advantage.

✔ **You're playing the role of victim.** Oh, woe is me! This response is the ultimate cop-out. Instead of accepting change and finding out how to respond to it (and using it to the advantage of your organisation and yourself), you choose to become a victim of it. Playing the role of victim and hoping that your colleagues feel sorry for you is easy to do: 'Poor Samantha, she's got a brand new crop of upstart competitors to handle. I wonder how she can even bring herself to come to work every morning!'

But today's successful businesses can't afford to waste their time or money employing victims. If you're not giving 100 per cent each day that you go to work, your organisation may well find someone who can.

✔ **You're hoping someone else can make things better for you.** In the old-style hierarchical organisation, top management almost always took responsibility for making the decisions that made things better (or worse) for workers. We have a newsflash: the old-style organisation is changing, and the new-style organisation that's taking its place has empowered every employee to take responsibility for decision making.

Global competition, information systems and technology, and the need for flexibility and responsiveness all require you to make decisions more quickly than ever. In other words, the employees closest to the issues must make the decisions; a manager who's seven layers up from the front line and 3,000 miles away can't do it. You hold the keys to your future. You have the power to make things better for yourself. If you wait until someone else makes things better for you, you're going to be waiting an awfully long time.

✔ **You're absolutely paralysed, like a rabbit in the headlights.** This condition is the ultimate sign of resistance to change and is almost always terminal. Sometimes change seems so overwhelming that the only choice is to give up. When change paralyses you, not only do you fail to respond to change, but also you can no longer perform your current duties. In today's organisation, such resistance is certain death.

Instead of allowing change to paralyse you, become a leader of change. Here are some ideas for how to do this:

- Embrace the change. Become its friend and its biggest cheerleader.

- Be flexible and be responsive to the changes that swirl all around you and through your organisation.

- Be a model to those employees around you who continue to resist change. Show them that they can make change work for them instead of against them.

- Focus on what you can do – not what you can't do.

- Recognise and reward employees who've accepted the change and who've succeeded as a result.

If you notice any of these warning signs of resistance to change – in yourself or in your colleagues – you can do something about it. As long as you're willing to embrace change instead of fighting it, you hold incredible value for your organisation, and you can take advantage of change rather than falling victim to it. Make responsiveness to change your personal mission: be a leader of change, not a follower of resistance.

Aiding Your Employees through Change

When your organisation finds itself in the midst of change – whether because of fast-moving markets, changing technology, rapidly shifting customer needs or some other reason – you need to remember that change affects everyone, not just you as a manager. And although some of your employees can cope with change with hardly a hiccup, others may have a very difficult time adjusting to their new environment and the expectations that come along with it. Be on the alert for employees who are resisting or having a hard time dealing with change, and then help them make the transition through the process.

The following tips can help your employees cope with change on the job:

✔ **Show that you care.** Managers are very busy people, but don't ever be too busy to show your employees that you care – especially when they're having difficulties at work. Take a personal interest in your employees and offer to help them in any way you can.

✔ **Widely communicate the potential for change.** Nothing is more disconcerting to employees than being surprised by changes that they didn't expect. As much as possible, give your employees a full briefing on potential changes in the business environment, and keep them up to date on the status of the changes as time goes on.

✔ **Seek feedback.** Let your employees know that you want their feedback and suggestions on how to deal with potential problems resulting from change, or about how to capitalise on any opportunities that may result.

✔ **Be a good listener.** When your employees are in a stressful situation, they naturally want to talk about it – this part of the process helps them cope with change. Set aside time to chat informally with employees, and encourage them to voice their concerns about the changes that they and the organisation are going through.

✔ **Don't give false assurances.** Although you don't want to needlessly frighten your employees with tales of impending doom and gloom, you must tell them the truth. Be frank and honest with your employees and treat them like the adults they are.

✔ **Involve employees.** Involve employees in planning for upcoming changes, and delegate the responsibility and authority for making decisions to them whenever practicable.

✔ **Look to the future.** Paint a vision for your employees that emphasises the many ways in which the organisation can be a better place as everyone adapts to change and begins to use it to their benefit.

Change can be traumatic for the people who are experiencing it. Stay alert to the impact of change on your employees, and help them work their way through it. Not only will your employees appreciate your support, showing their appreciation with loyalty to you and your organisation, but also morale will improve and your employees will be more productive as a result.

Encouraging Employee Initiative

One of the most effective ways to help employees make it through a change process in one piece is to give them permission to take charge of their own work. You can encourage employees to take the initiative in coming up with ideas to improve the way they work, and then to implement those ideas. The most successful organisations are the ones that actively encourage employees to take the initiative, and the least successful are those that stifle it.

So make sure that everyone knows what you're trying to achieve, and then get everyone involved. The following examples illustrate effective and not-so-effective strategies for managing change:

- **VXR Radio:** VXR Radio, a commercial music station, gave notice that its broadcasting equipment was to be replaced and upgraded. It required that all staff be trained in the new equipment so that when switch-over day came no glitches or hiccups occurred. One shift manager accordingly scheduled all her staff on training courses provided by the manufacturers of the new equipment over the three months' lead time. When the changeover came, her people transferred smoothly and effortlessly. They were involved in the new processes right from the start, they were fully familiar with the machinery and they knew how to operate it to broadcast standard.

- *The Times* **and** *The Sun* **versus the** *Financial Times***:** Following the revolution in newspaper printing in the UK in the 1980s, many newspapers moved from traditional printing presses and technology in Fleet Street to new premises and processes in Wapping. A major dispute erupted involving News International, then owner of *The Times* and *The Sun* newspapers, and members of the National Union of Journalists (NUJ) over new terms and conditions of employment associated with the move. For many weeks fighting occurred outside printing establishments, and journalists, managers and printers were victimised, harassed and beaten up.

  Contrast this with the experience of the *Financial Times*, whose staff also moved to premises in Wapping the same week without fuss, bother or conflict. The owners of the *Financial Times* simply told staff what they required, and then left the staff to implement the changes. Top managers provided the resources, information and reassurances necessary and the organisation achieved the move with full involvement – and no conflict whatsoever.

As a manager, you need to make your employees feel secure enough to take the initiative in their jobs. Not only does feeling secure help your employees more successfully weather the change that swirls all around them, as a result they also create a more effective organisation and provide better service to customers in the process. Ask your employees to take the following suggestions and put them into practice:

- Look for ways to make improvements to the status quo, and follow through with an action plan.

- Focus suggestions on areas that have the greatest impact on the organisation.

✔ Follow up suggestions with action – and, where necessary, implement your own suggestions and recommendations.

✔ Use what you're doing to look for areas of improvement throughout the organisation, not just within your department or business unit.

✔ Don't make frivolous suggestions. They reduce your credibility and distract you from more important areas of improvement.

Making Changes within Yourself

If you've done everything you can to deal with change at work and take control of your business life, but you're still feeling lost, you may be facing a much deeper issue that's not readily apparent on the surface.

When you read a book, do you ever wish that you'd written it? When you go to a seminar, do you ever think that you could teach it? Have you ever wondered what owning your own business is like, being your own boss and completely responsible for your company's profits or losses? If you answered 'yes' to any of these questions, you may not be truly happy until you pursue your dream. Maybe you want to start a new career or move to a new company. Or perhaps you have an opportunity with your current employer to make a job change that can take you to your dream. Maybe you want to go back to university to pursue an advanced degree. Or maybe you just want to take a holiday or a short leave of absence. It may very well be that all the change you need to make is within yourself.

Top five change management websites

Check out our top five favourite sites for managing change:

✔ **ManagementFirst:** www.management first.com/experts/change.htm

✔ **Managing Change:** www.managing change.com

✔ **Change Management Learning Centre:** www.change-management.com

✔ **Teach First:** www.teachfirst.org.uk

✔ **The Carnegie Foundation for Change:** www.dalecarnegie.co.uk

Chapter 16

Setting Standards and Enforcing Them: Employee Discipline

In This Chapter

▶ Disciplining your employees

▶ Setting standards

▶ Following the twin tracks of discipline – performance and behaviour

▶ Writing a script

▶ Developing improvement plans

▶ Putting improvement plans into action

*W*ouldn't it be nice if all your employees always carried out their tasks perfectly and loved the organisation as much as you do? Unfortunately, in the real world, employees do make mistakes, and some of them may exhibit poor attitudes towards work. Every organisation has employees (and managers) who make mistakes from time to time – everyone does so occasionally. However, when your employees make repeated, serious mistakes, when they fail to meet their performance goals and standards or when it seems that they'd rather be working somewhere else (anywhere but where they are now!) and they prove that by ignoring company policies, you have to take action to remedy the situation – immediately and decisively.

Employees who aren't performing to agreed standards or who allow a poor attitude to overcome their ability to pull with the rest of the team, cost your organisation more than do conscientious and hardworking employees. Poor performance and attitude directly and negatively affect your work unit's efficiency and effectiveness. Also, if other employees see that you're letting their colleagues get away with poor performance, they have little reason to maintain their own standards. Not only do you create more management headaches, but also the morale and performance of your entire work unit decrease as a result.

This chapter covers the importance of dealing with employee performance issues before they become major problems. We explain why you need to focus on performance and not personality. We also introduce and show you how to implement a consistent system of discipline that can work for you, regardless of your line of business.

Understanding the Need for Employee Discipline

Employee discipline has a bad name. Because of the abuses that some over-zealous supervisors and managers have committed, the word *discipline* conjures up visions of crazed management tirades, embarrassing public scoldings and worse – bullying, victimisation, discrimination and harassment. The reality is that many employees confuse the terms *discipline* and *punishment*, considering them to be one and the same. This belief can't be farther from the truth, at least when discipline is done well.

The word *discipline* comes from the Latin *disciplina*, meaning teaching or learning. In organisations, discipline comes from several sources:

✔ Within the individual, reflecting their personal, professional and occupational commitment

✔ Within the work group, reflecting the collective commitment and team spirit that are present

✔ Within the organisation, reflecting the set and established overall standards

Punishment, on the other hand, is derived from the Latin root *punire*, which itself derives from the Latin word *poena*, or penalty. Interestingly, the English word *pain* also found its beginnings in the Latin *poena*.

 This little digression serves to point out that employee discipline ought to be a positive experience. At least when you do it the right way! Through discipline you bring small concerns to your employees' attention so that they can take actions to correct them before they become major problems.

The primary goal of discipline isn't to punish your employees; you want to help guide them back to a satisfactory job performance. Of course, sometimes this step isn't possible, and you have no choice but to dismiss employees who can't perform satisfactorily. However, dismissal is the very last resort, and you only use it when you've exhausted all other options.

Two main reasons to discipline your employees exist:

- ✔ **Performance problems:** All employees must meet goals as part of their jobs. For a receptionist, a goal may be to answer the telephone on the third ring or sooner. For a sales manager, a goal may be to increase annual sales by 15 per cent. When employees fail to meet their performance goals, you have to administer some form of discipline.

- ✔ **Behaviour and misconduct:** Sometimes employees behave in ways that neither you as a manager nor the organisation can accept. For example, if an employee abuses the company sick leave policy, you have a valid reason for disciplining that employee. And you must always discipline employees who sexually harass or threaten other employees.

In practice, discipline ranges from simple verbal exchanges – 'William, your report was a day late. You must submit future reports on time' – to more serious matters, handled formally – 'Sorry, Mahmood, I warned you that I can't tolerate any further insubordination. I'm now treating this as a formal disciplinary matter.' A wide variety of options lies between these two extremes, the use of which depends on the nature of the problem, its severity and the work history of the employee involved. For example, if the problem is an isolated incident and the employee normally performs well, the discipline you dish out is less severe than if the problem is repeated and persistent.

Always carry out discipline as soon after the relevant incident as possible. As with rewarding employees, your message is much stronger and more relevant when it has the immediacy of a recent event. If too much time lapses between an incident and the discipline that you conduct afterwards, your employee may forget the specifics of the incident. Not only that, but you also send the message that the problem isn't that serious because you didn't bother doing anything about it for so long.

Managers practise effective discipline when they notice performance shortcomings or misconduct before these problems become serious. Effective managers help to guide their employees along the right path. Managers who don't discipline their employees have only themselves to blame when poor performance continues unabated or acts of misconduct escalate and get out of hand. Employees need the active support and guidance of their supervisors and managers to know what the organisation expects of them. Without this guidance, employees sometimes find it difficult to keep on the right path.

Following Procedures

This part of the manager's job is quite simple – you must follow procedures! Statutory provisions and procedures cover all aspects of employee discipline, so before you do anything or tackle anyone, you must commit yourself to following whatever procedures your organisation has in place. Failure to follow your own organisation's procedure normally renders any subsequent dismissal *automatically unfair*, no matter what the employee has actually done.

Disciplinary procedures exist to protect everyone involved – you, the employee and the organisation – and to ensure that you deal with everything in a fair, even and impartial way.

Your company probably has its own disciplinary procedures. If it doesn't, the procedures that the Advisory, Conciliation and Arbitration Service (ACAS) publishes are normally deemed to apply; you must follow these standards or be prepared to give substantial reasons why you didn't. If you don't follow the correct procedures, the disciplinary action you take is normally deemed in law to be automatically unfair (and this also applies to dismissal; see Chapter 17).

Your business's disciplinary procedures must meet the following criteria:

- ✔ They must be in writing, stating to whom they apply and how they're to be applied.

- ✔ The organisation must publish and issue them and make them available to all staff.

- ✔ They must consist of a series of warnings, both oral and written.

- ✔ They must give examples of gross misconduct that triggers summary dismissal when proved (see the section 'Dealing with misconduct: The second track', later in this chapter). In addition, your procedures must allow employees to be accompanied and/or represented when they're facing disciplinary matters; and all procedures must allow for an appeals process, even where summary dismissal is the outcome.

Managers and supervisors need to know the disciplinary procedures, what they can and can't do and when and where to go for help. Your organisation should train and brief all employees in the content of the procedures so that they understand the triggers for disciplinary action for both behaviour and performance issues.

When facing a disciplinary issue, employees are entitled to respond to your statement of the facts and to state their own case. If you're accusing employees of a serious breach of conduct or performance, they're entitled to face their accusers and refute the charges (if they can).

The law requires disciplinary warnings to include a clear statement of what's wrong; what needs to happen now and by when; how, when and where progress is to be checked, and who checks progress; and any further follow-up action deemed necessary.

Focusing on Performance, Not Personalities

You're a manager (or a manager-to-be). You're not a psychiatrist or a psychologist – even if you feel that you sometimes do nothing but give counselling to your employees. Your job isn't to analyse your workers' personalities or to attempt to understand why your employees act the way they do – no one can read minds about things like attitude. Your job *is* to assess your employees' performance against the standards that you and your employees agree to and to be alert to employees' violations of company policy. If your employees are performing above standard, reward them for their efforts. (Refer to Chapter 4 for information on rewarding and motivating your employees.) If, on the other hand, they're performing below standard, you need to find out why (possibly a process, motivation or training problem is out of a particular employee's control) and, if necessary, discipline them.

We're not saying that you shouldn't be compassionate. Sometimes employees' performance suffers because of family problems, financial difficulties or other pressures unrelated to the job. Although you can give your employees the opportunity to get through their difficulties – you may suggest some time off or a temporary reassignment of duties – they eventually have to return to meeting their performance standards.

If personal problems or other difficulties are overwhelming an employee, you need to encourage her to seek confidential help from professional sources, through your organisation's employee assistance or support programme, occupational health department or other professional support. Your job as a manager isn't to tackle this yourself; your job is to see that the employee is properly supported.

To be fair, and to be sure that discipline focuses on performance and not on personalities, ensure that all employees fully understand company policies and that you communicate these policies clearly. When your organisation takes on new employees, make sure they get an induction to key company policies. When your human resources representative drops off new employees at your office door, take the time to discuss your department's philosophy and practices. Periodically sit down with your employees to review and update their performance standards.

When you apply discipline, use it consistently and fairly. Always follow procedures. Although you must always discipline your employees as soon as possible after a shortfall in performance or act of misconduct, rushing to judgement before you have all the facts is a mistake. Take time out to investigate where doing so is necessary or desirable; and you must investigate fully when you're dealing with allegations of serious or gross misconduct. When you do confront employees with their misdemeanours, ask a clear question: 'Can you give me an explanation?'

You need to treat all employees exactly the same, regardless of seniority, occupation, length of service or hours worked. Not to do so simply invites trouble, in the form of action (potentially including legal action) that an employee may take against you, or lobbying from those you've treated more harshly.

Identifying the Two Tracks of Discipline

Two key reasons exist for disciplining employees: performance problems and misconduct (see the section 'Understanding the Need for Employee Discipline', earlier in this chapter). The twin-track system of discipline includes one set of discipline options for performance problems and another for misconduct. These tracks reflect the fact that misconduct, usually an employee's wilful act, is a much more serious transgression than a shortfall in performance. Performance problems often aren't the employee's direct fault and you can usually correct them with proper training or motivation.

These two tracks reflect the concept of *progressive discipline*. Progressive discipline means that you always select the least severe step that results in the change in behaviour or performance that you want.

You must have disciplinary procedures, and these must be available to all employees. Disciplinary procedures must state the nature of warnings and sanctions, and how long any warning is to remain on file. You use disciplinary procedures as the basis of recording the nature of the misdemeanour, the actions taken and the outcomes.

All warnings must be formally notified to the employee, whatever the eventual outcome. For example, if your employee responds to a verbal warning and improves as a result, then you can move on to your next management challenge. However, if the employee doesn't respond to a verbal warning, you then progress to the next step – reconvening the disciplinary matter with the view to issuing a written warning.

So, as you prepare to discipline your employees, first decide whether you're trying to correct performance-related behaviour or misconduct. Then decide the best way to get your message across. If the transgression is minor – a lack of attention to detail, for example – you may only need to conduct a short conversation. Anything more serious, requiring formal disciplinary action, requires you to notify the employee of that action in writing – (again!) follow the procedures!

Dealing with performance problems: The first track

If you've done your job right, each of your employees has a job description and a set of performance standards. The job description is an inventory of all the duties that accompany a particular position. Performance standards, on the other hand, are the measurements that you and your employees agree to use in assessing your employees' performance. Performance standards form the basis of periodic performance appraisals and reviews.

Although every organisation seems to have its own unique way of conducting performance assessments, employees usually fall into one of three broad categories:

- Outstanding performance
- Acceptable performance
- Unacceptable performance

When it comes to employee discipline, you're primarily concerned with correcting unacceptable performance. You always want to help your good employees become even better employees, but your first concern has to be to identify employees who aren't working to standard and to correct their performance shortcomings.

Many organisations have procedures to deal with poor performance that are separate from their approaches to bad behaviour and misconduct. Again, whichever is the case in your organisation, you must enforce the procedures fairly and evenly. Again, if you get as far as the formal stages in managing unacceptable performance, you must state your case in writing; allow the employee to respond; allow the employee to be accompanied or represented; and make a clear statement about what's to happen as a result of the particular case.

We list the following disciplinary actions in order of least to most severe. Don't forget: use the least severe step that results in the behaviour you want. If that step doesn't do the trick, move down the list to the next step:

- **Verbal guidance, counselling and support:** This form of discipline is certainly the most common step that managers take first when they want to correct an employee's performance. A manager verbally counsels a variety of employees many times a day. Verbal counselling can range from a simple, spontaneous correction performed in the corridor ('Jasmine, you need to let me know when our clients call with a service problem') to a more formal, sit-down meeting in your office ('Sam, I'm concerned that you don't understand the importance of checking the correct address prior to shipping orders. Let's discuss what steps you're going to take to correct this problem and your plan to implement them'). Some organisations treat this discussion as an informal warning, particularly if the individual has had many instances of verbal guidance and counselling without a visible improvement in performance. You may, or may not, choose to put a note in the individual's personnel file (not forgetting that the employee has a right to see what's in his file);

you ought, in any case, to make a note in your own diary of who you spoke to, and what you spoke about.

✔ **Written counselling:** When employees don't respond favourably to verbal counselling, or when the magnitude of performance problems warrants a different approach, consider written counselling. Written counselling formalises the counselling process by documenting your employees' performance shortcomings in a written memo. The supervisor presents written counselling to an employee in a one-to-one session. After the employee has an opportunity to read the document, you can discuss the employee's plans to improve his performance. This documentation becomes a part of your employee's personnel file.

✔ **Moves and transfers:** If, with the best will in the world, a particular employee is simply not getting the hang of the job, then a move to new duties may be best for all concerned. Consult with the employee and see what he thinks. However, if he's perfectly happy struggling with the job, you nevertheless have to make it clear that this situation can only go on for so long. Put a clear time limit on when the performance has to improve; and make it clear that, if no improvement is forthcoming, the two of you are going to have to sit down and make alternative plans. In all cases, support the employee as much as you can and give him the best possible chance to improve.

✔ **Dismissal:** When all else fails, dismissal is the ultimate form of discipline for employees who are performing unsatisfactorily. As any manager who's fired an employee knows, dismissing employees isn't fun. Consider it as an option only after you exhaust all other avenues.

Perhaps needless to say, in these days of unfair and wrongful dismissal and high levels of compensation, you must document employees' performance shortcomings very well and support them with facts. For further information on the ins and outs of this important form of discipline, see Chapter 17.

Dealing with misconduct: The second track

Misconduct is a wholly different animal from performance problems, so it has its own discipline track. Although both misconduct and performance problems can have negative effects on a company's bottom line, misconduct is usually considered to be much more serious than performance shortcomings because it indicates a problem with your employees' attitudes or ethics. And modifying performance behaviours is a great first step in eventually modifying workers' attitudes or belief systems.

Misconduct covers any aspect of employee behaviour. What constitutes misconduct varies between organisations and occupations, and managers have to make their own judgement on this, within the constraints of the given situation. It's usual to specify:

- ✔ **Serious misconduct,** such as persistent bad timekeeping or frequent absenteeism, which is likely to lead to sanctions and/or dismissal if the employee doesn't remedy it.

- ✔ **Gross misconduct,** which normally leads to dismissal when proved. Organisations normally have to provide written examples of what constitutes gross misconduct in their disciplinary procedures (see the section 'Following Procedures', earlier in this chapter). The usual examples are bullying, victimisation, discrimination and harassment; physical and verbal violence and abuse; fraud and theft; and misusing drugs and alcohol.

The discipline that results from misconduct has much more immediate consequences for your employees than does the discipline that results from performance problems. Although performance may take some time to bring up to standard – what with preparing a plan, scheduling additional training and so forth – misconduct has to stop right now! When you discipline your employees for misconduct, you put them on notice that you don't tolerate their behaviour.

Your organisation's disciplinary procedure must incorporate at least two levels of warning, verbal and written, to meet statutory requirements. Make sure that you adhere to this procedure. The only exceptions are for serious or gross misconduct, in which case you may proceed to a final warning or to dismissal where the case against the employee is proved.

As in the first track, you have a progressive approach from least to most severe. Your choice depends on the nature of the misconduct; and the employee's work record may also influence you (for example, if the employee has had recent warnings for misconduct, you may move on to the second or final warning).

- ✔ **Verbal order:** When you catch employees doing something wrong, you simply speak to them and tell them that you don't tolerate their behaviour. This has the desired effect in the overwhelming majority of cases. If the verbal order doesn't work and the employee doesn't change his behaviour, then you're into a formal disciplinary situation, and you need to issue a formal warning.

- ✔ **First warning:** When an employee's misconduct is minor or a first offence, but he hasn't responded to verbal orders and directions, the first warning provides the least severe option for putting him on notice that you're aware of the misconduct and determined to do something about it. At each warning, the employee receives a written confirmation of his warning, together with what happens next if his behaviour or conduct doesn't improve. In many cases where the verbal order didn't work, a first warning is all that the situation requires.

- ✔ **Second warning:** Unfortunately, not all your employees get the message when you give them a first warning. Also, the magnitude of the offence may require that you skip the first warning and proceed directly to the second or even final warning – this applies especially to persistent breaches of health and safety guidelines, or disrespectful conduct that falls immediately short of outright harassment. All written warnings signal to your employee that you're serious and that you're documenting his behaviour for his personnel file.

- ✔ **Final warning:** Where, despite all your best efforts, behaviour and conduct aren't improving, you proceed to a final warning. The final warning states clearly that if behaviour and conduct don't improve, dismissal is your next option. Make it clear in the final warning who'll review the employee's conduct and behaviour, when and where, and make sure that you stick to this timetable.

- ✔ **Suspension:** Where serious allegations are made against an individual, you usually suspend them from work while you conduct an investigation. Suspension should normally be on full pay; the employee is, after all, innocent until proved guilty. If you do suspend someone without pay, you must have substantial reasons for doing so and be prepared to give those reasons in writing.

- ✔ **Dismissal:** In particularly serious cases of misconduct, dismissal may be your first choice in disciplining a worker. This rule is particularly true for extreme violations of safety rules, theft, gross insubordination and other gross misconduct. Dismissal may also be the result of repeated misconduct that less severe discipline steps don't correct. See Chapter 17 for more information about dismissing employees.

Disciplining Employees: A Suite in Five Parts

One right way and many wrong ways to discipline employees exist. Forget the many wrong ways for now and focus on the right way. Whatever the disciplinary situation you're facing, follow your organisation's procedures and document everything.

Structure your approach around the steps outlined in the following sections. By following these five steps you can be sure that your employees understand what the problem is, why it exists and what they need to do to correct it.

Describing the unacceptable behaviour

Make clear exactly what your employee is doing that's unacceptable. When describing unwanted behaviour to an employee, be excruciatingly specific. Don't make vague statements such as 'You have a bad attitude' or 'You make a lot of mistakes' or 'I don't like your work habits'.

Always relate unacceptable behaviour to specific performance standards that the employee hasn't met or to specific policies that the employee has broken. Specify exactly what the employee did wrong and when the behaviour occurred. Be sure to focus on the behaviour and not on the individual.

Following are some examples of describing behaviour for you to consider:

✔ Your performance last week was below the acceptable standard of 250 units per week.

✔ You failed the drug test you took on Monday.

✔ The last three analyses you submitted to me contained numerous mathematical errors.

✔ You've been late to work three out of four days this week.

Expressing the impact to the work unit

When an employee engages in unacceptable behaviour – whether her work doesn't meet the organisation's standards or she engages in misconduct – the behaviour typically affects the work unit negatively. When an employee is consistently late to work, for example, you may have to have someone else to cover that employee's position until the offender finally turns up. Doing so takes your other employee away from the work that she should be doing, reducing the efficiency and effectiveness of the work unit. And when an employee engages in sexual harassment, if you don't immediately do something about it, you're in fact tolerating that behaviour, which can lead to the harassed person taking legal action against you as an employer.

Continuing with the examples that we use in the preceding section, following are the next steps in your discipline script:

✔ Because of your below-standard performance, the work unit didn't meet its overall targets for the week.

✔ This specifically breaks our drug-free workplace policy.

✔ Because of these errors, I now have to take extra time to check your work before I can forward it onwards.

✔ Because of your lateness, I had to pull Helen from her position to cover yours.

Specifying the required changes

Telling your employee that she did something wrong does little good if you don't also tell that employee what she needs to do to correct the behaviour.

As a part of your discipline script, tell your employee the exact actions that you want her to perform. Tell the employee that her behaviour must be in accordance with an established performance standard or company policy.

Following are some examples of the third part of your discipline script:

- You must bring your performance up to the standard of 250 units per week or better immediately.
- You're required to set an appointment with the company's employee assistance programme for drug rehabilitation.
- I expect your work to be error free before you submit it to me for approval.
- I expect you to be in your seat, ready to work, at 9 a.m. every morning.

Outlining the consequences

Of course, if the unacceptable behaviour continues, you need to have a discussion with the employee about the consequences. Make sure that you get your message across clearly and unequivocally and that your employee understands it.

Here are some possibilities for the fourth part of your script:

- If you can't meet the standard, I'll send you for further training to improve your skills.
- If you refuse to undergo drug rehabilitation, you're incapable of working effectively, and this may eventually lead to your dismissal.
- If the accuracy of your work doesn't improve immediately, I'll have to issue a written note to be placed on your personnel file.
- If you're late again, I'll request that the general manager convene a formal disciplinary hearing of your case.

Providing emotional support

Give your employee an emotional boost by expressing your support for her efforts. Make this support sincere and heartfelt – you do, after all, want your employee to improve, don't you?

Work to build a strong foundation of positive aspects and trust that you can draw on when dealing with the negatives:

- ✔ You have, after all, worked here for a very long time.

- ✔ You've never been in any trouble before.

- ✔ You usually show a great commitment to everything that you do.

And finally, accentuate the positive:

- ✔ But let's try to avoid that – I know you can do better!

- ✔ I really want this to work out, so let's find you the help you need.

- ✔ Can I do anything to help you overcome this situation?

- ✔ We can avoid that situation – I'm counting on you to turn this around!

Putting it all together

After you develop the five parts of your discipline script, put them together into a unified statement that you deliver to your wayward employees. Although you undoubtedly discuss the surrounding issues in some detail when you meet, make the script the heart of your discipline session.

The five parts of the script work together to produce the final product as follows:

- ✔ Your performance last week was below our standard of 250 units per week. Because of your below-standard performance, the work unit didn't meet its overall targets for the week. You must bring your performance up to the standard of 250 units per week or better immediately. If you can't meet the standard, I'll send you for further training to improve your skills. But let's try to avoid that – I know you can do better!

- ✔ You failed the drug test you took on Monday. This specifically breaks our drug-free workplace policy. You're required to make an appointment with the company's employee assistance programme for drug rehabilitation. If you refuse to undergo drug rehabilitation, you're incapable of working effectively, and this may eventually lead to your dismissal. I really want this to work out, so let's find you the help you need.

- ✔ The last three analyses you submitted to me contained numerous mathematical errors. Because of these errors, I now have to take extra time to check your work before I can forward it onwards. I expect your work to be error free before you submit it to me for approval. If the accuracy of your work doesn't improve immediately, I'll have to issue a written note to be placed in your personnel file. Can I do anything to help you avoid that outcome?

✔ You've been late to work three out of four days this week. Because of your lateness, I had to pull Helen from her position to cover yours. I expect you to be in your seat, ready to work, at 9 a.m. every morning. If we should be aware of any special circumstances, please say so now. Otherwise, if you're late again, I will request that the general manager convene a formal disciplinary hearing on your case. We can avoid that situation – I'm counting on you to turn this around!

Making and Implementing an Improvement Plan

Managers love plans – plans for completing projects on time, plans for meeting the organisation's financial goals in five years and plans to develop more plans. In the case of employee discipline, one more plan exists. The *performance improvement plan* is a crucial part of the discipline process because it sets definite steps for the employee to undertake to improve performance within a fixed period.

If your employee's performance transgressions are minor and you're giving only verbal counselling and guidance, working up a performance plan is probably overkill. Also, because employees must correct most instances of misconduct right now or else face the consequences, performance improvement plans generally aren't appropriate for correcting employee misconduct. However, if your employee's poor performance is habitual and you've started the disciplinary procedure, a performance plan is definitely what the doctor ordered.

A performance improvement plan consists of the following three parts:

✔ **Goal statement:** The goal statement provides clear direction to your employees about what it takes to achieve a satisfactory improvement. The goal statement, which is tied directly to your employees' performance standards, may be something along the lines of 'Completes all her assignments on or before agreed deadlines' or 'Is at his station ready to work at exactly 9 a.m. every day'.

✔ **Schedule for attainment:** What good is a plan without a schedule? Not having a schedule is like eating an ice-cream cone without the ice cream or watching television with the sound turned off. Every good plan needs a definite completion date, with fixed milestones along the way if the plan for goal attainment is complex.

    ✔ **Required resources/training:** The performance improvement plan must also contain a summary of any additional resources or training that can be brought to bear to help employees bring their performance up to scratch.

Figure 16-1 shows a sample performance improvement plan for a worker who makes repeated errors in typed correspondence.

Performance Improvement Plan

Jack Smith

Goal statement:

    ★ Complete all drafts of typed correspondence with two or fewer mistakes per document.

Schedule for attainment:

    ★ Jack must meet the above goal within three months after the date of this plan.

Figure 16-1:
A sample performance improvement plan.

Required resources/training:

    ★ Jack will be enrolled in the company refresher course in typing and reviewing correspondence. This training must be successfully completed no later than two months after the date of this plan.

After you put performance improvement plans in place, your job is to ensure that they don't just gather dust on your employees' shelves. Follow up with your employees to make sure that they're acting on their plans and making progress towards the goals you both agreed to. Yes, following up on improvement plans takes time, but that time is well spent. Besides, if you can't find the time to check your employees' progress on their improvement plans, don't be surprised if they can't find the time to work on them.

Check that your employees are following through with the goal statements you agreed to, that they're keeping to their schedules and that they're receiving the training and other resources you agreed to provide. If not, you need to emphasise the importance of the improvement plans with your employees and work with them to figure out why they haven't implemented them as agreed.

To assist your employees in implementing their improvement plans, schedule regular progress report meetings with them on a daily, weekly or monthly basis. More extensive improvement plans necessitate more frequent follow-up. Progress meetings serve two functions:

- They provide you with the information you need to assess your employees' progress in implementing their plans.

- They demonstrate to your employees, clearly and unequivocally, that their progress is important to you. If you demonstrate that the plans are important to you, your employees can make the plans a priority in their busy schedules.

Set up performance improvement plans with your employees and stick to them. One of the most difficult challenges of management is dealing with a poor performer who improves when under scrutiny and then lapses again. Adhere to your plan. If an employee can't maintain the necessary performance standards, then you may want to consider whether she's really suited for continued employment with your organisation.

Top five discipline websites

Wondering where to find the best information on the web about the topics we address in this chapter? Well, you've come to the right place! Here are our top five favourites:

- **Croner:** www.croner.co.uk

- **Trades Union Congress:** www.tuc.org.uk/

- **Resolving disputes at work:** www.berr.gov.uk/employment

- **Advisory, Conciliation and Arbitration Service (ACAS):** www.acas.org.uk/

- **Addressing disciplinary problems at work:** www.problemsatwork.org

---

Chapter 17

Handling Resignations, Dismissals and Redundancies

● ●

In This Chapter

▶ Understanding the various kinds of dismissal

▶ Taking necessary precautions before dismissing an employee

▶ Firing employees: A step-by-step approach

▶ Deciding at what time to dismiss employees

● ●

*B*eing a manager is a tough job. Of all the tough jobs that managers have to do, firing employees has to be the absolute toughest. No matter how many times you fire someone, dismissing an employee is never a pleasant thing to do.

The mechanics of what you have to do before you dismiss an employee – setting goals, gathering data, assessing performance, disciplining and completing the paperwork – aren't so tough. The tough part is all the emotional baggage that goes along with firing someone, especially someone you've worked with for a while and have shared good and bad times with. However, no matter how difficult it is, telling an employee that you no longer need his services is sometimes your only option.

This chapter deals with the reasons employees are dismissed and why they resign, the different kinds of dismissals and exactly how you can carry them out. You discover the difference between a redundancy and a dismissal, as well as the importance of following procedures and having documentation to support your actions.

Accepting Resignations

Employees have many reasons to resign from their jobs. You may find the thought that anyone voluntarily chooses to leave your particular brand of workers' paradise hard to believe, but leave they do, and for all kinds of reasons.

Sometimes employees find better promotional or pay opportunities with another firm. Sometimes employees find themselves in dead-end work situations or leave because of personality conflicts with their manager or other employees. Sometimes employees leave because of emotional stress, family needs, alcohol dependency or other personal reasons. Following are the main ways in which employees leave voluntarily:

- ✔ **Resignation:** Resignation occurs when an employee decides to leave his position with your firm with no prodding or suggestion to do so from you. Unfortunately, the best employees always seem to be the ones who resign. Although you can't force someone to stay with your organisation forever (nor would you want to), you can make sure that people aren't leaving because your organisation isn't adequately addressing problems. A certain department experiencing a high turnover of staff, for example, is a warning sign that work conditions are too stressful, or that you may have a bad manager or supervisor in the position. Conducting exit interviews with leavers can be a particularly useful tool for uncovering problems that you need to address. Don't let employees leave without first asking them why they decided to resign, and what the organisation can do better.

- ✔ **Resignation (encouraged):** An encouraged resignation occurs when you suggest to an employee that he leave his job. Such resignations are often used as face-saving measures for employees who you're about to fire. Instead of sacking them, you can offer them the opportunity to resign. This approach can help to dampen the hurt of being fired, plus it keeps a potentially damaging incident off the employee's record. Be careful that you do this in such a way as to avoid a *constructive dismissal* (when you conduct yourself in such a way that the only course of action open to a reasonable person is to resign and leave), otherwise you'll find yourself in front of an employment tribunal. You normally only encourage people to resign when both you and they are prepared to sign a compromise agreement in which both parties agree that this is the final solution to the matter in hand.

- ✔ **Retirement:** Retirement happens when employees reach the end of their career and decide to leave finally and forever. Occasionally, organisations working to cut costs quickly offer certain employees early retirement, extending the benefits of regular retirement to those who are willing to retire from the company before they've reached the normal age to do so. Retirement is generally a happy time for all involved, marked with celebrations and tokens of the organisation's affection and gratitude (such as a plaque, a gold watch or a very nice lunch).

Dealing with Dismissals

Dismissals are rarely as easy to deal with as resignations. Dismissals are seldom pleasant experiences – for manager or employee – and this ultimate sanction against an employee is a last resort.

Dismissals come in two types:

- **Redundancies and lay-offs:** Redundancies and lay-offs occur when an organisation decides to dismiss a certain number of employees for financial reasons. For example, your company loses several key contracts and the revenue that you projected was coming with them. In order to stay afloat, your firm may have no choice but to reduce payroll costs through lay-offs.

  Every company has its own policy for determining the order of lay-offs. In some organisations, the last employee hired is the first to go. In others, employee performance determines lay-offs. Most organisations give first refusal to laid-off employees for new jobs if and when the company's financial health improves.

- **Dismissal:** An organisation fires employees when these people have no hope of improving their performance, when their job descriptions need to evolve and the people in the jobs aren't able to evolve along with them, or when the employee commits an act of misconduct that's so serious that dismissal is the only choice.

Making employees redundant

Call it what you like – a reduction in workforce, downsizing, rightsizing, re-engineering or whatever. The causes and results are the same. Your organisation needs to reorganise its operations, or cut the payroll and related personnel and facilities costs, and some of your employees must go.

Although understandably traumatic for those employees involved, redundancies and lay-offs are different from dismissals because the employees losing their jobs generally have done nothing wrong. They're usually good employees who follow the rules. They're productive and do their jobs. They're loyal and dedicated workers. They may even be your friends. The real blame usually lies with external factors, such as changes in markets, mergers and acquisitions, and pressures of a more competitive global marketplace; where internal factors do exist they occur normally as the result of organisational or managerial ineptitude.

Always instigate a recruitment freeze during periods of likely and possible redundancies and lay-offs; and if the organisation has vacancies, offer these positions to employees at risk of redundancy before looking elsewhere.

When it becomes apparent that redundancies and lay-offs are inevitable, you must decide how many employees are affected, who they are and when the redundancies and lay-offs are to take place. You then need to notify and consult with everyone – those who are affected, those who may be affected and those who aren't affected as well. Make clear the extent of the problems, and notify people that the course of action you're taking is the only way out. You must use formal channels of communication to notify all employees and their representatives, including any trade unions that your organisation recognises.

Give as much notice of redundancy as possible. You have to follow statutory limits – up to 90 days' notice where more than 20 people are being laid off – but common sense in any case dictates getting the matter out into the open as soon as possible. After you've discussed redundancies and lay-offs at board-room level, you may as well broadcast them anyway – this type of information always gets out quickly!

The key is getting through what's after all an organisational and business crisis without having to resort to compulsory redundancies. This isn't always possible by any means, but you should try to achieve it if you possibly can.

Then follow your business's redundancy and lay-off procedure. The organisation should have codes of practice in its redundancy procedure that specify the position of and processes for

- ✔ **Early retirement,** in which an individual is allowed to retire before she'd normally do so

- ✔ **Voluntary redundancy,** in which an individual seeks and accepts severance from the organisation on redundancy terms

- ✔ **Compulsory redundancy,** in which an individual has to accept severance on redundancy terms

- ✔ **Redeployment and/or transfer,** in which an individual is assigned to another job that she's capable of and willing to do in another department or location

You must make clear the basis on which selection for compulsory redundancies is made. You mustn't discriminate on grounds of race, ethnicity or religion; sex or gender; pregnancy; disability; or membership/non-membership of a trade union. Keep any recognised trade unions involved and informed of the situation regarding redundancies.

Most organisations opt for 'last in, first out' (LIFO); if you don't follow this practice, you must specify otherwise by job title, grade, location of work and so forth. You must always give substantial reasons in writing for selecting particular employees for redundancy.

You proceed as follows:

1. **Prepare a final list of employees to be laid off.**

   After you turn the organisation upside down to find potential savings, you need to prepare a list of employees to be laid off. Write the list in rank order in the event of a change that may allow you to remove employees from the list. Consider your employees' experience and how long they've been with the organisation if you possibly can. This reinforces the need to make clear who's to be laid off on a basis that you can substantiate for business reasons. And be careful not to discriminate.

2. **Notify affected employees.**

   By now, many employees are probably paralysed with the fear that they're being made redundant. As soon as you finish developing the lay-off list – updating it to account for employees who may already have found new jobs on their own – notify the affected employees. Private, one-to-one meetings are the best way to handle notification of redundancy.

3. **Provide outplacement services to redundant employees.**

   If time and money permit, provide outplacement and counselling support to the employees you're laying off. Your organisation can provide training in subjects such as CV and application writing, financial planning, interviewing and networking, and allow the employees to use company-owned computers, fax machines and telephones in their job searches. If you can help your employees by providing job leads or contacts, by all means do so.

4. **Make the redundancies.**

   Conduct one-to-one redundancy meetings with employees to finalise arrangements and complete redundancy paperwork. Explain the redundancy package, continuation of benefits and any other company-sponsored redundancy programmes as appropriate. Collect keys, identification badges and any company-owned equipment and property. Escort (you can do this personally, or have a security guard or human resources representative fill the role) your newly redundant, former employees off the premises and wish them well.

5. **Rally the survivors.**

   Rally your remaining employees together in an all-hands meeting to let them know that, now that the lay-offs are complete, the firm is back on the road to good financial health. Tell the team that, to avoid future lay-offs, you have to pull together to overcome this immediate downturn in the business cycle.

Processing the types of dismissal

You must have procedures for dismissals and redundancies – and you must follow them. Any dismissal that the employee affected challenges in an employment tribunal is automatically found to be unfair if you don't follow the correct procedures.

Dismissal may be fair, unfair, wrongful or constructive.

✔ **Fair:** You may dismiss anyone, at any time, for negligence and incompetence; breach of the criminal law – fraud, theft, vandalism, violence or dishonesty; bullying, victimisation, discrimination or harassment; other gross misconduct, examples of which ought to be itemised in the organisation's procedures; and some other substantial reason, a catch-all description because you can't possibly specify every single set of circumstances when you may legitimately dismiss an employee.

For a dismissal to be fair, you must have evidence of the misconduct, and you must be able to produce this at the point at which dismissal is a possibility or likelihood. You must confront the employee with the evidence, and allow him the time and opportunity to respond. You must take account of any mitigating circumstances that the employee produces. Additionally, you must allow the employee to be represented and/ or accompanied at any hearing that may lead to dismissal. You must also allow an appeal. All of this needs to be itemised in the organisation's procedures; minimum standards along these lines are available from the Advisory, Conciliation and Arbitration Service (ACAS), and these are normally deemed to apply unless you can give a good reason why not.

✔ **Unfair:** Dismissal is normally automatically unfair if you breach procedures as outlined in the preceding point; or if you dismiss anyone on grounds of sex/gender, race, religion, age, membership of a trade union, refusal to join a trade union, pregnancy, parenthood or the fact that he has a conviction that is *spent*, meaning the person has served his sentence and the matter is now expunged from his record.

This applies regardless of job or occupation, length of service or hours worked. Even if the person has just started working for you, you may not dismiss him on any of the above grounds.

If you nevertheless dismiss someone on any of these grounds, the dismissal is normally found to be automatically unfair and the penalties for unfair dismissal get steeper each year.

✔ **Wrongful:** Dismissal is wrongful if you take actions that breach the employment contract; for example, if you remove the equipment that employees need to do their job, or turn them out of their office making it impossible for them to do their job properly.

✔ **Constructive:** Dismissal is constructive if the actions you take against an employee mean that the only course open to that employee is to leave the organisation. When this occurs, the individual normally takes you to tribunal and seeks to prove or demonstrate his case. Constructive dismissal can include such things as encouraging bullying, victimisation, discrimination or harassment; doing nothing about bullying, victimisation, discrimination or harassment when it's brought to your attention; or other forms of discrimination that you do nothing about. Constructive dismissal can also include giving people tasks that are impossible to perform; failing to deliver rewards and bonuses that you promised or indicated; and even making their working lives such a misery that *anyone* would want to leave.

Many employers go to a great deal of time and trouble to get some form of legal basis for what's otherwise a wrongful or unfair dismissal. For all the well-documented and high-profile cases (such as the bullying of female staff in City of London finance houses, or staff from ethnic minorities in several of the UK's police forces), some organisations and managers still try it on! Managers dig up every slight incident that may conceivably have occurred concerning a particular employee in the dim and distant past, and then present this as damning evidence of the employee's wrongdoing, negligence or incompetence – anything, in fact, rather than accepting their own organisational and managerial shortcomings. Tribunals and courts don't normally entertain this approach. If you have evidence for dismissal, document it, produce it, operate according to procedures – and then you have nothing to worry about.

Gathering good reasons for firing

As long as you aren't discriminating against your employees, and as long as you follow procedures when you dismiss them, you still have quite a lot of discretion in getting rid of workers. People generally agree on certain behaviours that warrant dismissal. Such behaviours include:

- ✔ **Verbal abuse of others:** Verbal abuse includes swearing, repeated verbal harassment, malicious insults and other similar behaviour. Your employees have the right to do their jobs in a workplace free of verbal abuse. And verbal abuse of customers and other business associates is just plain bad for business. (Keep in mind that if you don't take action by quickly firing a repeat offender, you put yourself and your company at risk of grievances by those employees being harassed.)

- ✔ **Incompetence:** Despite your continued efforts to train them, some employees just aren't cut out for their jobs. If you've tried to help them and they still can't perform their duties at an acceptable level of competence, parting ways is clearly in the best interests of both the employee and the firm.

- ✔ **Repeated, unexcused lateness:** You depend on your employees to get their jobs done as scheduled. Not only does lateness jeopardise the ability of your employees to complete their tasks on time, but it also sets a very bad example for your other employees who are punctual. If certain employees continue to be late to work after you warn them that you won't tolerate this behaviour, you have clear grounds for dismissal.

- ✔ **Insubordination:** Insubordination – both *repeated insubordination* (where a minor offence occurs repeatedly) and *gross insubordination* (a single major offence) – is normally grounds for dismissal as gross misconduct. Although supervisors commonly encourage their employees to question why a decision is made, after the decision is made, the employees must carry it out. If they're unwilling to follow your direction, the basic employer–employee relationship breaks down, and you don't have to tolerate it.

✔ **Physical violence:** Most companies take employee-initiated physical violence and threats of violence very seriously. Employees have the right to do their jobs in a safe workplace; employers have the duty to provide a safe workplace. Physical violence jeopardises your employees' safety and distracts them from doing their jobs. Never let an employee think that you don't take a physical threat seriously – the best way to communicate that is to call the police immediately. The workplace is no place for violence or threats of violence.

✔ **Theft:** You can't tolerate theft of company property or of the property of colleagues, employees or clients. Most companies that catch employees engaging in this nasty little practice dismiss them immediately and without warning. If you decide to dismiss an employee for theft, and you have concrete proof that the employee carried out the crime, you can do so knowing that you're on firm legal ground.

✔ **Intoxication at work:** Although being drunk or under the influence of drugs on the job is sufficient grounds for immediate dismissal, many companies nowadays offer their employees the option of undergoing rehabilitation with an employee assistance programme or enrolling with an organisation such as Alcoholics Anonymous. In many cases, employees can rehabilitate themselves and return to regular service.

✔ **Falsification of records:** Falsification of records is illegal; and is therefore never tolerated. This category includes providing fraudulent information during the recruitment process (universities the employee didn't attend, qualifications the employee doesn't possess, inaccurate information about previous jobs and so on) and producing other fraudulent information during the course of employment (fake expense reports, falsified timecards, cheating at professional or internal career path examinations and so on).

Some of these behaviours are considered gross or serious misconduct that merit immediate dismissal with no verbal or written warning and no second chance. If you can prove that such behaviour took place or witness it, you can dismiss the employee(s) involved immediately, according to your organisation's established procedures.

Easing into Dismissal

One of the hardest tasks any manager ever has to do is to fire an employee. Dismissing an employee isn't a pleasant way to spend an afternoon. Most managers prefer doing almost anything else. ('John, maybe we should go for a quick swim in the shark tank.') Although the reasons for dismissing employees are clear cut and relatively easy for managers to use as a basis for a dismissal, having that basis doesn't make the task any easier.

The next sections point out reasons you may want to dither over dismissals, and then talk about exhausting alternatives.

Trying to avoid the inevitable

Your job as a manager offers plenty of examples to prove that you can't avoid the inevitable. Nevertheless, when it comes to dismissing employees, you may join the legions of managers who use one or more of the following reasons to put off having that difficult discussion:

- **Fear of the unknown:** Dismissing an employee can be a frightening prospect, especially if you're getting ready to do it for the first time. Is your employee going to cry? Have a heart attack? Get mad? Beat you up? Most managers get worried about a first-time dismissal. If you're in that particular boat, read up on the firing process before you do it; it can provide you with both logical and emotional support. (Unfortunately, the last time never seems to come around until you retire.)

- **Emotional involvement:** Considering that you spend between a quarter and a third of your waking hours at work, becoming friends with some of your employees is natural. Doing so is fine until you have to discipline or dismiss one or more of your friends. Letting any employee go is tough enough, much less an employee with whom you've developed a personal, as well as professional, relationship.

- **Fear of a negative reflection on you:** If you have to dismiss one of your employees, what are you saying about yourself as a manager? In the case of a lay-off, is it your fault that the organisation didn't attain its goals? If you're firing an employee, did you make the wrong choice when you decided to hire that person? Many managers opt to put up with performance problems in their employees rather than draw attention to their own shortcomings, whether real or perceived.

- **Possibility of legal action:** The fear of legal action is often enough to stop the most strident of companies and their managers in their tracks. This possibility reinforces the point that you must have grounds for dismissal, and that you must follow the dismissal procedures.

- **Discomfort:** Many managers are reluctant to fire employees because 'they don't quite like to' or 'it's not very nice'. So they fail to tackle the problem (in which case it gets a lot worse), or they do nothing until a crisis has already broken.

Rodney Ledward was a gynaecologist who, during the course of his career, botched hundreds of operations, which caused untold suffering for, and sometimes permanent damage to, many of his patients. When the case finally came to light, it quickly became apparent that Rodney Ledward's history of malpractice was widely known. However, his managers had been reluctant to deal with the issue because he had a strident and difficult personality, and so tackling him would have been unpleasant!

You can, of course, hope that the problem just goes away – but don't hold your breath! Problem employees never just go away.

Few managers end up regretting firing a wayward employee too soon. Far more regret not taking action more quickly when the writing is on the wall.

Working up to dismissal

Can you dismiss an employee humanely? We like to think so. If you focus on being fair and professional, you have a good chance of minimising the negative impact while making the best of a situation that's not working. Here are some guidelines that can help you make this difficult transition a little easier before getting to dismissal:

- ✔ **Give the employee the benefit of the doubt.** You need to be sure that you're giving the employee a fair chance to succeed – not necessarily an endless number of chances, but a fair chance. This idea is especially important when the employee is new. You can say something like: 'I don't know how you've been managed in the past, but I want to make it clear what we expect of you in this position so that we can agree on some mutual goals for your job.' Summarise your expectations in writing and set up a time frame for reviewing progress on the employee's goals. Ask the employee to come to you if she has questions or needs help in meeting the expectations, and acknowledge when the employee has done some good work. Don't expect your employees to know what you want without open, two-way communication.

- ✔ **Make it clear when an employee isn't meeting your expectations.** You have a much easier time dealing with problems when they're small than when they become huge. Raise your concerns and the reasons for them being concerns. You can use a disclaimer, such as 'I know you're capable of improving in this area of your job', but you also at some point need to be clear that if improvement isn't forthcoming, the employee may lose the job. Document these discussions for clarity, reinforcement and to provide evidence if you need it later that you've made an honest attempt to manage the employee fairly.

- ✔ **Exhaust alternative approaches to dismissal.** Some managers find it useful to try one or more attempts to get through to an employee who isn't performing well. You can discuss other opportunities that may better match the employee's abilities, for example. Or you can offer the employee a 'career day': 'Tom, I want you to take a career day tomorrow. Take the day off and don't come to work. I'm still going to pay you, but I want you to go to the beach, a museum, your kid's school or even just watch television all day – and simply focus on one question: is this job really what you want to be doing with your life right now? Come back and give me your answer, and if you do really want to stay in your position, we have to talk about what needs to change in order for you to keep your job and not have to leave.'

✔ **Relate performance to pay.** 'Jane, we have some mutually agreed goals, but I haven't seen you actually change your behaviour or achieve any of the results we discussed. I don't like surprises, and I'm sure you don't either. So I want to make it clear that your next performance review is in a few months and if you haven't shown substantial improvement in your performance, you won't be getting a salary increase.' Typically, in this approach a person quickly falls in line or ends up leaving of her own accord – either way, you've solved your problem.

✔ **Extend probationary and trial periods.** 'Ronan, you seem dead keen on this job, but your performance isn't yet up to scratch. We very much want to keep you on. However, we must extend your probationary period for a further three months, just to make sure that you really are fitting in.' Again, when you take this approach the person quickly falls into line or ends up leaving of his own accord. And if you've specified a further trial period, then make sure that you review the person's performance when the period finishes.

If you've tried all of these approaches, and you still see no improvement, then you have no choice but to dismiss. That being the case; act quickly. The sooner you deal with the situation, the better – for the employee, for you and for the work group. You have to move from hoping your employees will improve to looking at the evidence to see whether they are, in fact, improving. Remember, sometimes the biggest incentive you can offer your work group is to get rid of people who aren't performing, thereby sending a clear message to everyone else that the group can't afford to have anyone who isn't pulling their weight. In reality, the reaction from other employees – who often know more about a colleague's performance than anyone else in the organisation can ever hope to – is, 'What took you so long?' Even during a dismissal you can still be gracious: 'I thought things would work out, but they haven't and you're going to have to leave.'

Heeding the Warning Before You Fire an Employee

Firing an employee is unpleasant enough without being dragged through the courts on a charge of unfair or wrongful dismissal. The problem is that, although most organisations have clear procedures for disciplining employees, some managers ignore these procedures in the heat of the moment. Seemingly, a manager's minor oversight can lead to major monetary damages awards in favour of former employees.

Before you fire an employee for any reason, make sure that you can meet the following criteria and, where necessary, defend your position. Take our word for it: you'll be glad you did!

- **Procedures:** Use your procedures, follow them to the letter and demonstrate – in writing – that you did so.

- **Documentation:** Remember the rule: document, document and then document some more. If you're firing an employee because of performance shortcomings, you better have the performance data to back up your assertions. If you're firing an employee for stealing, you better have proof that this employee is the thief. You can never have too much documentation. This rule is always true when you take employee relations actions, but particularly when you dismiss an employee.

- **Fair warning:** Make sure that you spell out performance standards clearly to employees in advance. Explain company policies and practices along with your expectations. Give your employees fair warning of the consequences of continued performance problems. The law is quite clear: dismissing an employee without warning, especially for performance-related behaviour, is generally considered unfair. However, certain kinds of employee misconduct, including physical violence, theft and fraud, are grounds for dismissal without warning.

- **Response time:** You must give your employees enough time to rectify their performance shortcomings. The amount of time considered reasonable to improve performance depends on the nature of the problem to be addressed. For example, if the problem is lateness, you can expect the employee to correct the behaviour immediately. However, if the employee is to improve performance on a complex and lengthy project, demonstrating improvement may take weeks or months.

- **Fairness and reasonableness:** Your company's policies and practices should be reasonable. The average worker should be able to achieve the performance standards you set with your employees, and penalties should match the severity of the offence. Put yourself in your employees' shoes. If you were being dismissed, would you consider the grounds for dismissal to be reasonable? Be honest!

- **Avenues for appeal:** Offer employees ways to appeal your decision to higher-level management. Again, the law requires that avenues exist for dismissed employees to present their cases to higher management. Sometimes a direct supervisor is too close to the problem or too emotionally involved, which can cause errors in judgement that someone who's not personally involved in the situation can see easily.

Firing an Employee Fairly in Three Steps

Although your job is to point out your employees' shortcomings and help your employees perform to the standard you require, the employees are ultimately responsible for their performance and behaviour. When you arrive at the last disciplinary step prior to firing an employee, letting him know that the responsibility and choice are his and his alone is important; you can't do this critical step for the employee. Your employee improves his performance or leaves. And if he decides to leave, have your employee express his choice in writing!

Assuming that the employee has made his choice, and that choice is to continue the misconduct or below-standard performance, the choice is then yours. And your choice is to dismiss before the employee does any more damage to your organisation.

Keep three key goals in mind when firing employees:

- ✔ **Follow procedures.** You don't want to be lumbered with a high-level compensation case for firing someone who deserved that action, simply because you didn't follow procedures.

- ✔ **Provide a clear explanation for the firing.** According to legal experts, many employees claim for unfair dismissal simply in hope of discovering the real reason they were fired.

- ✔ **Seek to minimise resentment against your company and yourself by taking action to maintain your employee's dignity throughout the dismissal process.** The world is a dangerous enough place without incurring the wrath of potentially unstable former employees.

Fire an employee in a meeting in your office or other private location. Make the meeting concise and to the point; set aside 20 to 30 minutes for the meeting. Dismissal meetings aren't intended to be discussions or debates. Your job is to inform your employee that he's being fired. This meeting isn't going to be fun, but keep in mind that you're taking the best course of action for all concerned. One more thing: have a witness with you when you dismiss an employee – especially when the person being dismissed is of a different gender. Ideally, bring someone along from human resources who can step in with a discussion of the administrative details of the dismissal, such as turning in keys and equipment, continuing benefits, severance pay and so forth. In addition, make sure the employee has the option of having a colleague or representative with him.

In this context, these are the three steps for firing an employee:

✔ **Tell the employee that you're dismissing him.** State simply and unequivocally that you've made the decision to fire him. Don't use euphemisms – 'We're letting you go'; 'We're allowing you to spend more time with your family' – this is degrading and demeaning, to the employee and also to you. Dismiss the employee face to face – however uncomfortable it is, it's what you're paid for. Be sure to note that you considered all relevant evidence, that you reviewed the decision and all levels of your organisation's management agreed to it, and that the decision is final. If you did your homework and used a system of progressive discipline (refer to Chapter 16) in an attempt to correct your employee's behaviour, the announcement should come as no surprise. Of course, no matter the circumstances, a firing shakes anyone to the core.

✔ **Explain exactly why you're dismissing the employee.** If the firing is the result of misconduct, cite the policy that the employee broke and exactly what he did to break it. If the firing is due to a failure to meet performance standards, remind the employee of past attempts to correct his performance and the subsequent incidents that led to your decision to fire him. Stick to the facts. Confirm the facts in writing – and the stated and written reasons *must* be the same, otherwise the dismissal is normally considered unfair.

✔ **Announce the effective date of the dismissal and provide details on the dismissal process.** A firing is normally effective on the day that you conduct your dismissal meeting. Keeping a fired employee around is awkward for both you and your employee and you should avoid this situation at all costs. If you're offering a severance package or other dismissal benefits, explain them to your employee as well as how he can make arrangements for gathering personal effects from his office. Go through the dismissal paperwork with the employee and explain how you'll pay any remaining wages due, including any notice period to which they're entitled.

Dismissal can be quite traumatic for the employee on the receiving end of the news. Expect the unexpected. Although one employee may quickly become an emotional wreck, another may become belligerent and verbally abusive. To help defuse these situations, consider applying the following techniques:

✔ **Empathise with your employee.** Don't try to sweeten the pill, but be understanding of your employee's situation. The news you've just delivered is among the worst that anyone can get. If your employee becomes emotional or cries, don't try to stop him – hand him a tissue and carry on with the discussion.

✔ **Be matter-of-fact and firm.** Even if your employee becomes angry, you must maintain a calm, businesslike demeanour throughout the dismissal meeting. Don't lead your employee to believe that he's participating in a negotiating session or that he can do something to change your mind. Be firm in your insistence that the decision is final and not subject to change.

✔ **Keep the meeting on track.** Although letting your employee vent his feelings is appropriate, don't allow the employee to steer the meeting from the main goal of informing him about the dismissal. If the employee becomes abusive, inform him that you'll end the meeting immediately if he can't maintain control.

You may find it helpful to prepare a *dismissal script* to read during the dismissal meeting. A script is beneficial because it helps to ensure that you don't forget to mention an important piece of information, and it provides instant documentation for your employee's personnel file (which you should retain). Practise the script before you go into the dismissal meeting.

Here's a sample dismissal script for an employee with continuing performance problems:

'Bronwyn, we've decided that today is your last day of employment with the firm. The reason for this decision is that you can't maintain the performance standards that we agreed to when we hired you last year. As you know, we've discussed your failure to meet standards on many occasions over the past year. Specifically, in the disciplinary hearing that we had on 5 October we notified you that you had one month to bring your performance up to standard or we may dismiss you. You didn't achieve this goal, and I therefore have no other choice but to terminate your employment, with immediate effect. Ali from personnel is here to discuss your final pay and benefits and to collect your office keys and voice-mail password.'

Determining the Best Time to Dismiss

Any manager probably has her own idea of what day of the week and time of the day to dismiss employees. Monday dismissals are the way to go because of A, B and C. Or Friday dismissals are best because of X, Y and Z. And is it better to carry out a dismissal as the first task in the morning, or should you wait until the close of business?

We think that dismissing an employee as soon as you decide you have to do so, regardless of the day of the week, makes the most sense. After you've decided that an employee needs to go, every additional day is a drain on the organisation – and on yourself.

So what time is the best to dismiss someone? The best approach is when her colleagues aren't there to witness the dismissal, prior to starting work or at the end of the day. The idea is to minimise the embarrassment for the dismissed employee. If you dismiss an employee early in the day, she has to face her colleagues and explain why she's packing up her belongings and why the security guard is preparing to escort her off the premises. Your intent isn't to embarrass or punish your employee – you want to make the dismissal process as painless and humane as possible. Allow an employee to save face by scheduling the dismissal meeting at a time when you can avoid public display.

Never be afraid to take advice from an employment lawyer, especially where there might be questions over the probability, likelihood or potential for discrimination or harassment. In these cases, compensation is uncapped, and you need to know precisely where you stand if the case goes wrong.

Top five dismissal websites

Wondering where to find the best information on the web about the topics addressed in this chapter? Well, you've come to the right place! Here are our top five favourites:

✔ **Confederation of British Industry:** www. cbi.org.uk/

✔ **Trades Union Congress:** www.tuc.org. uk/

✔ **Advisory, Conciliation and Arbitration Service (ACAS):** www.acas.org.uk/

✔ **Institute of Directors:** www.institute ofdirectors.com/

✔ **Croner:** www.croner.co.uk

Part VI
Tools and Techniques for Managing

'Look, Mr Brinkley, you don't fool me —
you don't have a proper accountant in
this company do you?'

In this part . . .

Although you don't have to be a technical wizard to be a manager, you can benefit from keeping abreast of some of the key tools and technologies that drive today's business. In this part, we consider the basics of accounting and budgeting and how to harness the power of technology. We also cover how to develop employee skills and talk about some of the most recent management trends.

Chapter 18

Budgeting and Accounting

- -

In This Chapter

▶ Creating your budget

▶ Applying professional budget tricks

▶ Understanding accounting basics

▶ Interpreting financial statements

▶ Exploring other ways of looking at money

- -

As a manager, you need to understand the basics of budgeting and accounting. When your colleagues start throwing around terms such as *staff budget*, *cash flow*, *profit and loss statement* and *balance sheet*, don't you want to do more than simply nod your head and respond with a blank stare? Here's some good news: you don't need an MBA to grasp these basics.

In this chapter, we cover the importance of budgeting in an organisation, as well as putting together a budget by using some of the professional tricks of the budget trade. We then introduce the survival basics of accounting.

Exploring the Wonderful World of Budgets

A *budget* is an itemised forecast of an individual's or company's income and expenses expected for some period in the future. Budgets provide the baseline of expected performance against which managers measure actual performance. Accounting systems generate reports to compare expected performance against actual performance to provide financial information on an organisation's financial status. With this information, managers with budget responsibility act as physicians to assess the current financial health of their businesses.

When you receive the latest accounting report, it says that sales are too low compared to budget. What does that mean? As a responsible manager (this means you!), you need to work out why. Maybe your sales force is having problems getting the product delivered to your customers quickly. Or perhaps your competition developed a new thingamajig that's taking sales away from your product. Whatever the problem is, you can't know if you don't understand the basics of budgeting.

Because business is changing all the time (find out all about change in Chapter 15), you may wonder why you bother having a budget. Without a long-term plan and goals, your organisation lacks focus and wastes resources as employees wander aimlessly about. A budget isn't just an educated guess that reflects your long-term plans and allows you to act on them; it's a personal commitment to making a designated future happen. The best budgets are flexible, allowing for changes in different key assumptions, such as income results. Of course, planning becomes more difficult as the world changes all around you, but plan you must.

Winston Churchill said: 'When circumstances change, so do I.' This must be your attitude to budgeting – changes in circumstances simply don't allow you to stick rigidly to a single course of action.

Budgets also fulfil another important purpose: they provide a baseline against which you can measure your progress towards your goals. For example, if you're 50 per cent of the way through your financial year but have actually spent 75 per cent of your budgeted operating funds, then you have an immediate indication that a potential problem exists if you don't see any significant change in your expenditure. You've under-budgeted your expenses for the year, or you're overspending. Whenever budgeted performance and actual performance disagree, or are in *variance*, the job of responsible managers is to ask why, and then to put right any problems that they find.

Depending on your organisation's size, the budgeting process may be quite simple or very complex. Regardless of your organisation's size, you ought to budget for everything. Following are examples of budget areas that just about every organisation needs:

- ✔ **Sales budget:** The sales budget is an estimate of the total number of products or services that the organisation will sell in a given period. Determine the total turnover by multiplying the number of units by the price per unit.

- ✔ **Staff budget:** Staff budgets consist of the number and name of all the various positions in a company along with the salary or wages budgeted for each position.

✔ **Production budget:** The production budget takes the sales budget and its estimate of quantities of units to be sold and translates those figures into the cost of labour, material and other expenses required to produce those units.

✔ **Administration and overheads budget:** Administration and overheads budgets contain all the different expenses that a department may incur during the normal course of operations. You budget for things like travel, training, office supplies and so forth as expenses.

✔ **Capital budget:** This budget is a manager's plan to acquire *fixed assets* (anything your organisation owns that has a long useful life), such as furniture, computers, facilities, physical plant and so forth to support the operations of a business.

Whether you're responsible for budgeting as a part of your managerial duties or not, you need to have a basic understanding of the process your business goes through to account for the money it makes and the money it spends.

Making a Budget

You have a right and a wrong way to do a budget. The wrong way is simply to make a photocopy of the last budget and submit it as your new budget. Some people simply add a bit here and there, and then hand the slightly revised budget in, hoping it's good enough.

The right way is to gather information from as many sources as possible, review and check the information for accuracy and then use your good judgement to guess what the future may bring. A budget is a *forecast* – a commitment to the future – and is only as good as the data that goes into it and the good judgement that you bring to the process.

Review the basic steps in putting together a budget:

1. **Closely review your budgeting documents and instructions.**

   Take a close look at the budgeting documents you're working with and read any instructions your accounting staff provide with them. Although your organisation may have done something the same way for years, you never know when that procedure may change.

2. **Meet with staff.**

   When you're starting the budget process, meet with your staff members to solicit their input. In some cases, you need the specific input of your employees to forecast accurately. For example, you may need to know how many trips your salespeople plan to make next year and where they plan to go. In other cases, you can simply ask for employee suggestions. One employee may ask you to include a pay increase in the next budget. Another may inform you that the current phone system is no longer adequate to meet the needs of employees and customers and that you should budget for a new one. Whichever the case, your staff can provide you with very useful and important budget information.

3. Gather data.

Pull out copies of previous budgets and accounting reports and then compare budgeted figures to actual figures. Work out whether you overspent or underspent and by how much. If no historical data is available, find other sources of information that can help guide the development of figures for your budget.

Determine how much business you plan to bring in during the next budget period, and what it will cost to bring it in. Consider whether you need to hire more people, lease new facilities or buy equipment or supplies. Furthermore, consider the possibility of large increases or decreases in sales or expenses and what effect they would have on your budget.

4. Apply your judgement.

Hard data and cold facts are very important in the budgeting process; they provide an unbiased, unemotional source of information on which to base your decisions. However, data and facts aren't everything – not by a long shot. Budgeting is part science and part art. Take the data and facts and then apply your own judgement to determine the most likely outcomes.

When you're new to management, you have little experience to draw on, so you have a natural tendency to rely more heavily on data. However, as you become more accomplished in management and budgeting, your personal experience and judgement come to the fore.

5. Produce a draft.

Depending on how your organisation does business, either fill out your budget forms and send them to your budget people for processing, or enter them in the budget model yourself. The result is a budget draft that you can review and modify before you finalise it. Don't worry if the draft is rough or is missing information. You have a chance to fill in the gaps soon enough.

6. Check results and redraft as necessary.

Check over your draft budget and see whether it still makes sense to you. Are you missing any anticipated sources of revenue or expenses? Are the numbers realistic? Do they make sense in a historical perspective? Are they too high or too low? Will you be able to support them when you present them to upper management? The fun part of budgeting is playing with your numbers and trying out different scenarios and what-ifs. When you're satisfied with the results, sign off on your budget and turn it in. Congratulations! You did it!

The accuracy of your budget hinges on two main factors: the quality of the data you use to develop your budget and the quality of the judgement you apply to the data you're working with. Although judgement is something that comes with experience, the quality of the data you use depends on where you get it. You can use three basic approaches to develop the data for building a budget:

- **Build it from scratch.** In the absence of historical data, when you're starting up a new business unit or when you just want a fresh view, you want to develop your budgets based strictly on current estimates. In this process, widely known as *zero-based budgeting*, you build your budget from scratch, determining the people, facilities, travel, advertising and other resources that you require to support it. You then cost out each need, and the budget is complete. Perhaps not too surprisingly, the answer that comes out of building a budget from scratch is often quite different from one that results from using historical data. Funny how that works; and funny, too, how many errors and omissions building from scratch can show in some cases.

- **Use historical figures.** One of the easiest ways to develop data for your budget is to use the actual results from the preceding budget period. Although the past isn't always an indication of the future – especially when an organisation is undergoing significant change – using historical data can be very helpful in relatively stable organisations and you may have an interest in seeing which numbers have gone up and which have gone down.

- **Use the combination approach.** Many managers do both. They use a combination of zero-based budgeting and historical figures for determining which data to include in their budgets. To use this approach, gather historical data and compare the figures to the best estimates of what you think performing a particular function costs. You then adjust historical data up or down, depending on your view of reality.

Budgeting and the Real World

In any organisation a certain amount of mystery and intrigue – some call it smoke and mirrors – hovers around budgets and the budgeting process. Indeed, whether your organisation is a one-person operation or the central government, you can use many tricks of the budget trade to ensure that you get all the resources you need and desire. *Note:* In these days of big-business scandals and shenanigans, we definitely aren't suggesting that you do anything illegal, immoral or unethical. The tricks we suggest in this section are quite legal, and they're time-honoured techniques for budgeting that all kinds of organisations around the world use every day.

The make-or-buy decision

One of the most common decisions that a business makes is whether to make – that is, build or perform with in-house staff – or buy-in goods and services that are necessary for the operation of the business. For example, say that you need a security guard for your reception area to ensure the safety of your clients. Do you take on someone new as an employee, or does contracting with a company that specialises in providing security services make more sense?

When you consider such a make-or-buy decision, the first point to think about is the cost of each alternative to your firm. Say that in Case A, you hire your security guard as a full-time employee for £6.00 an hour. In Case B, a security services firm provides a guard for £8.00 an hour. On the surface, hiring a security guard as an employee seems to make the most sense. If the guard works 2,000 hours a year, then in Case A you spend £12,000 a year for your guard and in Case B you spend £16,000 a year. By employing the guard yourself, you stand to save £4,000 a year. Right?

Maybe not. See why.

Case A: Hire in-house security guard

Hourly pay rate	£6.00
Fringe benefits rate (pension, employer's health care) @ 35%	£2.10
Overheads rate (including NI, holiday cover, accommodation) @ 50%	£3.00
Total effective pay rate	**£11.10**
Hours per year	× 2,000
Total annual staff cost	**£22,200**
Annual liability insurance increase	£4,000
Uniforms/cleaning	£1,000
Miscellaneous equipment	£500
Total annual cost	**£27,700**

Case B: Contract with security firm

Hourly pay rate	£8.00
Total effective pay rate	**£8.00**
Hours per year	× 2,000
Total annual cost	**£16,000**

Surprise, surprise. Instead of saving £4,000 per year by hiring an in-house security guard, you're actually going to spend almost £12,000 more each year because more costs are involved in hiring an in-house employee than just his hourly pay. You have to add all the fringe benefits, national insurance, any pension contributions and more, plus the employee's share of overheads – facilities, electricity, air-conditioning and so forth – to the basic wage rate to get a true picture of the cost of the employee to your organisation. Furthermore, you need to purchase additional liability insurance, uniforms, uniform cleaning and any other additional equipment.

On the other hand, when you contract with a security services firm, the firm bears the cost of fringe benefits, overheads, insurance, uniforms and equipment. You simply pay the hourly fee and forget it. Furthermore, if the guard isn't any good, you just make a phone call and a replacement is sent immediately. No messy dismissals or potential tribunal cases to worry about.

Now, which deal do you think is the better one? On the face of it, no contest; contracting with the security organisation makes more sense. However, you have to remember that you lose control over the quality of service provided; the guard isn't your employee, but the contractor's; and the security firm may have nobody who's any better to send to you if this one doesn't work out.

Second – and this applies to all sorts of outsourcing – you may find that the contracting organisation no longer wishes to do business with you at some time in the future; or else it goes broke. In both cases, you face having to find a new contracting organisation or take on your own employee in any case. Also, you may prefer simply to have everyone who works on your premises as an employee, and so you accept the increased cost in return for better overall control.

As a manager, finding out how to play the budget game is definitely in your interest. Generally, the goal of the budget game is to build in enough extra money to actually be able to get the job done. In the worst case, you have enough resources available to protect your employees and vital functions when the business goes sour. In the best case, you have money left over after you pay all your necessary expenses. You can turn the money back into the accounts department with much fanfare and accept the accolades from the powers that be for your expert resource management skills, or you can apply the money to the purchase of some equipment or other department needs. Of course, if you work for the government or for many large commercial corporations, your goal is to spend every penny of your budgeted amount so that your budget doesn't decrease in the following year.

You can play the budget game up front, when you develop the budget, or during the course of the budget period. The following sections tell you how to develop a solid budget.

Producing real budgets

This section lists some of the games that the pros play when they develop budgets. Again, these aren't immoral or unethical; they're simply what's necessary to survive and prosper in the real world. Although these techniques are most appropriate for new or unstable departments or projects, you can use them when developing any budget. We may be exaggerating just a bit on some of these points, but most of them have a very clear ring of truth.

✓ **Do some selective padding.** Simple, but effective. The idea is to pad your anticipated expenses so that your budget targets are easy to achieve. You end up looking like a hero when you come in under your budget, plus you get some extra money to play with at the end of the year. This situation is known as win–win. Do be careful, though – most senior managers have worked their way up and know how the game is played. If you go really over the top, they'll think that you're pulling their leg, and will reject your budget accordingly!

✔ **Tie your budget request to your organisation's values.** This is the 'Everything in the organisation is rosy' approach to budgeting. If you want to beef up your budget in a particular area, just pick one of your organisation's values – for example, quality – and tie your request to it. When your boss asks you to justify why you've tripled your office furniture budget, just tell him that your employees can't do quality work without large, hand-crafted walnut desks.

✔ **Create more requests than you need, and give them up as you have to.** You don't want to appear unreasonable in your budget demands – don't forget, you're a team player! When you draft your budget, build in items that are of relatively low priority to you overall. When your boss puts on the pressure to reduce your budget (and bosses always do), give up the things you didn't really care so much about anyway. Doing so ensures that you get to keep the items that you really do want.

✔ **Shift the time frame.** Insist that the budget items are an investment in the company's future. The secret is to tie these investments to a big pay-off down the road. 'If we double our staff budget, we'll be able to attract the talent that we need to expand our operations.'

✔ **Be prepared.** The best defence is a good offence. Know your budget numbers cold and be ready to justify each budget item in intimate detail. Don't rely on someone else to prepare for you – this can be your finest hour as a manager. Be a star and go for it!

Staying on budget

After your new department or project starts up, you need to monitor your budget closely to make sure that you don't exceed it. If your actual expenditure starts to exceed your budget, you need to take quick and decisive action.

Following are some of the ways that experienced managers make sure that they stay on budget:

✔ **Freeze non-essentials.** Some expenses, such as staff, overheads and electricity, are essential to an operation or project and you can't stop them without jeopardising the organisation's performance. Others, such as purchasing new carpeting, upgrading computer monitors or travelling first-class, are discretionary and you can postpone them without jeopardising performance. Freezing non-essential items of expenditure is the quickest and least painful way to get your actual expenditure back in line with your budgeted expenditure.

✔ **Freeze recruitment.** Although you may have budgeted for new staff, you can save money by imposing a recruitment freeze. Not only do you save on the cost of hourly pay or salaries, but you also save on the costs of fringe benefits, staff accommodation and overheads expenses. And because you aren't tinkering with your current employees' pay or perks, generally everyone is happy with your decision. Of course, you may need to fill some critical positions in your organisation, budget problem notwithstanding. You can determine which positions you have to fill if they become vacant, and which jobs other employees can cover.

✔ **Postpone products, services and projects.** The development and production phases of new products and projects can burn up a lot of money. By postponing the start-up and implementation of these new products and projects, you can get your budget back on track. Sometimes it only takes a few weeks or months to make a difference.

✔ **Delay payments to suppliers.** Instead of paying right on time, you can delay your payments over a longer period. If you're going to go down this route, you're generally best off working this out with your suppliers in advance (that is, if you want them to continue to be your suppliers in the future).

Delaying payments to suppliers used to be a manager's favourite for improving cash flow. Of course, you do have to balance your decision to delay payments against the supplier's ability to remain in business without being paid! Otherwise you may find next time that you've got no supplies – because you've got no supplier!

✔ **Hammer suppliers.** If you're in a powerful position and take a large volume from a particular supplier, you can use this to drive the price down. Again, however, you do have to balance such a decision against the supplier's capability and willingness to continue to do business with you on this basis. And if suppliers find outlets that are prepared to do business with them on more favourable terms, they may refuse to do business with you.

✔ **Freeze wages and perks.** These kinds of savings directly affect your employees, and we can guarantee that they aren't going to like that at all. Most employees are used to regular wage and salary increases. Although increases aren't as generous as they were a decade ago, employees still consider them to be essential. However, if you've made cuts and still need to cut more, then you really don't have any choice but to freeze your employees' wages, salaries and other things such as overtime and bonuses at their current levels.

✔ **Lay off employees and close facilities.** You're in business to make money, not to lose money. When sales aren't sufficient to support your expenses – even after enacting cost-savings measures such as the ones in this list – you must take drastic action. Action doesn't get much more drastic than laying off employees and closing facilities. However, if your budget is as far off as it must be if you reach this point, then cut you have to. Refer to Chapter 17 for more information on conducting employee lay-offs and redundancies.

Understanding the Basics of Accounting

The accounting system that takes up gigabytes of storage space on your company's network server depends on a few very basic assumptions. These assumptions determine how every pound and penny that flows into and out of your organisation is assigned, reported and analysed.

Some managers believe that they can get by with little or no knowledge of accounting and finance. This attitude is a mistake. As a manager, you must be just as familiar with these accounting basics as are the employees who work in your accounting department. Not only does this knowledge help to ensure that you understand and control your organisation's financial destiny, but also if you're in command of the financial side of your business as well as the technical side, then you're also much more likely to survive the next round of corporate lay-offs.

Working out the accounting equation

Daily events affect every business's financial position. A manager spends cash to buy a stapler and is reimbursed out of the petty cash fund. The company uses its overdraft facility to pay supplier invoices. Customers pay bills and those payments are deposited. Employees receive their salaries. Each of these *financial transactions* and many more has its place in the accounting equation.

The accounting equation states that an organisation's *assets* are equal to its *liabilities* plus its *share capital*. The accounting equation looks like this:

Assets = Liabilities + Share capital

This simple equation drives the very complex system of accounting used to track every financial transaction in a business, provide reports to managers for decision making and provide financial results to owners, shareholders, lenders, the taxation authorities and other stakeholders.

So what exactly does each part of the accounting equation represent? Take a look at each part and what it comprises.

Assets

Assets are generally considered to be anything of value – primarily financial and economic resources – that a company owns. The most common forms of assets in a business include the following:

✔ **Cash:** This asset encompasses money in all its forms, including cash, other accounts, money market funds and marketable securities, such as stocks and bonds. Every business likes to have lots of cash.

✔ **Accounts receivable (or debtors):** This asset represents the money that customers who buy goods and services on credit owe to your company. For example, if your business sells a box of CD-ROMs to another business and then bills the other business for the sale instead of demanding immediate payment in cash, this obligation becomes an account receivable until your customer pays it. Accounts receivable are nice to have unless the companies or individuals that owe you money run away, close down or decide to delay their payments for six months.

✔ **Stock:** Stock is the value of merchandise held by your business for sale and the finished goods that you've manufactured but haven't yet sold, as well as the raw materials and work in progress that are part of the manufacture of finished goods. Stock usually becomes cash or an account receivable when your organisation sells it. Stock that sits around on a shelf forever isn't the best way to tie up your company's assets. Keeping your stock moving all the time is much better, because you're generating sales.

✔ **Prepaid expenses:** Prepaid expenses represent goods and services that your firm has already paid for but not yet used. For example, your company may pay its annual liability insurance premium at the beginning of the year, before the insurance policy actually goes into effect. If your organisation cancels the policy during the course of the year, then the insurance company refunds part of the premium to your business.

✔ **Equipment:** Equipment is the property – machinery, desks, computers, phones and similar items – your organisation buys to carry out its operations. For example, if your company sells computer supplies to individuals and other businesses, you need to purchase shelves on which to store your goods, fork-lifts to move it around and phone systems on which to take orders from your customers. As equipment ages, it loses value. You account for this loss through *depreciation*, which spreads the original cost of a piece of equipment across its entire useful lifetime. When in doubt, depreciate.

✔ **Property:** Property includes the land, buildings and facilities that your organisation owns or controls. Examples include office buildings, manufacturing plants, warehouses, sales offices, mills, farms and other forms of property.

Assets are divided into two major types: *current assets* and *fixed assets*.

✔ **Current assets** can be converted into cash, normally within one year. Such assets are considered to be *liquid*. In the preceding list of assets, cash, accounts receivable, stock and prepaid expenses are considered current assets. Liquid assets are useful to have around in case you ever get into difficulties; however, you do need to remember that once people know that you're in difficulties, the prices that you're able to charge when trying to raise cash tend to go down.

✔ **Fixed assets** require more than one year to convert to cash. In the preceding list of assets, equipment and property are classified as fixed assets. If your business gets into trouble and you need cash, fixed assets probably won't do you much good unless you can use them as collateral for a loan.

Liabilities

Liabilities are generally considered to be debts that you owe to others – individuals, other businesses, banks and so on – outside the company. In essence, liabilities are the claims that outside individuals and organisations have against a business's assets.

The most common forms of business liabilities include the following:

✔ **Accounts payable (or creditors):** Accounts payable are the obligations that your company owes to the individuals and organisations from which it purchases goods and services. For example, when you visit your local office supply store to buy a couple of pencils and bill the purchase to your company's account, this obligation becomes an account payable. If you need to, you can negotiate delayed payments with suppliers in times of need, but you do need to be careful not to jeopardise your credit rating or business confidence.

✔ **Short-term loans:** Short-term loans are loans made to your organisation by individuals, financial institutions or other organisations that you're due to pay back within one year. If, for example, your firm takes a 90-day loan to increase its inventory of CD-ROMs to satisfy a rapid increase in customer demand, this is considered a short-term loan.

✔ **Expenses:** Expenses are those items that your company incurs and has to pay regardless of the volumes of business conducted. Examples include payroll, sick leave due to employees, taxes payable and interest due to lenders.

✔ **Bonds and debentures:** Some large companies issue bonds and debentures to raise money to finance expansion or achieve other goals. Bonds and debentures represent the money that a company owes to the individuals and organisations that purchase the bonds and debentures as an investment on which a fixed and assured rate of return exists.

✔ **Mortgages:** When organisations purchase property, they often do so by incurring long-term loans known as *mortgages*. Mortgages differ from standard loans in that they're usually secured on the property that the mortgage finances. For example, if your company defaults in its payments on the mortgage used to purchase your office building, ownership of the office building reverts to the entity that originally issued the mortgage, usually a bank or investment group.

Like assets, liabilities are also divided into two major types: *current liabilities* and *long-term liabilities*.

✔ **Current liabilities** are repayable within one year. In the preceding list of liabilities, accounts payable, short-term loans and accrued expenses are considered current liabilities.

✔ **Long-term liabilities** are repayable in a period greater than one year. In the preceding list of liabilities, bonds and debentures and mortgages are classified as long-term liabilities.

Share capital

All businesses have owners. In some cases, the owners are a few individuals who founded the company. In other cases, the owners are the many thousands of individuals who buy the company's stock through public offerings. *Share capital* is the shareholders' possession of the assets of a business after all liabilities have been paid. *Shareholders' liabilities* – their responsibilities if the business goes bankrupt – are limited to the face value of the shares themselves.

Retained earnings

Retained earnings are the profits left over from conducting business once shareholders have received their dividends. *Dividends* are what's paid out to those who put their money into shares in the company – their reward for their investment and risk. Retained earnings are then used to reinvest in the business, new product and service development, financing new ventures and developing and expanding into new markets.

Knowing double-entry bookkeeping

Double-entry bookkeeping is the standard method of recording financial transactions that forms the basis of modern business accounting. Invented in 1494 by Luca Pacioli, a bored Franciscan monk (he must have been really bored to invent accounting!), double-entry bookkeeping recognises that every financial transaction results in a record of a *receipt* (also known as an asset) and a record of an *expense* (also known as a liability).

Consider this example: your company buys £1,000 worth of CD-ROMs from a manufacturer to resell to your customers. Because your company has established an account with the disk manufacturer, the manufacturer bills you for the £1,000 instead of demanding immediate cash payment. Here's the double-entry version of the accounting equation illustrating the £1,000 purchase of CD-ROMs now in stock:

Assets	=	*Liabilities*	+	*Share capital*
£1,000	=	£1,000	+	£0
(Stock)		(Accounts payable)		

In this example, assets (stock) increase by £1,000, the cost of purchasing the CD-ROMs to stock your shelves. At the same time, liabilities (accounts payable) also increase by £1,000. This increase represents the debt you owe to your supplier of CD-ROMs. In this way, the accounting equation always stays balanced.

Identifying the Most Common Types of Financial Statements

An accounting system is nice to have, but the system is worthless unless it can produce data that's useful to managers, employees, lenders, suppliers, owners, investors and other individuals and firms that have a financial stake in your business. And believe us; a lot of people have a financial interest in your business.

All financial statements are nothing more than reports, intended for distribution to individuals outside the accounting department, that summarise the amounts of money contained in selected accounts or groups of accounts at a selected point or period. Each type of financial statement has a unique value to those people who use it, and different individuals may use some or all of an organisation's financial statements during the normal course of business. The following sections review the financial statements that you're most likely to encounter during your career as a manager.

The balance sheet

The *balance sheet* is a report that illustrates the value of a company's assets, liabilities and share capital – the company's financial position on a specific date. Think of it as a snapshot of the business. Although it can be prepared at any time, a balance sheet is usually prepared at the end of an accounting period, usually a year, quarter or month.

Figure 18-1 shows a typical balance sheet.

	31 January 2011
ASSETS	
CURRENT ASSETS	
Cash and cash equivalents	£458,000
Assets and liabilities	£11,759,000
Stock	£154,000
Prepaid expenses and other current assets	£283,000
Refundable income taxes	£165,000
TOTAL CURRENT ASSETS	£12,819,000
EQUIPMENT AND FURNITURE	
Equipment	£4,746,000
Furniture, fixtures and improvements	£583,000
	£5,329,000
Allowance for depreciation and amortisation	£(2,760,000)
	£2,569,000
COMPUTER SOFTWARE COSTS, NET	£3,199,000
NET DEPOSITS AND OTHER	£260,000
	£18,847,000
LIABILITIES AND SHAREHOLDERS' EQUITY	
CURRENT LIABILITIES	
Loans payable to bank	£1,155,000
Accounts payable	£2,701,000
Accrued compensation and benefits	£2,065,000
Income taxes payable	£0
Deferred income taxes	£990,000
Current portion of long-term debt	£665,000
TOTAL CURRENT LIABILITIES	£18,847,000
LONG-TERM DEBT, less current portion	£864,000
DEFERRED RENT EXPENSE	£504,000
DEFERRED INCOME TAXES	£932,000
STOCKHOLDERS' EQUITY	
Common stock	£76,000
Additional paid-in capital	£803,000
Retained earnings	£8,092,000
	£8,971,000
	£18,847,000

Figure 18-1:
A typical balance sheet.

As you can see, the balance sheet provides values for every major component of the three parts of the accounting equation. By reviewing each item's value in the balance sheet, managers can identify potential problems and then take action to solve them.

The profit and loss account

Assets and liabilities are all very nice, thank you, but many people really want to see the bottom line. Did the company make money or lose money? In other words, what was its profit, or loss? This job belongs to the *profit and loss account* (sometimes called the profit and loss statement).

A profit and loss account adds all the sources of a company's revenues and then subtracts all the sources of its expenses to determine its net income or net loss for a particular period of time. Whereas a balance sheet is a snapshot of an organisation's financial status, a profit and loss account is more like a film; we explain the various roles in the following sections.

Figure 18-2 illustrates a simple profit and loss account.

Turnover

Turnover is the value received by a company through the sale of goods, services and other sources such as interest, rent, royalties and so forth. To arrive at net sales, total sales of goods and services are offset by returns; and also by *allowances* such as discounts, special offers and other product- and service-based promotions (for example, handing out free product samples, or giving discounts for online bookings).

Expenses

Expenses are all the costs of doing business. For accounting purposes, expenses are divided into two major classifications:

- ✔ **Cost of goods sold:** For a firm that retails or wholesales merchandise to individuals or other companies, this figure represents the cost of purchasing merchandise or stock. By subtracting the cost of goods sold from revenue, you end up with the company's *gross profit*.

- ✔ **Operating expenses or overheads:** Operating expenses or overheads are all the other costs of doing business not already part of the cost of goods sold. Operating expenses or overheads are usually further sub-divided into *selling expenses*, which include marketing, advertising, product promotion and the costs of operating stores, and *general and administrative expenses*, which are the actual administrative costs of running the business. General and administrative costs typically include salaries, accounting, data processing and purchasing; and the cost of corporate facilities including rent, rates, heating, lighting, water, telecommunications and transport.

Twelve months ended
31 January 2011

TURNOVER

Gross sales	£58,248,000	
Less: Returns	£1,089,000	
Net sales		£57,159,000

COST OF GOODS SOLD

Beginning stock		£4,874,000
Purchases	£38,453,000	
Less: Purchase discounts	£1,583,000	
Net purchases		£36,867,000
Cost of goods available for sale		£41,741,000
Less: Ending stock		£6,887,000
Cost of goods sold		£34,854,000

GROSS PROFIT £22,305,000

OPERATING EXPENSES

Total selling expenses	£8,456,000	
Total general expenses	£1,845,000	
Total operating expenses		£10,301,000
Operating income		£12,004,000
Other income and expenses		
Interest expense (income)	£360,000	
Total other income and expenses		£10,301,000
Income before taxes		£11,644,000
Less: Income taxes		£3,952,000
Net income		£7,692,000
Average number of shares		3,500,000
Net income		£2.20

Figure 18-2:
A simple profit and loss account.

Net profit or loss

The difference between revenues and expenses (after adjustment for interest income or expense and payment of taxes) is a company's net profit or net loss. Also commonly known as a company's *bottom line*, net profit or loss is the cash you have on hand after you've paid all the bills, and it's the figure that everyone wants to know when they're assessing the firm's financial health. Many corporate executives and managers have found themselves on the street when their companies' bottom lines dipped too far into the loss side of the equation.

The cash-flow statement

The cash-flow statement shows the movement of cash into and out of a business. It doesn't take an Einstein to realise that when more cash is moving out of a business than is moving into the business for a prolonged period, the business may be in big trouble. Without cash to pay employees' salaries, suppliers' invoices, loan payments and so forth, operations quickly cease to exist.

Cash-flow statements come in several varieties:

- **The simple cash-flow statement** arranges all items into one of two categories: cash inflows and cash outflows.

- **The operating cash-flow statement** limits analysis of cash flows to only those items having to do with the operations of a business, and not its financing.

- **The priority cash-flow statement** classifies cash inflows and outflows by specific groupings chosen by the manager or other individual who requests preparation of the statement.

Analysing Business Health

If you don't know exactly what you're looking for, analysing a company's financial records can be quite a daunting task. Fortunately, over many years expert business financial analysts have developed ways to assess the performance and financial health and well-being of an organisation quickly.

Using financial ratios

By comparing the ratios of certain key financial indicators to established standards and to other firms in the same industries, interested parties can assess how well a business is doing. The key ratios are:

✔ **Current ratio:** This ratio is the capability of a company to pay its current liabilities out of its current assets. A ratio of 2 or more is generally considered good. Consider this example:

Current ratio = *Current assets* ÷ *Current liabilities*

= £100 million ÷ £25 million

= 4.00

✔ **Quick ratio:** The quick ratio (also known as the *acid-test* ratio) is the same as the current ratio with the exception that you subtract stock from current assets. This ratio provides a much more rigorous test of a firm's capability to pay its current liabilities quickly than does the current ratio, because you can't liquidate stock as rapidly as other current assets. A ratio of 1 or better is acceptable. Do note, however, that large organisations in practice tend to extend their overdraft facilities or limit dividends to shareholders if they need to, rather than selling off assets that they want to keep for the longer term. The acid test is, however, critical in analysing the cash flow and performance of small and medium-sized organisations.

Quick ratio = *(Current assets – inventory) ÷ Current liabilities*

= (£100 million – £10 million) ÷ £25 million

= £90 million ÷ £25 million

= 3.60

✔ **Debtors turnover ratio:** This ratio indicates the average time it takes for a firm to convert its accounts receivable into cash. A higher ratio indicates that customers are paying their bills quickly, which is good. A lower ratio reflects slow collections and a possible problem that management needs to address, which is bad. Your boss isn't going to like it.

Debtors turnover ratio = *Net sales ÷ Accounts receivable*

= £50 million ÷ £5 million

= 10.00

You can gain one more interesting piece of information quickly from the debtors turnover ratio. By dividing 365 days by the debtors turnover ratio, you get the average number of days that it takes your firm to turn over its debtors, which is commonly known as the *average collection period*. The shorter the average collection period, the better the organisation's situation is, and the better your job security is.

Average collection period = *365 days ÷ Debtors turnover ratio*

= 365 days ÷ 10.00

= 36.5 days

✔ **Debt-to-equity ratio:** This ratio measures the extent to which the organisation depends on loans from outside creditors versus resources provided by shareholders and other owners. A ratio in excess of 1 is generally considered unfavourable, because it indicates that the firm may have difficulty repaying its debts.

The debt-to-equity ratio indicates the *capital gearing* of the firm. People expect to see as much of the equity as possible in the form of share capital, because then little risk exists that the creditors will call in their loans. So the higher the volume of debt in relation to equity, the higher the *gearing* (or volatility) of the organisation; and when that gearing shows no signs of coming down, stock markets and other backers and interested parties begin to lose confidence in the organisation.

Debt-to-equity ratio = *Total liabilities ÷ Share capital*
= £50 million ÷ £150 million
= 0.33 or 33 per cent

✔ **Return on investment:** Often known by its abbreviation, *ROI*, return on investment measures the capability of a company to earn profits for its owners. Don't forget: profit is good and loss is bad. Because owners – shareholders and other investors – prefer to make money on their investments, they like an organisation's ROI to be as high as possible.

Return on investment = *Net income ÷ Share capital*
= £50 million ÷ £150 million
= 0.33 or 33 per cent

Using other measures

As a manager, you must be able to do the following calculations, and know and understand what they mean for your company, your business and your own department or domain. These calculations enable you to be very precise about where the resources for which you're responsible are used and consumed. They provide the basis for assessing the effectiveness of particular activities, and they enable you to measure and assess financial performance and give information that your company can review as often as necessary or desired.

You need to be able to work out income, expenditure, profit and loss per employee, per product or service, per product or service cluster, per location and per outlet. This information helps to ensure that everyone knows where money is being made and lost, and by whom.

✔ **For the employees:** Take the number of employees and divide the total turnover by this figure so that you know how much turnover is produced on average per employee.

✔ **For the products and services:** Divide total sales by the number of outlets you have, so that you can see average sales per outlet. You can also identify the relationship between sales of one product or service and others.

You can then develop this approach further so that the data works for you in your situation. For example:

✔ Percentage of payroll spent on front-line staff, administrative staff, corporate staff and head office.

✔ Products and services that attract people's attention in the first place; products and services that sell; and products and services that make money. For example, car companies use top-of-the-range models to attract; they then sell largest volumes of lower- to mid-range models; and they make their money through finance plans, service guarantees, add-ons and guaranteed insurance arrangements.

Top five accounting websites

If you want to find out more about accounting (and, hey, who wouldn't?), here are our top five websites:

✔ *Business Finance* magazine: `www.businessfinancemag.com`

✔ **Institute of Chartered Accountants:** `www.ica.org.uk`

✔ **Association of Certified and Chartered Accountants:** `www.acca.org.uk`

✔ *AccountingWEB*: `www.accountingweb.co.uk`

✔ **Accounting Conventions:** `www.businessdictionary.com`

Chapter 19

Harnessing the Power of Technology

In This Chapter

▶ Using technology to help you

▶ Understanding the pros and cons of technology

▶ Going for efficiency and productivity

▶ Putting technology to use

▶ Developing a technology plan

*L*ike everything in life, technology has good and bad points. With computers, for example, managers and workers alike have more ways to waste time than ever before. When all you could do with a keyboard was type, you couldn't get managers anywhere near one – they had secretaries to do that kind of stuff. Now, call it a computer, add email and the Internet, and you can't get managers away from it. Research shows that managers spend up to five hours of their working day on the computer. When you add the average of three hours a day in meetings, this doesn't leave much time to do the real work. And do you really need to spend half an hour typing, editing, spellchecking and colour printing a gorgeous, 64-shades-of-grey memo when a handwritten note or quick phone call works just as well? You may automatically assume that your employees are more productive simply because they have computers at their fingertips, but are you (and your organisation) really getting the most out of this innovative and expensive technology?

In light of this question, in this chapter we explain how to harness *information technology* – technology used to create, store, exchange and utilise information in its various forms. We examine the technology edge, and consider how technology can help or hinder an organisation. We look at how technology can improve efficiency and productivity, and how to get the most out of it. Finally, we describe how to create a technology plan.

Using Technology to Your Advantage

You can easily get the impression that information technology is taking over the world. Certainly, computers and telecommunications technology are ever more important. CEOs and senior managers all use computers and mobile phones exactly the same as everyone else, because they too (some would say above all) need to be instantly responsive when required. Overall, information technology can create tremendous advantages for you and your business, and you must capitalise on them – before your competition does.

Information and telecommunications technology is only as good as the people who use it. So whatever technology you implement, make sure that your staff know and understand how to use their equipment. Also ensure that they understand what they're *not* allowed to use the technology for – such as booking holidays in the firm's time, or downloading material from controversial or obscene websites).

First, understand the technology and what it can do for you, your organisation, and your staff. You need to take the decision whether to let technology use you or you use it to facilitate more effective, productive and high-quality work. Next, make sure that your staff are fully trained. Using expensive technology to less than full capacity simply because employees don't know what to do with it, is wasteful. Finally, recognise that technology is a 'sunk cost', as well as an investment on which you're looking for returns. This means that, whenever it becomes necessary, you have to be prepared to junk your technology and replace it in order to stay competitive. So you need to make sure that your technology works as effectively as possible for you before it becomes obsolete.

The following sections outline four basic necessities for putting modern technology to work for you.

Know your business

Before you can design and implement an effective information technology strategy for your business, you have to completely understand how your business works – what work is done, who's doing it and what resources they need to get their work done.

One way to get to really know your business is to approach it as an outsider. Pretend you're a customer and look at how your company's people and systems handle you. Do the same with your competitors to see how their people and systems handle you. Compare the differences and the similarities to determine how you can improve your own organisation as a result of what you discover.

Create a technology-competitive advantage

Few managers understand how technology can become a competitive advantage for their business. Although they may have vague notions of potential efficiency gains or increased productivity, they're clueless when dealing with specifics.

Information technology can create real and dramatic competitive advantages over other businesses in your markets, specifically by

- ✔ Using the Internet as a marketing tool, as a part of your corporate and institutional presentation and image building. The Internet can enhance and develop the image and presentation that you want for all your marketing activities, as well as being a vehicle for sales.

    Make sure that the messages you convey on the Internet are the same as or complementary to those put out elsewhere.

- ✔ Using the Internet as an additional marketing, sales, customer and client liaison vehicle.

- ✔ Using the Internet to discover potential (and we stress *potential*) staff, suppliers, customers and product and service outlets.

- ✔ Linking everyone in the company with each other, and with key suppliers, distributors, outlets, customers and clients.

- ✔ Providing up-to-the-minute information on pricing, products and services.

Any website that you develop must be kept up to date. If it's to be fully effective and complementary to the full range of your business activities, you need to check it once a week; some organisations do this once a day, and the best have staff dedicated to changing the website as soon as anything occurs that requires an update.

Develop a plan

If you're serious about using any technology to full advantage, you must have a plan for its implementation. You can find details about creating a technology plan later in this chapter (see the section 'Planning and Implementation'), but the following are several points to remember in the planning process:

- ✔ **Don't buy technology just because it's the latest and greatest thing.** Everybody loves gadgets – and everybody loves the latest gadget above all. However, just because an item is new doesn't mean that it's right for your business. Be sure that whatever technology you include in your plan makes sense for your business.

✔ **Plan for the right period of time.** Different kinds of businesses require different *planning horizons*, the time periods covered by their plans. If you're in a highly volatile market – wireless communications, for example – then your planning horizon may be only six months or so ahead. If you're in a stable market – say, a grocery chain – your planning horizon may extend three to five years into the future.

✔ **Make the planning process a team effort.** You're not the only one who'll be affected by all this new technology that you bring into your company. Keep customers and suppliers informed of any changes that affect them; and above all, involve your staff – they're the people, after all, who will use the new technology.

✔ **Weigh up the costs of upgrading your old system versus moving to a new system.** Every system eventually comes to the end of its useful life. So you have to choose whether to patch up what you have or replace it altogether. And you need to approach that decision from the point of view of how long the system is likely to remain useful into the future, whether you're patching it up or replacing it.

✔ **Make time to train your staff so that they're expert in whatever technology you use.** If you don't, you'll find yourself with expensive equipment that people aren't using to its full potential.

Always bear 'Moore's Law' in mind: the power of technology doubles every 18 months. You need to use this knowledge

✔ To assess whether your not fully up-to-date technology is serving its purpose nevertheless

✔ To see whether replacing or upgrading your technology would produce the returns over the period of time for which you want to use it

✔ As a broader guide to assessing what's available in terms of the business benefits that the technology can deliver rather than just its newness

You should also develop your expertise so that you recognise when your technology is genuinely obsolete and truly needs replacing (again, for business reasons rather than just because it's not the very latest thing).

Get some help

If you're a fan of technology and expert in it, that's great – but beware! Don't get drawn down the line of being blinded by technology for its own sake; always keep in mind its use in your organisation and how people less expert and enthusiastic than you are going to use it. Involve everyone, and if necessary engage a technician or technology consultant to advise on the process. If you do bring in a consultant, make sure that you involve the staff affected in making the changes.

Evaluating the Benefits and Drawbacks of Technology

Think for a moment about the incredible progress of information technology just in your lifetime. Can you believe that three decades ago the personal computer had yet to be introduced commercially? Word processing used to mean a typewriter and a lot of correction fluid or sheets of messy carbon paper, but computers have revolutionised the way in which business people can manipulate and deliver text, graphics and other elements in their reports and other documents. The mobile phone, the laptop, the iPad, the Blackberry and other business technology essentials are all recent innovations; and they're all certain to be developed greatly over the next few years.

So how can technology help your business? Information technology can have a positive impact in these very important ways:

- ✔ **By automating processes:** Not too many years ago, most business processes were manual. For example, your organisation's accounting and payroll departments most likely did their calculations entirely by hand, using only calculators to assist them. People can now accomplish in minutes what used to take hours, days or weeks. Other commonly automated processes are stock tracking, customer service, call analysis and purchasing.

- ✔ **By automating personal management functions:** Managers can now make available their personal schedules and diaries to everyone who needs them.

- ✔ **By creating the ability to carry personal data around at all times:** Managers can now keep abreast of everything that they need as the result of portable information technology.

- ✔ **By keeping in contact around the clock:** Managers can now be accessed at any time, for any reason. Although managers need to preserve their work–life balance, this ease of contact means that things such as crisis management can be engaged much more quickly.

Before you run off and automate or upgrade everything, keep this piece of information in mind: if your present system is inefficient or ineffective, simply upgrading the existing system won't necessarily make it perform any better. In fact, upgrading it can make your system perform worse than the manual version. Whatever you do, review and evaluate all processes in detail. Cut out any unnecessary steps as you go along, and make sure that your system is designed for the future and not the past. And if that sounds a time-consuming process, it's time well spent.

Just as information technology can help a business, it can also hinder it. Here are a few examples of the negative side of information technology:

- ✔ Widespread worker abuse of Internet access has reduced worker productivity by 10 to 15 per cent. Forrester Research, an American think tank, estimates that 20 per cent of employee time on the Internet at work doesn't involve their jobs; other studies in the UK by the Chartered Management Institute, put the figure as high as 30 per cent of time.

- ✔ Hackers have sent periodic waves of computer viruses and malicious attacks through the business world, leaving billions of pounds' worth of damage and lost productivity in their wake.

- ✔ Non-experts spend inordinate amounts of unproductive – and expensive – time trying to make things work, in spite of the fact that they're not qualified to do so.

- ✔ Email messages can be unclear and confusing, forcing workers to waste time clarifying the intention or covering themselves in case of problems.

- ✔ Employees are forced to wade through an ever-growing quantity of spam and junk email messages.

- ✔ The slick, animated and sound-laden computer-based full-colour presentations so common today often tend to drown out the message you're trying to get across. People lose sight of what they're supposed to absorb, do or act on as the result of the presentation.

If you're in any doubt about the amount of time that information technology can consume, consider the findings of Patrick Glynn. He surveyed his own organisation, the headquarters of one of the largest UK banks, and found that providing a substantial answer to an important email took about 20 minutes. At that rate you can process only three emails an hour; so if you have 30 important emails to answer, they effectively take up a whole day's work.

You have to take the bad with the good with information technology. But don't take the bad lying down. You know the problems and difficulties – so recognise them at the outset, and take active steps to prevent them occurring. You can do this by

- ✔ **Staying abreast of the latest information technology innovations and news.** Although you don't need to become an expert on how to install a network server or configure your voice-mail system, you do need to become conversant in the technology behind your business systems.

- ✔ **Hiring experts.** Although you must have a general knowledge of information technology, plan to hire experts to advise you on the specifics. Always seek expert advice on the design and implementation of critical information technology-based systems.

> ✔ **Managing by walking around.** Make a habit of dropping in on employees, wherever they're located, and observe how they use your organisation's information technology. Ask them for their opinions and suggestions for improvement. Research and implement changes as soon as you discover a need.

One point is certain: everyone's lumbered with the present state of technology and the great speed at which it develops. Therefore, you have to know and understand what current technology can do for you, as well as keep an eye on what new innovations or inventions can offer. So you have to become an expert in assessing and evaluating the potential of technology, the amount that it costs and the returns that it can (and can't) deliver for your organisation.

Improving Efficiency and Productivity

British industry has shifted from primary manufacturing and engineering activities to domination by the service sector. The service sector – whether public services, commerce, financial services, leisure, travel, tourism or retail – depends on the speed and quality of information and data processing to maintain, secure and develop competitive advantage.

The idea that businesspeople who manage information best have a competitive advantage in the marketplace seems obvious enough. The sooner you receive information, the sooner you can act on it. The more efficiently you handle information, the easier you can access it when and where you need it. The more effectively you deal with information, the fewer expenses you incur for managing and maintaining your information.

Managers often cite the preceding reasons, and others like them, as justification for allotting vast amounts of corporate resources to buying computers, installing email and voice-mail systems and training employees to use them. Unfortunately, for years researchers found no evidence to prove that office automation resulted in measurable productivity gains. This led many to label the phenomenon the *productivity paradox*, meaning that technology that's supposed to make it easier for someone to do a job, more quickly, to a higher standard and with fewer errors actually produces fewer results, less quickly. The problem now is that work is done at the machine's speed, rather than the speed at which the individual works.

Author Eliyahu Goldratt defined information as 'the answer to a question'. Many information systems are great at providing data, but not so hot at providing information (at least within this definition). As a manager, you need to first identify the questions that need answers, then who needs the answers (customers, suppliers, employees, management), how fast (now, within one minute, one hour, one day) and how frequently (daily, weekly, monthly). When the answers to these questions become clear, you have a rational basis on which to evaluate alternative technologies. A great deal of technology seems to be designed to provide an immediate answer to a question that you only need to ask once a month.

The key to effective planning and implementation of information technology systems is understanding what they're supposed to do for you. You also need to know the environment and context within which they're to be implemented and, above all, the results that they're supposed to deliver. For example:

- ✔ Ryanair and easyJet have transformed air travel in Western and Central Europe. They cut out the cost of employing travel agents to make bookings, requiring people to book online or, at a premium rate, through their own call centres. However, the online booking facility isn't an end in itself; it's underpinned by the major cost and price advantages that each of the companies delivers, relative to the competition, including European flag-carrier airlines. And when Michael O'Leary, the CEO of Ryanair, was asked whether by getting customers to book online he was eliminating those who didn't have computer access, he simply replied: 'We are the largest volume carrier in Europe; and we carry more passengers than British Airways.'

- ✔ Honda UK at Swindon has a fully automated supply-side process. As parts are removed from the shelves to go on to the production lines, they're automatically deducted from the stock level; when the stock level reaches a particular point, a request to suppliers is automatically generated. The supply-side contract means that suppliers must dispatch within two hours, and Honda must receive their requirements within four hours.

Other companies have taken an enlightened view of 'the technology in its environment' to great effect. Especially, they've recognised the limitations of what technology does. For example:

- ✔ Semco, a Brazilian manufacturing company and globally iconic organisation, closed down one computerised accounting and billing system because it did the job more slowly than clerks working with calculators.

- ✔ Mobile communications retailer Carphone Warehouse forbids its staff to send emails to each other unless, and until, they've first talked face to face, or unless the particular member of staff isn't on the premises for some reason. The company takes the view that far more gets done, far more quickly, when people talk to rather than write to each other.

Technology projects

If you're installing new technology in your organisation, you need to address the following questions: What do you want the technology to do for you? How will it be integrated into the rest of the organisation and its work? Which staff will use it? How much will it cost? How will we get our money back?

The answers to these questions must be your guide. The technology itself – both hardware and software – is of no consequence; what does matter is its use and value to the organisation. This and no other is the basis for choosing your equipment, computers and any other technology – they're working tools, not fashion items or 'must haves'.

Information technology projects can, and do, overrun on cost and installation times, and underperform when it comes to usage and value, particularly if you're driven by the technology itself rather than the answers to the questions above. The public sector, commerce and industry alike are riddled with major technology projects that have been under-designed, under-costed and under-evaluated. The UK's National Health Service national database was costed originally at £440 million; to date, it has cost £2.7 billion and is still not fully functional. This situation can happen to anyone, at any level. So be careful, and don't get sidetracked by the brand and cachet of the technology itself, especially when they're driven by fashion and fad rather than value.

So merely installing computers and other information technology doesn't automatically lead to gains in employee efficiency or product and service performance. As a manager, you must take the time to analyse and evaluate the environment in which the work has to be done. To be fully effective, the technology must integrate fully with the aims and objectives of the business, the ways in which it delivers products and services, and the capabilities and qualities of the staff doing the work.

Getting the Most Out of Information Technology

The personal computer shifted the power of computing away from huge mainframes and onto the desks of individual users. Now, computer networks are bringing a new revolution in business. Although the personal computer is a self-sufficient island of information, when you link these islands together in a network, individual computers have the added benefit of sharing that information with every other computer on the network. A computer network can create huge benefits for you and your organisation, for example:

✔ **It can improve communication.** A network will allow all employees in your organisation to communicate with each other quickly and easily. At the click of a button they can send messages to individuals or groups of employees, and they can reply just as easily. Furthermore, employees can use the network to access the financial, marketing and product information they need to do their job, from anywhere in the organisation.

✔ **It can save time and money.** In business, time is money. The faster you can get something done, the more tasks you can complete during your business day. Email allows you to create messages, memos and other internal communications, to attach documents to them if necessary, and to transmit them instantaneously to as many colleagues as you want. And these colleagues can be located across the room or around the world – and they all get the same message at the same time.

✔ **It can improve understanding of markets, products and services.** Information communicated via a network is timely, direct and standardised. Everyone gets the same message and so can develop the same understanding of the company's vision and values. Everyone receives the same information on the company's products, services and markets, and on how they're performing. As a result, all staff should have a much clearer understanding of the business environment than was previously possible.

✔ **It can improve and underpin staff cohesion.** Because everybody has the same access to information, and receives the same messages in an unfiltered way, much greater potential exists for mutual cohesion and commitment, provided that you use the network to support the organisation's core values and staff management practices. However, problems always occur if you deliver different messages to different groups of employees. Because so many people have access to so much more information, this practice will be revealed very quickly. Make sure your network communications are transparent and ethical (see Chapter 10 on communicating effectively and Chapter 14 on behaving ethically).

Obviously setting up a computer network involves expense, but it will underpin the culture, values, product and service knowledge of your organisation and reinforce its very foundations.

Whatever information you publicise or communicate online or via email must also be available to anyone who doesn't have a computer link to you. Make sure you always provide hard copies too. Also ensure that vitally important information is still posted on company notice boards or distributed to everyone in paper form.

Planning and Implementation

In the fast-changing world of technology, having a *technology plan* – a plan for acquiring and deploying information technology – is a must. Many businesses buy bits and pieces of computer hardware, software and other technology without considering what they already have in place, and without looking very far into the future. Then, when they try to hook it all up, they're surprised that their thrown-together system doesn't work.

Managers who take the time to develop and implement a technology plan don't have this problem, and aren't forced to spend far more money and time fixing systems problems. Follow these steps to ensure a smooth implementation process:

1. **Create the plan.**

   You provide the vision of the chosen technology – what it's supposed to deliver, how, when, where and to whom. In order to give this vision life, you have to be able to present it in ways that your colleagues and staff can understand, so get them involved. Without doubt, they'll be able to see potential that you haven't thought of, and also spot glitches or problems; after all, they'll be implementing and using the technology in the pursuit of your grand vision.

2. **Cost the plan.**

   You need to know how much your investment in technology will cost and what returns on your investment you're likely to get. You then need to relate this information to your departmental or organisational budget. Also consider a timescale for predicted returns.

3. **Screen and select suppliers.**

   Visit potential suppliers yourself. Take your technology plan – drawn up in step one, in consultation with your staff – with you. Show potential suppliers what you want, and ask them if they can deliver it. If they respond, 'No, we can't deliver this; but we can deliver something much better', listen to them, evaluate their proposal and go back to your staff to discuss it. Alternatively, if they respond, 'No, we can't deliver this; we'll deliver what we always deliver regardless of customer requirements', then just walk away.

4. **Implement the plan.**

   So everyone has agreed on the technology plan and you've chosen your supplier. Now comes the tricky part – implementation. Be in absolutely no doubt that glitches, delays, overruns and teething troubles will occur – they always do. At the implementation phase build in as much slack and leeway as necessary to allow for problems to arise and for you to resolve them.

5. Monitor performance.

And so finally your system is up and running. Congratulations all round! However, this is crunch time as you determine whether the system is really going to deliver what you planned. Teething troubles are inevitable, so make sure that you have a watertight service agreement with your supplier, committing them to sorting out any problems as soon as they occur. Make sure that your supplier's support staff are completely familiar with your system; if they aren't, insist that the supplier provides training for them.

If the worst happens and the system doesn't deliver what you and your staff expected, you must acknowledge the problem and deal with it. Don't respond like many large corporations and public service bodies by trying to make the unworkable work.

6. Train your staff.

Train your employees so that they can use the technology to its maximum advantage, getting the best possible returns before it becomes obsolete. Repeat this process each time that you change or upgrade your technology; don't assume that just because your staff can use one form of equipment, they can use all forms of it.

Remember that any technology is only as good as the people who use it.

'Everything takes twice as long as you think, and costs twice as much.' While never an excuse for organisational slackness or waste of resources, this truism underpins the point that nothing ever goes completely according to schedule.

Technology is a strategic expense; all organisations and their managers need to see technology projects as investments on which there are demonstrable and quantifiable returns. Make sure that whatever you do is guided by the business, product, service and market drivers of the organisation, and the results that the organisation expects you, as a manager, to deliver.

Top five information technology websites

You can find loads of IT info on the web, but these sites are the cream of the crop:

✔ *Wired* magazine: www.wired.com

✔ **Computerworld:** www.computerworld.com

✔ **IBM:** www.ibm.com

✔ **Accenture:** www.accenture.com

✔ **InternetWorld:** www.internetworld.co.uk

Chapter 20

Formulating Strategies for Being a Global Manager

- -

In This Chapter

▶ Understanding what globalisation is

▶ Seeing the opportunities and pitfalls in expanding overseas

▶ Having the necessary management skills, knowledge and understanding

▶ Recognising the problems and opportunities associated with outsourcing

- -

*W*e live in a world of multinational, international and global organisations, markets and activities, so if you want to be an expert manager you have to be able to survive and be successful and effective in it.

You need to start by choosing between some basic alternative approaches to globalisation and internationalisation, as follows:

- ✔ You and your organisation impose your preferred ways of doing things on every location in which you work because you can.

- ✔ You and your organisation impose your preferred ways of doing things on every location because you know and understand that your standards are high enough to transcend any local difficulties or differences.

- ✔ You and your organisation choose to fit in with the habits, customs and ways of working of every location in which you work.

Another way of looking at your approach is the extent to which you identify with the following:

- ✔ Think as a global organisation, and act as a global organisation.

- ✔ Think as a global organisation, and act in the best interests of all the places and regions where you have activities.

Nothing is inherently wrong with any of these approaches as long as you don't use your power and strength to act as a bully. Knowing and understanding your own and your organisation's perspective is important, however, because it affects the ways in which you conduct all your dealings with the particular locations in your role as manager. It also affects the ways in which the people in those locations perceive and understand you and your business.

This chapter covers everything you need to know and be able to do in order to take advantage of all the opportunities that today's globalised world has to offer organisations and their managers.

Defining Globalisation

Globalisation is the process of expanding business activities across national boundaries, cultures, time zones, locations, languages and social barriers. This process is driven by a variety of forces, as follows:

- **Global presence:** You operate in hundreds of different countries and locations across the world, with your offices, premises, products and services visible and available to all.

- **Global technology:** You have access to, or command of, technology that's universally used, understood and applied.

- **Global influence:** Your product and service quality and value, and project and project-based activities and delivery, are noted worldwide.

- **Global standards:** You set the standards for everyone in your industry; examples are companies such as Panasonic, Sony, Toshiba and Samsung in electrical goods; Boeing and Airbus in airlines; and Toyota and Nissan in car production and sales.

- **Financial size:** You have access to the sheer volume of finance and resources necessary to maintain and develop a global and international presence.

- **Market influence or dominance:** You're either the largest or a dominant provider; or else set the quality, product and service standards for the sector across the world.

- **Expertise:** You have the highest possible quality of expertise in the activities that you carry out and deliver, and you constantly seek to hire the best expertise available from wherever in the world you can find it.

The axes of globalisation

If you want to be recognised as a global organisation, you have to have a physical presence in particular parts of the world. At present, this means having and maintaining a presence in the United States, the EU countries, China and Japan. It also increasingly means extending that presence into India and other parts of southern Asia, Russia and the Middle East. Eventually, it will also mean expanding into Central and South America, and the African continent (currently, sustainable and commercially viable interests are only in the very north and very south of Africa other than some of the capital cities).

If you don't have a presence in these parts of the world, you'll lose influence based on physical presence to those who do. Bearing in mind that a physical presence always increases your influence (if only through the fact that people are physically aware of you) is thus essential. Also, the global or international organisation gains advantage as the result of its ability to use its financial and other resources to choose its particular locations; so be prepared to set up

in those places that presently have substantial influence on the ways in which people conduct business across the world.

If you need convincing of the necessity of a physical presence, consider the example of Research In Motion (RIM), the producers of the Blackberry. In 2010, RIM faced exclusion from the entire Middle East, in spite of the fact that its product sales were as buoyant and profitable as anywhere else in the world. Lacking any contact offices in the region, RIM faced exclusion from these countries, who were concerned that they couldn't oversee telecommunications and Internet traffic within their own borders. RIM was thus forced to open offices in the region so that it did have this crucial physical presence. As a knock-on effect, RIM then also gained close physical proximity and access to important and influential people in the region. RIM additionally realised that physical proximity and contact had to be central to its global strategy, regardless of the additional costs it incurred.

Global organisations and managers also have the ability to move quickly in order to respond to market opportunities wherever these may occur. Additionally, you need to be able to command supply and distribution chains and resources wherever these are required.

Moving quickly and commanding supply and distribution chains is essential to maintaining and developing a global presence, but large organisations aren't always flexible enough to be able to do this readily or easily.

Having Global Knowledge and Expertise

You need global and international knowledge and expertise to be effective worldwide. Crucially, you need to acquire and retain:

✔ **Understanding of and empathy with the cultures, language, customs and habits of the places in which you work:** Whatever the approach that you take to globalisation and even if (from the highest ethical position possible of course!) you want particular locations to do things your way, you still have to know and understand how the particular societies and markets operate.

✔ **Understanding of the laws and regulations in the places where you set up:** You don't want to be one of the (many) companies and organisations that spot a market opportunity only to then fall short because their standards don't match the laws of the particular locations.

✔ **True market knowledge and understanding:** Even if an opportunity exists, you know and understand the conditions in which you can exploit that opportunity, and under which the market is prepared to take your products and services.

Silver Spring

Silver Spring is a soft drinks company. Located in south-east England, it expanded following a series of mergers and acquisitions and is now one of the largest independent suppliers in the UK. Additionally, the company manufactures under licence for Coca-Cola and so has a very large and assured customer and production base.

As a result of expansion, Silver Spring found itself with spare productive capacity and so looked to expand overseas.

The company's main base isn't far from the Channel ports, so the French, Dutch, Belgian and German markets looked especially attractive. The company carried out market analyses, and discovered that these markets were indeed worth many millions of pounds (and euros). Silver Spring made plans to expand production so as to be able to supply these markets (and use its spare productive capacity).

And then, at last, wiser counsel prevailed! Someone from the company made contact with the French and German supermarket chains and co-operatives and asked some key questions:

✔ Did they want English soft drinks?

✔ Under what circumstances would they buy English soft drinks?

✔ What volumes would they want and how frequently?

And back came the answers. The big supermarkets and co-operatives were sure that Silver Spring produced excellent soft drinks; however, they were already very well supplied, stocking upwards of 500 different brands. Unfortunately, they were not looking for additional suppliers.

Always do your homework! You cannot expand into a market that doesn't need your products or services.

Why Go Global (and Why Not)?

When considering whether to do business in the global marketplace, you need to be able to answer the following questions:

- ✔ Do we have the finances and resources to be a global or international player?

- ✔ Do we have something that the world needs or wants?

- ✔ Do we have the infrastructure to take our activities all over the world?

If business opportunities exist, of course you use your managerial expertise to seek to exploit them. You develop your knowledge and understanding of the markets and locations in which you can make a profit.

But you must also consider timescales. How long will it take to establish yourself in a particular market? How long will it take you to turn a profit? And then, how long will it *really* take? When the costs involved in going global have been accounted for, what will the real effects on profit and company survival be?

You also have to look at the prospect not just of gaining a presence, but also consolidating, maintaining and developing that presence into long-term profitable activities. You need to be able to evaluate situations, prospects and locations for their potential. And you can only do this effectively if you've first gained a full understanding of the local conditions.

Above all, make sure that you don't go global purely in response to industrial or sectoral peer pressure, shareholder demands or for reasons of perceived prestige and vanity. Whatever the other organisations in your sector are doing, you have to be able to stand on your own two feet. Make sure that you take the decisions in your own interests, and not because someone else thinks you should be globalising.

Knowing Where to Set Things Up, and Why

An old industrial management maxim was that you set up close to your markets if your products gained weight during the production process; and close to your suppliers if they lost weight during the production process. This fundamental truth still holds good; however, additional factors are also important, such as:

- ✔ If you need a presence in global business centres – centres of technological, financial or operational expertise – then you have to go to those places.

- ✔ If you need a physical presence somewhere for your own reasons, then you need to establish it, pay for it, and be able to sustain it.

- ✔ If you engage in joint and multi-ventures, you probably need to have a physical presence where your partners operate.

You need to be clear that you have the resources capable of operating on a long-term and sustainable basis; and that everything you do is driven by business and managerial reasoning, and not peer pressure or excitement (see the nearby sidebar 'Seeking excitement' for more on that slippery slope).

Seeking excitement

Have you ever noticed how so many of the drives for globalisation end up with companies and organisations setting up new activities in exciting, exotic and mysterious parts of the world? And how few expand into locations perceived as drab and dreary? For example, organisations set up call centres in India and South Africa in spite of the fact that costs are lower (and the technology is the same) in Estonia, Latvia and Lithuania, and comparable in Ireland. Garment manufacture and precision-engineering companies have set up in Pakistan, Malaysia, China and Central America even though equivalent technology and facilities are available in Central and Eastern Europe where the transport infrastructure is also more predictable and assured.

And so on. Sometimes, too, people decide that they want to go to an exciting and exotic place – and then work backwards from this decision to find business reasons for doing so. Make sure that you don't look to go global purely for a change of scene.

Working Out whether You'll Really Turn a Profit

Obviously your immediate answer to this question is: of course! Nobody looks to go global in order to make a loss. However, to turn this profit, you have to be effective at

✔ Organising and managing across distances

✔ Organising and managing across cultures

✔ Organising, managing and harmonising different expertise and technology

✔ Developing an organisational ethos that recognises that going global brings a full range of commitments, as well as business opportunities

If you do have these organisational skills, you do indeed create the expansion and profits you seek. If you don't, you may experience these problems:

✔ You create financial commitments you can't meet, and so need to either divest your overseas ventures or cannibalise your core business in order to support them.

✔ You become overly dependent on particular locations and activities, and if things go wrong you may not be able to replace them.

And anything that can go wrong, will go wrong! For example:

✔ The floods in Pakistan and China in 2010 are certain to have lasting effects on the production of clothing, sporting goods and electrical products.

✔ Many of the goods described by global brands as counterfeit are in fact genuine but have been supplied directly to the black market by outsourced producers.

✔ Operating across great distances may involve transport hold-ups and delays due to bad weather (for sea and air transport), troubles at border crossings (road and rail transport) and breakdowns and accidents (all forms of transport).

So make sure you've thought of everything!

Debunking Some Management Myths

Management myths on globalisation, internationalisation and expansion abound, for example:

- **Growth is good.** Why is it? And even if growth is good for your company, is global and international expansion the right way to go? Have you, for example, fully exploited your domestic and local markets?

- **The world is waiting to welcome us.** Is it really? Many parts of the emerging world have lived to regret engagements with western companies and managers. They may take a very cautious approach to your organisation until you prove that you're trustworthy.

- **Having a website means our organisation's global.** The fact that people can access your website from anywhere in the world doesn't mean that you'll do business everywhere in the world.

If you're in any doubt, consider the experience of Boo.com, the online shoe retailer. Located in Sweden, Boo.com stated that they could, and would, sell shoes anywhere in the world; and they waited confidently for the orders to roll in. And waited and waited – until they went bankrupt. They'd forgotten that people don't buy shoes from around the world – they tend to go to the local shoe shop.

- **Global markets have more benign regulatory environments and are easier to compete in than domestic markets.** Many western companies have expanded abroad in the mistaken belief that running a business will be easier there than at home. To avoid falling flat on your face, analyse the potential business environment first!

- **We're really global.** This may be true; but equally some organisations claim to be global when they really aren't. For example, one UK civil engineering company describing itself as global has 38 offices around the world. Of the 38 offices, 33 are in the UK, one is in Florida, two are in Australia and two are in the Middle East. This isn't a global organisation; it's a domestic organisation with some peripheral activities. And an organisation that describes itself as global with the following divisions: UK, Europe, rest of the world, is actually overwhelmingly domestic, probably with some activities in Europe. No organisation that's truly global can run 'the rest of the world' from a single office.

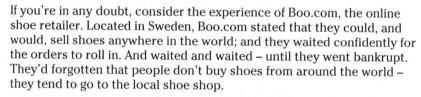

Outsourcing: The Cure for All Ills

A major drive in globalisation and internationalisation is the process of outsourcing. As an expert manager, you know and understand that outsourcing is fine provided that you do it for the right reasons.

As with so much in management, what you do isn't nearly as important as why you do it. If you outsource your production and service activities for the right reasons – to play to your own and the outsource provider's strengths – you have the basis for developing long-term and enduringly viable business activities. If you outsource for the wrong reasons – cost-cutting, expediency, shareholder pressure – you'll come up against all sorts of trouble.

Not so long ago, Richard was addressing managers from 'a major telecommunications company'. This company had just outsourced its human resources (HR) function, and one of the managers asked Richard whether he thought this was a good idea. Richard replied: 'If you've done it purely to strengthen the balance sheet, no; if you've done it to improve the quality of the HR provision, yes.'

The HR director was in the room and now spoke up. He said: 'We've outsourced this provision to remove the HR function from the balance sheet, to reduce the head count as a percentage of capital employed. However, we're going to get a much better service. The outsource provider has guaranteed that we'll get an effective response to issues within 12 hours, and problems addressed within 48 hours. So we're going to get a better service than before.'

And what happened? Well, the outsource provider was taken over by another consultancy and the telecommunications company had to renegotiate their contract. When they were unable to agree on terms, they were forced to take their HR provision back in-house. The whole process had been a waste of time and money.

In any case, the original objective in this example may well have been obsolete. Savvy investors now look much harder at outsourcing and other decisions that are designed purely to improve the perceived (and often illusory) strength of the balance sheet. If you decide to outsource, make sure it's for sound business reasons not just to save money.

Keeping your contracts under control

If you outsource, you pay agreed fees for products, services, expertise and technology. In return, you lose a certain amount of control over what's done in your name and how it's done. If your providers aren't located nearby, you need systems in place so that you can meet up quickly if necessary. You also need to make sure that contracts with providers satisfy the interests of both parties; if you use a dominant position to impose your own conditions on outsource providers, they'll resent you (even if they have no choice but to work with you).

And, if you do need to sort things out face to face, remember that either you have to get to them or they have to get to you. Consider the following:

✔ It took a senior manager from a top-brand clothing company eight hours to get from his office in America to Lahore in Pakistan; and a further three days to get to his supplier's location in rural Pakistan.

✔ It took Mattel executives ten days to get to a producer's factory in Mexico to investigate possible contract breaches occurring there.

✔ The volcanic ash cloud which swept over Europe in 2010 stranded at least one Microsoft executive en route to a technology provider in India.

You must have the managerial infrastructure to support anything and everything that you outsource.

Keeping your reputation intact

As we stress throughout this chapter, what you outsource isn't nearly as important as why and how you do it. One of the questions that you need to ask is: how will outsourcing this particular activity affect our reputation?

The answer lies in your knowledge and understanding of the outsource provider's business ethics and practices and their knowledge of yours. Banks and finance houses have damaged their reputations because they've outsourced customer service activities to companies that have no understanding of or empathy with their customer base. Technology companies have outsourced design activities to small firms that have come up with new products that are technologically perfect but lack the capacity to develop on a full commercial basis.

Take Reebok's decision to outsource its brand development to a small specialist firm as a salutary example. The specialists came up with Zyklon as a name for a range of shoes and clothing. Reebok went ahead and produced the range. Only after the products hit the retail market did anyone recognise that Zyklon was the gas used in the extermination camps by the Nazis.

Recognising that outsourcing's hard work

If you're not clear about why you're outsourcing, you'll create a whole lot of trouble for yourself. And if you are clear about why you're outsourcing, you'll create a whole heap of hard work! Whatever the situation, you have a full managerial job on your hands!

But the main – and deadly serious – thing to never forget is that, whatever your choice, it comes with hard work underpinned by expert knowledge and understanding. As we repeatedly stress, what you do is far less important than why and how you do it. As long as you can put your hand on your heart and say that you made the decision to outsource or go global in the best interests of the organisation and its business, that you know and understand the opportunities and pitfalls, no one can fault you.

Top five global management websites

Here are the best five websites on going global:

- ✔ *Financial Times*: www.ft.com

- ✔ *The Guardian*: www.guardian.co.uk/world/globalisation

- ✔ **BBC News:** www.bbc.co.uk/world service/programmes/global isation

- ✔ **Indymedia UK:** www.indymedia.org. uk/en/topics/globalisation

- ✔ **International Monetary Fund:** www.imf. org/external/np/exr/key/global.htm

---

Chapter 21

Keeping Track of Management Trends

. . . .

In This Chapter

▶ Knowing that managers must be professional

▶ Getting back to basics

▶ Recognising fashions and fads

▶ Using more substantial trends

▶ Understanding and addressing the symptoms of stress

. . . .

*I*f you look at the history of management and at what people's knowledge and understanding of what management is, you can see that they've developed piecemeal over the years. You can also recognise that some very clear principles of management and of managerial expertise exist. These clear foundations and principles are as follows:

✔ Treat everyone fairly and with respect.

✔ Produce good quality products and services that reflect the value that people place on them in terms of the price they're prepared to pay.

✔ Meet people's expectations and demands in terms of quality, service and value.

✔ Strive for continuous improvement in all aspects of performance, product and service quality, and resource utilisation.

✔ Set absolute standards of ethics, conduct, behaviour and performance.

All these principles are reinforced by what we call the Greatest Management Principle in the World: you get what you reward (see Chapter 4 for details).

When you reward people for working hard, being fair and delivering excellent products, services and service, you lay the foundations for being an excellent manager. This chapter looks at how to build on these foundations to develop your professionalism and expertise, to make you as effective as possible in everything you do.

Many of the most successful and profitable organisations concentrate hardest on the basics of business professionalism and expertise – enabling employees to deliver excellent products and services through effective management – and dip into specific management trends only when they believe they can make an active contribution to performance and profitability.

Being a Professional Manager

By any stretch of the imagination, management isn't yet a profession in the same way as medicine and the law, for example. These professions are distinguished by the following features:

- ✔ A distinctive body of knowledge required by all those who aspire to practise

- ✔ Formal qualifications granted as the result of acquiring a body of knowledge and expertise

- ✔ Entry barriers to practice such as specific qualifications and some experience

- ✔ Distinctive morality, such as doctors adhering to the Hippocratic Oath, requiring that members of the profession use their expertise to the best of their ability at all times and never abuse it for their own ends

- ✔ High value, in that professionals make a distinctive and positive contribution to organisations, individuals and society in general

- ✔ Self-regulation, in which professions set their own rules, codes of conduct, standards of behaviour and performance (for example, the British Medical Association and the Law Society)

- ✔ Lifetime membership, which can only be terminated by the actions of the governing bodies of the professions themselves

Managers – even expert managers – don't yet have to possess any formally recognised qualifications, training or expertise as a condition of being able to practise. This creates a paradox whereby those people who are required to be formally qualified are often managed by people who don't. Managers run GP practices, for example, and are responsible for organising the doctors' and nurses' time, productivity and even budgets.

Some people want to professionalise management; but others disagree and think that you learn management through

> ✔ **The school of hard knocks:** People learn the hard way, by doing and by making their own mistakes.

> ✔ **The Branson alternative:** People like Richard Branson have had no business or management education; if they can be so successful without training, why do you need it?

Clearly, these are prejudicial positions and don't stand up to scrutiny! The arguments against them are:

> ✔ **The school of hard knocks:** Everyone makes mistakes and learns from them, including doctors, lawyers and others who've undertaken professional education and training. But making mistakes when you have some idea of what you're supposed to be doing at least means you have a chance of working out where you're going wrong.

> ✔ **The Branson alternative:** Ask the person supporting this view, 'Have you founded something the size of the Virgin empire?' If the answer is no, or not yet, then having a helping hand along the way, provided through learning and education, does nothing but good. And Branson himself states that he's not a good manager (though he's clearly an excellent leader, visionary and pioneer).

So you need to make up your mind to be professional, look at trends and take every opportunity to learn.

Building the Basics

Clearly, all kinds of new opportunities exist in every industry. Simultaneously, however, they also create all kinds of new obstacles for managers and their employees. How, for example, can a manager best direct an employee when they may not even have physical contact with each other for weeks or months at a time?

Answers to questions like this lead many managers to step out of the fast-paced, business-at-the-speed-of-light environment and return to the basics of managing people. These basics include:

> ✔ **Making time for people.** You have no substitute for face-to-face time when it comes to building trusting relationships. Managing is a people job, and you need to take time for your employees. (Refer to Chapter 10 for ways to improve communication with your employees.)

✔ **Embracing change.** You recognise that change is a reality, and the effects it has on your employees. If you don't keep employees well informed, they wonder what's going on and morale my flag. Use the inevitability of change to develop face-to-face working relationships, improve communication and boost the quality of information available.

✔ **Increasing communication as you increase distance.** The greater the distance between manager and employee, the greater the effort both parties have to make to keep in touch. But don't depend on your employees to take the initiative; you need to keep the channels of communication flowing freely and often. (See Chapter 12 for ways to manage faraway employees.)

✔ **Using technology (and not letting it use you).** Technology can obviously be a great benefit, but make sure it serves a concrete purpose for you. Use it as a way to beef up your communication with employees, for example, not just as a way to distribute data. Reinforce this policy with regular email and mobile phone contact. (Refer to Chapter 19 for ways to use technology effectively.)

✔ **Setting performance targets.** Wherever your employees work and however often you see them (or not), make sure that they stay focused on and committed to their agreed goals. Specify timescales and deadlines, and reinforce them with regular contact through every means available.

✔ **Sharing results.** Keep your employees constantly informed of progress, so that everyone knows when they've done a good job and when things haven't gone so well. Again, you can deliver this kind of news more easily when you make sure communication and contact are as effective as possible.

✔ **Continuous improvement.** Recognise that everything about your organisation and its products and services (and your own conduct, behaviour and performance) can, and should, be improved. Something that was efficient and effective today becomes cumbersome tomorrow and obsolete the day after that. So always look at everything you do from the perspective of how you can improve it.

So managers have to work hard to be available to others. If you value strong working relationships and clear communication (we're assuming you do!), you need to return to basics, spending more and higher-quality time with your employees rather than less.

Refocusing on the basics has led to the increasing professionalisation of management – an understanding that, whoever they manage and in whatever industry or sector, managers have to be proficient, and strive to excel, in all of the areas listed above. Indeed, some would say that we've reached the point where, if you're not taking a professional attitude and aren't committed to being an expert manager, maybe management isn't right for you.

Adopting the Best of Management Trends

The graveyard of management innovation is littered with the wreckage of countless systems that were once hot, and now aren't. Zero defects, one-minute management, quality circles and total quality management all had their time in the sun, and are now on the back shelf. Every management trend has its own unique life cycle – usually short and expensive.

The fact is, most trends have value. Unfortunately, few organisations actually make the fundamental process and structural changes required to truly transform the organisation. After the programme's novelty wears off – often only a few short weeks or months after its introduction – the organisation goes back to business as usual. But even the most fleeting management fad has the potential to create effect some positive change within organisations. The secret is to concentrate on their real contribution to the never-ending search for success.

In the following sections, we take you through some trends that have substance, long-term potential and real benefits for your organisation. We describe and evaluate each managerial initiative and action and look at how, when implemented and executed properly, they can greatly enhance your managerial and organisational performance.

Outsourcing

In Chapter 20 we describe outsourcing as 'the cure for all ills'. And it has its place, for sure. If you want to try this approach successfully, however, you need first to decide which elements of your business could potentially be outsourced – such as payroll, security or IT maintenance – and then to find companies to provide these services for you that you feel able to work with.

Outsourcing is a trend driven by the need to make best use of your own scarce resources by contracting other people to work on specific areas in which they have expertise. Crucially, outsourcing is a business and managerial decision, just like everything else. So if you're considering working with outsource providers, you need to be clear that:

- They will enhance your business effectiveness and reputation, not diminish it.
- They follow the approach to quality and assurance that you need.

✔ You're happy to work with them because they're thoroughly professional and adhere to the highest standards of integrity.

✔ You're making the decision for reasons of business improvement and enhancement, not as a matter of expediency.

Make sure that any outsource providers do what they say they will do, when they say they will do it. Your customers and clients don't want to hear excuses from you along the lines of, 'We're really sorry that we didn't deliver what we promised but we outsourced this activity, and it's therefore not our fault.' Failure to deliver what you promise *is* your fault – and that's how your customers and clients will perceive it.

Moreover, if the driving force behind outsourcing is cost reduction, then make sure that your costs do indeed reduce! Especially if you're outsourcing to distant locations (for example, Asia, Central America), things are likely to remain cheap only until a problem occurs. If you can't get to the particular location for weeks, the expense that problem incurs may wipe out your cost savings.

Creating a learning organisation

A *learning organisation* is an organisation skilled at creating, acquiring and transferring knowledge, and at modifying its original assumptions, purposes and behaviour to reflect new knowledge and insights. Ever since Peter Senge's ground-breaking book *The Fifth Discipline* was published in 1990, creating and leading an organisation in which continuous learning occurs has been at the top of many managers' lists of management techniques to consider.

The problem with the old way of doing business is that organisations are built on the premise that the world is predictable. If you can just build a model that's large and complex enough, you can anticipate any eventuality. This particular view has a problem: the world isn't predictable. The global world of business is chaotic – what's true today is washed away tomorrow as the next wave of change hits. The only constant in today's organisations is change.

The learning organisation is designed around the assumption that organisations are going through rapid change and that managers should expect the unexpected. Indeed, managers who work for learning organisations welcome unexpected events because they consider them to be opportunities, not problems. Instead of static organisations that are strictly hierarchical, learning organisations are flexible. This structure makes managers able to lead change instead of merely reacting to it.

How do you go about designing a learning organisation? Several characteristics are particularly important as you consider turning your organisation into a learning organisation. The more of each characteristic that your organisation exhibits, the closer it is to being a true learning organisation, one that thrives in times of rapid change:

- **Encourage objectivity.** Over the course of our careers, we've seen managers make many organisational decisions simply to please someone with power, influence or an incredible ego. Managers make such subjective decisions not through a reasoned consideration of the facts, but through emotion. As a manager, you must encourage objectivity in your employees and colleagues, and practise it in your own decision making.

- **Seek openness.** For an organisation to grow, employees have to be willing to tell each other the truth. To make this openness possible, you must create a safe environment for your employees to say what's on their minds and to tell you any bad news without fear of retribution. You cannot build a learning organisation in an atmosphere of fear.

- **Facilitate teamwork.** Deploying employee teams is a very important part in the development of learning organisations. When an organisation relies on individuals to respond to change, it's at the mercy of individual responses, particularly resistance. In contrast, when an organisation relies on teams to respond to change, it can mobilise many more employees much more quickly. And a fast response can mean the difference between life and death in the ever-changing global business environment.

- **Create useful tools.** Managers in learning organisations need tools that enable employees to obtain the information they need to do their jobs quickly and easily. Computer networks, for example, have to be set up with access for all employees, and they need to provide the kinds of financial and other data that decision makers require. The best tools are those that get the right information to the right people at the right time.

- **Consider the behaviour you're rewarding.** 'You get what you reward' – so what actions are you rewarding, and what behaviours are you getting in return? If you want to build a learning organisation, reward the behaviours that help you achieve that goal. Stop rewarding behaviours that are inconsistent with this objective, such as subjectivity and individualism. The sooner you accomplish this mission, the better.

Making a flat organisation

Flattening an organisation involves removing layers of management. Doing so allows an organisation to widen the span of control (the number of people directly supervised) of the remaining managers, and push authority farther down the chain of command.

Fewer layers of management, and increased decision making and participation by non-management workers, typically results in:

- Less bureaucracy
- Faster decision making
- Improved ability to react to changing markets
- Increased reliance on self-managing teams
- More empowered and happier employees
- More satisfied and happier customers
- Reduced costs
- Increased profits

Instead of focusing on the structures and maintenance of hierarchy – departments, titles and so on – flat organisations

- Focus on their customers, both internal and external
- Encourage all employees to become directly responsive to customer needs
- Promote decision making by those employees closer to customers
- Eliminate bottlenecks in the flow of information
- Support open sharing of information

As more and more organisations turn away from the restrictive culture that's a natural by-product of hierarchy, the flat organisation is becoming an obvious choice – and the best opportunity to capitalise on fast-changing markets.

Unlocking open-book management

Many managers still think of strategy, accounts, financial performance, profits, losses and turnover as issues of concern only to a select few in the organisation, though the reality is that they're important to everyone who actually works in the organisation. Managers may use this approach as a way to solidify power at the top of their organisation, and to prevent everyone else from providing their own input and suggesting improvements to vital financial processes.

Apart from anything else, legal changes driven by both the British government and the European Union mean that companies and their managers have to change this attitude. Employees have statutory rights to know and be told what's being done in their name, for example if the company is planning to change its strategy, implement lay-offs and redundancies, revolutionise its technology or change working practices. Trade unions – if the organisation recognises them – are entitled to be consulted on a wide range of matters, as are all employees through a consultative body or forum.

So the trend is to be as open as possible – it benefits everyone. Much of the present open-book approach originally had its roots in what became briefly known as the 'new realism'. The 'new realism' was another fad that required employee representatives, including trade unions and organisations, to co-operate with rather than confront each other.

The first serious and strategic attempts to implement open-book management were introduced for sound business reasons by Japanese companies when they first set up in the UK. For example, Sanyo UK based in Lowestoft in Norfolk established a joint consultative committee that consulted its staff, including the recognised trade union, and kept them constantly informed and updated on the following:

- ✔ Productivity and output figures
- ✔ Defects and complaints
- ✔ Profitability, both overall and in relation to particular products
- ✔ Staffing levels and output requirements
- ✔ Training and development requirements
- ✔ Working practices, including flexibility of working hours and job roles

Sanyo and other companies make sure that their staff are fully trained in the financial aspects of the organisation, and understand what productivity and output figures mean both to them individually and to everyone else involved.

The result is that employees see a mutual commitment and responsibility on the part of the company and its managers. Employee involvement in all aspects of the organisation and its operations is that much greater, and employees are required to participate in decision making and establishing performance targets, rather than merely encouraged to do so.

The best organisations underpin open-book management with a single-status approach, meaning that any information goes to all staff, rather than to selected groups.

Opening the books up to everyone is also very profitable. Employees have an active stake in the company's performance and understand the direct connection between their own performance and organisational profitability. In some cases, this relationship is also underpinned and reinforced by profit-sharing schemes and performance bonuses tied directly to company performance.

Using consultants

The trend of using consultants was originally driven by the appeal of getting an expert, external – and detached – view of the present state of an organisation. Consultants could identify and address opportunities and problems. If you engage external consultants, make sure that the main driving force remains the present and future interest of your organisation.

The good, bad and ugly uses of consultants

When he worked in local government, Richard had two very closely related experiences of using consultants that summarised everything that you should and shouldn't use consultants for. His department had commissioned a report from one of the very top UK consultancies of the time about the restructuring of all council services. The report duly arrived, together with the bill (which in today's terms would be about £200,000).

One part of the restructuring was related to the privatisation and outsourcing of some key provisions that had, up to then, been delivered in-house. This required expert advice, so Richard duly trotted off to meet with a local government employment law firm to get their views. Richard himself now takes up the story:

'When I went to the law firm, they sent two senior partners to meet me. They had attended to everything that we wanted. They conducted a full review of the report that we'd been given, and had produced a report specifically about our council, detailing both the overall issues that we would have to tackle, and also the specific problems that would occur in our organisation. They then handed me a report produced specifically for us (which in today's terms cost the council about £10,000). This provided a set of rules and guidelines which we were able to use for the whole of the restructuring. They delivered a first-class and very substantial and long-lasting contribution to the work of the council.

As I was getting up to take my leave, I asked them:

"On the report, is there anything that we specifically need to be aware of?"

The two partners looked at each other, and one of them said:

"Yes, as a matter of fact there is. Other than the fact that they've changed the place names, this report is exactly the same as the one which this consultancy firm produced for another council a few months ago."'

This story says it all about the good, bad and ugly use of consultants. You use consultants when you want problems solving that you can't easily tackle; when you need their expertise – expertise which you yourselves don't have; and also when you need a dose of performance over-drive or energy to get things done more quickly than would otherwise be the case.

And – however much they've charged you – always check that they deliver their work with *you* in mind. Avoid at all costs being drawn into a line of work just because you've been charged high fees and, above all, be certain that you've not just been given an off-the-shelf prescription which will certainly not fit your exact needs!

Many management trends are marketed and promoted by consultancy organisations in order to give themselves a brand and summary to focus on. There's nothing wrong with this; lots of good work and ideas come from consultancy organisations. But if a consultancy does come up with ideas for you, make sure that you examine them in full before accepting their recommendations. And never accept something just because you've paid top dollar for it!

You also need to be aware of the pitfalls involved in using consultants; take a look at the nearby sidebar 'The good, bad and ugly uses of consultants'.

Consultants are there to solve your problems, to work themselves out of a job by meeting your needs and delivering solutions. You should never let them work themselves into a job.

Other fashions and fads

In the recent past, managers in all organisations and sectors have sought to use some or all of the following approaches, usually to make their lives easier:

✔ **Business process re-engineering (BPR):** Attention to administration, supervision and procedures for the purposes of simplicity, clarification and speed of operation. The strength of BPR is that improvements are always possible. In practice, however, people tend to apply BPR prescriptively to everything without reference to its wider effects on their organisation; and many people have now come to recognise BPR as simply a redundancy programme.

✔ **Six Sigma:** A zero defects approach attending to six areas of organisational practice – quality, defect, process capability, variations, stable operations and design. Six Sigma's contention is that, if you can produce zero (or near zero) defects in each of these areas, you're able to cut costs and, of course, greatly improve customer satisfaction.

✔ **Right first time, every time:** This approach looks lovely and is something that all managers aspire to! But of course it's a direct contradiction of the view that you can improve everything; and also a complete denial of human fallibility – nobody gets everything right first time or every time!

✔ **Benchmarking:** Benchmarking sets standards of performance against which to compare and rate your own and other companies' activities. Benchmarking is fine – everyone needs to know what's going on in the world outside. However, in the wrong set of circumstances, benchmarking drags all managers firmly back into their comfort zone; after all, as long as you can prove (at least to yourself) that you're not the worst performer in the industry, you can relax. In practice, whether you're the best or worst in the sector or anything in between doesn't matter – you have to stand on your own two feet.

Avoid the *circular flow of consultancy*, whereby you call in consultants and tell them that you have a problem; the consultants spend lots of time and money evaluating your organisation; and then come back and tell you that you have a problem.

Of course, if you're clear in your own mind about what you want out of particular approaches or the use of consultants, then no problem exists at all. But it must always be you that's driving the process; and you do so by ensuring that everything is

- ✔ Related to product and service performance, customer needs and wants, and organisational processes and capability to deliver

- ✔ At the core of management and staff training programmes

- ✔ A corporate priority, resourced and supported at the top of the organisation

- ✔ Given time to work

- ✔ Not relinquished as soon as the next fad comes along

Managing Stress

The trend of recognising and managing stress at work is driven by a number of factors, namely:

- ✔ Having employees off work for extended periods of time as a result of stress-related illnesses is very expensive

- ✔ Employees work much better for longer periods of time when they aren't constantly placed under great pressure to get the job done

- ✔ Occupations that are known to involve high levels of stress (such as the medical profession) encounter great difficulty attracting and retaining new recruits

Stress at work remains a highly emotional, subjective and contentious issue. On the one hand, the British Health and Safety Executive produces data stating that up to 50 million working days are lost each year in the UK as a result of stress. On the other hand, many organisations and managers still consider that anyone who complains of stress has no character, courage, backbone or commitment to the organisation. And in-between, quantifying and defining what sources of stress at a particular workplace actually exist is very difficult – one person's stress is another person's challenge.

Obviously some degree of workplace pressure is inevitable. You may be doing a great job yourself, but you have to work with others who see things differently, have different priorities and their own preferred ways of operating. Pressure can be created by dealing with change, different individual working styles, aspirations, approaches and priorities.

Stress in your personal life can magnify the stress you experience at work. Are you struggling to pay your mortgage? Is juggling childcare difficult? And, at work, are you constantly under pressure to perform? How do you get on with your colleagues and employees; do you feel as though you're fighting a constant battle to keep everyone happy? Are your relationships with your suppliers and customers cordial or fraught?

Consider your answers to these questions and, if they reveal that problems do exist, sit down and take a long hard look at what you do, how you do it and how you interact with people. Prioritise tasks, making sure that what you turn to first is indeed your top priority. Organise yourself and your staff to meet daily targets, and then concentrate on creating the conditions whereby people have time to look further forward. Schedule activities so that you don't find yourself piling up yet more work on existing pressure points, and build time into your schedules for delays, maintenance and repair – we all know that in practice nothing ever goes as planned.

All managers and organisations must deal with stress in these ways because when employees allow stress to overcome them, they lose their effectiveness. And when employees lose their effectiveness, the organisation loses its edge.

Most stress management training focuses on treating the symptoms of stress and not on curing the causes within the organisation. We see a problem with this approach. The training programmes teach workers relaxation techniques to decrease their level of stress, but they don't force top management to make better and faster decisions. The training shows employees how to reinforce and develop their self-esteem, use their time better and be more productive; but it doesn't address the roots of the problem – bad decision making, faulty or inadequate equipment and, above all, staff shortages. So alongside stress management training, you need to take whatever actions you can to alleviate as many of the workplace pressures as possible.

You can't wait for someone else to do something to reduce your stress. Find out how to manage stress yourself. Fortunately, managing stress isn't as hard as you may think. Effective stress management boils down to this: change the things that you can change and accept the things that you can't change – and know the difference between the two.

Committing to Being an Expert Manager

If you look at the professionalisation of management (including studying and evaluating management trends), you can see that a body of professional knowledge, understanding and expertise does exist. Use this foundation to develop a professional attitude – committing yourself to doing things to the best of your ability, and to conducting yourself and behaving to the highest possible standards.

This expertise will be increasingly valued by all organisations as they seek to gain the maximum returns from their investment in their managers. The reverse is also true: no organisation can afford to carry managers (or indeed anyone) who aren't expert, capable and hard-working.

Far fewer managers will exist in the future. And organisations will require far more of them – not in terms of volume of work, but in terms of quality and expertise. Organisations paying their managers high salaries expect them to deliver sustainable high levels of performance. And you can only do so if you're truly an expert manager, committed to your organisation and willing to learn, develop and improve at every stage of your career.

Top five management trend websites

Wondering where to find the best information on the web about the topics we address in this chapter? Well, you've come to the right place! Here are our top five favourites:

✔ **Tom Peters:** www.tompeters.com

✔ **The Stress Management Society:** www.stress.org.uk

✔ *Business 2.0* **magazine:** www.business2.com

✔ **Chartered Management Institute:** www.managers.org.uk

✔ *Management Today* **magazine:** www.managementtoday.com

Part VII
The Part of Tens

'I think you're finding the transition from worker to manager rather difficult, Bolsover.'

In this part . . .

These short chapters are packed with quick ideas that can help you to become a better manager. Dip into them whenever you have a spare moment for advice at your fingertips.

Chapter 22

Ten Common Management Mistakes

In This Chapter

▶ Failing to accept change as part of the job

▶ Not setting clear goals

▶ Neglecting to make time to communicate with employees

▶ Avoiding delegating responsibility

▶ Failing to remember what's really important

Managers make mistakes. Mistakes are nature's way of showing you that you're developing. Thomas Edison once said that it takes 10,000 mistakes to find an answer. Acknowledging that you made a mistake – and then putting it right – is a great management lesson. Of course, you don't want serial bunglers in charge of your organisation; nobody does. But far too often you come across managers who guess at what they think they should do, and then utilise vast quantities of organisational resources trying to make the impossible work. This approach is a waste of everyone's time, effort and energy, and it can become very expensive.

This chapter lists ten traps that new and experienced managers alike can fall into.

Not Making the Transition from Worker to Manager

When you're a worker, you have a job and you do it. Although your job probably requires you to join a team or to work closely with other employees, you're ultimately responsible only for yourself. Did you get to work on time? Did you attain your goals? Was your work done correctly? When you become a manager, everything changes. Suddenly, you're responsible for the results of a group of people, not just for yourself. Did your employees attain their goals? Did your employees do their work correctly? Are your employees highly motivated?

Becoming a manager requires the development of a whole new set of business skills – people skills. Some of the most talented employees from a technical perspective become the worst managers because they fail to make the transition from worker to manager.

Not Setting Clear Goals and Expectations

Do the words *rudderless ship* mean anything to you? They should. Effective performance starts with clear goals. If you don't set goals, your organisation has no direction and your employees few challenges. Without goals, your employees have little motivation to do anything but show up for work and collect their payslips.

Your employees' goals begin with a vision of where you and they want to be in the future. Meet with your employees to develop realistic, attainable goals that guide them in their efforts to achieve the organisation's vision. Don't leave your employees in the dark. Help your employees to help you, and your organisation, by setting goals and then by working with them to achieve those goals. (See Chapter 6 for more on goal setting.)

Failing to Delegate

Some surveys rank 'inability to delegate' as the number one reason managers fail. Despite the continuous efforts of many managers to prove otherwise, you can't do everything by yourself. And even if you can, doing everything by yourself isn't the most effective use of your time or talent as a manager. You may very well be the best statistician in the world, but when you become the manager of a team of statisticians, your job changes. Your job is no longer to perform statistical analyses, but to manage and develop a group of employees.

When you delegate work to employees, you multiply the amount of work that you can do. A project that seems overwhelming on the surface is suddenly quite manageable when you divide it up among 12 different employees.

Furthermore, when you delegate work to employees, you also create opportunities to develop their work and leadership skills. Whenever you take on a new assignment or work on a continuing job, ask yourself whether one of your employees can do it instead (and if the answer is yes, then delegate it!).

Failing to Communicate

In many organisations, most employees don't have a clue about what's going on. Information is power, and some managers use information – in particular, the control of information – to ensure that they're the most knowledgeable and therefore the most valuable individuals in an organisation. Some managers shy away from social situations and naturally avoid communicating with their employees, especially when the communication is negative in some way. Others are just too busy. They simply don't make the effort to communicate information to their employees on a regular basis, letting other, more pressing business take precedence by selectively 'forgetting' to tell their employees what they need to know.

The health of today's organisations, especially during times of change, depends on the widespread dissemination of information throughout an organisation and the communication that enables this dissemination to happen. Managers must empower employees with information so that employees can make the best decisions at the lowest possible level in the organisation, quickly and without the approval of those higher up. This takes time and energy, but is a much better use of organisational resources. (Chapter 10 talks about communication.)

Not Making Time for Employees

To some of your employees, you're a resource. To others, you're a trusted associate. Still others may consider you to be a teacher or mentor, and others see you as a coach or parent. However your employees view you, they have one thing in common: all your employees need your time and guidance during the course of their careers. Managing is a people job – you need to make time for your people. Some workers may need your time more than others do. You must assess your employees' individual needs and address them.

Although some of your employees may be highly experienced and require little supervision, others may need almost continual attention when they're new to a job or task. When an employee needs to talk, make sure that you're available. Put your work aside for a moment, ignore your phone and give your employee your undivided attention. Not only do you show your employees that they're important, but when you focus on them, you also listen to what they have to say. (Tips and pointers on making time for employees are in Chapter 4.)

Not Recognising Employee Achievements

In these days of constant change, downsizing and increased uncertainty, finding ways to recognise your employees for the good work they do is more important than ever. The biggest misconception is that managers don't want to recognise employees. Most managers do agree that rewarding employees is important; they just aren't sure how to do so and don't take the time or effort to recognise their effort.

Although pay rises, bonuses and promotions have decreased in many organisations as primary motivators, you can take many steps that take little time to accomplish, are easy to implement and cost little or no money. In fact, the most effective reward – personal and written recognition from one's manager – doesn't cost anything. Don't be so busy that you can't take a minute or two to recognise your employees' achievements. Your employees' morale, performance and loyalty will surely improve as a result. (We cover evaluating and rewarding employees in Chapter 7.)

Failing to Develop

Most managers are accustomed to success, and they initially spent a lot of time on self-development to make that success happen. Many were plucked from the ranks of workers and promoted into positions as managers for this very reason. Often, however, they catch a dreaded disease – *hardening of the attitudes* – after they become managers, and they only want things done their way.

Successful managers find the best ways to get tasks done and accomplish their goals, and then they develop processes and policies to institutionalise these effective approaches to doing business. This method is great as long as the organisation's business environment doesn't change. However, when the business environment does change, if the manager doesn't adjust – that is, doesn't *develop* – the organisation suffers as a result.

This situation can be particularly difficult for a manager who's found success by doing business a certain way. The model of the manager as a solid rock bearing up to storms is no longer valid. Today, managers have to be ready to change the way they do business as their environments change around them. They have to constantly develop, experiment and try new methods. If managers don't adapt, they're doomed to extinction – or at least irrelevance.

Resisting Change

If you think that you can stop change, you're fooling yourself. You may as well try standing in the path of a hurricane to make it change its course. Good luck! The sooner you realise that the world – your world – includes change, whether you like it or not, the better. Then you can concentrate your efforts on taking actions that make a positive difference in your business life. You must discover how to adapt to change and use it to your advantage rather than fighting it.

Instead of reacting to changes after the fact, proactively anticipate those heading your way and make plans to address them before they hit your organisation. Ignoring the need to change doesn't make that need go away. The best managers are positive and forward-looking. (Chapter 15 talks about managing change.)

Going for the Quick Fix over the Lasting Solution

All managers love to solve problems and fix the parts of their organisations that are broken. The constant challenge of the new and unexpected attracts many people to management in the first place. Unfortunately, in their zeal to fix problems quickly, many managers neglect to take the time necessary to seek out long-term solutions to their organisations' problems.

If you diagnose a serious disease, you have to perform major treatment; however, many managers, when faced with serious problems, still do their best to treat them with the equivalent of a sticking plaster. So if you have a problem, find out what caused it and treat it on its own merits. When you find the cause of the problem, you can develop real solutions that have lasting effects. Anything less isn't really solving the problem; you're merely treating the symptoms.

Taking It All Too Seriously

Of course, work is serious, and you've got to be good at it and concentrate on the things that are important. You carry the weight of staff, shareholder, customer and supplier expectations on your shoulders and that's often a very heavy burden, especially in times of difficulty.

But keep everything in perspective. Whatever the state of your business, you need to maintain a sunny and positive attitude, and make sure that it spreads to everyone else around you. Nobody wants to work for a misery – or, worse, still a bully – so don't be one! Being positive and upbeat also makes your life much more straightforward, in that you find it a lot easier to set and maintain standards. People come to you much more readily with things that need to be tackled; and so more gets done, more quickly.

And when you finally leave, what do you want people to remember you for? Achievements, of course, but what else? That you made everyone's life unbearable? Or that you delivered everything with a good heart? So, be good at your job – and enjoy it!

Chapter 23

Ten Common Management Myths

. . . .

In This Chapter

▶ Exploding the myths

▶ Recognising the effects of these myths on your employees

. . . .

As a manager, you need to be aware of the myths that surround everything you do. Each of the myths in this chapter is actually a barrier to progress. If you can recognise these myths (and be honest, recognise when you yourself start to think along these lines) and then take remedial action, you're going to have a much more productive working life.

You Can't Trust Your Employees to Be Responsible

If you can't trust your employees, who can you trust? Assume that you're responsible for hiring at least a portion of your staff. Now, forgetting for the moment the ones you didn't personally hire, you probably went through quite an involved process to recruit your employees. Remember the mountain of applications you had to sift through and then divide into winners, potential winners and losers? After hours of sorting and then hours of interviews, you selected the best candidates – the ones with the best skills, qualifications, character, expertise and experience for the job.

You selected your employees because you thought that they were talented people deserving of your trust. Now your job is to give them your trust without any strings attached.

You usually reap what you sow. Your staff members are ready, willing and able to be responsible employees; you just have to give them a chance. Of course, not every employee will be able to handle every task you assign to him. If that's the case, find out why. Does he need more training, time or practice? Maybe you need to find a task that's better suited to his experience or disposition. Or perhaps you simply hired the wrong person for the job. If that's the case, face up to your mistake and sort it out before you lose even more time and money. To get responsible employees, you have to give them responsibility.

You Have to Constantly Watch Your Employees

Watching what your employees are doing all of the time means you're micro-managing! And micro-managing is a waste of everyone's time, especially your own. So, at the end of every working day, if you haven't achieved your goals, work out why this is the case. And be honest with yourself: how much of the time that you lost was spent in watching what your employees were up to, how they were going about their jobs and who they were chatting to? Worse, did you stand over them while they tried to work things out and then start telling them how to do it? And worse still, did you then start getting involved with things that you know less about than them (such as fiddling with their computers – always fatal!) and hold your employees up as well as yourself?

Stop wasting time. You don't have to watch your staff at work, and you shouldn't. The *what* and the *why* is clearly up to you – the *how* you should always leave to your employees.

If you want people to behave like adults, treat them like adults.

When You Delegate, You Lose Control of a Task and Its Outcome

If you delegate correctly, you don't lose control of either a task or its out-come. What you lose control of is the way in which the outcome is achieved. Picture a map of the world. How many different ways can a person get from San Francisco to Paris? One? One million? Some ways are quicker than others. Some are more scenic, and others require a substantial commitment of resources. Do the differences in these ways make any of them inherently wrong? No.

In business, you have countless ways to get a task done. Even for tasks that are spelt out in highly defined steps – 'We've always done it that way' – you can leave room for new ways to make a process better. Why should your way be the only way to get the task done? 'Because I'm the boss!' Sorry, wrong answer. Your job is to describe to your employees the outcomes that you want and then to let them decide how to accomplish the tasks. Of course, you need to be available to coach and counsel your employees so that they can learn from your past experience if they want to, but you need to let go of controlling the *how* and instead focus on the *what* and the *when*.

You're the Only One Who Has the Answers

You must be joking! If you think that you alone have all the answers, you shouldn't be a manager. As talented as you may be, unless you're the company's only employee, you can't possibly have the only answer to every question in your organisation.

On the other hand, a certain group of people deal with an amazing array of situations every day. Those in the group talk to your customers, your suppliers and one another – day in and day out. Many members of the group have been working for the company far longer than you, and many of them will be there long after you're gone. Who are these people? They're your employees.

Your employees have a wealth of knowledge about your business contacts and the intimate, day-to-day workings of the organisation. They're often closer to the customers and problems of the company than you are. To ignore their suggestions and advice isn't only disrespectful but also short-sighted and foolish. Don't ignore this resource – you're paying for it anyway, whether or not you use it.

You Can Do the Work Faster by Yourself

You may think that you're completing tasks faster when you do them than when you assign them to others, but this belief is an illusion. Yes, discussing and assigning a task to one of your employees may require slightly more time when you first delegate it. However, if you delegate well, things quickly improve. Letting go of this task frees you up to be doing the things that you should be doing anyway.

Not only does doing a specific task yourself actually cost you more time, but you're also robbing your employees of a golden opportunity to develop their work skills.

When you do a task yourself, you're forever doomed to doing it – again and again and again. But when you teach someone else to do the task and then assign them responsibility for completing it, you may never have to do it again. Not only that, your employees may come to do the task faster than you can. Who knows, they may even improve the way that you've always done it.

Delegation Dilutes Your Authority

Actually, delegation does exactly the opposite – it *extends* your authority. You're only one person, and you can do only so much. Imagine all 10, 20 or 100 members of your team working towards your common goals. You still set the goals and the timetables for reaching them, but each employee chooses her own way of getting there.

Do you have less authority because you delegate a task and transfer authority to an employee to carry it out? Clearly, the answer is no. What do you lose in this transaction? Nothing. Your authority is extended, not diminished. The more authority you give to employees, the more authority your entire work unit has, and the better able your employees are to do the jobs you hired them to do.

As you grant others authority, you gain an efficient and effective workforce – employees who are truly empowered, excited by their jobs and work as team players – and you gain the ability to concentrate on the issues that deserve your undivided attention.

Your Employees Get Recognition for Doing a Good Job, Not You

Letting go of this belief is one of the biggest difficulties in the transition from being a doer to being a manager of doers. When you're a doer, the organisation rewards you for writing a great report, developing an incredible market analysis or programming an amazing piece of computer code. When you're a manager, the focus of your job shifts from your performance in completing individual tasks to your performance in reaching an overall organisational or project goal through the efforts of other people. You may have been the best marketing assistant in the world, but that's no longer important. Now you're expected to develop and lead the best marketing team in the world. The skills required are quite different and your success relies on both the efforts of others and your organisation's support – and your skills in delegation.

Wise managers know that when their employees shine, they shine too. Give your employees credit for their successes publicly and often, and they'll be more likely to want to do a good job for you on future assignments. Don't forget: when you're a manager, you're primarily being measured on your team's performance – not so much on what you're personally able to accomplish. Chapter 4 covers everything you ever wanted to know about employee motivation and rewards.

Delegation Decreases Your Flexibility

When you do everything yourself, you have complete control over the progress and completion of tasks, right? How wrong that is! How can you possibly be flexible when you're balancing multiple priorities, dealing with crises and trying to do your own job – all at the same time. Being flexible is pretty tough when you're doing everything yourself. Concentrating on more than one task at a time is impossible. While you're concentrating on that one task, you put all your other tasks on hold. That isn't flexibility.

The more people you delegate to, the more flexible you can be. As your employees take care of the day-to-day tasks necessary to keep your business running, you're free to deal with those surprise problems and opportunities that are always coming along and to make sure that lurching from crisis to crisis is kept to an absolute minimum.

Your Employees Are Too Busy

If that belief isn't a cop-out, we don't know what is. What exactly are your employees doing that means they don't have the time to learn something new – something that can make your job easier *and* boost the performance of your work unit?

Think about yourself for a moment. What about your job makes you want to return day after day? The salary? The perks and privileges? Partly maybe – but we're willing to bet that the main reason is the satisfaction you feel when you take on a new challenge, rise to it and succeed.

Now consider your employees – their job satisfaction is no different to yours. They want to test themselves against new challenges and succeed too. But how can they if you don't give them these challenges? Too many managers have lost good employees because they failed to meet those employees' needs to stretch and grow in their jobs. And too many employees have become bored rigid because their managers refuse to encourage their creativity and natural yearning to develop. Don't learn this lesson the hard way!

Your Workers Don't See the Big Picture

Actually, this myth may be true, but only because you make it so. How can your employees see the big picture if you don't share it with them? They're often specialists in their jobs or fields of expertise. They naturally develop severe cases of tunnel vision as they pursue the completion of their assignments or process their routine transactions. As we discuss in Chapter 1, your job is to provide your employees with a vision of where you want to go and the priorities of what needs to be achieved, and then allow them to find the best way to attain those goals.

Unfortunately, many managers withhold vital information from their employees – information that can make them much more effective in their jobs – in the hope that by doing so managers can maintain a close rein on their behaviour and stay 'in control'. By keeping their employees in the dark, these managers don't create the better outcomes that they hope for. Instead, they cripple their organisation and their employees' ability to learn, grow and become a real part of the organisation.

Chapter 24

Ten Great Ways to Engage Your Employees (and Keep Them Engaged!)

In This Chapter

▶ Gaining your employees' commitment

▶ Giving recognition, praise and rewards

*T*o engage your employees – that is, gain their commitment to what you what them to do – you have to respect them as people, value them as colleagues and treat them with integrity, honesty and openness at all times. And one part of this treatment (some say the biggest part) is to make sure that all your employees know when they've done a good job, and to create the conditions in which they can do so.

Above all, don't be the misery who says: 'If my people don't hear from me, they know they're doing a good job. But I soon get on to them if they make mistakes!' What a way to spend your working life!

Engagement has little, if anything, to do with money. Of course, money is important – everyone needs it, and receiving bonuses is nice. But remember, you can't buy loyalty, trust and respect; you have to earn them.

Showing your employees how you feel about them and their work needn't involve a lot of time or money. Use the engagement strategies in this chapter to create a motivating work environment in which every employee feels valued, trusted and respected. And if you really want to find out how to recognise and reward employees, then Bob's book, *1001 Ways to Reward Employees*, lists vast numbers of real-life positive rewards, most of which cost little or nothing but which enhance motivation, morale, trust and respect out of all recognition.

Being Supportive and Involved

Your employees need information and support in order to do their jobs. Give them what they need when they need it to do their best work. If they make a mistake in the process, support them and help them to develop as a result of that mistake. You can expect mistakes in any job, but how you handle them can be critical to building trust, knowledge and performance. All employees want their manager's support after making a mistake.

Furthermore, involve your employees when you're making key decisions – especially when those decisions affect them and their work. Ask them for their opinions and ideas. Doing so further shows that you respect and trust them – and that they actually have ideas worth sharing.

Handling Mistakes Expertly

Everyone makes mistakes – doing so is human! And making mistakes at work is no different. What's different, and what makes the world of difference to your employees, is how you respond to mistakes.

If you develop a reputation as someone who needs others to blame, scapegoat or victimise each time something goes wrong, no employee will engage with you. So when things do go wrong, sit down with your employees and work out what happened and why. Then agree with everyone what needs to happen next, so that you can avoid the mistake re-occurring. That way, everyone is involved in the solution – and so everyone learns.

If the mistake is in your department or division, as the manager you'll be blamed anyway. That goes with the territory of being a manager. In public, therefore, you accept the blame; and then in the confines of your department, you go back and work out with your staff what went wrong. And if you can't handle the public blame (or worse, if you only want the public praise for when things go right), then you shouldn't be a manager.

Granting Autonomy

Employees want and need to have the space to perform their work in the way they see fit. No one likes a supervisor or manager always hovering over their shoulder, micro-managing their every move, reminding them of the exact way everything should be done and making corrections every time they make a slight deviation. Guess what? Your employees may actually come up with a better way to do the task than your way, if you give them a chance.

Tell employees what you want done, provide them with the necessary training and resources and then leave them to it. When you give them what they need, you increase the likelihood that they'll perform to, or even beyond, your expectations.

Allowing Flexible Working Hours

Another great, no-cost way to engage your employees is to allow flexibility in their working hours, which includes when they start work and when they finish, the ability to leave work early when they need to and time off. Because most employees are trying to balance multiple priorities on both the work and home fronts, time is very important. As such, flexible hours and time off from work have become increasingly valuable commodities. Also bear in mind that the law requires organisations to offer flexible working hours if possible; so if you deny an employee's request outright, what does that say about your company's attitude to the law?

People generally want to spend more time with their family and friends and less time in the office. Unfortunately, current downsizing and re-engineering mean that employees have more work to do, not less. Giving your employees flexible hours can help them keep fresh and focused when they're actually at work.

Offering Training and Development

Guaranteed employment may be gone for everybody, but guaranteed employability is still very much alive in today's job market. As a result, employees are increasingly interested in developing new skills where they work. They can enhance their abilities and the value they offer the organisation. Remember, too, that most employee development happens on the job, not in the classroom. New work challenges and responsibilities and the chance to represent your manager or group are ways to develop, grow and master new skills.

Being given new opportunities to perform is very motivating for employees; building a fire under them isn't. So find ways to build a fire within your employees to make work a place where they want and are able to do their best as they develop and grow. Talking with employees about their long-term hopes and career plans is also important. You develop a strong mutual bond with each employee. If you know where someone wants to be in five years' time, you can think about aspects of their current job and circumstances that can help them prepare for the future. Don't deny ambition – foster and nurture it.

Giving Your Time

Employees need time to get to know their managers; and managers ought to spend time getting to know their employees. Knowing your employees as individuals strengthens your mutual bonds of trust, respect and loyalty.

Having access to your manager is a big motivator. Access does not mean being located physically close to your manager, however. Access and accessibility have less to do with physical proximity and more to do with a manager's responsiveness in taking employees' questions and concerns seriously and providing information, resources or assistance to employees in a timely manner.

Above all, if you have anything to tell people, tell them. And if you can't do so face to face, then use email, voice-mail, a mobile phone – anything to ensure that your employees know what they need and have to know. And if your staff ask questions that you can't answer immediately, make sure that you find the information they need and get back to them. Doing so is a mark of the trust and value that you place on your employees.

Providing Opportunities for Work and Job Enlargement

You're working busily away when one of your employees comes to see you. She says: 'I've just thought of a way we might be able to reduce administration time by 30 per cent. It'll take a bit of working out – do you want me to do it?' Do you say 'Yes, give it a go and keep me informed of progress' or 'That's not your job – get back to work'? Which response will have the greatest positive impact on staff engagement and, as a result, the work of your department?

If your staff see ways of improving and enlarging their jobs, then unless you have compelling operational reasons for not letting them go ahead, you should always encourage them. As well as getting better performance, you create higher engagement – because it's now *their* job (not just the one that your company gave them when they started work).

Don't forget voice-mail and texting as ways of making sure that people know that their achievements are recognised.

Giving Praise and Recognition Where It's Due

Everyone likes recognition for a good job well done. So always praise your staff if an opportunity arises. Send copies of thank you letters for jobs well done to everyone involved; or if suppliers or customers want to thank your staff in person, let them do it. David Sullivan of Sullivan Development Services used to produce champagne and a buffet for all his staff each time the company received written thanks for a good job. That way, everyone in the organisation knew that their work was important and valued. Taking time at the beginning or end of department or company-wide meetings to thank performers or allowing employees to acknowledge one another at group meetings can also be very effective. Using the company newsletter to post positive information, name top performers or thank project teams is another possibility for making people feel important and special when they've achieved.

Make sure that you always have a positive and encouraging attitude even when no specific praise is necessary. That way, you feed overall staff engagement because everybody likes to be a part of something that's positive. Also, when you are negative, people sit up and take notice – because you're negative so rarely!

Solving Problems Quickly

If one of your employees comes to you with a problem, she's expecting you to solve it. This means that you have to set aside as much time as is necessary to sort out whatever is the matter; and then return to your employee with either

- ✔ The solution she wants
- ✔ A clear and transparent explanation of why things can't be done her way

You need to provide one of these responses as quickly as possible. That way, you keep your employees happy (and therefore productive) as well as engaged.

Being a good problem solver is no more than your staff expect. But if you don't address and solve employees' problems you gain a reputation for being uncaring and unsupportive. Solving problems quickly doesn't produce a visible positive effect – but not doing so certainly has a huge negative effect!

Rewarding Employees Fairly

Of everything involved in recognising your employees, recognition and money are the hardest to get right and the easiest to foul up. If managers give out financial rewards for a job well done, these must apply to everyone involved, and everyone involved must be able to achieve them. If what you're rewarding was genuinely an individual effort, fair enough, reward the individual. But so few people work in complete, genuine isolation or on their own initiative that an individual effort is in fact most unlikely. Be aware that not rewarding everyone involved can cause deep resentment among those whose efforts you haven't recognised. For example:

- ✔ Excellent salespeople require excellent administrators to ensure persistently high performance, and yet those who work in support of sales teams often don't get the bonuses paid to the sales staff themselves.

- ✔ Excellent market traders and commodity and stock brokers require an effective back office to ensure that their trades reach maximum value, and yet the back-office staff rarely share in the sometimes huge bonuses paid to the traders.

If you're not careful, failure to recognise everyone involved can cause divisions and damage morale – exactly the opposite of what you intended. With this clear in your mind, you can consider the full range of monetary rewards available. You can use honoraria (voluntary fees) and one-off payments. Or, if the situation demands, you can use bonuses and percentage rises to ensure that the payments are fully institutionalised. Many organisations use monetary rewards in return for employee suggestions. Some employees prefer to be paid on commission, because they perceive that they're then being rewarded for their own direct efforts.

Many managers additionally make use of incentives like theatre tickets, holiday vouchers, seasonal hampers and restaurant meals as further ways of providing recognition.

Chapter 25

Ten (Plus Two) Classic Business Books You Need to Know About

. . . .

In This Chapter

▶ Finding traditional business tomes

▶ Locating useful management books

. . . .

An incredible variety of business books is available. Becoming bewildered by the choice is easy, and sorting out which books are of the greatest benefit to you is difficult.

So you have to start somewhere. And in the list that follows, we've already done the hard work for you. Every manager should buy and read these classic business and management books before reading any others (except this one of course!).

In Search of Excellence

In Search of Excellence by Thomas J. Peters and Robert H. Waterman (Harper & Row, 1982) is the book that transformed the whole approach to management thinking and practice, above all by bringing real managers, in real companies, out into the open. A bestseller that J. K. Rowling of Harry Potter fame would be proud of, *In Search of Excellence* held the mirror up to 63 companies and evaluated the characteristics that ought to be present in top-performing organisations, and those characteristics that were in fact present in the organisations studied. Surprise, surprise – everything was there! Bias for action, closeness to customer, attention to product and service quality, strength and expertise of leadership – each was present in the excellent companies, and has to be a management priority if the company or organisation is to succeed.

Some may argue that the book is now dated; and others cite the downturn in the performance of many of the companies studied as evidence that the work of Peters and Waterman wasn't flawless. Well, nothing ever is – not even business and management books! But read *In Search of Excellence* anyway – it brought management out into the open, and the principles (if not all the examples) still hold good for the most part.

Managing for Results

In *Managing for Results* (Harper & Row, 1964) – a real classic in the field of management and written by the greatest management writer of them all – Peter F. Drucker takes the development of his management theories a step further by showing readers what they must do to create an organisation that prospers and grows. Drucker encourages readers to focus on opportunities in their organisations rather than on problems. The book suggests that managers take a hard look at an organisation's strengths and weaknesses to develop effective plans and strategies. Drucker also states that managers have to be competent across the whole field of management, as well as expert in their own particular area; and especially, this expertise must cover strategic capability and staff and human resource management.

The Human Side of Enterprise

The first wake-up call for managers everywhere, this book proclaims that (big surprise) people play a major role in the success of any business. *The Human Side of Enterprise* by Douglas McGregor (McGraw-Hill, 1960) produced the birth of Theory X and its negative assumptions of human behaviour ('People are lazy') and Theory Y, which focuses on the positive assumptions of human behaviour ('People want to do a good job'). McGregor argues that relying on authority as the primary means of control in industry leads to 'resistance, restriction of output, indifference to organisational objectives, the refusal to accept responsibility, and results in inadequate motivation for human growth and development'. The book remains relevant reading for managers today, many of whom still haven't a clue why employees are so important.

The Peter Principle

The Peter Principle by Dr Laurence Peter and Raymond Hull (Morrow, 1969) states that in a hierarchy every employee tends to rise to his level of incompetence. This book is an amusing look at how hierarchies work in organisations and what managers can do to ensure that they don't assign employees to tasks beyond their capabilities. A must!

Competitive Strategy

This book by Michael E. Porter (Free Press, 1980) concentrates on the need for clarity of purpose; and this clarity of purpose is founded in a core foundation or generic position. The concept is really quite simple – if you don't have clarity of purpose, you can't expect others to understand what you're delivering, or on what basis.

The core foundation or generic position needs to concentrate on either securing cost leadership or cost advantage, or on securing brand leadership and quality advantage based on differentiation. If securing cost leadership or differentiation and brand advantage isn't possible, you'll lose out to those organisations that do have one or other of these positions. Securing brand leadership and brand advantage means that you can charge premium prices for your products and services, provided that the benefits delivered through differentiation are those that are of value to the customer. Securing cost leadership or cost advantage means you have much greater flexibility in the prices that you can charge; and especially, the cost leader has the greatest strength in withstanding price wars. If you don't hold one of these positions, you must have something else that's of value to the customer – for example, convenience or location – or else the confidence of those who operate closely with you in the particular sector and who need your products, services or expertise.

Finally, strategy has to have a focus, concentrating on mass markets or on narrow, specialist and precisely defined niches that are capable of supporting viable levels of business.

Competitive Strategy is essential reading for anyone serious about developing their knowledge and expertise.

The One Minute Manager

Written in a unique parable format, *The One Minute Manager* by Kenneth Blanchard and Spencer Johnson (Morrow, 1982) became an instant business classic. Even today, the book is a perennial resident on most business bestseller lists. *The One Minute Manager* teaches readers three very simple but important management skills (One Minute Goal Setting, One Minute Praisings and One Minute Reprimands), and it does so in an entertaining but informative way. A true classic.

Management Stripped Bare

This book is a cheerful debunking of fads and fashions, management speak and the actions (or inactions) taken by managers to avoid facing the real issues that directly affect the success and viability of their organisations. The core message of *Management Stripped Bare* by Jo Owen (Kogan Page, 2002) is very clear: until those in management positions stop talking about 'hitting the ground running' and 'thinking outside the box', and start clarifying their own purpose and developing real expertise in delivering it, organisations will continue to underperform. A really informative, substantial and entertaining read.

In Search of European Excellence

Robert Heller was the first British management guru, and was responsible, many years ago, for founding what is now the Chartered Management Institute as well as the business magazine *Management Today* (another management must-read!).

Written nearly 20 years after Peters and Waterman's book (see earlier in this chapter), *In Search of European Excellence* (Harper Collins, 1998) concentrates on the experiences of some of the largest and best-known British and European multinational corporations, companies and public service bodies. The currency of many of the lessons from Peters and Waterman – clarity of purpose, strength and expertise of leadership, product and service quality, flexibility and responsiveness – are still found to hold good. Heller draws particular attention to the shortcomings in performance and confidence in companies and organisations where, for whatever reason, these principles and practices no longer apply, or have been allowed to slide.

This book is enlivened with examples from companies and organisations familiar to us all, and is another must.

The Fifth Discipline: The Art and Practice of the Learning Organization

This book by Peter Senge (Century, 1990) introduced the concept of the learning organisation. It encourages organisations to apply systems thinking, seeing interrelationships instead of just isolated events, incidents and problems. Senge argues that organisations should make learning a continuous process rather than treat it as a series of distinct, unrelated events. He claims that everyone in an organisation has a responsibility to help create a learning organisation, with top managers playing a crucial role in the process. He also encourages organisations to realise the importance of reflection, as well as action, in business ('Yes, but who's going to help the customer?' – only someone who's first discovered how to do it properly).

Understanding Organisations

The foremost and most famous of all British management thinkers, Charles B. Handy started his career as a corporate executive at what is now oil company Royal Dutch/Shell, before moving into the world of business schools and management teaching and development.

Understanding Organisations (Penguin, 1996) offers comprehensive, clear and concise coverage of every aspect of how people behave in organisations, and what managers therefore need to know, understand and be able to apply. This includes the tricky areas of roles, character, attitudes and values, as well as the mainstream of leadership, motivation, groups and conflict. The book is full of useful examples of how theories of behaviour are applied in practice and, again, is a very entertaining read.

Body and Soul: The Body Shop Story

Body and Soul by Anita Roddick (Ebury Press, 1992) tells the story of the founding, development and subsequent globalisation of British natural cosmetics company The Body Shop. The sheer energy and enthusiasm of the company's founder Anita Roddick, her husband Gordon and everyone else involved comes shining through on every page.

Body and Soul describes the clear set of guiding principles and strong ethical base on which the company was created, and the commitment to all stakeholders – especially suppliers in developing countries – that has subsequently been so critical to the company's success. The book also concentrates on the crucial aspects of product and service quality, branding and differentiation, and especially the images of different cosmetics and the portrayal of the women who use them.

The Body Shop was founded in the early 1970s, during a worldwide economic downturn, so the last thing that anyone needed was a new brand of cosmetics. Nevertheless, The Body Shop succeeded and grew. Roddick and her husband intended the company to be distinctive and different from the rest of the cosmetics industry, and in spite of the external pressures and customs of the industry, it succeeded.

So read this book as a guide to the sheer energy, commitment and enthusiasm you require in order to succeed, and to the fun and adventures that you can have doing it. And bear in mind as you read it that in 2006 The Body Shop was sold to L'Oréal – one of those 'other' cosmetic companies.

Maverick

If Drucker is the greatest authority on management, then *Maverick* by Ricardo Semler (Century, 1992) is the greatest story. Ricardo Semler tells of how he transformed his family firm, a company making commercial white goods and pumps, from one that was, in his own words, 'moribund, into a company that thrives, chiefly by refusing to squander our greatest asset – the talents of our people'.

The story takes place not in Europe or the United States, but in Brazil. And so Semler achieved everything he did within the ever so slightly difficult confines of an inflation rate of 3,000 per cent (or 10 per cent per day), and a failure rate in the Brazilian capital goods sector of one in three.

And everything exists in this organisation – fully flexible working, self-managing teams, motivation and commitment, and concentration on product and service quality. And it's all underpinned by open books, full access to information and a profit-sharing scheme in which 23 per cent of retained profits are given to the staff. The company has a hierarchy of two levels only, and everyone has full and universal access to managers, including the top managers and Semler himself. *Maverick* is required reading at many business schools – and it's an absolute must for anyone who aspires to manage anything, anywhere.

Index

• *Numerics* •

80/20 principle of productivity, 101–102, 109
360-degree evaluation process, 126
The 1001 Rewards & Recognition Fieldbook
(Nelson), 76
1001 Ways to Energise Employees
(Nelson), 76
1001 Ways to Reward Employees (Nelson),
31, 33, 34, 76, 347

• *A* •

academic references, checking, 55
Accenture website, 128, 306
accident prevention, 201
accounting
analysing business health, 290–293
basic equation for, 282–284
budgets, 273–281
double-entry bookkeeping, 285–286
financial ratios, 290–292
financial statements, 286–290
websites, 293
Accounting Conventions website, 293
AccountingWEB website, 293
actions for milestones
determining, 116–117
relationships (sequencing), 117–118
scheduling, 118
actions versus words, 219
activity trap, avoiding, 109–110
ad hoc groups, 179
Adidas, 149
administration and overheads budget, 275.
See also budgets
Advanced Performance Institute
website, 112
advertising for recruitment, 49

Advisory, Conciliation and Arbitration
Service (ACAS), 153, 254, 270
aesthetic environment, in SPECTACLES
analysis, 133
Airbus, 197
Alice in Wonderland (Carroll), 98
apostles (customer type), 147
ASAP-cubed system, 71
assets
current versus fixed, 283–284
defined, 282
revaluation or devaluation of, 135
staff as most valuable, 148
types of, 283
assignment choices for employees, 65
Association of Certified and Chartered
Accountants website, 293
assumption, risk due to, 203–204
attainable goals, in SMART checklist, 101
attitude, as recruitment concern, 45
Aurelius, Marcus (Roman Emperor), 135
authority
delegation of, 344
importance to employees, 66
shift with teams, 172
autonomy, granting, 66, 348–349

• *B* •

BA (British Airways), 93, 174, 205
Baines, Ian (telecommuter), 191
balance sheet, 286–288
Balanced Scorecard Institute for
Performance Management website, 128
Bank of England website, 140
barriers to communication, 161–163
basics, refocusing on, 321–322
Batchelor's Foods, 179–180
benchmarking, 329
benefits. *See* wages and benefits

Berdahl, James (marketing VP), 34
Bing, Stanley (columnist), 35
biscuit motivation, 63
blame
  avoiding, 348
  communication poisoned by, 163
  ineffectiveness of, 13
blame, avoiding, 13, 163, 348
Blanchard, Kenneth (*The One Minute Manager*), 355
Blittle, Lonnie (assembly-line worker), 34
Body and Soul (Roddick), 357–358
The Body Shop, 31, 100, 136, 357–358
Bolles, Richard Nelson (*What Color Is Your Parachute?*), 50
bottom line, 290
Bowker, Richard (manager), 200
BPR (business process re-engineering), 329
Branson, Richard (CEO), 32, 321
British Airways (BA), 93, 174, 205
browsers and passing trade, 147
budgets. *See also* accounting
  decision making based on, 278–279
  defined, 273
  developing data for, 277
  need for, 274
  purposes of, 274
  in the real world, 277, 279–280
  staying on, 280–281
  steps for creating, 275–276
  tips for developing, 279–280
  types of, 274–275
  variance with, 274
building a tasty manager, 14
Business 2.0 magazine website, 332
business environment
  The Body Shop example, 136
  company reputation in, 136
  environmental scanning, 134–135
  factors to account for, 136–137
  green issues, 138–140
  identifying other issues, 135
  obligations in, 137–138
  PESTEL analysis of, 130–131
  risk management issues, 198

SPECTACLES analysis of, 133
SWOT analysis of, 131–134
websites, 140
Business Finance magazine website, 293
Business for Social Responsibility website, 228
Business Mentor website, 94
business process re-engineering (BPR), 329

• C •

capital budget, 275. *See also* budgets
career development plans, 88–90
Carnegie Foundation for Change website, 238
Carphone Warehouse, 302
Carroll, Lewis (*Alice in Wonderland*), 98
Cartwright, Roger (*Mastering the Organisation in its Environment*), 133
cash-flow statement, 290
challenges of management
  achieving trust, 18–19
  constant change, 16–17
  dismissals, 262
  new business model, 17–18
  partnership with employees, 16–18
  people skills required for, 15–16
  recruitment, 43
change management
  aiding employees, 235–236
  embracing change, 231–235, 322
  encouraging initiative, 236–238
  examples of, 237
  four stages of change, 232–233
  handling crises, 230–231
  need for, 229
  resisting change, 233–235, 339
  urgency versus crisis management, 230
  websites, 238
  in yourself, 238
Change Management Learning Centre website, 238
Chartered Institute of Personnel and Development website, 27, 128

Chartered Management Institute website, 27, 94, 332
Churchill, Winston (statesman), 31, 274
Ciba-Geigy, 139
circular flow of consultancy, 330
Clarke, Andy (CEO), 204
clients, understanding, 146–147
coaching
  characteristics of, 80–81
  coach, defined, 79
  developing employees, 86
  importance in learning process, 79–80
  metaphors for success, 83–84
  for performance improvement, 121
  show-and-tell method of, 82–83
  supportive role of, 81, 84–85
  techniques for, 84–85
code of ethics
  complying with, 211
  creating, 209–211
  Ethics Resource Center example, 212
collaborative leadership
  examples of, 38
  Orpheus principles for, 39–40
Colman's Foods, 38
command team, 178
commitment to expertise, 332
committees
  as formal teams, 178
  joining, 223
communication. *See also* documentation; feedback; listening; written communication
  bad, causes of, 161–162
  barriers to, 161–163
  channels and effects of, 157
  deciphering office politics, 218–221
  of dismissal, 268
  about downsizing, 257–258
  for employee development, 90
  of expectations, 24
  with flexible workers, 186, 188, 189
  forms of, 156
  horizontal organisation aiding, 171
  importance of, 23–24, 155, 156, 158, 336–337

as leadership skill, 32–33, 40
as manager's responsibility, 23–24
non-verbal, 166
performance appraisals for, 121
positive feedback, 24
red flags for problems in, 10–11
about rewards, 63–64
spoken, effectiveness of, 156
with stakeholders, 143–145
supportive environment for, 68
in teams, 174
teams aiding, 172
technology for, 158–161
telecommuting's effect on, 190, 191
toxic, 163–164
websites, 168
withholding information, 162–163, 346
Communications Management Ltd website, 168
community relations, 144, 150–151
company policy manual, 221
competition, reduced by teams, 172
Competitive Strategy (Porter), 355
complacency
  risk due to, 203, 204
  about shrinkage, 119
computer network, 303–304
Computerworld website, 306
Confederation of British Industry website, 270
confidence
  inspiring in stakeholders, 144–145
  as leadership trait, 36
  of staff in you, 149
conflict management in teams, 174
consensus, seeking, 40
constructive dismissals, 260
consultants, using, 328–330
control
  as classic management function, 19
  squeezing employees, avoiding, 13
  in Theory X management, 11–12
co-operation, promoting, 172
corporate citizens, 216
corporate responsibility guide website, 228

Corporate Social Responsibility
    website, 228
cost of goods sold, 288
counting, measuring instead of, 118
crime, managing risk of, 201–202
crisis management, 230–231
Croner website, 254, 270
cross-functional teams, 179–180
cultural environment, in SPECTACLES
    analysis, 133
current assets, 283–284
current liabilities, 285
current ratio, 291
customers
  in SPECTACLES analysis, 133
  understanding, 146–147

• *D* •

debtors turnover ratio, 291
debt-to-equity ratio, 292
decisiveness, 37
delegation, 336–337, 342–344
Deloitte website, 94
Department for Environment, Food, and
    Rural Affairs website, 140
Department for Transport website, 140
developing employees. *See* employee
    development
development, continual, 338–339
Diamond, Bob (CEO), 137
DigitalCompaq, 190
discipline. *See also* dismissals; motivation;
    negative consequences; punishments
  actions for, 245–248
  compassion in, 243
  describing the unacceptable behaviour,
    248–249
  expressing the impact to the work
    unit, 249
  focusing on, avoiding, 71, 72
  focusing on performance, not
    personalities, 243–244
  following procedures for, 241–244

legal issues, 242, 244
for misconduct, 243, 246–248
need for, 239, 241
office politics revealed by, 214
outlining the consequences, 250
for performance improvement, 121
performance improvement plan for,
    252–254
for performance problems, 241, 243–246
as positive experience, 240
progress report meetings, 253–254
progressive, 244
providing emotional support, 250–251
punishment versus, 240
sources of, 240
specifying the required changes, 249–250
steps for, 248–252
timing of, 241
twin-track system of, 244
websites, 254
dismissals. *See also* downsizing
  avenues for appeal, 266
  avoidance of, 263–264
  challenges of, 262
  constructive, 260
  defusing emotions around, 268–269
  documentation for, 266
  fair, 260, 266
  following procedures for, 266, 267
  guidelines for fairness, 264–265
  if discipline fails, 246, 248
  legal issues, 260–261, 265–266
  for misconduct, 247, 248, 261–262
  performance appraisals documenting, 122
  providing feedback before, 82
  reasons warranting, 261–262
  steps for, 267–269
  timing of, 268–270
  unfair, 260
  websites, 270
  wrongful, 260
distance
  as barrier to communication, 162
  managing from, 187–188
  virtual management websites, 191

documentation
  for dismissals, 266
  for protection, 226
double-entry bookkeeping, 285–286
downsizing. *See also* dismissals
  balancing development with, 92–93
  benefits of, 171
  for budget reasons, 281
  giving notice for, 257–259
  helping employees through, 93
  problems with hierarchical organisation, 170–171
  procedures for lay-offs, 257–259
  providing outplacement services, 259
  recruitment freeze during, 257
Drucker, Peter (management guru)
  on change management, 229
  Management, 75
  Managing for Results, 354
  on measuring instead of counting, 118
  on teams, 170
Dutton Engineering, 38

• *E* •

economic crisis
  managers' decisions leading to, 1–2
  media's role in, 152
  risks leading to, 205–206
economic incentives, 65, 74–75
economics
  in PESTEL analysis, 130
  in SPECTACLES analysis, 133
Economy, Peter
  expectations of parents for, 72
  Leadership Ensemble, 38–39
  overwhelmed experience of, 2
  useless training experienced by, 14
80/20 principle of productivity, 101–102, 109
The Elements of Style (Strunk and White), 167
employee development. *See also* learning; training employees
  balancing downsizing with, 92–93
  benefits of, 87
  career development plans, 88–90
  coaches' role in, 86
  described, 86, 87
  employees' role in, 89
  importance of, 349
  by Japanese companies, 88
  job enlargement, 350
  learning aspect of, 87
  manager's role in, 68, 89–91
  mentoring for, 91–92
  performance appraisals for, 122, 125
  top ten methods for, 91
  training aspect of, 87
employee letter, ultimate, 20
employee manual, Nordstrom's, 20
employees
  aiding through change, 235–236
  developing, 68, 86–91
  encouraging initiative in, 236–238
  engaging, 347–352
  gaining commitment to goals, 107
  involving in recruitment, 47
  keeping aware of expectations, 24, 264, 336
  knowledge of, respecting, 343
  leaders' integrity desired by, 37
  leadership desired by, 29
  making time for, 66, 337–338, 350
  micro-managing, avoiding, 342
  partnership with, 16–18
  solving problems of, 351
  squeezing, avoiding, 13
  staff budget, 274
  supporting, as function of managers, 23
  top ten desires of, 65–66
  traits to look for, 44–45, 50–51
  trusting, 341–342
  understanding and respecting, 148–149
employment agencies, 48
empowerment
  benefits of, 173–174
  defined, 173
  as manager's responsibility, 22–23
  need for, 22–23
  real world, 180–181
  of remote teams, 173
  of teams, 173–174, 180–181
  of workers, 39

encouraged resignations, 256
energisation, 21, 32
engaging employees
  allowing flexible working hours, 349
  being supportive and involved, 348
  general tips for, 347
  giving praise and recognition, 351
  giving your time, 350
  granting autonomy, 348–349
  handling mistakes expertly, 348
  offering training and development, 349
  providing job enlargement, 350
  rewarding fairly, 352
  solving problems quickly, 351
Environment Agency website, 140
environment, business. *See* business
  environment
environmental issues
  examples of handling poorly, 139
  in PESTEL analysis, 130
  profitability, 139–140
  resource management, 138–140
  in SPECTACLES analysis, 133
  waste disposal, 139
e-skills UK website, 94
ethics
  anagram for good choices, 213
  creating a code of, 209–211
  defined, 207, 208
  living ethically, 211–213
  traits of ethical people, 208–209
  websites, 228
Ethics Resource Center, 212, 228
evaluating employee candidates
  checking references, 55–56
  reviewing your notes, 56–57
  second (or third) interviews for, 57
expectations
  comparing performance to, 120
  high, as motivational, 72
  keeping employees aware of, 24, 264, 336
  performance appraisals for setting, 121,
    124, 125
expenses. *See also* budgets
  freeze for budget reasons, 280
  in profit and loss account, 288

experience
  interviewing candidates about, 53
  as recruitment concern, 45, 60
expertise, commitment to, 332
external rewards, 37

facilitation (leadership skill), 33–34
fair dismissals, 260, 264–266
fairness
  goals related to, 102
  in rewards, 352
Fast Company website, 182
feedback. *See also* communication
  before firing someone, 82
  group, posting, 115
  for individuals, keeping private, 115–116
  performance appraisals for, 124
  performance, MARS system for, 116–120
  provided by coaches, 81
  seeking from employees, 236
feuding, departmental, 163
The Fifth Discipline (Senge), 324, 356–357
fighting change, 233–235, 339
financial backers, communication with, 146
financial crisis
  managers' decisions leading to, 1–2
  media's role in, 152
  risks leading to, 205–206
financial ratios, 290–292
financial statements
  balance sheet, 286–288
  cash-flow statement, 290
  profit and loss account, 288–290
Financial Times, 237
firefighters, 216
firing. *See* dismissals; downsizing
fixed assets, 275, 284
fixed liabilities, 285
flat organisations, 325–326
flexibility, teams providing, 176
flexible workers
  communication with, 186, 188, 189
  defined, 184
  issues faced by, 186–187

managing and supporting, 188–189
managing from a distance, 187–188
organisational culture changes with,
    186–187
preparing for, 185–186
recognition for, 189
technology for, 188
telecommuting by, 190–191
virtual management websites, 191
flexible working hours
legal requirements for, 65, 183
managing shifts and non-standard hours,
    188–189
providing, 65, 349
formal teams, 177–178
forward thinking. *See* vision
fraud, dismissal for, 262. *See also* shrinkage
Freedom of Information Act, 211
French, John (military commander), 99
functions of management. *See also specific
    functions*
classic, 19
communication, 23–24
empowerment, 22–23
energisation, 21
supporting employees, 23

• *G* •

Gap, 149
Global Issues website, 140
global management
alternative approaches to, 307
choosing locations, 312
deciding about, 310, 311
defined, 308
forces driving, 308–309
knowledge and expertise needed for,
    309–310
myths on, 314
outsourcing, 314–317
physical presence needed for, 309
profitability issues for, 313
Research in Motion example, 309
Silver Spring example, 310
websites, 317

Glynn, Patrick (bank executive), 300
goals
activity trap counteracting, 109–110
characteristics needed for, 100
common, in teams, 172
communicating to teams, 105–107
employee commitment to, 107
functions of, 98–100
less is more for, 104–105
linking rewards to, 69
losing sight of, 108–109
maintaining focus on, 109–110, 322
measures for, 114–116
need for, 336
NHS example, 105
performance appraisals for setting, 121,
    124, 125
in performance improvement plan, 252
power to make them happen, 110–112
Pret A Manger example, 108
prioritising, 97, 104, 107–110
relating to employees' role, 102
responsibilities for, 97
set by coaches, 80–81
simple and concise, 103
SMART checklist for, 101–102
updating, 104
values translating into, 102–103
vision linked to, 98–100, 106, 336
websites, 112
Goals-2-Go website, 112
Goldratt, Eliyahu (writer), 301
government, compliance with, 152–154
Greatest Management Principle in the
    World, 62, 64, 319
green issues. *See* environmental issues
groups. *See* teams
groupware, 181

• *H* •

Handy, Charles B. (executive)
on technological change, 17
Understanding Organisations, 357
Harvester pub/restaurants, 38
Hauptfuhrer, Robert (CEO), 33

Hayek, Nicolas (Swatch founder), 100
HBOS, 152
Healthy Working Lives website, 206
Helmont Ltd, 150
Herald of Free Enterprise ferry, 200
hierarchical organisations, 170–171
high-performance teams, 179–180
hiring. *See* recruitment
holidays or time off, 64, 65
Holland, John (telecommuter), 190
Honda UK, 302
honesty
  with employees, 148, 236, 347
  as essential to integrity, 36–37
  with everyone else, 151
  with financial backers, 146
  as foundation of code of ethics, 210
  goals related to, 102
  openness fostering, 68
  as recruitment concern, 50
  rewarding, 120
  with stakeholders, 143–145
horizontal organisations, 171. *See also*
    teams
horizontal teams, 39
Hull, Raymond (*The Peter Principle*),
    354–355
Human Resources website, 112
The Human Side of Enterprise
    (McGregor), 354
Huntington Life Sciences, 153

• *I* •

IBM, 93, 306
icons in this book, explained, 6
In Search of European Excellence (Peters
    and Waterman), 356
In Search of Excellence (Peters and
    Waterman), 353–354
incentives. *See* rewards
incompetence, dismissal for, 261
informal teams, 178–179
information and communication
    technology (ICT), 159, 233. *See also*
    technology
information technology (IT). *See*
    technology
initiative, as recruitment concern, 45
innovation, teams aiding, 176
inspiration. *See also* motivation
  by coaches, 81
  confidence as trait for, 36
  as leadership skill, 31–32
  as manager's main job, 12
Institute of Chartered Accountants
    website, 293
Institute of Directors website, 40, 270
Institute of Risk Management website, 206
insubordination, dismissal for, 261
integrity
  with employees, 347
  with everyone else, 151
  as foundation of code of ethics, 210
  as leadership trait, 36–37
  with stakeholders, 143, 145
  with suppliers, 150
  toxic communication compromising, 163
intelligence, as recruitment concern, 45
interest, as barrier to communication, 162
internal rewards, 37
internationalisation. *See* global
    management
Internet, finding employees via, 49, 56
Internet resources. *See* websites
InternetWorld website, 306
interviewing employee candidates
  don'ts, 53–54
  do's, 51–52
  key steps for, 53
  legal issues for, 54
  questions to ask, 50–51
  second (or third) interviews, 57
  taking notes, 52
  taking time to prepare, 49, 51–52
intoxication, dismissal for, 262
Introduction to Performance Appraisal
    website, 128
IT (information technology). *See*
    technology
italics in this book, 3

• J •

Johnson, Spencer (*The One Minute Manager*), 355
JP Morgan Chase, 38
Judge Business School website, 40

• K •

King, Lawrence (ORIS Group director), 119
knowledge power, 111, 172, 223

• L •

lateness, dismissal for, 261
lay-offs. *See* downsizing
leaders
  communication by, 32–33
  great examples of, 31
  inspiration by, 31–32
  primary traits of, 29
  support and facilitation from, 33–34
leadership
  as classic management function, 19
  collaborative, 38–40
  employees' desire for, 29
  further information, 30
  management versus, 30–31
  sharing and rotating positions of, 39
  skills required for, 31–34
  traits of, 35–37
  as two-way interchange, 33
  vision needed for, 29–31
  websites for advice on, 40
Leadership Ensemble (Economy), 38–39
Leadership For Dummies (Marrin), 30
learning. *See also* employee development; training employees
  as aspect of development, 87
  career development plans, 88–90
  importance to employees, 65, 345
  on-the-job coaching for, 82–83
  learning organisations, 324–325
  performance appraisals for setting goals, 122, 125
  supporting employees', 79–80

Learning and Skills Council website, 27
Ledward, Rodney (gynaecologist), 263
legal issues
  for discipline, 242, 244
  for dismissals, 260–261, 265–266
  flexible working hours, 65, 183
  in PESTEL analysis, 130, 131
  for recruitment, 46, 54
  in SPECTACLES analysis, 133
liabilities, 284, 285
listening
  active, cultivating, 164
  by effective leaders, 40
  importance of, 156, 164
  taking notes, 166
  tips for, 165–166
  when interviewing job candidates, 53
lobbies, dealing with, 154
Lockheed Martin, 195
London Business School websites, 27, 40
losses, managing risk of, 199–200
loyalists (customer type), 147

• M •

macho management style, 11–12
make-or-buy decision, 278–279
Management (Drucker), 75
management speak, avoiding, 168
Management Stripped Bare (Owen), 356
Management Today website, 40, 332
management trends. *See* trends
management websites, 27
ManagementFirst website, 27, 238
Managing Change website, 238
Managing for Results (Drucker), 354
Managing the Flexible Workforce (Pettinger), 76
managing your manager, 224–225
Manpower Services Commission (MSC), 103–104
markets, understanding before entering, 135
Marks & Spencer, 149
Marks, Michael (executive), 32
Marrin, John (*Leadership For Dummies*), 30

MARS system
  determining actions, 116–117
  relationships between actions and
    milestones, 117–118
  scheduling, 118
  setting milestones, 116
*Mastering the Organisation in its
  Environment* (Cartwright), 133
Maverick (Semler), 358
McCormack, Mark (CEO), 127
McGovern, Phil (manager), 23
McGregor, Douglas (*The Human Side of
  Enterprise*), 354
McKnight, William (CEO), 22
measures for goals
  examples of, 114
  keeping individual measures private,
    115–116
  positive feedback using, 115
  posting group measures, 115
  recognising incremental progress, 115
  in SMART checklist, 101
meddling, avoiding, 163
media, handling, 151–152
Meek, Catherine (president), 34
meetings
  with flexible workers, 186
  progress report, 253–254
Melcrum website, 168
mentors. *See also* coaching
  mentoring employees, 91–92
  sponsorships with, 225
  websites, 94
mercenaries (customer type), 147
Meredith Belbin's team roles, 182
merit pay, 127
micro-managing, avoiding, 342
milestones
  actions for, 116–117
  relationships between actions and,
    117–118
  scheduling, 118
  setting, 116
Mind Tools website, 112
Ministry of Defence (MOD), 44

misconduct, 243, 246–248, 261–262. *See
  also* discipline
mission, passion for, 40
mistakes, common, 335–340
Mitsubishi, 93
moaners and whiners, 216
modelling, 25
monetary rewards, 65, 74–75
monofont text in this book, 3
Moore, Joe (adviser), 162
Moore's Law, 298
MotivAction website, 182
motivation. *See also* discipline; inspiration;
    rewards
  biscuit, 63
  for day-to-day successes, 73–74
  focusing on the positive, 71–73
  Greatest Management Principle in the
    World, 62
  high expectations for, 72
  as manager's responsibility, 76–78
  monetary, 65, 74–75
  no-cost methods for, 77
  supportive environment for, 67–68, 72–73
  websites, 78
Motorola, 100
Mourinho, José (football coach), 84
movers and shakers, 216
moves, for discipline problems, 246
MSC (Manpower Services Commission),
    103–104
Murphy's Law, 195, 197
myGoals.com website, 112
myths, management, 314, 341–346

• N •

NASA's Teams and Teamwork website, 182
National Health Service (NHS), 105, 199
negative consequences. *See also* discipline;
    punishments
  cautions for, 61
  defined, 61
  focusing on, avoiding, 71, 72
  positive consequences versus, 62, 72

Nelson, Bob
  ASAP-cubed system of, 71
  The 1001 Rewards & Recognition
    Fieldbook, 76
  1001 Ways to Energise Employees, 76
  1001 Ways to Reward Employees, 31, 33,
    34, 76, 347
  overwhelmed experience of, 2
  Please Don't Just Do What I Tell You! Do
    What Needs to Be Done, 20
  recruitment technique of, 51
  survey conducted by, 65
  team briefings by, 33
net profit or loss, 290
network building, 222–223
network, computer, 303–304
Nieman, Andrea (administrative
    assistant), 33
Nike, 149
nimbleness, teams providing, 175
Nissan UK, 173
non-verbal communication, 166
Nordstrom's employee manual, 18–19
Northern Rock, 152
notes
  as documentation, 226
  reviewing when evaluating candidates,
    56–57
  taking during recruitment interviews, 52
  taking when listening, 166

office politics
  assessing, 214–215
  building a network, 222–223
  at company parties, 223–224
  deciphering communications, 218–221
  defined, 207
  getting help from others, 223
  identifying key players in, 215–216
  importance of understanding, 213
  managing your manager, 224–225
  organisation chart of, 217–218
  in PESTEL analysis, 130
  protecting yourself, 226–227
  unwritten rules of, 221–226
  websites, 228
Office Politics website, 228
O'Leary, Michael (CEO), 31, 140
The One Minute Manager (Blanchard and
    Johnson), 355
The 1001 Rewards & Recognition Fieldbook
    (Nelson), 76
1001 Ways to Energise Employees
    (Nelson), 76
1001 Ways to Reward Employees (Nelson),
    31, 33, 34, 76, 347
on-the-job method of coaching, 82–83
open-book management, 326–327
openness
  with employees, 148, 347
  as key to supportive environment, 23
  in learning organisations, 325
  with stakeholders, 143, 144
operating expenses, 288
opportunities, in SWOT analysis, 131
optimism (leadership trait), 35–36
organisation chart
  official, 217
  of political environment, 217–218
organisation (classic management
    function), 19
Orpheus Chamber Orchestra principles,
    38–40
Oticon, 180
outsourcing
  control issues for, 315–316
  examples of, 315, 316
  as hard work, 316–317
  maintaining your reputation, 316
  reasons for, 314–315, 323–324
overheads, 275, 288
Owen, Jo (*Management Stripped Bare*), 356

● *P* ●

Pareto principle, 101–102, 109
participative management style, 12
parties, company, 223–224

Pearl of Wisdom icon, 6
performance appraisals
  avoiding surprises, 125, 126
  benefits of, 121–122, 127
  collaborative, 124
  examples of, 127
  preparing for, 126, 128
  process of, 123–125
  360-degree evaluation process, 126
  tips for, 125
  upward, 126
  websites, 128
  written, 124
performance improvement plan, 252–254
performance monitoring
  actions for milestones, 116–117
  balance needed for, 113
  interpreting the results, 120–121
  keeping individual measures private,
    115–116
  measures for goals, 114–116
  measuring instead of counting, 118
  milestones for, 116
  positive feedback using, 115
  posting group measures, 115
  recognising incremental progress, 115
  relationships for sequencing actions,
    117–118
  schedules for, 118
  shrinkage reduction, 118–120
performance problems, 241, 243–246, 261.
    See also discipline
personal power, 111
PESTEL analysis, 130–131
Peter, Laurence (*The Peter Principle*),
    354–355
The Peter Principle (Peter and Hull),
    354–355
Peters, Tom (management guru)
  on handling stakeholders, 146, 148
  on risk management, 199
  In Search of European Excellence, 356
  In Search of Excellence, 353–354
  website, 332
Peterson, Donald (CEO), 33

Pettinger, Richard
  on Errol Flynn managers, 220
  industrial training board experience of,
    103–104
  Managing the Flexible Workforce, 76
  overwhelmed experience of, 3
  on reasons for outsourcing, 315
  on using consultants, 328
  'wait a minute' technique of, 203, 213
  'wild' questions asked by, 203
planning
  balancing with doing, 103–104
  as classic management function, 19
  crises avoided by, 231
  for technology, 297–298, 302, 303, 305–306
*Please Don't Just Do What I Tell You! Do
    What Needs to Be Done* (Nelson), 20
Poling, Harold A. (CEO), 32
politics. *See also* office politics
  managers' decisions leading to crisis
    in, 1–2
  in PESTEL analysis, 130
  in SPECTACLES analysis, 133
Porter, Michael E. (*Competitive Strategy*),
    355
position power, 111
positive consequences. *See also* rewards
  defined, 61
  expectations for, 61
  focusing on, 71–73
  negative consequences versus, 62, 72
positive outlook, 29, 340, 351
power
  to make goals happen, 110–112
  movement with downsizing, 171
  sources of, 111
praise
  general lack of, 72
  guidelines for, 71
  importance to employees, 65–66, 72, 351
  for performance, 120
Presentations.com website, 168
pressure groups, handling, 153, 154
Pret A Manger goals, 108
PricewaterhouseCooper, 206, 212

prioritising goals, 97, 104, 107–110
probation before dismissal, 265
probing for information, 220–221
problemsatwork.org website, 254
production budget, 275. *See also* budgets
professional associations, recruitment
 through, 48
professionalising management, 320–321
profit and loss account, 288–290
profitability
 of globalisation, 313
 of going green, 139–140
 of risk management, 206
progressive discipline, 244
project teams, 177
ProjectSmart website, 168
promises, making, 227
promotions, documenting, 122
Puma, 149
punishments. *See also* discipline; negative
 consequences
 discipline versus, 240
 for good performance, 62–63
 as negative consequences, 61

• *Q* •

qualcom.com website, 49
quality improvement groups, 177
quick fixes, avoiding, 13, 339
quick ratio, 291

Railtrack, 200
Ramsey, Alf (football coach), 84
Ratner, Gerald (manager), 204
recognition. *See* praise; rewards
recruitment
 advertising for, 49
 being objective, 58–59
 challenges of, 43
 checking references, 55–56
 employee traits to look for, 44–45, 50–51
 evaluating candidates, 55–57

finding good people, 47–49
freeze during downsizing, 257
freeze for budget reasons, 280–281
hiring employees, 58–60
importance of, 45–47
interviewing candidates, 49–54, 57
involving employees in, 47
job description for, 46, 51
keeping in touch with top candidates, 60
legal issues for, 46, 54
Ministry of Defence example, 44
person specification for, 46
top choices unavailable, 60
trusting your instincts, 59–60
wages and benefits concerns, 51
website example, 49
websites for advice on, 60
from within, 48
reduction in workforce. *See* downsizing
redundancies. *See* downsizing
Reebok, 316
re-engineering. *See* downsizing
references, checking, 55–56
referrals for employees, 48
regulators, compliance with, 152–154
relationship power, 111
relationships between actions and
 milestones, 117–118
relevant goals, in SMART checklist, 101–102
Remember icon, 6
Research in Motion (RIM), 309
resignations, 255–256
resisting change, 233–235, 339
resources
 for career development plans, 89
 coaches providing, 85
 managing, 138–140
 in performance improvement plan, 253
respect
 creating an environment of, 68
 for employees, 148–149, 343
 for everyone else, 151
 goals related to, 102
 in office politics, 215
 for stakeholders, 143
 for suppliers, 150

responsibility, as recruitment concern, 45
retained earnings, 285
retirement of employees, 256
return on investment (ROI), 292
rewards. *See also* motivation; positive
    consequences
  asking employees what they want, 66–67
  biscuit motivation, 63
  clear communication about, 63–64
  for day-to-day successes, 73–74
  ensuring appropriate credit, 227
  external versus internal, 37
  fairness in, 352
  for flexible workers, 189
  further information, 76
  Greatest Management Principle in the
    World, 62, 319
  guidelines for a system of, 69
  importance of, 338
  incentives versus entitlements, 74–75
  in learning organisations, 325
  linking to goals, 69
  monetary, 65, 74–75
  monitoring the effect of, 65, 69
  no-cost methods for, 77
  office politics revealed by, 214
  performance-based, 63, 64, 69–71, 75–76
  for poor performance, 62–63
  as positive consequences, 61
  praise, 65–66, 71
  results and process measures for, 71
  Saga company example, 73
  seeking out the positive, 72–73
  for shrinkage reduction, 120
  time with manager as, 66
  unintended consequences of, 64
  what employees want, 65–66, 76
right first time, every time, 329
rightsizing. *See* downsizing
RIM (Research in Motion), 309
Risk Assessment Templates website, 206
risk management
  accident prevention, 201
  assumption requiring, 203–204
  British Airways example, 205

business environment issues, 198
complacency requiring, 203, 204
constant attention needed for, 198–199
for crime, 201–202
defining risk, 196
disaster examples, 200
importance of, 195
internal issues, 197–198
Lockheed Martin example, 195
for losses, 199–200
for management decisions, 202–203
moving forward after mistakes, 205–206
Murphy's Law, 195, 197
NHS example, 199
profitability of, 206
steps for, 204
volcanic ash example, 197
websites, 206
wild questions for, 203
Roddick, Anita (CEO), 31, 100, 357–358
ROI (return on investment), 292
roles
  creating clarity of, 39
  of team members, 176–177
rotating leadership positions, 39
Rumsfeld, Donald (US Secretary of
    Defense), 196
Ryanair, 302

• S •

safety, supporting employees', 68
Saga company, 73
Said Business School website, 40
salaries. *See* wages and benefits
sales budget, 274. *See also* budgets
Sanyo UK, 327
Sarbanes-Oxley Act website, 206
scapegoating, avoiding, 163, 348
scheduling
  milestones and actions, 118
  in performance improvement plan, 252
secrets, avoiding, 163
sectoral environment, in SPECTACLES
    analysis, 133

self-managed teams, 179–180
self-protection, 226–227
Sellafield nuclear power station, 151
Semco, 302
Semler, Ricardo (*Maverick*), 358
Senge, Peter (*The Fifth Discipline*), 324, 356–357
share capital, 285
shareholders, influence of, 135
shareholders' liabilities, 285
sharing leadership positions, 39
show-and-tell method of coaching, 82–83
shrinkage
  complacency about, avoiding, 119
  defined, 118
  programmes for reducing, 119–120
Silver Spring, 310
Six Sigma, 329
slowing down, avoiding, 233–234
SMART checklist for goals, 101–102
social environment, in SPECTACLES analysis, 133
South West Water, 139
speaking. *See also* communication
  effectiveness of, 156
  writing similarly to, 167
specific goals, in SMART checklist, 101
SPECTACLES analysis, 133
sponsorships, 225
squeezing employees, avoiding, 13
stability, as recruitment concern, 45
staff budget, 274. *See also* budgets
stakeholders
  communities, 150–151
  customers and clients, 146–147
  defined, 143
  expectations for treatment of, 143
  financial backers, 146
  government and regulators, 152–154
  handling discomfort in, 145
  inspiring confidence in, 144–145
  media, 151–152
  pleasing when possible, 144
  pressure groups, lobbies, and vested interests, 154

staff, 148–149
  suppliers, 149–150
  websites, 154
standards, setting, 124, 125
strengths, in SWOT analysis, 131
stress management, 330–331
The Stress Management Society website, 332
Strunk, William, Jr. (*The Elements of Style*), 167
styles of management
  the best way, 12–13
  flavour-of-the-month, 10
  macho, 11–12
  participative, 12
Sullivan, David (entrepreneur), 351
The Sun, 237
super-teams, 179–180
suppliers
  budget tips related to, 281
  Helmont Ltd example, 150
  local versus distant, 150
  mistreatment of, 149
  respect and integrity toward, 150
supportive environment
  creating, 67–68, 72–73, 348
  creation by coaches, 81, 84–85
  for flexible workers, 188–189
  as leader's responsibility, 33–34
  as manager's responsibility, 23
  trust and openness as key to, 23
suspension, for discipline, 248
Swatch, 100
SWOT analysis
  acronym explained, 131
  conducting on competitors, 132
  conducting on your business, 132
  justifying categorisations in, 133–134
  limitations of, 132

● *T* ●

talk the talk trend, 35
task forces, 178
task power, 111

Teach First website, 238
Teambuildinginc.com website, 182
teams. *See also* coaching
  ad hoc groups, 179
  Batchelor's Foods example, 179–180
  benefits of, 169–170, 175–176
  British Airways example, 174
  coaches' role in, 81
  coaching metaphors for, 83
  communicating goals to, 105–107
  communicating vision to, 106
  empowering, 173–175, 180–181
  formal, 177–178
  horizontal, 39
  informal, 178–179
  in learning organisations, 325
  managers versus members, 15–16
  managing, 174–175
  member roles in (table), 176–177
  Nissan UK example, 173
  Oticon example, 180
  recruitment concerns for, 45
  self-managed, 179–180
  support for members by, 23
  technology for, 181–182
  types of, 176
  websites, 182
techies, 216
technology
  benefits and drawbacks of, 295, 296,
    299–301, 322
  changes unleashed by, 17
  for communication, 158–161
  competitive advantage from, 297
  computer network, 303–304
  for efficiency and productivity, 301–303
  evaluating investing in, 159, 160
  example uses for, 302
  for flexible workers, 188
  gadgets and gizmos, 159–160
  getting expert help for, 298, 300
  global, 308
  ICT, benefits of, 159, 233
  IT websites, 306

  knowing your business, 296
  Moore's Law of, 298
  in PESTEL analysis, 130
  planning and implementing, 297–298, 302,
    303, 305–306
  in SPECTACLES analysis, 133
  for teams, 181–182
  videoconferencing, 160–161
  working hours increased by, 158
telecommuting, 190–191
Teller, Joe (manager), 199
temporary agencies, 48
termination. *See* dismissals; downsizing
terrorists (customer type), 147
theft, dismissal for, 262. *See also* shrinkage
Theory X management, 11–12
Theory Y management, 12
threats, in SWOT analysis, 131
360-degree evaluation process, 126
time off or holidays, 64, 65
time-bound goals, in SMART checklist, 102
The Times, 237
timing
  of discipline, 241
  of dismissals, 268–270
Tip icon, 6
Tom Peters website, 332
town gossips, 216
Townsend Thoresen, 200
toxic communication, 163–164
Trades Union Congress website, 254, 270
training employees. *See also* employee
    development; learning
  described, 87
  importance of, 349
  for performance improvement, 121, 253
  in technology use, 306
training in management
  instant gratification approach to, 15
  key steps for applying, 27
  useless activities in, 14
  Welch's instructive example, 26
transfers, for discipline problems, 246
transition from worker to manager,
    335–336, 344–345

trends
  basics of management, 321–322
  benchmarking, 329
  business process re-engineering, 329
  commitment to expertise, 332
  consultant use, 328–330
  flat organisations, 325–326
  flavour-of-the-month, 10
  foundations of management, 319
  learning organisations, 324–325
  open-book management, 326–327
  outsourcing, 315–317, 323–324
  professionalising management, 320–321
  right first time, every time, 329
  Six Sigma, 329
  stress management, 330–331
  talk the talk and walk the walk, 35
  websites, 332
trial period before dismissal, 265
True Stories icon, 6
trust
  creating an environment of, 18–19, 68
  of employees, 341–342
  integrity leading to, 36–37
  as key to supportive environment, 23
  in office politics, 226
turnover, in profit and loss account, 288
Tusa, John (BBC director), 171

• _U_ •

Understanding Organisations (Handy), 357
unfair dismissals, 260
University College London websites,
    94, 168
upward appraisals, 126
urgency versus crisis, 230

• _V_ •

values, goals related to, 102–103
variance with budget, 274
Venables, Terry (football coach), 83
verbal abuse, dismissal for, 261
vertical organisations, 170–171

vested interests, dealing with, 154
vetoers, 216
victim role, avoiding, 234
videoconferencing, 160–161
violence, dismissal for, 262
virtual management websites, 191
vision
  coaches providing, 85
  communicating to teams, 106
  degree of challenge for, 32
  goals linked to, 98–100, 106, 336
  as leadership trait, 29–31
VXR Radio, 237

• _W_ •

wages and benefits
  freeze for budget reasons, 281
  incentives versus entitlements, 74–75
  merit pay, 127
  as recruitment concern, 51
  relating performance to, 265
  as rewards, 65, 74–75
walk the walk trend, 35
Warning! icon, 6
waste disposal, 139
Waterman, Robert H.
  In Search of European Excellence, 356
  In Search of Excellence, 353–354
weaknesses, in SWOT analysis, 131
websites
  accounting information, 293
  address conventions in this book, 3
  change management, 238
  communication advice, 168
  discipline information, 254
  dismissal information, 270
  employee development, 94
  environmental management, 140
  ethics information, 228
  global management, 317
  goals information, 112
  IT information, 306
  leadership advice, 40
  management advice, 27

websites *(continued)*
  management trends, 332
  mentoring information, 94
  motivation advice, 78
  office politics advice, 228
  performance appraisal, 128
  recruitment advice, 60
  recruitment example, 49
  risk management, 206
  stakeholder management, 154
  team information, 182
  virtual management, 191
Weinstock, Arnold (CEO), 127
Welch, Jack (US business leader), 26
Wenger, Arsene (coach), 83
What Color Is Your Parachute? (Bolles), 50
Whistleblowers' Charter, 211
White, E. B. (*The Elements of Style*), 167
winning, defining effectively, 13
Wired magazine website, 306
withholding information
  avoiding secrets, 163
  as barrier to communication, 162–163
  sight of big picture lost due to, 346

Woodward, Clive (rugby coach), 83
work ethic, as recruitment concern, 44
work improvement groups (WIGS), 177, 179
working hours
  flexible, 65, 183–191
  technology's affect on, 158
Work911 website, 128
World Bank Group, 212
written communication. *See also*
    documentation
  company policy manual, 221
  deciphering office politics, 219–220
  developing skills in, 167
  for discipline problems, 246–248
  importance of, 166
  management speak, avoiding, 168
  performance appraisals, 124
  tips for, 166–167
wrongful dismissals, 260

• Z •

Zyklon, 316

FOR DUMMIES®

Making Everything Easier! ™

UK editions

BUSINESS

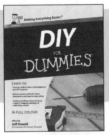

Marketing Kit FOR DUMMIES
Ruth Mortimer
Greg Brooks
Alexander Hiam, MBA
978-0-470-74490-1

Business Plans Kit FOR DUMMIES
Steven Peterson
Peter Jaret
Barbara Findlay Schenck
Colin Barrow
978-0-470-74381-2

Project Management FOR DUMMIES
Nick Graham
Stanley Portny
978-0-470-71119-4

Asperger's Syndrome For Dummies
978-0-470-66087-4

Boosting Self-Esteem For Dummies
978-0-470-74193-1

British Sign Language
For Dummies
978-0-470-69477-0

Business NLP For Dummies
978-0-470-69757-3

Cricket For Dummies
978-0-470-03454-5

REFERENCE

British Politics FOR DUMMIES
Julian Knight
978-0-470-68637-9

DIY FOR DUMMIES
Edited by
Jeff Howell
IN FULL COLOUR
978-0-470-97450-6

Researching Your Family History Online FOR DUMMIES
Dr Nick Barratt
Sarah Newbury
Jenny Thomas
Matthew L. Helm
April Leigh Helm
978-0-470-74535-9

Diabetes For Dummies, 3rd Edition
978-0-470-97711-8

English Grammar For Dummies
978-0-470-05752-0

Flirting For Dummies
978-0-470-74259-4

Football For Dummies
978-0-470-68837-3

IBS For Dummies
978-0-470-51737-6

Improving Your Relationship For
Dummies
978-0-470-68472-6

HOBBIES

Growing Your Own Fruit & Veg FOR DUMMIES
Geoff Stebbings
978-0-470-69960-7

Allotment Gardening FOR DUMMIES
Sven Wombwell
978-0-470-68641-6

Electronics FOR DUMMIES
Dickon Ross
Cathleen Shamieh
Gordon McComb
978-0-470-68178-7

Lean Six Sigma For Dummies
978-0-470-75626-3

Life Coaching For Dummies,
2nd Edition
978-0-470-66554-1

Nutrition For Dummies, 2nd Edition
978-0-470-97276-2

**Available wherever books are sold. For more information or to order direct go to
www.wiley.com or call +44 (0) 1243 843291**

24940 (p1)

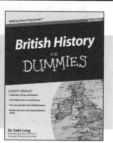

FOR DUMMIES®

The easy way to get more done and have more fun

LANGUAGES

978-0-470-68815-1
UK Edition

978-1-118-00464-7

978-0-470-90101-4

MUSIC

978-0-470-48133-2

978-0-470-66603-6
Lay-flat, UK Edition

978-0-470-66372-1
UK Edition

SCIENCE & MATHS

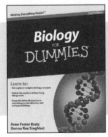
978-0-470-59875-7

978-0-470-55964-2

978-0-470-55174-5

Art For Dummies
978-0-7645-5104-8

Bass Guitar For Dummies, 2nd Edition
978-0-470-53961-3

Christianity For Dummies
978-0-7645-4482-8

Criminology For Dummies
978-0-470-39696-4

Currency Trading For Dummies
978-0-470-12763-6

Drawing For Dummies, 2nd Edition
978-0-470-61842-4

Forensics For Dummies
978-0-7645-5580-0

Index Investing For Dummies
978-0-470-29406-2

Knitting For Dummies, 2nd Edition
978-0-470-28747-7

Music Theory For Dummies
978-0-7645-7838-0

Piano For Dummies, 2nd Edition
978-0-470-49644-2

Physics For Dummies
978-0-7645-5433-9

Schizophrenia For Dummies
978-0-470-25927-6

Sex For Dummies, 3rd Edition
978-0-470-04523-7

Sherlock Holmes For Dummies
978-0-470-48444-9

Solar Power Your Home
For Dummies, 2nd Edition
978-0-470-59678-4

The Koran For Dummies
978-0-7645-5581-7

Wine All-in-One For Dummies
978-0-470-47626-0

Yoga For Dummies, 2nd Edition
978-0-470-50202-0

Available wherever books are sold. For more information or to order direct go to www.wiley.com or call +44 (0) 1243 843291

24940 (p3)

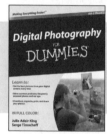

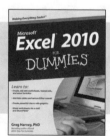